# BATTLEFIELD
# BRAVERY

*"Those who have not been there,
talk a lot of damned nonsense"*

Lt. Colonel Wilfrith Elstob, V.C.,
talking about the battlefield.

# BATTLEFIELD BRAVERY

## The Courage of Ordinary Men
## 1914–1919

A. Satterley and G. Scott

Reveille
PRESS

Reveille Press is an imprint of
Tommies Guides Military Booksellers & Publishers

Gemini House
136–140 Old Shoreham Road
Brighton
BN3 7BD

www.tommiesguides.co.uk

First published in Great Britain by
Reveille Press 2013

For more information please visit
www.reveillepress.com

© 2013 A. Satterley and G. Scott

ISBN 978-1-908336-80-4

Cover design by Reveille Press

Printed and bound in Great Britain by
CPI Antony Rowe, Chippenham and Eastbourne

# Contents

# Preface

Desperately working to get his mates out of a tunnel beneath the battlefield was a coal miner from Northumberland. Pressing on with his precious load of letters and parcels from wives, girlfriends and fathers, through the explosions of heavy shells, there is a post office worker. An errand boy from Chiswick is surrounded by his dead and wounded comrades, loading artillery shells and firing; alone at his gun, he did not survive the day. Up there a public school boy is leading men towards enemy wire, behind which is a concrete bunker and spitting machine gun. From the left a troop of cavalry, swords at their sides, clatter over a cobbled road; led by a grey-haired gentleman he points his bright sword and kicks his horse. His men follow, some of them laughing and joking. If we want to know something about heroes, we'll find it in the Great War. But what exactly is bravery, what exactly is heroism? The more I thought about it, the less, I realised, I understood it. These Tommies, what fear did they know? How could they stand up and face death, execution by machinery? Were they, to a man, conned by an Imperialist Victorian education? Perhaps there is something more believable, more interesting, going on here.

It gets more difficult; these were people we knew; they were our grandparents who stand in our dim memories in their front rooms behind net curtains looking out over the sea, or the red brick terrace. Not heroes. They were ordinary people who lived in the brick and stone houses that we live in today. They are that close to us. It is for this reason that I had to get involved in the First World War. I was never in battle, but my grandfather was. I knew him, but he never spoke about his war. He only once showed me the dark grey specks of shrapnel, a keepsake from Jerusalem, 1918 – he was marked until the end of his life and there's still that steel in his ashes. That war was his hardest test; the hardest test of his generation and the hardest test of the British Army. In that war we may expect to find brave heroes, but I did not find them. Instead, underneath the old mask of heroism, I found something far more fascinating and complex than I ever expected.

In the many pages that follow, the reader will see this hero doing his job, enduring his job, and see behind the myths of heroism. It may appear, for a time, that I have attempted to destroy the hero, and it may seem that I have succeeded, but my aim has been to understand how the ordinary man was transformed into a hero and why our society continues to honour and remember its war heroes, a hundred years on.

In my view, it may have taken that length of time for us to remember that war *can* be glorious, certainly not of itself, but in the flash of a grim moment between mates.

This book tells a surprisingly humanitarian story.

# Introduction

Ordinary folk are capable of remarkable things. The hardest of tasks has been accomplished. Quietly proud men of the Great War talked about it amongst themselves, if they didn't share it with families. They were the ordinary soldiers of the Great War who were called heroes but who didn't understand why. This book *is* about heroes.

**THE BRAVE HEROES**

They no longer exist, not in the old sense. The dead are remembered every November, but we have forgotten about the heroes, we don't know them at all, we don't know what they symbolise any more. I don't think anyone has seriously looked at who they were and what they did since 1919 (except to make lists of Victoria Crosses). In 1919, the last gallantry medals were pinned on chests or put in hand by registered post. Each in a little box to keep in a drawer, with name, rank and number typed on the outside; the same as pressed into the battle-worn identity tag or carved upon his stone war grave. The medal was delivered in its own little grave, already dead, and often buried in a drawer. Dead and buried were the story and the hero along with it.

But they were not, first and foremost, heroic. Not if we ever looked inside their minds or listened to what they told us. Yes, we talk nonsense about heroes, but in reality they were just ordinary men who did what was required of them. Functional, they were, when the lid was lifted off Hell. Right across the battlefield they achieved – something – in a mucky war that has come to represent the height of futility and waste.

But a medal is a beautiful thing, plucked from Passchendaele by one who was there. Beneath the coloured silk ribbon and floreate suspender, a soldier's name and details indented on the edge. Within a medal box, there is a savage, real drama, a highlight in a life accented by churned filth.

Shiny silver bravery medals – reflective souvenirs of a tarnished war.

I look at a medal and see my reflection, my own face looking out from it; 'there, but for the grace of god, go I'. I'm thankful that someone else went there instead of me. The shine further suggests the war was not always tarnished black, but contained beacons of light which illuminated the way. Soldiers in the line undoubtedly saw the light of heroism. They described it, named their heroes and remembered them. The state that prosecuted the war saw it too, took up and recorded them. It was, to a very surprising extent, a humanitarian bravery that was honoured. It is, therefore, worth wiping the old muck off this story.

There is an enormous gap in the literature of the battlefield. There is all horror and no good – nothing to learn from it but the folly. For 800,000 slaughtered there were just 573 who unfurled their crimson wings as 'Victoria Cross Heroes'. We can easily find some of those 573 paraded in print like a butterfly collection, but where did the other 196,619 bravery medals disappear to? Did their blue, red, white and purple ribbons not settle on men too? It might be the only thing we know about them; five minutes desperation in a long family life. Selective resurrection is what heroes win, but the same is true of most famous people.

While many books have been printed about the relatively few Victoria Crosses, very little effort has been made to document and understand the vast bulk of awards made for military bravery and distinguished service. We focus on the Great War of 1914–1918, as representing perhaps the hardest test of the British Army and of the British people. The VC is mentioned in many parts of this work, as there is much to learn from it, but the point of doing so is to contextualise the majority of awards as part of a greater honours system.

The major aim of this book is to document and understand the heroes of the Great War. Who were they and what did they do? Why did they do it? Who decided which of them would be a hero and how did the hero understand this? How do unit honours lists compare and how did they grow over the four years? We consider gallantry against the background of technological and tactical evolution, against the changing composition of the Armies. We consider the men and their deeds within an environment of boredom, labouring, fear, happiness even, and sudden death. We contemplate what types of battlefield behaviour and emotions allowed about three percent of men to receive the particular distinction of a medal for bravery or distinguished service.

We concentrate on life at the sharp end of fighting, for that is where bravery medals were won. We acknowledge that life on the various fronts was dominated by long periods behind the lines, training, resting, letter writing, working, digging and carrying. Much less time was spent simply occupying reserve trenches and even less in the actual front line fighting.[1] The time spent actually fighting was not great for most Army units. Much time was spent not feeling intense fear or apprehension, but with boredom, camaraderie and resentment.[2]

A major conclusion of the work is that the words 'bravery' and 'courage' mask an array of battlefield motives and emotions that were the real reason men performed their 'brave' acts. In fact the range of motives is so large as to suggest that bravery is an almost meaningless concept. With specific regard to the medals won by the British Army in World War One, the work also emphasises that some of the greatest courage is not represented by medals but went unrewarded. For example, the courage needed to helplessly endure shelling, the courage to face the enemy guns in no-man's-land during an attack and the courage required by burial parties searching corpses and gathering human remains. It was common to witness deaths that were neither peaceful nor quick, for the numbers of severe wounds encountered in this war was entirely unprecedented in scale. The war was so hard for some men and women that they ran out of courage, so vast that 'carers' ran out of sympathy. Military chaplains and nurses had to comfort large numbers of men in a terrible dying condition, almost daily. The chaplain had to write a never ending series of letters of condolence to families who sought his comfort. There were no special medals for such work, work which drained reserves of courage until there was none left. Medals were given for a restricted range of particular military services rather than for the full range of bravery and courage.

During this work we have tried to understand why it is that a great many winners of bravery medals modestly assert that they were only doing their job, or did nothing special. Apparent modesty is a characteristic of those commonly perceived as brave heroes, alongside courage and strength. Yet, all attempts to identify brave warriors before they go into battle have failed. In practice, brave, courageous warriors have appeared almost at random from the ranks of ordinary people. Surprisingly, perhaps, in this book we do not make a point of finding and describing heroes; instead we try to reveal a story of ordinary people with ordinary human traits, performing their work almost always in lethally dangerous environments. We show how, in battle, heroes emerge, and we reveal the key role of the onlookers who witness and benefit from heroism. Only then are we able to understand why heroes become celebrated and why their recognition and commemoration is important. But this does not happen by their own choice, and it is emphasised that in battle heroism and cowardice are blood brothers; a man may be both coward and hero at different times. In fact, the one can be the other.

## SOURCES

Available information for this kind of study is voluminous. To date, few attempts have been made to integrate with other disciplines, particularly battlefield psychology. We have consulted general history books, compilations of first-hand British and German soldier's accounts, regimental and battalion histories relating to the Northumberland Fusiliers (the infantry regiment chosen as our example for this work), academic journal articles and material published online. We have dealt with the awards made to the various support arms of the Army in a similar way to the infantry; all the major Corps are included in this study. Unpublished documentary material such as battalion War Diaries preserved in the WO95 Series at the National Archives, Kew, have been consulted. These yield much information on the actions for which gallantry awards were won. The 'Soldiers Died in the Great War' digital database (SDGW) provides a near complete record of deaths in battle and of daily attrition during the war.[3] The National Archives website provides searchable access to the Medal Index Card records (MICs) which preserve each soldier's entitlement to medals for general service and, in a separate series, those awarded for gallantry.

Another key source is the *London Gazette* in which the official notification of every gallantry award can be found, sometimes including details of the action. Normally the *London Gazette* provides the name, rank and number of the recipient, the regiment in the case of 'other ranks' and often a brief description of the act for which the award was won (the 'citation'). From about September 1917 the home town of the awardee may also be given in the case of other ranks. The unit or battalion with which the recipient was serving is rarely given and must be sought elsewhere, if available, for example in the campaign medal rolls (issued for general service rather than bravery) at the National Archives, Kew. Rarely does a citation provide information such as the date and place of the act, which may have been present in the original recommendation for the award, but which was removed before publication in the *Gazette*. This is a major deficiency in the *London Gazette* citation data that we have attempted, as far as possible, to overcome. Whilst the *London Gazette* announcements do generally occur in a predictable sequence, following major actions for example, in the absence of firm data the task of assigning an award to a battle can be uncertain. In the case of the DSO and MC, it is always worth bearing in mind that there is a complete series of annotated *London Gazettes* in the WO389 series at the National Archives which do provide some limited information on the location and date of the act.

Whereas citations were generally published in the *London Gazette* for gallantry awards of the Victoria Cross (VC), the Distinguished Service Order (DSO), the Military Cross (MC) and the Distinguished Conduct Medal (DCM), no citations for the Military Medal (MM) were published in the *Gazette*. Citations for the MM survived in unpublished records until 8 September 1940 when the warehouse containing Army records at Arnside Street, London was hit by bombs and destroyed by fire. Luckily, the Northumberland Fusiliers Museum at Alnwick has a note of the battalion with which almost all MM winners served.

# SECTION I:
# BEHIND THE LINES

# Recognition of Battlefield Bravery

~⟶

An awards system was in place during the First World War that was designed to provide different rewards according to military rank as well as for different levels of gallantry. These awards are illustrated below in order of seniority:

**Victoria Cross (VC)**

**Distinguished Service Order**

**Military Cross (MC)**

**Left: Distinguished Conduct Medal (DCM) Right: Military Medal (MM)**

Award procedures dictated, to some extent, who could be awarded different types of medals and for what kinds of act.

Most prestigious is the Victoria Cross, instituted by Queen Victoria in January 1856 and cast from bronze. It is the highest British award for gallantry and is only rarely awarded for the most exceptional acts of valour in battle. For example, of about 100,000 men who served with the Northumberland Fusiliers during the First World War, only two officers and three other ranks won the Victoria Cross.

The Distinguished Service Order was instituted in 1886 and was open to all commissioned officers, but in practice was mainly awarded to captains and higher ranks during the Great War. It could be awarded for gallantry in battle as well as for distinguished service over a period of time. Even good staff work could result in an award of the DSO, in recognition of the contribution of senior officers to the planning and implementation of victory.

The Military Cross was instituted nearly four months after the start of the war, on 31 December 1914, and was open to captains, lieutenants and warrant officers (i.e. junior officers, although awards to majors are known). Almost all were awarded for battlefield gallantry, but the MC could also be awarded for staff work and organisation behind the lines.

The Distinguished Conduct Medal was instituted in 1854 during the Crimean War and was open to other ranks only, although during the 1914–18 war and, especially after the institution of the Military Medal in 1916, it was mainly an NCO's award.

The Military Medal was instituted on 25 March 1916 and was also open to other ranks only. Some were awarded retrospectively for acts carried out in 1914 and 1915 but the vast majority of these medals was awarded for actions from summer 1916 onwards.

## NEW YEAR AND KING'S BIRTHDAY HONOURS LISTS

Awards appearing in the so-called 'Honours Gazettes' require special attention, not least because they illustrate the full breadth of the honours system which rewarded large numbers of acts that did not involve the stereotypical charging of machine guns. Honours awards were different from immediate awards; the immediate award was 'for a specific act of gallantry' whereas an Honours award would be made when 'no specific act can be recorded'. Typically, therefore, Honours awards were made for gallantry or good service over a period of time.

The DSO, MC and the DCM could be announced in New Year and King's Birthday Honours editions of the *London Gazette* and these are referred to as periodic (i.e. non-immediate) awards. These editions were published on the 1 January and the 3 June each year, or if these days fell on a Sunday, the nearest working day. Announcements of MM awards are never found in these gazette editions, the medal could not be awarded as part of an Honours list. The MM could be given for specific acts of gallantry 'during a specific period of active operations', but only as an immediate award. Some MMs were allowed for multiple acts of bravery over a period of many months and the citation usually lists these acts. While official guidelines were that the MM should not normally be given for actions covering more than two to three days, some slipped through.

Procedures to be followed by officers making recommendations were stipulated in an Army pamphlet of February 1918, which clarified many aspects of the awards system then in place.[1] As far as Honours Despatches are concerned, rewards were allotted to units for distribution as senior officers saw fit, as long as the recommendations were up to standard and the candidate was deserving. Paragraph 28 of the February 1918 booklet states; *the number of awards placed at the disposal of the Commander in Chief is sufficient to admit of the reward of every case which reaches the high standard required.* Clearly, this was open to abuse, but in general it was a process meant to ensure that those deserving of reward, obtained that reward, and it worked well. Among the soldiers, of course, there was grumbling and cynicism about some of these rewards, but Tommy grumbled about everything.

All periodic awards were very well earned; there were far too many deserving cases being brought to notice to start giving a medal to men who did not deserve one. In this regard, however, it is worth noting that whilst staff officers could be awarded DSOs and MCs for battle planning behind the lines, the other ranks' DCM was only to be awarded 'for services in action' (i.e. for services under fire, during air raids, bombardments or other enemy action that produces conditions equivalent to actual combat).[1] Whilst some early war periodic DCMs had been awarded for other reasons, these were rare. The overwhelming majority of DCMs were awarded for gallantry or distinguished services in action with the enemy. A rare example of a DCM awarded for services rendered many miles behind the lines, is that to Acting Sergeant John R. Boxall of the Army

Service Corps, who was awarded the medal 'for conspicuous ability, tact and zeal in the performance of his duties as Chief Clerk in the office of the Assistant Director of Supplies, Boulogne' during 1915. This man dedicated his life to the Corps, for he was awarded the MBE in the King's Birthday Honours list of 1932 and his Territorial Efficiency Decoration as Honorary Major of the Royal Army Service Corps in 1951, before retiring in 1956 and finally being struck off the list of the Army Reserve of Officers in 1967.

The function of the Honours despatches and Honours awards was to make sure that those who might not have done sufficient to earn an immediate reward for gallantry, but who were nevertheless the backbone of fighting and support units, were eligible and did receive their due recognition. There were many who worked night and day for months or years and thereby made a very real contribution to the war; theirs was a sustained effort in the face of the enemy rather than a single act. The importance of these men to the British Army, to their units and to their immediate compatriots is easily under-estimated. Among their number are Sergeant Majors who helped a unit to be successful on the battlefield; there are the battalion cooks who more than anyone else cheered the men up when they most needed it; and there are the Quarter Master Sergeants and Company Sergeant Majors who – often under heavy shell fire and in the open – made certain that whatever the conditions, supplies of rations, blankets, trench waders, wire and ammunition all made it up the line to the men when it was needed. Upon these men the British Army depended, and they could be depended upon to deliver. Their contribution was more than a single act on a battlefield, it was in fact war-winning.

## THE QUOTA SYSTEM

The quota system and its evolution during the war, is relevant only to the understanding of officers' gallantry awards. The number of awards was limited so as to maintain a high standard. In each theatre of war, the quota system was so organised that an army division or brigade had a fixed monthly allocation of awards of each medal. At quiet times there were ample awards to go round, but during intensive periods of battle, the quota might be used up fast, meaning that only the best of a great many recommendations might be approved for reward. In 1914 and 1915, quotas for officers' awards were in fact far too low, meaning that early war awards are scarce and that many deserving candidates received nothing. Quotas for officers' awards were gradually increased as the war went on, until in 1918, they were removed completely. There were never limits for awards made to other ranks (DCM, MM), but a great many deserving acts still went unrewarded for a great many reasons.

Monthly quotas for France and Flanders are summarised in the following table:

| RANK | AWARD | Authority for Approval | MONTHLY QUOTA (Immediate Awards) | | | | | |
|---|---|---|---|---|---|---|---|---|
| | | | August 1914 | Mid-1915 | November 1915 | October 1916 | 1st April 1917 | 3rd May 1918 |
| All Ranks | VC | HM the King | | | | | | |
| Officers | DSO | CinC France | 5 | 20 | 30 | 200 | 200 | Unlimited* |
| | MC | CinC France | – | | | 3 per DSO | 500 | Unlimited* |
| NCOs & Ptes | DCM | CinC France | Unlimited | Unlimited | Unlimited | Unlimited | Unlimited | Unlimited* |
| | MM | Corps Cmdr | – | – | – | Unlimited | Unlimited | Unlimited* |

**Table 1: Immediate Award Quotas, France & Flanders, 1914–18**

For other theatres of war, the quotas were:

Mesopotamia, Immediate Awards:
Prior to 1 January 1918, 10 DSOs and 20 MCs per month, increasing to 20 DSOs and 40 MCs a month thereafter.

Italy, Immediate Awards:
6 DSOs and 15 MCs a month as from 1 March 1918 (reduced from 20 DSOs and 50 MCs a month, the allotment before that date).

There were, in addition, quotas for periodic awards for France and Flanders. Separate bi-annual allocations were made down to battalion level. In practice, this meant that unit commanders had an allocation of a specified number of awards of different types to find awardees for. Those whose recommendations had been overlooked for an immediate award or Mention in Despatches might, in this manner, receive an award in an honours gazette.

In the last four months of the war, after all award quotas had been removed, some 36,000 awards were made and another 21,500 periodic awards were made in the King's Birthday Honours Gazette of 1919.[2] This Gazette is sometimes referred to as 'the Peace Gazette'. Large numbers of late war awards led to a debate on the standard of rewards, specifically whether the standard had been relaxed in 1918 (this question is dealt with later, as the view persists to this day).

## ANNOUNCEMENT AND CITATION

It is very much worth noting that the citations for the New Year and King's Birthday Honours awards were often printed in later Gazettes, which means that an award associated with a particular *London Gazette* date may be the date of publication of the citation, not that of the original announcement. As a result, periodic awards may not always be recognised as such; the important date is the initial announcement.

In a similar fashion, there are citations relating to immediate awards of the Military Cross that were gazetted separately from the original announcement. For example, MCs announced in the 19 November 1917 *Gazette* had the corresponding citations published in the 22 March 1918 *Gazette*. In order to understand the possible date of the action for which the award was made, it is necessary to check that the *London Gazette* date given is the original announcement date and not the later date that the citation was published. If the date of publication of the citation is used, the award may easily be placed in the wrong historical context. Reference to Table 2 should help to correctly identify periodic awards and correlate original gazette announcements with separately published citations.

Note that in respect of all periodic awards of the DSO and MC, no citations were published in the *London Gazette* and, for most of these awards, it seems that no citations survive, although occasional information can sometimes be found in unit histories, war diaries or other records.

| Award | Announced | Citation Gazetted | Comments |
|---|---|---|---|
| DSO | 03 June 1915 | 03 July 1915 | Birthday Honours (Periodic Awards) |
| DSO | 01 January 1916 | 14 January 1916 | New Year Honours (Periodic Awards) |
| DCM | 01 January 1916 | 13 February 1916 | New Year Honours (Periodic Awards) |
| DCM | 11 January 1916 | 10 March 1916 | New Year Honours Supplement (Periodic Awards) |
| DCM | 03 June 1916 | 21 June 1916 | Birthday Honours (Periodic Awards) |
| DSO | 24 June 1916 | 27 Juky 1916 | Immediate Awards |
| MC | 13 July 1916 | 20 October 1916 | Immediate Awards |
| MC | 27 July 1916 | 19 August 1916 | Immediate Awards |
| DOM | 01 January 1917 | 13 February 1917 | New Year Honours (Periodic Awards) |
| DSO | 17 March 1917 | 17 April 1917 | Immediate Awards, Mesopotamia |
| DSO | 17 March 1917 | 26 April 1917 | Immediate Awards, Mesopotamia |
| DSO | 17 March 1917 | 11 May 1917 | Immediate Awards, Mesopotamia |
| DSO | 17 March 1917 | 26 May 1917 | Immediate Awards, Mesopotamia |
| DSO | 17 March 1917 | 18 June 1917 | Immediate Awards, Mesopotamia |
| MC, DSO | 26 April 1917 | 18 June 1917 | Immediate Awards, Mesopotamia |
| DOM | 04 June 1917 | 09 July 1917 | Birthday Honours (Periodic Awards) |
| MC, DSO | 26 September 1917 | 08 January 1918 | Immediate Awards |
| MC, DSO | 18 October 1917 | 07 March 1918 | Immediate Awards |
| MC, DSO | 27 October 1917 | 18 March 1918 | Immediate Awards |
| MC, DSO | 19 November 1917 | 22 March 1918 | Immediate Awards |
| DOM | 19 November 1917 | 06 February 1918 | Immediate Awards |
| MC, DSO | 26 November 1917 | 06 April 1918 | Immediate Awards |
| Bars to DCM | 26 November 1917 | 06 February 1918 | Immediate Awards |
| MC, DSO | 17 December 1917 | 23 April 1918 | Immediate Awards |
| DCM | 01 January 1918 | 17 April 1918 | New Years Honours (Periodic Awards) |
| MC, DSO | 18 January 1918 | 25 April 1918 | Immediate Awards |
| MC, DSO | 04 February 1918 | 05 July 1918 | Immediate Awards |
| MC, DSO | 18 February 1918 | 18 July 1918 | Immediate Awards |
| MC, DSO | 04 March 1918 | 16 August 1918 | Immediate Awards |
| MC, DSO | 26 March 1918 | 24 August 1918 | Immediate Awards |
| DCM | 03 June 1918 | 18 October 1918 | Birthday Honours (Periodic Awards) |
| Bars to DCM | 03 June 1918 | 13 January 1919 | Immediate Awards |
| DCM | 01 January 1919 | 03 September 1919 | New Years Honours (Periodic Awards) |
| MC | 15 February 1919 | 30 July 1919 | Immediate Awards |
| DCM | 18 February 1919 | 10 January 1920 | Immediate Awards |
| MC | 08 March 1919 | 04 October 1919 | Immediate Awards |
| DCM | 11 March 1919 | 28 November 1920 | Immediate Awards |
| MC, DSO | 02 April 1919 | 10 December 1919 | Immediate Awards |
| DCM | 15 April 1919 | 25 February 1920 | Immediate Awards |
| DCM | 03 June 1919 | 11 March 1920 | Birthday Honours (Periodic Awards) |

**Table 2: Dates of award announcements versus date of citation,**
***London Gazette*, 1914-1918.**

## MULTIPLE AWARDS

Regarding second – and further – awards of the same medal, whereby a clasp or bar was attached to the ribbon of the first award, these were required to be immediate awards. Second, third or fourth awards of the same medal could not be Honours awards. In practice this meant that if a man became deserving of a second Honours award, he could not receive a bar to his decoration. He would have to receive a Meritorious Service Medal if his actions were not in the face of the enemy, or a Mention in Despatches, if they were. Therefore, an Honours DCM with later MID or later MSM appears more interesting in the light of this rule. If a man already in possession of an Honours decoration later became deserving of an immediate award, he could receive a bar to the decoration or an MM in the normal way. A bar to a gallantry decoration, if gained in 1918, was always an immediate reward for gallantry in the face of the enemy. In general it is also worth noting that winning a bar to a decoration was considered a great distinction, and the standard for winning the bar was therefore higher than for the original decoration. There are many examples of men in possession of a decoration who were recommended for a bar, but were refused it on the grounds that they already had the medal.

## OTHER REWARDS FOR BRAVERY

In addition to medals awarded for gallantry in action, there were other ways of rewarding valour that were inherited from the nineteenth century and much earlier. Men were promoted in the field for gallantry – they could be mentioned in despatches and there was the Divisional Card of Honour which many of those who received the Military Medal also received in connection with their act of battlefield gallantry.

Sometimes men received additional leave, for example Sergeant Sugden and Private Dunmore of the Machine Gun Corps. The pair had gone out together over to the enemy lines and, Sugden using his excellent German, had ordered a troublesome enemy trench mortar detachment to surrender with its weapon. This, the unsuspecting Germans dutifully did, presumably having understood the British

Sergeant's kind request perfectly. A peaceful resolution to the problem of the trench mortar was rewarded with a fortnight's leave for the pair of them, and the British lines were quiet for a month.[3]

## RECOMMENDATION AND APPROVAL

The process of recommending men for reward was a precise one. A stream of reports on all forms of battalion operations flowed constantly from the front line troops and ended up on senior officer's desks. Much of the material consisted of administrative and operational reports, but some of these contained recommendations for honours and awards. What typically happened was, after each battalion action, participants were de-briefed and reports sent up to the Command structure for digestion, dissemination and action. Individuals involved were interviewed by their Commander, usually a junior officer, who wrote a report summarising details of the events. Those who had performed an act that fell within the guidelines for an award, were brought to the notice of superiors and, by closely following official procedures, were recommended for a bravery award.

Often it was a junior officer, for example a company commander, who wrote a recommendation, which may then have been revised and written up by hand under the auspices of the unit commander. In the case of a recommendation for a Victoria Cross, signed witness statements were required before being sent to brigade and divisional headquarters, and then upwards to Corps and Army Commanders. VC recommendations were then endorsed by the Commander-in-Chief of the British Armies in France before being sent to Whitehall in London and eventually to the King. If approved at every step, the award of the Victoria Cross would be announced in Divisional or Brigade Orders as well as the *London Gazette*. Authority to award the DSO, MC and DCM lay not with the King, but with the Commander-in-Chief in France, whereas authority to award the MM lay with the Corps Commander or other officers appointed by him. The chain of authorisation for the MM was therefore the shortest, but it was in fact the award process for the Victoria Cross which shows the quickest turnaround from act to

*London Gazette* announcement, such was the importance placed on getting awards rapidly to the men.

If at all possible, an award ceremony was held in which the soldiers concerned were singled out for praise in front of the battalion, and received the ribbon of the decoration to wear on the left breast, from a senior officer. The medal itself was usually sent direct, in its box, to next of kin at the address provided by the soldier. Sometimes this occurred months after the award of the ribbon, by which time the soldier might have been killed or injured. After the award of the ribbon, many soldiers returned home on leave to an organised civic reception at which something of a fuss was made of them (the nature of this 'fuss' is documented in Section III, under the heading After the Act).[4] At all times, a great effort was made to speed the award process so that the time between act and award was minimised. In general, recommendations were submitted and awards announced in Brigade Orders within a few weeks of the acts of gallantry. This is shown by the announcements that appeared in the unit War Diaries which typically pre-date the official announcement in the *London Gazette* by several weeks. Very often, the men found out they had won an award some time before its publication in the *London Gazette*. Over the period of the war, the average time delay between act of gallantry and announcement of the award in the *London Gazette,* was increasingly stretched in parallel with the increasing intensity of the battles, the volume of recommendations received and the practice of splitting initial announcements and publishing large numbers of citations in later Gazettes which took up a lot of space:

Awards for 1916: Gazetted 4–8 weeks after the action.
Awards for late 1917: Gazetted 6–12 weeks after the action.
Awards for Spring 1918: Gazetted 3–6 months after the action.
Awards for late 1918: Gazetted 6–9 months after the action.

The above should be regarded as generalised, because there are both faster and slower turnaround times for awards, as well as some spectacular exceptions. Late in the war, the deeds of some prisoners of war returning from POW camps became known and resulted in retrospective awards being made. The *London Gazette* dated 30 January 1920 is sometimes known as 'the POW Gazette'; a slight misnomer as it is by no means clear that all of the men whose names appear therein were actually prisoners of war. Furthermore, none of the awards appearing in this gazette come with a published citation, so it is impossible to verify each and every personal circumstance.

Recommendations for awards relating to men taken Prisoner of War, or who were posted as 'missing' after an action, could only be approved if it could be ascertained from an official report that the man was still alive at the time the recommendation was signed by the officer making it. In addition, those taken prisoner could only receive an award if capture occurred 'through no fault of his own' – i.e. the man had not surrendered willingly. In this case, heroism was defined by those who preferred to die than to surrender voluntarily; to sacrifice themselves rather than attempt to save themselves.

## POSTHUMOUS AWARDS

Regarding posthumous awards, the general rule that a man must have survived the act for which he was to receive an award, was established with respect to the Victoria Cross during the 19th Century.[5] This idea was summarised in the following statement made by Lord Panmure – that the VC 'was an order for the living', and so could not be conferred upon the families of dead men. That the VC was loosely considered an order, reveals the historical linkage to pre-existing ancient orders such as the Order of the Thistle and the Order of the Bath, which certainly were orders for the living. Some of these ancient orders required the insignia to be returned to the Chancery upon death of the holder. But the Victoria Cross was not an order, it was a gallantry award, and it took many decades after its institution before the rules concerning posthumous rewards were finally solidified. It took until the middle of 1918, in fact, to clearly spell this out in an Army booklet entitled *Instructions Regarding Recommendations for Honours and Awards*. In paragraph 46 of this booklet there is the following statement: *all orders, decorations and medals can be granted posthumously.... provided that the officer initiating the recommendation signed it before (the man's) death.* [6] Further, if the officer was unable to sign before the man's death due to the 'severe stress of military operations', then the officer should make a note on the recommendation to that effect, and it would be considered. However, these being new clarifications to the rules, no such posthumous awards could be made relating to services prior to 15/16 July 1918. A man still could not be recommended for an award if he was killed during the action for which he was recommended. The general rule applied throughout the war was that a man must have survived the act for which he was recommended, at least until an officer had written a recommendation and had signed it. The only exception to this rule was when the severe stress of operations prevented the officer from performing his normal duty.

Posthumous awards of this sort do not only appear in the second half of 1918. An exceptional batch of retrospective, posthumous awards was placed in the *London Gazette* of 27 July 1917, edition number 30209, pages 7771–7772 in which 'His Majesty the KING has been graciously pleased to approve of the award of the Military Medal for bravery in the Field to the undermentioned Non-Commissioned Officers and Men, since deceased, who has (sic) been *killed in action or died of wounds or disease subsequent to the date of the award* of the Military Medal to them by the Commander-in-Chief in the Field'. A list of fifty-six names follows, of which four were serving with the Northumberland Fusiliers. All four of these Fusiliers died on the 1 July 1916 so their awards were announced over a year after their deaths. There are other, yet more exceptional examples: Company Sergeant Major Gillborn of the Northumberland Fusiliers was awarded a DCM in the *London Gazette* of 3 December 1918, for expelling the enemy from stables and a trench at Hooge four years earlier in October 1914. He was killed in action very shortly afterwards and, posthumous awards not being allowed under the rules of late 1914, his claim for an award resurfaced only much later. No doubt the claim was allowed on the basis that he was killed after performing the act of gallantry.

Rules on posthumous awards such as this one were clarified as the war proceeded, leading to occasional retrospective awards.

The significance of the posthumous ruling is that many men who died heroically in the fighting, could not receive any decoration other than a Victoria Cross or a Mention in Despatches. The presence of an oakleaf emblem on the rainbow ribbon of a Victory Medal awarded to the next of kin of a man killed in action, can sometimes hide a dramatic story.

## RETROSPECTIVE AWARDS

There were also some 'catch-up' *Gazette* editions containing awards of the Military Medal for various actions during the campaign. In the first half of 1916, submissions were requested for retrospective MM awards, the proposals to be received from Commanders by 1 July 1916. In late 1916, therefore, back-dated awards of the MM were announced in the *London Gazettes* of 12 September (Gazette edition 29749), 27 October 1916 (Gazette edition 29805) and 11 November (Gazette edition 29819). A note on the last page of these gazette editions is easily missed:

*NOTE: These Military Medals have been awarded for services rendered on various occasions during the progress of the Campaign, and the ranks now shown are not in all cases the ranks held by the recipients of the decorations when the acts of gallantry were performed.*

MMs appearing in these *Gazettes* are very difficult to assign to a particular action, as it is known that many of them were for the first half of 1916 and some of them were retrospective awards going back as far as 1915, for actions in France and Flanders 1915 as well as for Gallipoli. Yet others are known to be awards for the Battle of the Somme, for the 1 July 1916 and later. In addition, retrospective awards are known to be included in the *London Gazettes* of 21 September 1916 (Gazette edition 29758), although no such note is found on the last page of this edition. This *Gazette* contains some MM awards for the campaign on the Gallipoli Peninsula in 1915. In terms of the Military Cross, a tranche of retrospective awards made to Warrant Officers was announced in the *London Gazette* of 19 August,1916. MCs for as far back as 1914 are included in this *Gazette*.

In general, it is advisable to check carefully for notes in any *London Gazette* edition of interest.

## DEADLINE FOR IMMEDIATE RECOMMENDATIONS

Recommendations for immediate awards had to be submitted immediately, rather than being 'held over… until such time as recommendations for an Honours Gazette are called for'. The pamphlet *Instructions Regarding Recommendations,* paragraph 30, states that 'unless recommendations for immediate rewards reach the Commander in Chief within one month from the performance of the acts of gallantry, they will not be considered unless there are exceptional reasons'.[7] This ruling is a significant one, because it means that after every action, officers had to submit recommendations quickly so that they would pass through their superiors and up the chain of command to arrive with the CinC within a month. As a result, recommendations were received and approved more or less consecutively, in date order, and published in the *London Gazette* in date order. This is precisely what has been found with regard to the *London Gazette*; awards appear in batches and are in date order, they are not mixed up randomly and this means that the date of the act of gallantry can be estimated from the *London Gazette* date. This is helpful in deciding, for example, which sections of the unit War Diary to look through when further information is needed on a particular award. This is particularly the case for the MM, as many citations have not survived and other means must be employed to understand what the medals were awarded for.

Once again, a few exceptions to the one month ruling occur. One example is well illustrated by the following: Records of the 55th Division preserve recommendations for eleven awards relating to acts carried out by the 1st Battalion of the Northumberland Fusiliers during April 1918. These eleven men were on attachment from their parent Division at this time, and so recommendations were typed up by 55th Division and forwarded to the parent unit for onward transmission. The recommendations were received by the parent unit but, due to a misunderstanding, were not forwarded to the CinC for approval. They sat in files for two months and under normal circumstances no awards would have been made. Once the oversight came to light, Major General Jeudwine, Commanding 55th Division, submitted them with a covering letter asking that 'in the interests of those recommended' they be considered. The delay, he said, was due to the parent Division assuming that they had been submitted through the 55th Division, when they had *not* been. The letter was sufficient to get two officers of the Northumberland Fusiliers the MC and eight men the MM, but these awards were published in the *London Gazette* out of sequence as a result of the mistakes made in timely submission. This is the only such case of late submission recognised during the study of the whole of the Northumberland Fusiliers' decorations for the First World War. It seems to have been a rare occurrence, indicating that the great majority of awards are published in time sequence in the *London Gazette* That said, allowances have to be made for recommendations coming in from far afield – Mesopotamia and Egypt suffer an additional delay between date of act and publication in the *London Gazette*.

**RECOGNITION OF TRENCH RAID PARTICIPANTS**
Awards for trench raids also require special consideration as there were particular guidelines in place for their treatment. The pamphlet *Instructions Regarding Recommendations* states in paragraph 35 that '... the number of officers and other ranks of the raiding party, together with the number of MMs awarded by the Corps Commander for the same raid, should be stated'; presumably when recommendations for DSOs, MCs and DCMs were submitted to the CinC.[8] There was certainly an effort to reward those who took part in trench raids more freely than for other types of action, and the number of MMs made for each raid was required so that the number of other decorations could be held in proportion. A particularly successful raid might attract ten or more MMs for

a small group of men, well above the normal award rate, and the numbers of other decorations would be similarly above average. The Northumberland Fusiliers' most successful raid attracted two DSOs, five MCs, a bar to the DCM, three DCMs, a bar to the MM and twelve MMs. On this raid, nine per cent of participants received a decoration for gallantry, i.e. approximately five times the whole-war average award rate for the regiment and comparable to the awards list of a successful battalion-scale attack. Factors in the high rate of reward for trench raids, must include a high likelihood of meeting enemy face to face and that in some, but not all raids, the men were volunteers. The act of volunteering for a raid was looked upon very favourably in the Army, not only because volunteering set an example to others and was therefore to be encouraged whenever it occurred, but also because voluntary self-sacrifice is a prime ingredient of classical heroism.

**VARIATIONS IN SUBMISSION RATE**
Some units gained far more awards than others. Mostly for easily understood reasons, such as in the theatre of war when a unit was deployed and its role was front line fighting troops or support troops. In other cases there are differences for less easily understood reasons. Within a single infantry regiment, the Northumberland Fusiliers, substantial differences in award rate at brigade and battalion level have been uncovered, which cannot easily be explained in terms of external factors, such as severity of fighting or the battalion's role (pioneers versus front line infantry). The recommendation and approval process was imperfect, relying to a degree on subjective considerations by senior Army officers possessing a great range of personalities, but even this cannot sufficiently explain some of the differences between battalions.

Some battalions may not have been putting forward as many recommendations for awards as others. They were not in the habit of applying for medals when far greater, more immediate problems demanded their attention. These battalions received encouragement to submit more recommendations as the war went on. Some units, the Guards Regiments for example, were officered by highly articulate men with a public school education. The Guards were proud regiments with a strong awareness of the importance of augmenting the regimental honours list. Their officers were very good at the wording of recommendations, and might even have had 'influence' over the awards process. This in itself cannot be offered as a full explanation for the high numbers of awards made to the Guards Regiments, who were also undoubtedly the elite infantry units of the British Expeditionary Force. Yet other factors in addition to these must be considered in relation to the Guards and also the Highland Regiments' particularly long honours lists. And yet, there were two units which felt that the MM was beneath them and did not apply for this medal; these were the Black Watch, the 2nd Battalion and the Highland Light Infantry. These factors are discussed in a later chapter.

There were Colonels, Brigadiers and Generals who had very different attitudes as to what acts fell inside and outside of a soldier's job description. Subjectivity arising from the character of individual officers could result in different standards being set in different units. If what Paddy Griffith has pointed out with regard to the diversity of tactics employed by the BEF at battalion, brigade and divisional levels is true – that tactical incoherency was a function of the 'anarchy of personal whims' of individual commanders – then we can be certain that the gallantry award process was subjected to a similar anarchy of personal whims.[9] An officer's willingness to write or authorise a recommendation will have varied over time for a great many reasons, not the least of which was personal stress and fluctuating workload. Each time the responsible officer was replaced, a different personality influenced the decision to recommend or not to recommend, a different linguistic competency influenced the wording of the written report and his varied priorities dictated how many recommendations might get written up for each action. The importance of wording should not be under-stated; those senior officers charged with reviewing the thousands of submitted recommendations were looking for particular ingredients, and they would reject recommendations which contained the wrong sorts of ingredients. For example, in a recommendation for an immediate reward, a lack of conciseness or wording which emphasised services over a long period of time would almost certainly fail to result in a decoration.

So much for the anarchy among officers, but the privates and NCOs themselves came from a rich tapestry of civilian and regimental social backgrounds. If the Guards and Highland Regiments arrived in the firing line bearing an immense weight of fighting tradition and expectation, then there were certainly line battalions whose 'corporate identity' developed into one that was disengaged from the aims and conduct of the war. Some Army units, from battalion to divisional level, just didn't do war very well, tended not to deliver and were not that good at fighting. As a point of interest, just over 3 per cent of those who joined the Army between 1914 and 1918 were court-martialled at some stage, this number being substantially in excess of those awarded a gallantry medal in the same period.[10] Of course, the number of court-martials awarded was not limited by a quota system, so we may simply conclude that the Army had its 'dud' units and disciplinary problems in the same way as it had its elite units and heroes.

The decision to award medals was equally mysterious at times, and with attempts made to keep the supply of awards limited and not flood the troops with them, not everyone who deserved a medal received one. But occasionally it was the reverse: Captain Lawrence Gameson received the award of the French Croix de Guerre which was a surprise to him.[11] A batch of these awards had been made available to the 15th Division and, as he had been attached as Medical Officer to the divisional artillery, according to the General who pinned the medal on him, 'the artillery had done him the great honour by giving away one of their medals to an officer who was only attached'.

An incident of greater significance has been recorded by a machine gunner of 151st M.G. Company; Bill Leftley found himself in no-man's-land with probable empty enemy positions in front of him; only he realised the situation and so got into the trench alone. He surprised some Germans who immediately offered to surrender, no doubt thinking there was more than one British soldier. Leftley was 'scared stiff that the first German should rumble the actual situation and shout a warning to his mates, but all went well' and twenty prisoners were duly handed over to an infantry officer.[12] Apparently, although it seems highly unlikely, Leftley was recommended for the Victoria Cross, but as he had no witnesses, his story was rejected as 'a joke' and instead, Leftley received the French Medaille Militaire and the infantry officer got the Military Cross. Such dubious stories of injustice, transformed into rumours and petty grievances, probably did much to undermine the confidence of some of the rank-and-file in the entire awards system.

## TREATMENT OF COLLECTIVE GALLANTRY AND REWARDING THE LEADER

During the establishment of the Victoria Cross during 1855–56, Prince Albert had expressed the desire that selection of recipients of the Cross should be made by a system of voting. This was committed as Clause 13 of the VC Warrant, and allowed for award by ballot. The object of clause 13 was to ensure that the VC was distributed fairly in the opinion of the men who were actually there and who had personally witnessed the acts of their comrades. In practice, the clause was also used to restrict the numbers of VCs conferred to a handful of men in the most successful general actions, such as the Charge of the Light Brigade during the Crimean War. In such cases, whereas it could be argued that all who took part deserved the award, only a few would receive it, 'in recognition of all who were present'.[2] This philosophy was almost certainly applied in combination with the idea that those in positions of responsibility (for the leading of men) should receive the honour on behalf of all who were present. Throughout the First World War, batches of awards made for single actions can be found which clearly show that the man leading the operation received the most prestigious award and a handful of junior leaders and privates received the less prestigious awards. It was not uncommon for all officers present to be decorated whilst only a small proportion of privates received a medal. A part of the reason for this is certainly that the leadership was receiving the honour on behalf of all of those present, in an effort to restrict the number of awards made and thus to maintain exclusivity. It is also argued that leadership in itself was an extremely important component of many awards, and that the War Office and military staff were recognising and encouraging junior leadership. Whatever combination of factors came to bear, the result was that NCOs and officers were a more highly decorated group than ordinary private soldiers This is discussed in detail later.

Whilst the above may sound discriminatory, giving the officer in command a medal and the soldiers nothing, was neither discriminatory nor evidence of a bad old class system at work. It was absolutely right. The critical point in this regard is that in battle, or in other potentially lethal circumstances, it is the job of the leader to initiate events which may reasonably be expected to lead to his own death. There is a far greater element of self-sacrifice involved in initiating such actions than there is in following, and voluntary self-sacrifice is, as has been stated previously, a primary and major ingredient of classical heroism.

## SUSTAINED GALLANTRY AND DISTINGUISHED SERVICE

Not all so-called bravery medals were presented as rewards for glittering acts of bravery. A rudimentary appreciation of acts resulting in the award of the Victoria Cross tends to suggest that bravery is perhaps the only important element represented by gallantry medals. Yet, when an interest is taken in other awards, it is apparent that many were won for distinguished services over a period of time. In some cases, the period of time was stated in the award citation as 'the duration of the war' or a number of years.

Whereas sustained bravery over a short period of time was a prime ingredient of Victoria Cross citations, distinguished service over a period of time was not overlooked. Great effort was made to ensure that glittering acts of bravery, which naturally caught the attention, did not overshadow other important services on the battlefield. Distinguished service may contain elements of bravery but it is not only that; many NCOs and officers worked very hard, highly competently, to maintain the functionality of their units, whether battalions, companies, field hospitals or repair workshops, and also to maintain the psychological and physical wellbeing of their men. Distinguished service was usually less spectacular but was equally, or even more, vital to the success of operations, especially when these operations lasted weeks or months. Whether by inspirational man management or by brilliant organisation of units in the chaos of a battle, certain men quietly distinguished themselves over long periods, repeatedly, and in very trying circumstances. The honours and awards committees ensured that those who had performed over and above normal expectations in such circumstances, received due recognition. This was partly the function of the periodic awards published in the King's Birthday and New Year Honours Lists, but was also taken care of by immediate awards of the DCM and DSO. Senior officers who received the Order of the Bath had usually provided distinguished service over a period of time, quite often while in contact with the enemy. During the First World War, the importance of distinguished service was well understood by the Army and the War Office. In the chapters which follow, the critical importance of the men who helped to win the war by means of unstinting devotion to duty will be highlighted. In this way, greater balance is brought to the understanding of bravery medals and what they represent. Particularly in long, drawn-out operations, it is not only the isolated glittering act carried out on the spur of the moment that brings ultimate victory, but in large measure it is also sustained gallantry, inspirational leadership and distinguished service.

## TACTICAL CHANGES; THE EFFECT ON GALLANTRY AWARDS

The development and proliferation of tactics within the BEF began almost as soon as the so-called 'Old Contemptibles' were being thrown back towards the Channel ports. The shock of those weeks was taken on board by the leadership, as they realised they could conceivably lose the war. After Christmas 1914, the early attacks of 1915 – at St. Julien in April 1915 and at Loos in September to October 1915, for example – were a vital part of the 'learning curve', not only for the leadership but also at the level of NCOs and privates. No large scale offensives and few significant battles were attempted, everyone had plenty of time to consider how they might do things better, be it attack with fewer casualties and throw the enemy out of his positions, or defend better and deny the German Army its desires. As Paddy Griffiths noted, the war up to mid-1916 was the time of 'greatest amateurism, blundering and fumbling', and 'the BEF was heavily engaged in major battle for little more than thirty days between the Christmas fraternisations of 1914, and 30 June 1916'.[13] This, as much as the absence of the MM, explains the paucity of pre-1st July gallantry awards (their scarcity does not indicate a higher standard).

The Generals were not incompetent and bungling. Lessons learned in desperate and confused actions of 1914–1915 were disseminated, among Generals in their conferences, formally at training centres and informally by Tommy in his trenches during 'stand-to' over a cup of tea.

Alongside tactical changes were the arrival and integration of new weapons and the progressive devolution of responsibility for tactics onto the shoulders of NCOs rather than field officers. The Napoleonic control of battalions by an officer at their head had long since disappeared from the British Army, but the remains of high level command and control still remained in 1914. This feature particularly hampered the activities and effectiveness of cavalry operations. As the importance of platoon tactics, and then section tactics, became understood and implemented on the battlefield, so junior NCOs and privates were expected to make the tactical decisions. A great many British infantry attacks of 1914–1916 used fire and manoeuvre but remained liable to think in terms of attacking in waves, or straight lines in battalion strength. This was the downfall of the 1 July 1916, and of the use of battalions who had not been shown how to attack like the 1st Battalion of the Northumberlands.

The BEF evolved from a force based around riflemen with fixed bayonets supported by a couple of heavy machine guns (two heavy Vickers or Maxim machine guns per battalion in 1914 [14]), to a swarm of semi-isolated, self-motivated sections supporting each other as they moved in open order onto battlefield targets. The infantry platoon of 1917–18 had become the major unit of attack and was composed of a section of riflemen, one of bombers, a rifle grenade section and a Lewis gun party backed up by the plunging fire of the Stokes mortar (capable of firing at such a rate that as many as fifteen bombs could be airborne before the first one had landed on target). Each infantry section had become a miniature all-arms unit, having tools for fire suppression (Lewis gun), light artillery (bunker-busting and tank stopping rifle grenades and Stokes mortars) and mobile 'storm troops' in the form of riflemen and bombers.[15] None of them was expected to wait for orders when they knew what, in general, they ought to be doing. That the First World War was dominated by artillery is well known, but it is often forgotten that the war was won by the infantry rather than by tanks, ships or aircraft.

As early as the Somme, but particularly during 1917 and 1918, the concept of a target included a weak point in the enemy line through which troops could infiltrate, as much as it might mean a defended enemy position. The innumerable training centres had shown the men how to do the job in principle and parent units had finished that off by further training and by example. Fire, manoeuvre and infiltrate had become the prime expertise of the British soldier by 1918, not that of the German.[16] The British Army was, by that time, confident of winning and, with relatively light casualties, because they had achieved tactical supremacy in attack over the German Army long before the German waves broke upon under-prepared British defences during the Spring of 1918.

Organisational changes helped too: The Machine Gun Corps had been reorganised in February 1918 to be independent from the infantry and was provided with its own transport. At least one machine gunner thought that the Machine Gun Corps: 'proved that their system of transport was so efficient that, notwithstanding the fact that the infantry had advanced as quickly as the men could march, when the front line was actually checked and held up near the river bank, the machine guns came into action immediately. It is doubtful whether under the old system of fighting – the machine guns with the infantry battalion – this could have been achieved'.[17] By 1918, the firepower of the British Army was immense, thanks to the arrival of a new range of infantry weapons, new tactics based on increased mobility and exploitation, and new organisational and transport structures.

Just as the chaotic battles of the Hundred Days are perhaps the least understood of all, the medals won for bravery by the participants during that time represent some of the most professional soldiering of the BEF, even with its large conscript cohort, in that long artillery and infantry war. In the second half of 1918, the army was winning more medals for greater military success. The infantry were operating section tactics, infiltrating and isolating enemy positions, making bigger captures of arms and prisoners; artillerymen were driving hard up to the front to offer direct, mobile support to the infantry; aircraft were bombing and strafing targets in overhead support and tanks and machine guns were jumping forward to suppress and destroy resistance. Furthermore, the cavalry were on reconnaissance patrol gathering information on enemy dispositions and feeding it to the advancing forces, whilst ready to charge, chase and run down. In 1918, many local actions were fought under the command of NCOs, the platoon and section leaders; the very men who received the bulk of the bravery medals.

The effect of tactical changes over the course of the war was to devolve responsibility downward through the ranks, until it rested upon the junior officers and senior NCOs. This directly resulted in the increasing likelihood that these men would win large numbers of gallantry medals.

## ABUNDANCE OF AWARDS IN 1918

At many levels within the Army and the Government, the closing year of the First World War saw concerns voiced over the apparently high numbers of awards being conferred. As a result, after the Armistice and prior to the Second World War, an awards quota system was put into operation for all Army gallantry awards including those not previously subjected to a quota – the MM and DCM – whereby a certain number of awards was allotted to the different theatres of operations on a monthly basis. This was an attempt to iron out some of the perceived problems of award rate encountered during the First World War, both at Army level and at unit level. The quota system still exists within the Army today; a legacy of the latter parts of the First World War. But was the award rate actually too high in 1918 and had the standard of awards been eroded?

| Battle Phase | Fatalities | Fatalities per MM | MM | DCM | MC | DSO |
|---|---|---|---|---|---|---|
| Retreat from Mons, 1914 | 370 | – | 0 | 6 | 1 | 1 |
| 1915 – 30 June 1916 | 2927 | – | 77 | 51 | 16 | 4 |
| Somme July–Nov 1916 | 4301 | 14.2 | 302 | 32 | 49 | 7 |
| Winter 16–17 | 699 | 12.7 | 55 | 9 | 16 | 2 |
| Arras/Scarpe April–June 1917 | 1889 | 11.7 | 161 | 12 | 35 | 6 |
| Third Ypres 1917 | 2075 | 8.5 | 244 | 38 | 36 | 5 |
| Winter 17–18 | 173 | 3.9 | 44 | 8 | 8 | 0 |
| 1918 Offensive/Asiago | 2243 | 8.6 | 261 | 37 | 60 | 8 |
| Hundred Days/Piave | 1187 | 5.1 | 231 | 34 | 69 | 7 |

Table 3: Northumberland Fusiliers, awards and fatalities versus time

If late war awards were made both consistently and fairly when compared to earlier war awards, then an unjustified reaction in the immediate post-1918 period may have left a lasting influence on the British awards system that continues to affect military and public perception to this day. The question is not an easy one to answer, as award rate depended upon the intensity and success, or otherwise, of battles, and is disguised by the continued announcement of awards right up to 1920, long after the war had ended. Certain distortions have to be removed from the data before the question can be explored. The number of decorations for gallantry awarded to the Northumberland Fusiliers, each month in the periods indicated, is shown in Figure 1. During the Somme battle, the regiment was receiving an average of 90 awards per month. During 1917 this fell to about 60 awards per month but in 1918 it climbed spectacularly to nearly 170 per month (for the Spring Offensives) and 125 per month (for the Hundred Days). Superficially, it looks as if the award criteria had been severely relaxed. However, the British Army was firstly hardest pressed and then at its most successful during 1918. The difficult attritional battles of 1916 and 1917, which history has recorded as a waste of life in return for little military gain, arguably merited fewer gallantry awards because they were not accompanied by obvious military success. The Army was relatively small from 1914 to 1915 and was involved in rather few significant actions. The Army of 1916 was involved in what must have seemed, if compared to the actions of any previous war, unmitigated disasters, and the Army was never in the habit of showering troops with decorations for battles which did not add to Britannia's laurels.

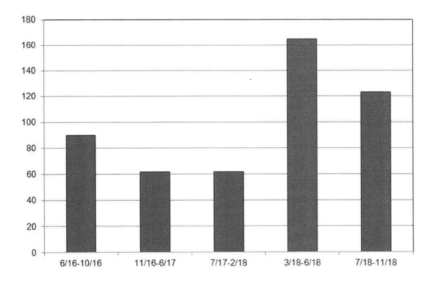

**Figure 1: Medals won per month, Northumberland Fusiliers, 1916–1918**

It may be seen from Figure 2 (on page 46) that the fighting of late 1918 was no less lethal than in any previous year, in fact the only three consecutive months in which the Northumberland Fusiliers suffered fatalities greater than 200 were August, September and October 1918. Also, long before the Hundred Days, the award rate

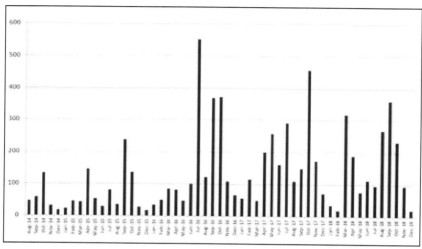

**Figure 2: Monthly Fatalities, 1916-1918**

had been climbing; this was not a phenomenon restricted to 1918, it was already occurring in 1917. Figure 3 shows how, as the war progressed, the numbers of awards for certain very successful battles, rose steadily. Even in February 1917, one battalion (the 23rd) gained more awards (twenty-two) for a single trench raid of a few hours duration, than any battalion had gained in any of the hard, prolonged and costly battles on the Somme of the previous year. There does not appear to be a clear point in 1918 at which the rate of award rose, but instead, the rate of reward for the most successful actions climbed steadily in the post-1916 period. The largest issue of awards to a single battalion was made for a series of actions carried out by the 2nd Battalion between 4 and 8 November 1918. However, the largest number of awards made for a single battle was the 73 gallantry medals issued after the highly successful Battle of the Menin Road on 20 September 1917, a 10th and 11th Battalion action (32 and 41 awards respectively). The principle that medals for bravery should be associated more with successful military actions (and less with the unsuccessful) goes right back to the Crimea and crops up repeatedly through the 19th Century. The award of the Victoria Cross, for example, was considered by War Office and government as an approbation of the conduct of the General officer commanding a victorious Army in the field.[18] As another example, it was Lord Wolseley who suggested that a total of four Victoria Crosses ought to be sufficient reward for the saving of the guns at Sanna's Post, 1900, which action; 'was not of a nature to reflect credit on our Army'.[19] Thus, three further VC recommendations for Sanna's Post were blocked. The gradual climb in number of awards in 1917–18 therefore, not only reflects growing success of British operations, but also the gradual erosion of the German Army's will to fight and resist over the same time period.[20]

Higher award rates in 1918 are therefore expected for a number of reasons. The Army of 1918 was larger than at any time before, there were more soldiers involved in actual fighting and the British Expeditionary Force in France and Flanders was holding a much longer section of the line than in earlier years. They had taken over more and more of the line from the French in order to ease pressure on them. During 1918, also, the eastward movement of the front line gathered pace and hence became far more dangerous because more and more operations occurred in the open. Trench warfare of 1915–1917 provided relatively good shelter for men most of the time, and full exposure to enemy fire only occurred on those uncommon occasions when the Army went over the top. The actions of 1918 were quite different, too; between March and late May, Germany's second great attempt to win the war by taking the offensive was defeated. Very soon after the last German attacks had died away, the Allied Armies launched their own determined and vigorous offensive which battered a worn down enemy and broke their strongest defensive lines on the way to complete victory by early October 1918.

Late in the war, there was greater military success and greater tactical professionalism. There is no evidence to suggest that medals were issued in abundance to maintain morale of the troops. There is plenty of evidence to the contrary, gathered by the British censor teams who were looking at soldiers' letters home, that the will to fight was alive and well during 1918. There were no problems with despondency or morale even during the headlong retreats of the

Spring.[21] Tommy was not in need of a freer distribution of medals to maintain his will to fight; rather he was well fed and well supplied and he had complete confidence in the inevitability of final Allied victory. During the Hundred Days of the Summer and Autumn of 1918, he found his own encouragement in the continuing retreat of the enemy and the scale and rapidity of the victories being achieved. It is therefore thought that the more abundant issue of medals in 1918 had much more to do with the abundant military successes achieved in that year by a larger Army on a wider frontage, than any official effort to ingratiate depressed and fearful conscript soldiers by means of symbolic trinkets. A higher award rate cannot simply be dismissed as the result of relaxed standards.

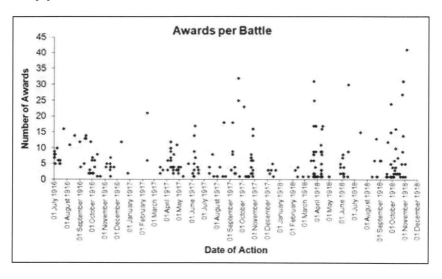

**Figure 3: Numbers of medals won in each action,**
**Northumberland Fusiliers, 1916–1918**

## EVOLUTION OF THE HERO

The hero is an idea, and that idea changed significantly as warfare developed from 1855, the year of institution of the Victoria Cross, to 1918.[22] If the VC is studied in isolation from the wider honours system, of which it is a part, it is possible to miss the fact that certain VC acts of the Victorian period became DCM and MM acts in World War One. Smith asserts that the Victorian concept of the hero was alive and well in 1914 during the retreat from Mons; 'all the elements of standard Victorian heroism, desperate defence, personal sacrifice, and defiance of the enemy' were present among the 1914 VC heroes, even saving the guns ('that most holy of preindustrial heroic acts'). However, what Smith has not recorded is that there was a great many of these exact same acts rewarded between 1915 and 1918, but the most Victorian of them merited increasingly the DCM or MM and not the VC. The Victorian hero can still be found, among DCM and MM winners, who were first into the enemy trenches, who performed highly symbolic acts such as carrying the 'Royal Standard of Scotland' across no-mans-land during an attack. Among men of the machine gun corps we find many DCMs for defence to the last man before grabbing the weapon and getting out (in one case, a tripod left behind was pluckily rescued, almost from among the enemy). In the Army Service Corps, we find many DCMs for saving the guns, using steam driven gun tractors rather than horses. Throughout all units, officer rescue still merited a higher award rate than rescue of other ranks, and there are many rescues which warranted official recognition (outside of the Royal Army Medical Corps). Most classically Victorian VC acts did in fact merit reward beyond 1914. What actually changed with regard to the VC was simply this; in a more violent war, with far more outstanding displays of gallantry coming to notice coupled with official reluctance to issue the cross too freely, awards emphasised hard fighting over symbolism. The nature of the 'Supreme Hero' evolved, but the Victorian Hero persisted in the less prestigious rewards.

## DISTRIBUTION OF GALLANTRY MEDALS

Having reviewed the types of reward and some of the rules, we must begin the task of identifying who won the medals during World War One (which units and which men). There were many reasons why some units won more medals than others. By looking at who won medals for battlefield bravery, we begin to see patterns which have not been described before. An interpretation of what these patterns mean leads us to an understanding of what was important to the British Army during World War One – bravery in itself, skilful leadership or something different. In this chapter, therefore, we take a high level tour of gallantry awards made to the whole British Army before, in Section II, we examine the details of what exactly the medals awarded to various corps, the cavalry and the infantry were granted for.

A total of 197,192 bravery medals were awarded over the period of the First World War.[23] Abbott & Tamplin, in the 2nd edition of their 1981 book, *British Gallantry Awards*, state that there were 573 awards of the Victoria Cross, 9,767 DSOs, 40,236 MCs, 25,072 awards of the DCM and 121,544 MMs to the British and Commonwealth Armies. These numbers include the bars marking second, third and sometimes fourth awards of the decoration to the same recipient for repeated acts of bravery or distinguished service. The number excludes mentions in despatches which any man could receive, and Orders of the Bath, for example, which were conferred upon high ranking officers for gallantry in action (usually Colonels and higher).

## Distribution by Unit

In order to discover who won medals for bravery, we have sampled the WO372 series of Medal Index Cards (MICs) at the UK National Archives (WO372/23 and WO372/24 series). Figure 5 summarises these results. What is immediately apparent is that 62 per cent of medals was won by the infantry. This reinforces the concept that it was an infantryman's war; the infantry outnumbered all other units, the war was fought by the infantry and it was won by the infantry. No other arm comes close in terms of absolute numbers of medals gained. By contrast, the Army Service Corps was a large unit engaged in supply duties. The success of the infantry was reliant upon the men who supplied them, but the Army Service Corps only received 2 per cent of all medals awarded for gallantry, mainly because they did not do much actual fighting. It is clear that the units which operated in the front line won more awards for gallantry than those which operated mainly behind the lines.

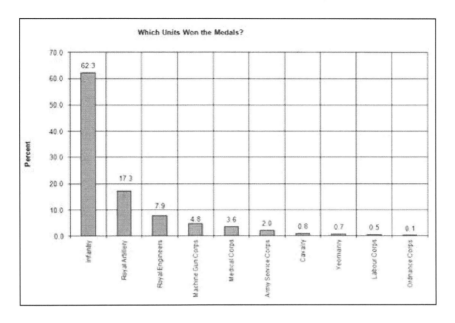

**Figure 4: Percentage of medals won by different army units, 1914–1918**

Of all who served, very few were decorated for gallantry (Figure 5). The Medal Index Card data reveal that approximately 2.3 per cent of other ranks within the infantry received a gallantry award (DCM or MM). The artillery held the highest proportion of gallantry award winners among the other ranks at 3 per cent and it is the support corps and cavalry that received the lowest proportion. The global proportion of gallantry award winners is 3.5 per cent of those who served overseas during the Great War (assuming figures of 200,000 gallantry medals and 5.7 million who served overseas – the approximate number of Victory medals awarded).

While it is easy enough to understand why the infantry received so many medals, it is interesting that proportionately more artillerymen had medals for gallantry on their chests than any other unit. The artillery was the most decorated of the Corps. The reason for this is the artillery was always in demand and had much less rest out of the line than the infantry. Artillery batteries were

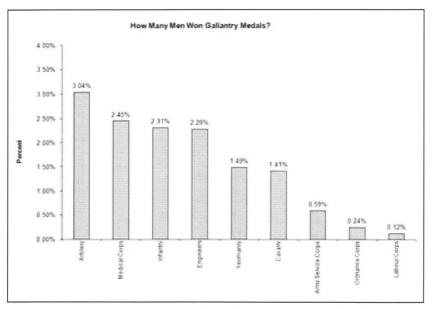

**Figure 5: Percentage of other ranks winning gallantry medals, by unit**

attached to a Division, but were very often called upon to remain in the line at work, when their parent Division had been withdrawn for resting. Therefore, with more days spent fighting, the artillery naturally came by more awards. The three Corps with less than 1 per cent were operating behind the front line much of the time, where shelling and aerial bombing of supply routes, supply dumps and men was continual. These units obtained fewer 'fighting' awards, but made up for this by earning a far higher proportion of medals for meritorious service over a period of time.

The infantry total of 2.3 per cent is broken down in Figure 6 revealing that 3.6 per cent of other ranks in the Guards Regiments won a gallantry award, compared to approximately 2 per cent for most ordinary infantry regiments. The Highland regiments appear in second place with nearly 3 per cent of men gaining awards. The Northumberland Fusiliers languish well down in second to last position with 1.75 per cent of other ranks winning gallantry awards; half that of the Guards regiments and well down on the average county regiment. The category 'regiment' includes any infantry unit with a name including the word regiment, in other words, most of the ordinary county regiments are included here. An interpretation of these relative values is provided later.

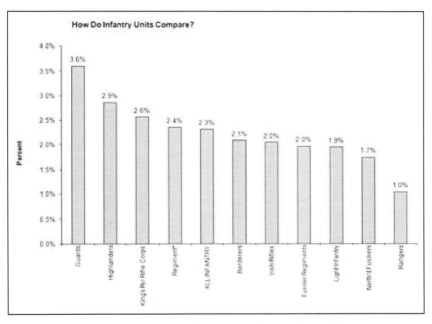

**Figure 6: Percentage of infantry other ranks winning
gallantry medals**

This figure should not be misinterpreted as a description of which units were the bravest. There are many factors influencing the relative positions of units on this plot.

The Guards regiments were unquestionably an elite formation at the outset in 1914, but they retained this quality and reputation right through to the very end of the war in spite of losing many battalions worth of men as casualties. A Scots Guards private, Stephen Graham, was impressed to see how the Grenadier Guards attacked a strongly held piece of German trench in late 1918, their 'discipline, courage and fame committed them then, as ever, to doing the impossible in human heroism and endurance'.[24] That the Guards were special is beyond doubt, but it was the Grenadier Guards who were the most special, carrying on their regimental traditions in the worst conditions of the trenches without dilution or relaxation. The regiment demanded particular behaviour from Guardsmen, they possessed an *esprit de corps* that required them never to flinch even in the face of the impossible. They had other advantages over line regiments; the Guards were only composed of regular army battalions, there were no Territorial or Service battalions, so they received some of the best recruits – their battalions were artificially populated with the most promising and the best men. Nowhere was this truer than with regard to their officers, who were the best that Britain could field in terms of background, ability and education. Some of these officers were highly capable in the writing of recommendations, and worked conscientiously to see that their men got the medals they deserved. These aspects of their tradition, structure and composition explain how the Guards did so well in obtaining such a high proportion of gallantry medals.

Similarly, the Scottish regiments had made for themselves (and partly invented for themselves) a fearsome reputation that men felt compelled to uphold. A standard of performance had been established and embellished in popular histories of 19th century battles and there was an expectation that no man would damage the reputation of the Scots in battle. Scotsmen felt they had to live up to that fighting tradition, to the point that they needed to be restrained at times.

Incredible bravery, to the point of recklessness, was a trademark of these formations that was not lost on the Germans, who knew that Guardsmen and Scotsmen would not be stopped by explosives, bullets or cold steel. The Rifle Corps also may be viewed as elite and officered by good quality men. Thus, reputation alone helped these units to achieve success, which in turn brought to them more honours and decorations than other units. However it also brought higher casualties in several of their actions.

Lower award rates among the line regiments can be ascribed to their having more territorial and service battalions who were more likely to spend less time in the attack and more time holding the line in support and reserve trenches (Ball, 2006). Other kinds of battalion serving in line regiments were not fighting units but instead were support units who were not expected to take part in attacks. A high proportion of support battalions has an effect on the award rate for the regiment. The Northumberland Fusiliers had four pioneer battalions, the highest number of any infantry regiment during World War One. Most other regiments had just one or two pioneer battalions, and many regiments did not raise any pioneers at all. It was the mining towns of the north-east of England that generated the highest proportions of pioneers and these units did not have the chance to win large numbers of gallantry medals. This partly explains why the Northumberland Fusiliers and the Light Infantry appear rather low in the rankings. The Durham Light Infantry with its pioneer battalions was also a large regiment.

## Distribution by Rank

An analysis of the Distinguished Conduct Medal reveals that across most of the British Army, half of these medals went to men holding the rank of sergeant or more senior. The other half went to privates, lance corporals and corporals. Considering that sergeants and higher were in a definite minority (20 per cent of the total manpower or lower), there is a clear bias towards sergeants and warrant officers. The table below shows just how consistent the 50:50 ratio was across all arms:

| DCM | A.Cyc.C | A.S.C. | R.A. | R.E. | R.A.M.C | M.G.C. | Cavalry | Tanks | North'd Fus |
|---|---|---|---|---|---|---|---|---|---|
| Sgts+ | 52% | 48% | 52% | 44% | 50% | 57% | 49% | 48% | 55% |
| Pte/ Cpl | 48% | 52% | 48% | 56% | 50% | 43% | 51% | 52% | 45% |

**Table 4: Awards of the Distinguished Conduct Medal by unit and by rank, part 1.**

How great this bias was has been calculated for the Northumberland Fusiliers; whereas 4.5 per cent of sergeants and warrant officers received gallantry decorations, only 1 per cent of privates and corporals received decorations. In absolute terms, this means that sergeants and higher were nearly five times more likely to receive decorations for gallantry than privates and corporals. Regarding the officers of the Northumberland Fusiliers, it is known that in the Tyneside Scottish Brigade (composed of four battalions), 104 awards were won by approximately 695 officers who served, i.e. 15 per cent were decorated. In the Tyneside Irish Brigade, also composed of four battalions, 573 officers are known to have served and of these, 77 were decorated, i.e. 13 per cent.

| DCM | A.Cyc.C | A.S.C. | R.A. | R.E. | R.A.M.C | M.G.C. | Cavalry | Tanks | North'd Fus |
|---|---|---|---|---|---|---|---|---|---|
| Sgts, WOs | 52% | 48% | 52% | 44% | 50% | 57% | 49% | 48% | 55% |
| L/Cp, Cpl | 27% | 12% | 29% | 36% | 15% | 24% | 28% | 27% | 22% |
| Pte, Spr, Gnr | 21% | 40% | 18% | 20% | 35% | 19% | 23% | 25% | 23% |

**Table 5: Awards of the Distinguished Conduct Medal by unit and by rank, part 2.**

Referring now to Table 5, we see that for nearly every Army unit, 80 per cent of all DCMs went to NCOs and only 20 per cent to privates. The split is fairly constant across most units (except the Army Service Corps and the Royal Army Medical Corps). These ratios are so constant as to suggest a deliberate allocation by Army authorities; this is surely not a result of chance. In combination with the observations on bias (in favour of NCOs) made above, this suggests that it may have been policy to confer decorations on sergeants and higher at five times the rate to privates and corporals. No evidence to substantiate this possibility has yet come to light (although it is known that the Navy was carefully monitoring and managing the allocations of its rewards in periodic gazettes by rank and location during World War Two – this practice originated somewhere). It was not lost on the private soldier of 1916 that the newly instituted MM did not come with a gratuity and was therefore worth a lot less to the recipient than a DCM. Some ventured to suggest that this was the main reason the MM was instituted, to save money.

That the DCM came with a generous gratuity of £20 and a pension, may also help to explain why it was the long-serving, experienced and reliable sergeants and warrant officers who received half of all DCMs, and that 80 per cent of all DCMs went to NCOs. In turn, this observation lends weight to the argument that the MM was not entirely junior to the DCM in terms of the level of bravery required to win one, it was in many cases the equal of the DCM in all but the rank of the recipient.

## Proportions of New Year and King's Birthday Honours Awards, by Corps

| HONOURS | A.Cyc.C | A.S.C. | R.A. | R.E. | R.A.M.C | M.G.C. | Tanks | North'd Fus |
|---|---|---|---|---|---|---|---|---|
| DCM | 58% | 60% | 52% | 51% | 30% | 28% | 34% | 30% |
| MC | 20% | 60% | 32% | 45% | 28% | 16% | 20% | 23% |
| DSO | 100% | 98% | 85% | 85% | 77% | 72% | 48% | 41% |

**Table 6: Proportion of Periodic (Honours) Awards by unit**

With regard to Periodic (Honours) Awards, Table 6 shows that the proportion of honours awards varied considerably across the Corps and the infantry. Front line units received a much higher proportion of immediate awards and units operating largely behind the lines received a higher proportion of honours awards for distinguished services over a period of time.

## UNDERSTANDING THE MILITARY MEDAL

In this section we review the medal for which the least is known – the Military Medal (MM). We also begin to introduce some of the important concepts which are enlarged upon during the remaining sections of the book. The MM is considered the most junior of medallic awards of 1914–1918. It did not attract any financial benefits and was awarded in comparatively large numbers (close to 120,000 when second and third awards are included). The medal was awarded mainly for actions from 1916 onwards, but some retrospective MM awards have been noted for 1915 actions.[25]

The distribution of MM awards between different Army units reveals that the infantry walked away with the lion's share – 67 per cent – of MMs. This statistic clearly illustrates that the MM was awarded mainly for the fighting part of military operations. Many other tasks, although dangerous and requiring courage, did not attract awards of the MM.

- Infantry        67 per cent
  (mostly for large attacks, but many for patrol work, runners, trench raids, for work as Battalion stretcher bearers, all the things the infantry had to do)
- Artillery       13 per cent
  (mainly for gallantry and devotion to duty under shellfire, but also we see runners, ammunition explosions and a good portion of 'lifesaving')
- Engineers    6 per cent
  (mainly for devotion to duty under shellfire whilst engaged in construction work and cable repairs – vital for communications)

- RAMC            4 per cent      (all 'lifesaving awards')
- Cavalry/Tanks  2 per cent
- Other Corps    2 per cent      (mostly for gallantry under shellfire)
- RAF              1 per cent      (all for gallantry behind the lines during enemy air raids)

We have seen how the DCM was largely an NCO's reward. The extent to which the MM was a private's award is shown below:

- Pte          47 per cent
- L/Cpl         9 per cent
- Cpl          16 per cent
- Sgt+        28 per cent (total NCOs, 53 per cent)

If we assume that an infantry battalion was made up of 80 per cent Ptes and 20 per cent NCOs, then an explanation is needed for the fact that only 47 per cent of sampled MMs have the rank of private, gunner or sapper indented on the edge; 20 per cent of the men won 53 per cent of MMs, making the NCOs a medal-rich contingent. The importance of battlefield leadership in often confused military actions, cannot be overstated. Privates would fight hard if their leadership was solid and privates would run if their leadership ran first. The significance of junior leadership was not lost on the enemy. Leaders were specifically targeted by German soldiers because they knew that if they could eliminate them from the battlefield, an attack could be more easily beaten.

Moving to the types of action for which the Military Medal was awarded, we see that 49 per cent of all sampled MMs were won for specific acts during a large scale attack, and most of these awards are those to the infantry. It is important to note that bravery medals were never won for simply 'going over the top' and getting shot down or blown up; all the awards made for infantry attacks were for specific acts such as attacking and silencing a machine gun position, for clearing a trench or for getting the wounded in under heavy shell and machine-gun fire. However there are many other actions represented by the MM:

- Attack                         49 per cent
- Gallantry under shellfire      12 per cent
- Lifesaving                     9 per cent
- Trench Raids                   7 per cent
- Runner                         6 per cent
- Defending                      5 per cent
- Fighting Patrol                4 per cent

It is notable that just 12 per cent of MMs were awarded for gallantry under shell fire which accounted for 50 per cent of deaths and injuries early in the war and rising to 85 per cent later.[26] Shelling accounted for a further large number of psychological battle casualties, including the well known victims of 'shell shock'. What is abundantly clear from first-hand accounts is that heavy bombardments required some of the greatest courage to endure. It is, therefore, surprising that acts of gallantry under shell fire led to the award of so few medals.

Ranked third in abundance, 9 per cent of awards were made for 'lifesaving', split almost equally between the Royal Army Medical Corps and other units. Considering that the Medical Corps probably evacuated more wounded than anyone else, it is interesting that so many lifesaving acts by non RAMC men resulted in the award of MMs. Part of the explanation may be that many lifesaving acts were carried out by battalion stretcher bearers who were not part of the Royal Army Medical Corps, but were performing the same function on the front line. Another probable explanation may be that some lifesaving awards were for excavating buried comrades, an act not confined to the Medical Corps or battalion medical staff.

Trench raids account for 7 per cent of MM awards in the available sample. A surprisingly high value considering that raids were typically carried out 'occasionally' by a fraction of a battalion; from small parties to company strength was typical, but some were indeed battalion scale in strength. Raiding was not routine work. By contrast, routine patrols went out nightly in many cases, in order to observe and gain intelligence on the enemy as well as to gain familiarity with the ground. Trench raids were at most a monthly event, indeed some battalions only raided once or twice in the entire war. The contrast between 7 per cent of MMs awarded for raids versus 4 per cent for patrol work is a far greater one than is immediately apparent, and the reason for this difference can be explained very well; the allocation of rewards for successful trench raids was held artificially high by Army Headquarters specifically to encourage raiding.[27] The same is true for the German Army, in which General von Stein made it clear that the participants of raids, 'will be publicly praised in a Corps Order of the Day and they will each receive a signed certificate of recognition. If the patrol has been successful, if enemy soldiers have been recovered dead or alive, or if there have been important seizures of material, the participants will receive the Iron Cross or other decorations. Whenever there has been a particularly successful patrol operation, there is always a large scale distribution of Iron Crosses'.[28] In the case of trench raids, it is plain to see that Army Headquarters decided that raid participants were more heroic than the normal. Other decisions about heroism, its nature and suitable reward, were made by the State and the Army.

Awards made to 'runners' (6 per cent of total) provide an interesting insight into what was considered militarily important on the battlefield between 1914 and 1918. Primarily, runners carried important information to officers which allowed them to coordinate the battle. For example, reports from front line infantry that a line of enemy trenches had been taken, but that the battalion flank was exposed as a result of failure by a neighbouring unit and they were in urgent need of ammunition. Such information allowed action to be taken at a time in history when the fog of battle was particularly dense. Secondarily, perhaps, their courage was recognised because they volunteered, and if they were successful, they might well be reporting to a senior officer who was in a position to press a recommendation for him. Many other soldiers died isolated in forward positions and shell holes before their courage became known to senior officers.

## PERIOD OF TIME MMs

The exact status of the Military Medal as an immediate award for acts of gallantry in battle is difficult to define because of the general lack of surviving citations. Although it was intended as a reward for acts carried out over a short period of time, including single actions of no more than a few days' duration, this medal was used to reward prolonged periods of distinguished services over many months, even after the regulations regarding its award were clarified in February of 1918. A series of recommendations for MMs actually gazetted is found in the 57th Division Routine Orders, dated 12 December 1918. Several of these recommendations relate to good services over a period of time, but that for number 681034 Gunner H. Lund, Royal Field Artillery, (T.F.) represents an excellent example of a period of time award (place names are blanked out in the original document): 'This man has served with the Battery for eighteen months continuously. He, as limber gunner, has been continuously at the gun-position for months at a time, and has always carried out his duties with noteworthy zeal. At .......... he served his gun through the heaviest hostile barrages until badly gassed when he refused to go to hospital. His gun was left in action mainly owing to his efforts in spite of the bad conditions. During the ....... battle in April 1918, he was again conspicuous, his gun firing 5,000 rounds in nine days. During the offensive from August to October, 1918, near ........ he served his gun continuously. He has always been most cheerful, and his steadiness has been of the greatest value in most trying circumstances'. The MM, commonly thought to be for single acts of bravery only, was sometimes presented for distinguished services over a long period. What proportion was for a period of time will never be known, but most were for specific battlefield acts carried out in a single day or single action lasting at most a few days. This was the position adopted in the guidelines for honours and awards issued in February 1918.

## CONCLUSIONS

We conclude that officers were roughly three times more likely to be decorated for gallantry than sergeants and fifteen times more likely to be decorated than privates and corporals. Sergeants were roughly five times more likely to be decorated than privates and corporals. The total proportion of men receiving decorations for gallantry in battle during the First World War was only about 2 per cent of all those involved. Some units saw over 3 per cent of those who served gain a medal, for example the Grenadier Guards and the ever-present artillerymen, whereas other units saw only 1 per cent of their number receive a special distinction. The proportion varies according to the nature of each unit's duties, the composition of the unit and the location of their activities relative to the front line where the greatest number of medals was earned. The great majority received no additional recognition for their service, other than a handful of campaign medals.

To receive a medal for gallantry was certainly a great distinction; the authorities succeeded in keeping these distinctions special by means of issuing them very sparingly to only the most deserving cases. There is no case to be made that medals were handed out too freely in the British and Commonwealth Armies.

Considering the distribution of gallantry medals in their totality, it may be seen that 68 per cent of all awards were won by 20 per cent of a unit's strength – the commissioned officers and NCOs. The most junior ranks, privates, gunners, sappers and cavalry troopers, composing about 80 per cent of most units, only received 32 per cent of awards, and 92 per cent of these awards were MMs with no financial benefits attached. Of those most junior ranks who did receive a medal for bravery, only 8 per cent were lucky enough to receive a DCM. To see a DCM on a private's chest was something unusual, but what that private had to do to get one of these rarities changed substantially as the war progressed. It is easy to interpret all of this as class prejudice, but instead it is thought to have little to do with class and much to do with the practicalities of waging a war against a formidable enemy. The higher a man's rank, the more responsibility for leadership he had, and the more heavily the consequences of his actions were felt by himself, his immediate colleagues and by the Army as a whole. The pivotal role of the junior leadership on the battlefield meant that these men were more likely to be decorated or die in the endeavour. Those who followed were 'acting under orders'; they were obliged by their contracts of service to do their jobs. That the junior leadership was rewarded with a disproportionate number of medals is a deeply significant observation in terms of understanding battlefield bravery; what it is, how it is recognised, and what it isn't.

Medals were not granted for courage alone. Had medals been issued to reward courage, there should have been far more awards made to those who endured shell fire as well as to those who stepped out of trenches and walked into a hail of bullets and shell fragments. Gallantry medals from the First World War were presented for specific types of acts and there was a series of courageous actions for which there was a policy of making no reward. The act of going into battle and of being shot at and wounded or killed, whilst requiring some of the greatest courage, was considered part of a soldier's job. That said, it is paradoxical that the winners of gallantry medals routinely state that; 'I was only doing my job'. Such is commonly stated by those viewed as heroes, and the two separate viewpoints will be fully squared up later.

Alongside additional evidence presented elsewhere in this book, it is suggested that battlefield leadership was of primary importance and that bravery on its own was not the only component of awards. The war was not won by means of the glittering act of personal bravery carried out on the spur of the moment. That there was great bravery and courage displayed by most soldiers in the front line trenches, particularly when under heavy artillery bombardment or going over the top, is readily understood. Likewise, that most of these courageous or brave acts went unrewarded is clear when we consider the scarcity of awards on men's chests. So what was it that was being rewarded in the war of 1914–1918? Section II of this book attempts to illustrate what that was.

# SECTION II:

# IN THE FIRING LINE

# Battlefield Acts

This Section comprises an overview of the nature of infantry, cavalry and corps gallantry and distinguished service during the Great War, mainly with reference to the Western Front. In this section, the underlying parameters and motives for the display of individual and collective bravery are examined and highlighted, along with what the junior leadership was doing on the battlefield and the true value of that leadership. How Tommy was motivated to stand and fight is also examined. But primarily what the following chapters explain is what men did in order to receive recognition and what was required of them to receive higher distinctions. What they did looks very much like 'just their job', but many of the stories do seem peculiarly inspiring and exciting, or at the least highly remarkable. The diversity of actions for which men received decorations is staggering; the distinctions between each unit in itself is of great interest. Notably, that icon of bravery which arose during the Great War and has coloured popular judgement of battlefield bravery ever since, the act of single-handedly charging a machine gun position may be viewed for what it is – exceptional, and rare. The act of storming a machine gun post is not typical of the vast majority of battlefield acts that resulted in the award of medals for gallantry and distinguished service, but it is an act that can help us understand the nature of heroism as experienced by the hero and by those men who saw it.

We mainly review the DCM, the MC and the DSO. The VC is only briefly considered for comparative purposes, as it is not the purpose of this work to describe again what the VC was conferred for. However, some examples of VC awards are provided so as to put the major volume of awards into context. An attempt to understand more clearly the Military Medal, as we have seen, suffers from a severe lack of data but in the case of the Tank Corps, for which all MM citations have survived, some conclusions may be drawn which help us to understand the entire awards system in World War One. A small selection of foreign awards is considered which has provided some informative conclusions concerning the relative importance of personal bravery versus distinguished service. One example of a Mention-in-Despatches is presented which throws light upon the treatment of those forced to surrender and who were taken Prisoner of War. We also focus upon the act of lifesaving as well as the persistence of the 'Victorian Hero' through to 1918.

For each unit the relative scarcity of the various battlefield acts, the relative abundance of immediate awards and Honours awards plus the split between ranks is presented. Not all units have received attention; some were too small and awards too rare; e.g., the Veterinary, Cyclist and Ordnance Corps as well as awards to women. The Army Chaplain's Department has also received little attention in this work.

# The Royal Artillery

This chapter contains an overview of the activities and bravery awards of the Royal Horse Artillery, the Royal Field Artillery and the Royal Garrison Artillery. These units operated guns of varying sizes, from mobile to light field guns drawn by the Royal Horse Artillery, who were expected to act in direct support of the cavalry (which also had its own machine gun sections). The Royal Field Artillery operated the famous 18-pounder field piece as well as howitzers. Batteries often operated short distances behind the front line in direct support of infantry operations, which was particularly true of howitzer batteries. Royal Field Artillerymen also operated trench mortars which moved into the line to perform shoots on particular targets. Some trench mortar batteries remained in the line for significant periods, providing heavy support to light infantry weapons and an answer to enemy trench mortar activity.

The Royal Garrison Artillery (RGA) operated the larger, heavy, siege and railway guns which tended to be situated further behind the lines in more permanent artillery positions. Their guns had to be towed by large horse teams or by a steam tractor into and out of position; battery positions were sometimes serviced by light rail lines constructed by the railway companies of the Royal Engineers. Few in number at the start of the war, the RGA grew in numbers and importance over time.

Gun positions of many artillery units were constructed by the Field Companies of the Royal Engineers with the muscle of spare infantry or Labour Corps men. In addition to gun pits, the artilleryman's world included ammunition dumps and, usually, accommodation close by, for example dug-outs or tents. Having a place to sleep nearby suggests the permanence of the gun lines, the lack of regular rotation out of the firing line and the long periods of time the artillery units spent at the front. Whilst infantry Divisions were cycled between the front line, reserve trenches and back areas, many artillery units remained in the line while the rest of the Division gained rest and training. Such was the demand for artillery support and the permanence of the guns in their positions. This is one reason why just over 3 per cent of artillerymen gained decorations for gallantry during the war; a very high proportion, which puts them second only to the men of the Guards regiments, of whom 3.6 per cent won decorations.

The Royal Artillery gained just over 17 per cent of all Great War gallantry awards and most of those were awarded to men at the gun line, who were frequently enduring enemy counter-battery fire, or to those who were acting as linesmen with Brigade signallers. These latter awards are in essence identical to those made to linesmen of the Royal Engineers and their actions are considered in a later chapter. Approximately 18 per cent of Artillery DCM awards was made to linesmen and a further 8 per cent to men operating the signalling equipment, typically telephones, in Forward Observation Posts (FOPs) or in dug-outs under shell fire. About one quarter of Artillery DCM awards went to the signallers. An even greater proportion of Military Crosses was awarded to signals and communications officers; some 32 per cent went to Forward Observation Officers (FOO) and an additional 2.5 per cent of MCs was awarded solely for gallantry under shell fire whilst laying or repairing telegraph wires. The Forward Observation Officer generally had with him a small team of NCO and private brigade signallers which included a telephone operator.

In 1914, the Royal Horse and Royal Field Artillery were essentially mounted units. Their guns and ammunition limbers were towed by horses and were trained to do battle by shooting at visible targets, using predominantly shrapnel. In the early days of the war in France, they deployed in full view of the enemy, fired into enemy masses and were themselves peppered by rifle and machine gun bullets. Whilst so doing, the artillerymen of 1914 got into classic Victorian scrapes, arriving and fighting under a hail of fire and extracting themselves in dire circumstances with horses and men being shot all around them. Not until after 1914 would the artillery fully revise its expectations by adopting more wholeheartedly the doctrine of indirect fire, guided by Artillery Observation Officers who were in contact with the battery by telephone from FOPs.

## THE VICTORIAN GUNNER

The traditional Victorian concept that the artillery should provide direct fire support for infantry is exemplified by the early battles of 1914, when, for example, Wheeler Quarter Master Sergeant R. Edwards of 6th Battery, Royal Field Artillery was decorated for 'conspicuous bravery at Le Cateau on 26 August', but also for 'repairing equipment under heavy fire, frequently helping to run up single guns into the infantry firing line'. His DCM was announced in the *London Gazette* of 17 December 1914.

While the British Expeditionary Force was being pushed back from Mons in August and September, artillerymen and guns came into direct contact with German infantry and similarly deployed field guns. Driver W. Austin of the 41st Brigade, RFA was at Villers Cotterets when, 'although wounded, he remained at duty, and by his courage saved a gun from capture'. This was a significant act because at the time too many field guns were being lost by virtue of their deployment in the firing line. Gunner W. J. Harrison of 27 Battery, RFA gained his DCM, 'for bravery and devotion to duty in withdrawing guns by hand under heavy fire near Ligny on 25 August'. Major Henry E. Vallentin, Harrison's Commanding Officer, gained his DSO, 'For bravery and devotion in withdrawing guns by hand under a heavy fire, near Ligny, France'. Note that the citation is the same, but the rank of the recipient determined the reward. Ligny was already famous as the location of Blucher's victory over the French 199 years previously in June 1815. Saving horses as well as guns was also rewarded; Farrier Sergeant T. Harrison of 115th Battery, RFA; 'for very gallant conduct on 14 September in saving horses which had become entangled in a blocked road, and man-handling guns away from a position which had become untenable from a very heavy shell fire, after the Officer Commanding Battery and Captain had been wounded'. Much of the Army depended upon expensive horse power and could ill afford to lose good, and difficult to replace, animals.

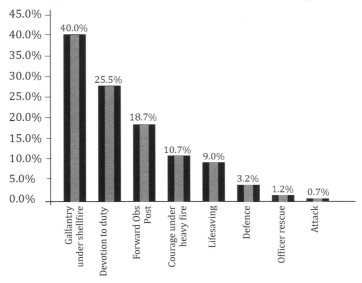

## Distinguished Conduct Medal, Artillery, Categories

| Activity | % |
|---|---|
| Period of time | 23.0 |
| Line Laying/Repair | 18.4 |
| Maintain gun in action | 11.8 |
| Communications | 8.1 |
| Supplying Battery | 7.8 |
| Firefighting, Exploding Ammunition | 7.6 |
| Gun Extraction | 4.7 |
| Removing wounded | 3.9 |
| Messages | 2.9 |
| Supporting infantry | 2.7 |
| Guns Forward | 2.2 |
| Buried men | 2.2 |
| Tending Wounded | 2.0 |
| Gun Repair | 1.2 |
| Serving Ammunition to Guns | 1.0 |
| Ammunition Dump | 0.2 |
| Rangetaker | 0.2 |

| Unit | % |
|---|---|
| Royal Field Artillery | 58.0 |
| Royal Horse Artillery | 16.2 |
| Unknown RGA | 12.3 |
| Siege Battery | 7.9 |
| Heavy Battery | 2.8 |
| Trench Mortar Bty, RFA | 0.9 |
| Trench Mortar Bty | 0.7 |
| Mountain Battery | 0.5 |
| Anti-Aircraft Battery | 0.5 |
| Trench Howitzer Battery | 0.2 |

| Rank | % |
|---|---|
| Sergeants | 52.4 |
| Privates/Corporals | 47.6 |

| | |
|---|---|
| Honours DCMs | 52.2% |

**Figure 7: Analysis of the Distinguished Conduct Medal, Royal Artillery**
*Results of a sample of 431 Immediate and Honours DCM Awards*

## Military Cross, Artillery, Categories

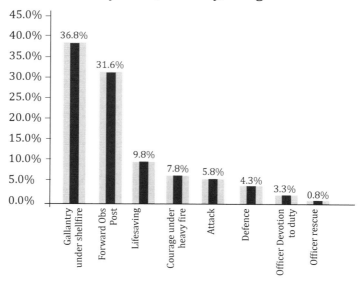

| Activity | % |
|---|---|
| Communications | 20.1 |
| Maintain gun in action | 14.5 |
| Firefighting, Exploding Ammunition | 11.8 |
| Line Laying/Repair | 9.8 |
| Guns Forward | 9.2 |
| Gun Extraction | 6.8 |
| Supporting infantry | 6.5 |
| Removing Wounded | 3.8 |
| Period of Time | 3.6 |
| Buried men | 3.6 |
| Messages | 3.3 |
| Tending Wounded | 2.7 |
| Supplying Battery | 1.8 |
| Ammunition Dump | 1.8 |
| Serving Ammunition to Guns | 0.9 |
| Gun Repair | 0.0 |
| Rangetaker | 0.0 |

| Unit | % |
|---|---|
| Royal Field Artillery | 65.5 |
| Royal Horse Artillery | 2.3 |
| Unknown RGA | 20.5 |
| Siege Battery | ? |
| Heavy Battery | ? |
| Trench Mortar Bty, RFA | 9.8 |
| Mountain Battery | 0.5 |
| Anti-Aircraft Battery | 1.0 |
| Trench Howitzer Battery | 0.5 |

| Rank | % |
|---|---|
| Major + | 4.5 |
| Capts and Junior | 90.0 |
| Warrant Officers | 5.5 |

| | |
|---|---|
| Honours MCs | 32.5% |

**Figure 8: Analysis of the Military Cross, Royal Artillery**
*Results of a sample of 400 Immediate MC Awards*

## Distinguished Service Order, Artillery, Categories

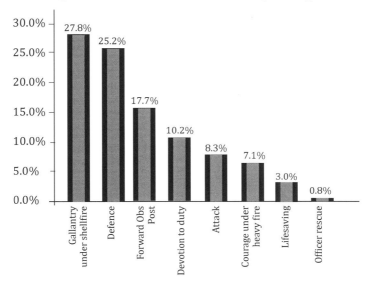

| Activity | % |
|---|---|
| Supporting infantry | 23.2 |
| Maintain gun in action | 16.9 |
| Guns Forward | 11.6 |
| Period of Time | 10.7 |
| Gun Extraction | 9.3 |
| Communications | 9.3 |
| Firefighting, Exploding Ammunition | 8.9 |
| Supplying Battery | 2.2 |
| Removing Wounded | 2.2 |
| Line Laying/Repair | 1.8 |
| Tending Wounded | 1.8 |
| Buried men | 0.9 |
| Messages | 0.9 |
| Serving Ammunition to Guns | 0.4 |
| Ammunition Dump | 0.0 |
| Gun Repair | 0.0 |
| Rangetaker | 0.0 |

| Unit | % |
|---|---|
| Royal Field Artillery | 80.5 |
| Royal Horse Artillery | 6.4 |
| Unknown RGA | 12.0 |
| Siege Battery | ? |
| Heavy Battery | ? |
| Trench Mortar Bty | 1.1 |
| Mountain Battery | 0.0 |
| Anti-Aircraft Battery | 0.0 |
| Trench Howitzer Battery | 0.0 |

| Rank | % |
|---|---|
| Lieut. Colonel | 14.3 |
| Major | 63.5 |
| Captain | 10.9 |
| Lieutenant | 5.6 |
| 2nd Lieutenant | 5.6 |
| Honours DSOs | 78.8 |

**Figure 9: Analysis of the Distinguished Service Order, Royal Artillery**
*Results of a sample of all 266 Immediate DSO Awards*

During October 1914, the artillery was still providing direct fire support to infantry operations; Sergeant G. T. Spain of 'F' Battery, Royal Horse Artillery received a DCM; 'For conspicuous gallantry during the attack on 23 October, in working, and later commanding a single gun with great effect, in support of the Gordon Highlanders'.

## DCM AWARDED BY BALLOT

The award of the DCM by ballot was never a procedure incorporated into the Royal Warrant for the medal, but awards of the DCM by ballot do rarely seem to have occurred. One such contains a direct reference to the thirteenth clause of the Royal Warrant for the Victoria Cross, which could be awarded by ballot, 'in the event of a gallant and daring act having been performed by (*a body of men, and when*) ..... all are equally brave'.[1] This idea originated with Prince Albert in 1855 during the establishment of the Victoria Cross.[2] In 1914, 47904 Gunner C. B. Carry of 'J' Battery received a DCM in such a fashion when: 'The whole of his section behaved with conspicuous gallantry at Gibra, France, on 8 September, and he has been selected by the vote of his comrades for commendation'. The comrades of the pre-war volunteer Artillery were slain by rifle, machine gun and shrapnel fire at their guns in 1914; the DCM citation of Bombardier T. H. Holmes (106th Battery, RFA) reads: 'for conspicuous gallantry in assisting to serve a single gun, until and after all but one of the sub-section had been killed or wounded'. Some of the early war DCMs for lifesaving retain a distinctly Victorian flavour; consider the award made to Bombardier F. Holton, 121st Battery, RFA: 'for gallantry at Ciri on 16 September, under a very heavy shrapnel and high explosive shell fire, went out and helped to carry into safety Gunner Davies, telephone operator, who had been wounded and was unable to move'. It reads like many DCM citations arising from the Boer War, and like some Victoria Cross citations from earlier conflicts, except that in 1914 the rifle fire was more accurate.

## SAVING THE GUNS

Not only during the Retreat from Mons in 1914, but also during the heavy German counter-attacks at Cambrai in November 1917 and during the Spring Offensives of 1918, do we see the artillery caught up in desperate rearguard actions. In defence, guns were maintained in action to the last by the stubborn, or those who would not be beaten. An excellent example of this type of rearguard action is afforded by the following citation for the DCM won by Sergeant F. S. Jenkinson, a man who already had an MM to his name: 'For conspicuous gallantry and devotion to duty while acting as battery sergeant major at the guns. He kept the forward section in action under very heavy bombardment of gas and high explosive. One gun was put out of action by a direct hit, and he made repeated attempts to get the other guns away, firing on the enemy with open sights till the last moment. He showed great pluck and determination'. A series of Military Crosses was announced in the *London Gazette* of 22 June 1918, being awards for the opening days of the German Offensives. Of these, Second Lieutenant David E. Collier of the 214th Siege Battery, Royal Garrison Artillery displayed great determination on 21 March 1918 when with the enemy just 1,000 yards away and approaching, he received orders to disable the guns and leave. He, however, 'succeeded in limbering up the section and withdrawing both the guns in full view of the enemy and under intense machine-gun fire'. Lieutenant Sidney Johns, attached to an Anti-Aircraft Battery, RGA, found himself: 'at one time between the infantry and the advancing enemy, and under heavy machine-gun fire' yet succeeded in getting one of his guns away safely: 'But for his coolness and determination, the gun would have been lost'.

Artillerymen who left withdrawal too late sometimes found themselves reaching for their rifles. Again on 21 March 1918, Lieutenant Ewan Mackie of 293rd (London) Brigade, Royal Field Artillery, was with his battery when it came under machine-gun fire, but by means of his 'courage and determination maintained the whole battery in action, engaging over open sights..... until all his guns were out of action'. Then, 'he manned the intermediate trench with the gunners and engaged the enemy with machine gun and rifle fire'. His MC citation, also in the 22 June 1918 *Gazette*, attributes the determination of the entire battery to fight it out to this officer's 'marked skill and gallantry'. MCs awarded for defensive actions of this nature are very scarce; just about 4 per cent of artillerymen gained distinction for saving the guns or for fighting with enemy infantry during the Spring Offensives.

## GUNNERS IN THE LINE

The example of Captain Harry Ridealgh's experiences during the Battle of Cambrai in late 1917 illustrates the dire situations a Forward Observation Officer, attached to the infantry and calling down artillery fire, could find himself in. The story is accentuated by the award of a Victoria Cross to one of Ridealgh's NCOs. Harry Ridealgh was a Yorkshire Quarryman, an explosives expert from Poole-in-Wharfedale. He started off as a pre-war Territorial Sergeant in the 4th (West Riding) Howitzer Brigade, part of the 49th (West Riding) Division, and landed in France in May 1915. He was granted a temporary commission in November 1915. In late 1917, he was Forward Observation Officer for D Battery, 276 Brigade RFA which was equipped with 4.5 Quick-Firing howitzers. The battery was operating close to the front line at Petit Priel Farm. Ridealgh won the Military Cross with the following citation which was published in the *London Gazette* of 8 January 1918: 'For conspicuous gallantry and devotion to duty as brigade forward observing officer. He went forward with the infantry and established his post and, while waiting for daylight, started to mop up. In one perfectly dark dugout he discovered five of the enemy and ordered them out. As they refused, he killed two and took the other three prisoners. He afterwards again advanced with the infantry, reached and endeavoured to dismantle two hostile guns which were still red hot with recent firing, and having established another post, remained there passing back information under very heavy shell fire and circumstances of the greatest difficulty until compelled to retire by the hostile counter-attack'. Ridealgh was forced to vacate his FOP and it seems most logical that he retreated towards his battery position. When the attackers approached Ridealgh's battery, they met great resistance. D-Battery was holding up the German attack at point-blank range. Sergeant Gourlay, one of Ridealgh's men, was in charge of a section of two howitzers which were fired all day over open sights at 100–200m range, single-handedly stalling the German attack on that part of the line. At one point, when a machine-gun opened up on him, Gourlay hauled his one remaining half-tonne howitzer out of its gun-pit, levelled it at the machine gun and blew it and its crew up with a single shot, winning D-Battery a Victoria Cross, while Ridealgh received the MC. The difference between the two decorations is that Ridealgh did a good job, probably he felt that he had done no more than his duty and no more than many of his brother officers had done, but Sergeant Gourlay had achieved the halting of the German Army single-handed. He, too, might have said that he was only determined not to let them pass, and only did his duty as a gunner Sergeant, but his actions came to official notice as a result of a recommendation being filed by his Commanding Officer. And so Gourlay was elevated to the status of reluctant Hero, and decorated by the King.

## RESCUING THE BURIED

One of the defining characteristics of trench warfare and life on the gun line was the risk of being buried alive by shell fire. The lucky were dug out, but many were crushed and suffocated. In the early part of 1916, Corporal T. Edney was serving with 84 Siege Battery, Royal Garrison Artillery: 'he went to the assistance of two men who had been buried by a shell, extricated both, and carried one of them 300 yards into safety under heavy shell fire'. Corporal H. Hill, of the 10th Siege Battery was rewarded in the winter of 1915–16, 'when a building was hit by a shell and some men buried, he at once called for volunteers and dug out and carried to a place of safety the buried men. All this was under heavy fire'. Battery Sergeant Major R. T. Ainge of Bristol was caught up in the Spring 1918 German attack and won an immediate DCM: 'when two officers and some men of the battery were badly wounded and buried in a dug-out this Warrant Officer did splendid work in getting them away under continuous shell fire, showing a total disregard for his own safety'. At a similar time, Gunner H. A. Jennings was awarded his DCM, 'When his battery commander was buried, owing to a direct hit on a dug-out, he rescued him and carried him under heavy gas-shell fire to a dressing station. He then returned and assisted wounded men until he himself was gassed'. On 26 October 1918, Gunner G. H. Guise of the 1st Kent Heavy Battery, Royal Garrison Artillery did enough to get a DCM in the Birthday Honours list of 1919, for rescuing buried men at his battery position whilst under heavy shell fire: 'He was almost completely buried in a shell crater; three other men were entirely buried. Although unable to move, he continued to draw attention to the spot where the men were buried, and he directed the operations of the rescue party, and refused to be moved himself until satisfied that his comrades' safety was assured'. One Field Artillery officer, 2nd Lieutenant Pieter Hendrik Schalk Beruidenhout, was presented with the Military Cross after this heroic underground exploit: 'when his dug-out was blown in by a shell which killed some men and wounded others, although much shaken himself, he bore the whole weight of the roof on his shoulders for some time and prevented it falling in on the wounded'. This occurred at Fricourt on the Somme on 5 July 1916. Beruidenhout was also noted for his conspicuous gallantry when carrying out 'dangerous reconnaissances', no doubt creeping about no-man's-land looking for potential targets for his battery.

**TENDING AND EVACUATION OF WOUNDED**
Shell fire tore gunners to pieces and severely injured gun crews. Gunner W. L. Gale, RGA, in late 1917 gained a DCM: 'in rescuing a gunner who had had his arm blown off, fetching a stretcher and carrying him into a small iron shelter where he and a comrade remained with him keeping a pressure on the artery .... The whole of the time the shelling was most intense'. Having been commissioned into the Royal Artillery as a young medical student, it is no surprise that 2nd Lt. Reginald Jackson took the responsibility for wounded men when the batteries with which he was serving came under heavy counter-battery fire on 24 July 1916: 'Having experience as a medical student, he voluntarily assisted wounded men with utter disregard of personal danger, while the batteries in the neighbourhood were under heavy shell fire'. Being in possession of specialist knowledge, this young man would have felt only too

pleased to be able to do something useful for the wounded rather than watch impotently. This may be an example in which the possession of particular skills empowered a man, provided the impetus to show what he could do. He might have denied, as many did, that he did anything special that day, but instead, 'I only did what anyone else would have done in my position'.

It was not only at the gun line that men were hit; supply columns constantly moved up and down from battery positions and suffered from shell fire. During the battle of the Somme, Acting Bombardier W. H. A. Creighton, Royal Horse Artillery, was in charge of four ammunition wagons, getting them up to the battery positions. 'An enemy heavy howitzer shell having killed three horses and wounded all the drivers of one team, he ordered the other three wagons to go on, and remained himself to dress the wounded men. While doing so another shell killed the remaining horses and one of the drivers. He continued dressing the remaining two men, carried them to the dressing station, and returned to collect the harnesses of the dead horses'. Whilst at the wagon lines to the rear of his battery position, and in the process of assembling and transporting stores and ammunition forward, Battery Sergeant Major W. J. Harling of East Ham was with 460th Battery, Royal Field Artillery. Near Becelaere; 'On the night of 4/5 October 1918, when a dug-out was hit, he extricated four men under fire, bandaged the wounded, and got them safely away. On the night 7/8 October, the lines were again heavily shelled and he spent two hours attending to wounded men and horses and further helped to extinguish three burning ammunition wagons'. These were eventful nights, indeed.

## BURNING AND EXPLODING AMMUNITION

Gun positions required feeding with ammunition, it was piled within easy reach of the guns and was constantly being transported by means of horse and mule drawn wagons. Ammunition fires were an ever present threat, in addition to enemy high explosives, shrapnel and gas shells. Gunner R. C. Dadd, Royal Horse Artillery, from peaceful Whitstable in Kent, reacted when: 'during a heavy shelling of his battery position, the camouflage was set alight. He and another gunner took the lead in putting out the fire, which, but for their prompt action and disregard of danger, would have caused very serious danger to guns and ammunition'. He later ran back to the gun position 'under very heavy shell fire to the position to fetch a stretcher' after a man was wounded. The citation for his DCM further emphasises that Dadd, 'set a splendid example of fearlessness and devotion'. Having already proven himself worthy of a Military Medal for an earlier act of bravery in the field, Sergeant J. W. J. Airey added a DCM to his awards when: 'the ammunition in a gun-pit had been set on fire by the heavy enemy shelling', probably at the commencement of one of the 1918 German Spring Offensives. He 'rushed out of shelter and worked with unremitting energy to extinguish the fire, which he eventually overcame successfully, though he had to pull down the camouflage, which was blazing. His prompt and courageous action, which was carried out under fire of an intense description, saved an explosion which would undoubtedly have had very severe consequences'. Underlining this man's repeated gallantry, the citation records that he was always fearless, and volunteered 'for any work of however dangerous a nature'. Junior officers might expect to receive the Military Cross for a display of leadership in such situations, for example 2nd Lieutenant Harold Talbot Vizard of 'C' Battery, 71st Brigade, Royal Field Artillery, who on 14 March 1916, was in a gun pit containing 60 shells. The pit was set alight by heavy shell fire but rather than run for it, he set an example of calmness and courage to his men: 'with great initiative 2nd Lieutenant Vizard had the ammunition removed and remained in the pit till the fire was extinguished'. Men found other ways to extinguish a fire; Gunner T. Feasey of D-Battery, 76th Brigade Royal Field Artillery was near Ruesnes on 4 November 1918, when 'the enemy set fire to a large dump at the battery position. He at once rushed up and put out the fire by covering it with earth. By his gallantry and promptitude he saved the gun close by'. Whilst coming under enemy counter-battery fire, Sergeant T. Digby, Royal Horse Artillery, distinguished himself when 'an enemy shell burst just in front of his gun, a piece of it penetrated into the wagon body from which smoke and flame began to come out. He withdrew the shell, the India rubber fuse cover of which was on fire, and put the fire out'. One is reminded of several Victoria Cross awards dating from the Crimean War, for example, which related to similar incidents of extinguishing the burning fuses of enemy shells and of throwing fizzing shells over the parapet (or overboard) to explode safely.

## AT THE AMMUNITION DUMP

Naturally enough men were employed at ammunition dumps where they had the opportunity to perform, repeatedly, acts that would have been sufficient to win them a Victoria Cross in previous wars. During the German advance of Spring 1918, 60804 Sergeant E. G. H. Basher, a South African artilleryman, won the Distinguished Conduct Medal: 'for conspicuous gallantry and devotion to duty'. His is a long and detailed citation, appearing in the *London Gazette* of 3 September 1918. He was stationed at a corps ammunition dump, 'established in four different places successively'. 'During five days' hard and difficult work, when each dump at which he was on duty became in turn a favourite mark for enemy shells and air bombs, he was of the greatest assistance to the officers responsible for the supply of ammunition during severe fighting'. The published citation further records that he performed his work, 'though suffering from severe concussion from the explosion of a shell' and that 'he maintained the issue of the ammunition in spite of heavy shelling and many fires and explosions'.

Similar services were carried out by other men who were awarded the Military Medal rather than the DCM, for example, 676558 Sergeant W. H. Davis of D-Battery, 275th Brigade Royal Field Artillery. William Hutchinson Davis served in France from 29 September 1915, and his MM was announced in the *London Gazette* of 17 September 1917. The recommendation states: 'In the Battery position at Ypres on 19 July 1917, a dump of howitzer cartridges became ignited by enemy shell fire. The dump was in close proximity to a track, which was at the time occupied by transport, and also nearby was a dump of boxed ammunition. This NCO went and extinguished the fire, which was spreading to the boxed ammunition, showing a complete disregard of danger to himself both from the dump and the persistent and accurate fire of the enemy. His courage undoubtedly saved many casualties'. The recipient came from Kendal, Cumbria and was awarded the Territorial Force Efficiency Medal (a long service award) in May 1921.

## AT THE GUN LINE

Forward of the ammunition dumps, the artilleryman's experience on the gun line was dominated by the arrival of enemy shells, and particularly of aimed counter-battery fire, which as we have seen caused ammunition fires, set fire to camouflage, to men's clothing and other equipment. It was not only the blast and the shell fragments that caused commotion and damage; through it all he had to continue to lay down the barrage and engage his targets. From transport or from gun limber, ammunition was served to the guns, with fuses correctly set. Inserted into the smoking breech, the breech was locked and the gunner's lanyard was given a sharp pull to send the projectile flying to its target. Thousands of rounds might be supplied to and fired by a gun in the space of a few days.

## GETTING THE GUNS FORWARD

Gallantry medals were awarded for getting the guns forward and into position, for the actual firing of the guns under heavy enemy counter-battery fire and for extracting guns when threatened by enemy advance or heavy shell fire. Corporal F. W. Accleton won a DCM during the Somme battle of 1916: 'When a heavy shell blew him from the saddle and wounded his horse, he held on to his horse, steadied the team and brought the gun into action'. Battery Sergeant Major J. H. Avis, 'when assisting an officer to take three guns up to his battery at night they came under heavy artillery barrage, but by dint of skilful leading and prompt use of such cover as was available, the battery was reached and the guns brought into action'. Second Lieutenant Ernest Wallace Christie took his horse-drawn guns forward into action, at the gallop, when enemy shelling caught them in the open. The citation for his MC tells us that, 'At Poelcapelle, on 28 September 1918, whilst driving into action, two teams were hit and five men wounded. This officer showed great coolness and resource in getting the remaining teams clear and removing the wounded to a place of safety'. This officer's quick decision making and leadership in a critical situation probably inspired his men with confidence and materially assisted in maintaining his men's will to fight back. With guns in position, they had to register on an aiming point. 'On the night of 26 August 1918, near Mercatel, when the battery came into action at night and no aiming point was available', 19993 Corporal J. Gilbertson of Silloth, Cumberland, 'stood at a crossroads for two hours and held an electric torch over his head as each gun wanted its line. The cross roads were being constantly shelled'. In spite of being a single act, this was a Birthday Honours DCM.

**SERVING AMMUNITION TO THE GUNS**
It was whilst enduring heavy and accurate counter-battery fire that many heroic deeds were performed by artillerymen. During the course of July 1916, Major von Mellenthin of the German Field Artillery Regiment 6 wrote that: 'We had our hands full. The (gun) barrels steamed, no one could touch them. The gunners had to open and close the hot breeches with pieces of wood'. Many artillerymen received bravery decorations for remaining in action or putting out ammunition fires under heavy counter-battery fire. Major Mellenthin again: 'One gun after another was knocked out .... we were firing 2000–3000 rounds per battery per day. The French sent over incendiary bombs and gas shells as well. Everything caught fire – the guns, the rations, the men's equipment. Some of the gunners were buried alive and others, stupefied by gas, suffered for hours even days'. Explosions of high explosive shells could singe men's beards and moustaches and leave their clothes burning and smouldering, never mind the effects of incendiary shells.[3]

The number 5 and number 6 of each gun detachment was required to set the fuses and carry ammunition to the guns from limbers or dumps placed for immediate use. It was a dangerous job. Corporal H. P. Boatman of 'H'-Battery, Royal Horse Artillery, received the DCM; 'For conspicuous gallantry on 12 October

1914, at Strazeele. Although wounded, he continued to supply ammunition to the battery until totally disabled by a second wound'. Working in a battery of the Royal Garrison Artillery while the Germans advanced towards him in the Spring of 1918, number 26588 Battery Sergeant Major W. Brice of Yeovil, 'For four hours assisted materially in getting a section of guns into position. During the heavy bombardment which immediately followed, he supervised the service of ammunition with exemplary coolness, and when the battery position had to be vacated he rendered valuable assistance in organising the battery riflemen to assist the infantry'. Number 41046 Sergeant J. E. H. Cowley of Finsbury, 'Under intense bombardment he took charge of a second gun and kept it in action as well as his own until one was knocked out'. Between 18 September and 11 November 1918, Sergeant J. Crabbe of the 1st (North Riding) Heavy Battery, Royal Garrison Artillery had set a 'splendid example to his detachment'. In one particular incident, 'when his battery position was subjected to heavy shell-fire, he kept his gun in action until it received a direct hit'. During a German attack on Hooge on 30 July 1915, Corporal H. Eldridge of the 123rd Battery, Royal Garrison Artillery won the DCM when he and two others, of the same detachment: 'all the other men of which were either killed or wounded by very heavy shell fire from three directions, but they kept their gun in action and maintained its rate of fire, till finally Corporal Eldridge was wounded and rendered helpless'. When a shell exploded right under Sergeant P. L. Hill's gun 'and destroyed half his detachment .... although knocked off his feet and badly shaken, (he) collected the rest of the men and continued firing the gun'. The important component of this Sergeant's DCM recommendation was undoubtedly this: 'It was entirely owing to his example under this heavy fire that the section remained steady'. Here, the influence of one man, demonstrating to others what may be accomplished in spite of everything, had an important impact on the remaining men. Junior officers in particular performed this function, for example when 2nd Lieutenant Arnold Scott James of 282 Siege Battery, RGA: 'at all times, by his example and disregard of danger, kept the detachments working coolly and efficiently, despite the most intense hostile shelling'. Again, the importance of junior leadership in hardening the resolve of the men around them is apparent. Even when all others were killed around them, some found the determination to carry on alone in the maelstrom: Corporal A. Gittins, from Bury, Lancashire, deservedly earned the DCM (probably at Cambrai, 30 November 1918): 'For conspicuous gallantry and devotion to duty. When a shell completely knocked out one detachment, he single-handed loaded, laid and fired the gun still under heavy fire and, though greatly exhausted, continued to do so'. Similarly, Sergeant E. Kent, 'continued to serve his gun single-handed after the whole of the detachment except himself had become casualties'. Bombardier E. Griffiths' DCM was announced in the *London Gazette* of 21 October 1918, with the following citation: 'Whilst forming one of a detachment engaged in carrying out an important shoot on the enemy's wire, the position was heavily shelled. In spite of hits on the parapet and in the gun pit, the detachment stuck to its work and completed the shoot'. Many of these awards were made to men who stuck it out rather than went for cover. Without a doubt, some men died alone serving their gun, no-one else left to observe them go, and these determined souls received no medal at all.

## SERVICING AND REPAIRING THE GUNS

During long periods of firing and under heavy fire, guns needed mending or servicing to keep them in action. Gun barrels became so worn out that they were not allowed to fire, for fear of their totally inaccurate shooting. High explosive rounds fell short frequently enough, causing casualties and consternation among friendly troops, without allowing worn out guns to fire wildly off side. The men who performed gun repair duties were the Fitters, yet they received few medals for doing so, between 1 and 2 per cent of all artillery DCM awards were made for repairing guns. Most of these were periodic awards. One such award of the DCM for this type of work was announced in the *London Gazette* of 3 September 1919, and was awarded to 285854 Fitter W. K. Aldborough of the 121st Heavy Battery, Royal Garrison Artillery. The citation states that:

'He has displayed rare devotion to duty throughout the recent operations before Amiens and Arras, and it is largely due to his courage and energy that guns were kept in action at a time when it was of the utmost importance that they should be so. He worked day and night without rest, frequently under hostile shell fire and bombing without complaint, and, in the absence of a staff-sergeant fitter, his skill and sound workmanship were of the utmost value'. Operating with the 69th Siege Battery, Royal Garrison Artillery, Smith Gunner (Acting Fitter Corporal) A. Galloway of South Shields, received his DCM in the same *Gazette* edition (3.9.19): 'For exceptional gallantry, skill and devotion to duty under heavy shell fire on 28 March 1918. When his battery was under a heavy concentrated fire and had many casualties he regularly went round the guns and attended to minor damage'. He also undertook to serve at the guns when casualties made it necessary, 'under heavy and accurate fire'. An immediate DCM award for the fighting in the same period, Spring 1918, was made to Fitter Corporal R. Birkin, who: 'When a battery was being very heavily shelled and most of the guns were damaged he went from gun to gun, repairing them where possible and keeping them in action when practically all the battery were casualties, until he was badly wounded. He showed great pluck and determination and absolute disregard for danger'.

## THE TRENCH MORTAR BATTERIES

Men of the trench mortar batteries were right in the front line, of course, but there were fairly small numbers of awards made to these artillery detachments (under 2 per cent of the combined artillery DCM total but nearly 10 per cent of MCs). On the Ancre, 16 February 1917, Temporary Lieutenant George Douglas Filby ordered his trench guns out from safety and into shell holes, 'in full view of the enemy, and succeeded in knocking out two enemy strong points'. In this instance, courageous leadership and example resulted in military success. Mortar teams were often under heavy enemy fire. On 9 April 1918, for example, Corporal J. W. Chadwick was attached to a Heavy Trench Mortar Battery operating near Bethune. 'Out of communication with his officer, he kept his mortar in action until it was destroyed by shell fire.' After failing to get into contact with his officer, 'he fought with the infantry' and was wounded. His New Year Honours DCM was announced in the *London Gazette* of 3 September 1919. In the same *Gazette*, Corporal H. Duckham received his DCM for service with trench mortars: 'During the fighting in March and April he showed marked courage on more than one occasion. On 21 March 1918, in Holnon Wood, he continued firing until all his ammunition was expended. Twice his gun pit was hit by enemy shells and the mortar buried in earth and debris, but he dug it out again and fired his remaining rounds. Later, during the same operations at Hangard Wood, Amiens, on 9 April 1918, during a raid, he again kept his gun in action under heavy artillery fire, and contributed greatly to the success of the raid'. Here again, men and materials were blown up and buried in the shell storm. 3708 Gunner J. Deane was attached to a medium trench mortar battery when: 'He rescued a machine gun under very heavy fire and brought in many wounded men. On another occasion, he repeatedly dug out trench mortars which had been buried'. One of the useful functions of the trench mortar was its ability to cut enemy wire, dropping heavy charges from close range. Acting as Observation Officer for trench mortars operating in support of the 1 July 1916 attack at La Boisselle was 2nd Lieutenant Louis De Velly, who 'observed fire most effectively from an exposed position and thoroughly cut the enemy wire'. Second Lieutenant Henry Spencer Bell received the MC when engaged in wire cutting near Armentieres on 4 November 1916, he successfully 'directed the fire from "No-Man's-Land"'. Ordered to 'cut wire at all costs', 2nd Lt. Charles Davis Morgan 'carried out his instructions, although shelled out of one position after another' and despite his guns being 'frequently buried'. His MC was announced in the *London Gazette* of 25 August 1916, for actions on 27 June, in the preparatory phase of the bombardment which culminated in the 1 July attack. Sometimes the trench mortars were used to shoot smoke screens, although gallantry awards for such work are rare. For example, at High Wood on 28–30 July 1916, Temporary 2nd Lt. Charles Price, RFA was attached to the 5th Bn. Special Brigade, Royal Engineers for smoke screen operations. Price made the necessary reconnaissance to identify appropriate positions in which to place his trench guns and, on the next night, successfully got them into position 'under heavy fire'. When the attack on High Wood commenced, so his MC citation states: 'the smoke barrage from these guns was largely instrumental in securing the success achieved. Though wounded and suffering great pain, he stuck to his post and refused to go to the dressing station till his work was completed and his men and guns brought successfully back'. Throughout, he performed the expected duties of an officer in charge of such an operation and delivered the required result. Getting himself wounded and sticking to his post provided an element of self-sacrifice to his actions, helpful in pushing an award recommendation. In addition, he instilled confidence in his men, that he would stick it out, set the example, and care for them enough to get them all back safely. Men needed fatherly leadership of exactly this sort. Price showed determination and skill of a high order, but whether he thought he was 'brave' while busy with his allotted task, while carrying out orders according to a pre-arranged schedule and plan, seems rather unlikely. He became a brave hero after the act.

## THE TRENCH HOWITZER BATTERIES

Awards to men of trench howitzer batteries are also very scarce, and the following examples relating to actions in 1915 (a New Year Honours DCM award for 1916) illustrates how they performed under heavy, close range, enemy fire: 43034 Corporal W. Hurley, 'For conspicuous gallantry in serving his guns throughout three days under a continuous heavy shell and rifle fire'. At about the same time, two junior officers in charge of Trench Howitzer batteries, Temporary 2nd Lts. Francis Russell Watson and Owen Whitaker, gained Military Crosses for their leadership in front line trenches. Watson got his battery forward and into captured positions at Hooge on 9 August 1915 and from there identified targets and eliminated an enemy bombing party who were attempting to counter-attack, and then 'located and knocked out a machine gun in a house on the right flank'. Whitaker's MC is interesting as it appears to show that anger and vengeance may have been motivating factors in his behaviour, rather than 'bravery': 'For conspicuous gallantry on the Yser Canal on 14 August 1915, when a portion of our trenches was under fire for over three hours from several of the enemy's trench mortars and aerial torpedoes'. Whilst enduring this sort of heavy fire from the universally detested enemy trench mortars, and being stuck like rats in a trap within the confines of a narrow trench, men's urge to seek revenge grew. When 2nd Lt. Whitaker's howitzer detachment were hit and all his men killed or wounded, he: 'with his soldier servant (Gunner Raynor) .... took the place of the detachment, continued to work a gun and placed two bombs in the enemy's trenches before expending all the ammunition on the spot. They were under very heavy fire from the enemy's trench mortars all this time'. Their commitment to the task in those conditions may very well have been stirred by adrenaline, anger and vengeance, which masked fear and overrode the instinct for self-preservation. Perhaps, too, the award of the Military Cross for these events was not entirely welcome, being so closely associated with the sudden destruction of the men in his detachment, men he knew, nurtured and led.

**THE ANTI-AIRCRAFT BATTERIES**
Worn out men from various units, or those undergoing recovery from shell shock were sometimes drafted to the Anti-Aircraft batteries that became a feature of the back areas as the aerial threat increased. These batteries were manned by a core of experienced gunners and specialist experts in the field. About 4 per cent of Artillery DCMs and 1 per cent of MCs was won by men of anti-aircraft batteries. Without the ability to accurately track moving targets, effective anti-aircraft battery fire came down to luck and good judgement alone. Use of an optical instrument known as a rangefinder, if available, helped matters considerably, but even then the anti-aircraft gunners did not have access to the sophisticated range-finding equipment that the Royal Navy was using. Almost as soon as a range was identified and time fuses set, the target had moved. Corporal E. A. Beales was attached to 'C' A.A. Battery, Royal

Garrison Artillery and managed to win a DCM in the New Year Honours list of 1 January 1919. He was a recognised 'expert' range-taker, the citation states: 'He has served in France since April 1915, in anti-aircraft sections and nearly the whole time in forward areas. He is a highly skilled and expert range-taker and has shown so much ability in the performance of this duty that he was given charge of one of the few two-metre range-finders. He worked it, and another, until both were destroyed by shell fire. His ability and devotion to duty are of the highest order'. Also listed in the 3 September 1919 *Gazette* was the citation for another anti-aircraft gunner, 191095 Sergeant J. Crankshaw of the 114th A.A. Section, Royal Garrison Artillery. The award was: 'For gallantry in action at Arras on 28 March, 1918 and, subsequently, on several occasions during heavy shell fire, when he showed great courage, coolness and disregard of personal safety in keeping his gun in action'.

**THE MOUNTAIN BATTERIES**
Other scarce awards are those won by men of the Mountain Batteries of the Royal Garrison Artillery. Sergeant F. Cavill was serving with No. 7 Mountain Battery, RGA in 1915. He won the DCM: 'For conspicuous gallantry whilst in charge of a mountain gun. By his skill and bravery he materially assisted the advance and subsequent withdrawal of the gun', meriting a New Year Honours award for 1916, citation published in the *London Gazette* of 11 March 1916. In the same *Gazette*, another Honours DCM went to 13988 Sergeant H. G. Frond of No. 2 Mountain Battery, RGA for his services in France and Flanders. His award was, 'For conspicuous gallantry. Whilst advancing to occupy a position, under heavy shell and rifle fire, Sergeant Frond exhibited great bravery and skill and brought his gun into action without loss. Subsequently, he displayed fine initiative and resource, although he was twice wounded during the following ten days'. The 27th Mountain Battery was in action in German East Africa during August 1916, where two of its officers won the Military Cross as Forward Observation Officer (Lt. William Lynedoch Curwen) and for getting his gun up into the line to successfully engage and destroy enemy machine gun positions (Captain Dudley Haskard).

## SUPPLYING THE BATTERIES WITH AMMUNITION

Such was the experience of men on the gun line during battle. Behind the guns there were the transport drivers, principally bringing ammunition up, but also there are rare awards for getting rations and water up to the guns. Those who were specially recognised, overcame varying types of obstacle to get supplies through to the batteries, the most common being heavy shell fire, but there were also blocked roads, direct shooting and landmines. Operations depended heavily upon the supply of ammunition reaching the guns, as without it, targets went unmolested and SOS calls for fire, from the infantry, could not be answered. A failure of ammunition supply, every artilleryman knew, would have very serious implications. As in all of the other services, men felt obliged to carry on doing their duty to their comrades, regardless of personal danger.

Corporal F. G. Bevens of 95 Battery, Royal Field Artillery, gained his DCM: 'For conspicuous gallantry on 5 May 1915, when in charge of three ammunition wagons, which were bringing ammunition to the battery on the Menin Road, near Ypres. One wagon was blown up by a shell and Corporal Bevens was wounded, but with great gallantry he took the remaining two wagons to the battery under heavy fire although suffering great pain'. This award was gazetted on 5 August 1915. During the Somme battle of 1916, Sergeant J. A. Hunter (RFA) was tasked with getting ammunition wagons up to the guns 'under heavy shell fire. When teams and drivers were badly knocked about by heavy shell fire, Sgt. Hunter showed great coolness and pluck in getting the road clear. He carried wounded to the dressing station and continued the supply of ammunition'. Similarly, Gunner W. P. Connolly, a native of Widnes in Cheshire, won the DCM when: 'A convoy of ammunition came under hostile shell fire. Several casualties to teams and drivers were caused and the N.C.O. in charge was wounded. He at once took charge, cut the wounded clear and superintended the rehorsing of the ammunition wagons. He saw to the removal of the wounded and then led the convoy up to the position and delivered the ammunition. His great coolness and courage saved a difficult situation and proved an incentive to the rest of the men'. 22335 Battery Sergeant Major W. A.

Freeman won the DCM: 'When the battery ammunition wagons were moving along a narrow road five 5.9 shells fell in rapid succession about the centre of the column, causing many casualties to men and horses and damaging many vehicles. Battery Sergeant Major Freeman showed great coolness and gallantry under fire, rapidly clearing away the wounded men, dead horses and broken vehicles, and so reopened the road for the columns of other units extending for over a mile behind his own wagons'. Working as a driver getting ammunition forward, 676981 Gunner Horace Williams won a Military Medal when he: 'showed a conspicuous example of courage and skill, and repeatedly brought ammunition to the gun position during very hard fighting in front of Cambrai in October 1918 under heavy shell fire, setting a splendid example of devotion to duty to all ranks'. Williams was an accomplished horse handler, winning prize medals in the 57th Divisional Horse Show in both 1917 and 1918. The level of competition at these shows was very high, for men put great effort into them and they were very much enjoyed.

Gunner T. Fellowes of Kettering won the DCM when: 'Wagons were being pressed forward with ammunition to an advanced battery position, and two landmines exploded under his wagon, killing or wounding the men and horses. Though severely wounded himself, he harnessed two horses to an undamaged wagon and delivered the ammunition to the battery position. His courage throughout was remarkable'. The award was published in the *London Gazette* of 15 November 1918.

## SUPPLYING RATIONS AND WATER TO BATTERY POSITIONS

Battery Quarter Master Sergeant J. H. Johnson, 'During three days of intensive operations he did splendid work in maintaining the ammunition and water supply, under constant fire, setting a very fine example of coolness and ability under trying circumstances'. His DCM was an immediate award gazetted on 26 January 1918, but most awards of the DCM for getting stores other than ammunition up were Honours DCMs. In the Birthday Honours list for 1919, for example, we find 687480 Driver H. Gristwood who served with A Battery, 160th Brigade, Royal Field Artillery. His DCM citation

Horace Williams, Ammunition Limber Driver, Royal Artillery

**Figure 10: The Military Medal, British War Medal, Victory Medal and Divisional Horse Show Medal belonging to Gunner Horace Williams, Royal Field Artillery.**

reads: 'For conspicuous gallantry and devotion to duty during the recent operations behind Gheluwe from 7 October to 15 October 1918. When the battery was in an open position he brought up rations night after night without fail, frequently having to pass through very heavy fire. In addition to the shell fire he had to contend with difficult ground to get over. It was entirely due to his determination that the battery was kept supplied with rations'. During the second half of 1917, 201489 Driver H. Henthorn from Oldham had displayed: 'conspicuous gallantry and devotion to duty during lengthy operations. He nightly delivered rations and water at the gun position, frequently under very heavy shell fire. On one occasion, when the wheel driver was blown off his horse by a shell, he took on his team unaided, and safely delivered the ammunition'. Similarly, 680548 Sergeant J. Southworth, Royal Field Artillery, Territorial Force, won the MM for services throughout the war but particularly for his work on an ammunition column: 'This man has served with the Battery continuously since the Division came to France, as gunner, bombardier, corporal, sergeant, and frequently as Acting Sergt-Major. He has displayed qualities which have made him respected by all ranks and trusted by officers. On the night 30 September 1918, by his initiative and doggedness in charge of an ammunition convoy, he succeeded in delivering to the gun position 1,500 rounds of ammunition in spite of many casualties. He has at all times shown himself cheerful in trying circumstances, calm in danger and efficient in administration'. It is extremely unusual to see reference to administrative work in an MM recommendation, particularly in a late war award, and also that the recommendation is clearly for distinguished services over a very long period.

## Relationship with Animals

Under the circumstances of many gallantry awards, controlling the horses and mules was difficult and dangerous. Examples of awards which mention this aspect are very scarce indeed, but this DCM awarded to Battery Sergeant Major E. Day of the Royal Horse Artillery was mainly for control of the horses: 'When the teams and wagons of the guns in action showed signs of getting out of control owing to being heavily shelled, he took charge, and by his personal example he succeeded in steadying them. He displayed the utmost disregard of danger, and inspired all ranks by his courage and coolness'.

## THE ARTILLERY CLERK AND THE STORM OF PAPERWORK

In the New Year Honours list of 1916 there was a small number of awards made to Artillery Clerks, a form of award that generated much resentment among the fighting arms. One good example is the DCM awarded to 8714 Acting Sergeant Major, Artillery Clerk C. J. Chaundy of Headquarters, 1st Divisional Artillery, RGA. He earned his decoration: 'For conspicuously good and hard work throughout the campaign. He has set a fine example of energy and devotion to duty to all with him'. Being far removed from a gallantry award, many felt that this and others like it in the New Year and Birthday

Honours Gazettes of 1916, undermined the value of those awards won in battle. Critics forgot that the DCM had always been available to reward meritorious service over a long period whilst in the field, but their voices were heard and the 'immediate' award of the Meritorious Service Medal was instituted in the course of 1916 to cover such work when not in the face of the enemy.

## BATTERY COMMUNICATIONS

Crucial to the Artillery was communications, most of which occurred by telephone, by runner or by motorcycle despatch rider. That 26 per cent of artillery DCMs were won by linesmen has been alluded to earlier in this chapter, but some of the rarest gallantry awards went to visual signallers (flags and semaphore). Gunner H. G. Binley of 33rd Brigade, Royal Field Artillery received notification of his DCM award in the Birthday Honours Gazette of 3 June 1915, the citation reads: 'For conspicuous gallantry on numerous occasions in repairing telephone lines under heavy fire. When no other means of communication were available he transmitted messages from the front by flag signalling'. Another example also comes from the early part of the war, this time from October 1914. Corporal R. J. Bird's DCM was announced in the *London Gazette* of 1 April 1915: 'For gallant conduct on 25 October 1914, in joining his Battery Commander under very dangerous circumstances, and succeeding in keeping up communication by semaphore with his Battery, under very heavy shell and rifle fire'. Flags were not the only method of visual signalling, there was also the signalling lamp. While waiting for telephone cables to be repaired, the lamp came into its own: Acting Corporal A. Johnson of 16th Battery, RFA received the DCM, 'For conspicuous gallantry; he successfully worked visual signalling in the open under a heavy shell fire while the telephone wires were being repaired'. During the Somme battle of 1916, 52006 Bombardier P. Hughes proceeded forward with the infantry during an attack, and when the advance was held up by barbed wire entanglements, he: 'showed great courage in sending back messages by lamp from an exposed position of the enemy's trenches'. His DCM award was published in the *London Gazette* of 20 October 1916. These alternative methods were available to the artillery signallers throughout the war, not only in the earlier stages. For example, 87188 Corporal A. E. Hollingdale received a DCM in the 1918 Birthday Honours list, having used almost every form of communication in the course of his duties: 'This N.C.O. has displayed courage, resource and ability on many occasions as telephonist, and also as linesman under severe shell fire. On one occasion he obtained valuable information by visual signalling, and twice passed through hostile barrage to deliver messages. Recently his pit was hit by a shell, but though badly gassed, he remained at duty till relieved'. This particular award demonstrates the set of skills that all artillery signallers had to be proficient in, from the use of code on the telephone, to use of visual signalling equipment and as a last resort, to be prepared to deliver messages by hand. Such awards for semaphore and other visual signalling are very scarce, compared to the large numbers of awards for laying and maintaining telephonic cables.

Awards made to telephonists are also uncommon; the awards sometimes include reference to mending wires under fire and so they are often for activities similar to those of the linesman. For example, 45886 Corporal P. H. Kendall of 129 Battery RFA won his DCM: 'For conspicuous and consistent gallantry and good work as telephonist. He has repeatedly repaired wires under fire'. Whereas this was an Honours award, the following was an immediate award made solely for work as telephonist; 7905 Gunner P. Kenna, RFA, received the DCM in the *Gazette* of 22 September 1916: 'For gallantry and exceptionally good telephone work in all weathers and at all times of day and night during operations'. Artillery observation posts and headquarters positions were key targets for enemy shelling as these coordinated the British artillery's targets, requests for stores and ammunition, as well as its movements. Men who were not on the gun line or out mending lines were still in continual danger from being spotted and shelled out of existence. In the battles of 1915, 879 Gunner A. Driver of the 11th (West Riding) Battery, Royal Field Artillery, received the DCM whilst acting as telephonist for his role in dealing with the consequences of targeted German artillery fire:

'After the observation station had been destroyed by shell fire, Gunner Driver returned and entered the building at great personal risk, owing to heavy fire, to obtain bandages for the wounded. On another occasion he took a telephone instrument to the observation position, through a heavily shelled area'.

## THE FORWARD OBSERVATION OFFICER AND THE INFANTRY LIAISON OFFICER

A discussion of the courage shown by artillerymen cannot be considered complete without reference to the many officer's awards made for their work as Forward Observation Officer (F.O.O.) and as Infantry Liaison Officer. Roughly one in three Military Crosses was awarded to F.O.O.s for their work in identifying targets from their observation posts in the front line and for telephoning the information back to the battery. They spotted the fall of shot, communicating accurate corrections and accompanied the infantry so as to offer them rapid artillery support when needed. Liaison Officers won at least 3 per cent of Artillery MCs, but this number is likely far too low as in many citations the officer's role may not be stated clearly. Many citations indicate working with infantry but do not state that the man was assigned as Liaison Officer. Their job was to accompany the infantry as mobile F.O.O.s, calling down fire on targets as they arose, perhaps a machine gun position or a strong point, or perhaps a crowd of the enemy organising themselves for a counter-attack. The liaison officer sometimes accompanied infantry in trench raids, reacting as instantly as possible to calls for fire. Of course, he or one of his team would need to be laying telephone cables, typically from a drum as they went, so that communications were maintained.

The work of the Forward Observation Officer was dangerous as once discovered, his static post would become the target for aimed shell fire, in an attempt to knock him out of the battle. Sometimes, of course, the F.O.O. operated more in the open, from a shell hole for example, but in this case he had to keep his head down and be sure that his signalling could not be seen by the enemy. A very typical Military Cross citation for acting as F.O.O. during 1916 is afforded by this one relating to Temporary Lt. Reginald Pridmore of 'D' Battery, 241st Brigade Royal Field Artillery: 'As F.O.O. he displayed great coolness under fire, notably on one occasion when his O.P. was very heavily shelled. Both he and his look-out man were partially buried, but he carried on and sent in valuable reports'. The MC to 2nd Lt. Lawrence Patterson was awarded in the same *Gazette* for getting the guns of his battery correctly aimed, or 'registered', onto their targets. The award was for: 'great pluck, notably on one occasion when he laid a wire under machine gun and rifle fire and maintained communications until he had registered all his guns'. Once the guns were shooting a barrage or were ordered to engage specific targets of opportunity, the F.O.O.s would watch the fall of shot and send back corrections. Often a call for fire support from the infantry would reach the Observation Post, and this would be converted into instructions to engage the target by the F.O.O. During the Battle of Arras, on 23 April 1917, for example, 2nd Lt. Victor Hollis of 281 Brigade Royal Field Artillery 'was in constant touch with the infantry and gained, by reconnaissance, information which was of the utmost value in enabling the situation to be dealt with'. So the F.O.O. was not expected always to sit tight in his post, but when he saw it was necessary he was expected to show initiative and get out, make personal reconnaissances, identify targets, liaise with infantry and assist to blast the infantry forward whilst minimising their casualties. These represent 'combined operations' awards to F.O.O.s and this sort of activity was occurring as far back as 1915. A good example from that year, and possibly one of the first such awards, is provided by the Military Cross given to Lieutenant Francis R. G. Milton of the 63rd Brigade, Royal Field Artillery. The citation for his award states: 'For conspicuous ability in artillery duties. As Liaison Officer during an attack this officer maintained communications under continuous shell fire, gave ample information to the guns and, as a result, the infantry were closely supported'. Later in the war, the newness of embedding artillery officers in infantry formations during operations had gone. During the battle of the Somme, near Longueval on 14 July 1916, 2nd Lt. Kenneth Oscar Nash was attached to an infantry battalion as liaison officer, 'and when the battalion had many casualties among its officers he collected a party of infantry and his own signallers and led another attack against the enemy trenches'. Sticking to his assigned duties as liaison officer far better, Lt. Arthur Wellesley Newman of 243 Brigade Royal Field Artillery 'closely supported a bombing attack, and by his accurate shooting into an intricate system of trenches accounted for many of the enemy'. He was lucky that his telephone cable remained intact, for had it been broken he would not have been capable of winning the Military Cross. This action occurred at Ovillers on 21 August 1916. Both of these officers' MCs were announced in the *London Gazette* of 20 October 1916.

Later in the war, the liaison officer was absolutely standard procedure and the whole team was more capable of engaging multiple targets, accurately and quickly. In the Gazettes of late 1918, we see how the art of infantry–artillery cooperation had become very powerful: Acting Captain Algernon F. R. D. Ryder had already won the MC before winning his second, 'in August and September 1918, he showed the greatest courage and resource in making daring personal reconnaissances and reporting hostile movements to the infantry and in bringing up guns, which enabled heavy casualties to be inflicted on the enemy'. Another aspect of the infantry–artillery cooperation in late 1918 was the phenomenon of bringing guns up in close support, in order to engage the enemy at essentially point-blank range. Lieutenant Robert Hamilton of 161 Brigade Royal Field Artillery, for example, 'was in command of guns on close support of the infantry at Trefcon on 7 September 1918'. The infantry had encountered resistance and had called for fire support. Rather than opt for indirect fire support as might have occurred earlier in the war, Hamilton 'brought up one gun under an intense machine-gun fire, with which he overpowered at point-blank range the machine guns that were harassing the infantry, who were then able to occupy the village'. Similarly, Acting Major Kenlis Atkinson won the MC on 30 September 1918 during the battle for the suburbs of Cambrai: 'Following close behind the infantry over the Canal de L'Escaut, he brought his guns into action under extremely heavy artillery and machine-gun fire, and destroyed several machine gun nests, which enabled the infantry to establish themselves in their position'. Lieutenant Roderick MacGregor won his MC when in charge of a battery of howitzers which he pushed forward in close support of the infantry in spite of suffering heavy casualties in men, horses and stores. In part he won his MC for 'being the first gun of the division' to get 'well forward', one of his guns having been blown up by a landmine on the way.

## CRITICAL LEADERSHIP ACTIVITIES OF ARTILLERY OFFICERS

Officers of the artillery won MCs for encouraging their men to further endurance, by setting an example of fighting spirit and showing a will both to endure and to win. These were the ingredients of leadership that were so important in determining men's will to fight it out in spite of intense danger, fatigue and sometimes even war weariness. Some MCs were awarded to those officers who toured their battery when under heavy fire, setting an example by walking out in the open, confidently, while the men toiled in the gun pits. This was important in convincing the men that the danger was less than it really was, and seeing an N.C.O. or officer do this, risk his life in the open, even for a short time, encouraged men to be optimistic about their own chances of survival. These points are applicable to much of the successful junior leadership displayed and rewarded with medals right across all units of the British Army. As the MC citation of Acting Captain Harold Turner (Royal Garrison Artillery) printed in the *London Gazette* of 22 June 1918 states: 'Thanks chiefly to his own splendid example of courage and coolness the whole battery acquitted itself magnificently' under heavy enemy counter-battery fire the whole day.

Immediate awards of the DSO to artillery officers illustrate the level of command required to perform the senior field officer's tasks.Often in charge of a complete artillery brigade, their responsibility was to deploy their guns to best advantage, to undertake reconnaissances on behalf of the batteries, to liaise with other arms and to maintain the morale of the men under their command. All this had to be performed over a wide frontage and, at times, in highly fluid situations. Rather than requiring ever greater bravery to win the higher honour of the DSO, these men required management skills combined with the charisma and determination to have orders implemented in a timely and correct fashion. Upon their shoulders rested a great responsibility. For example, Lt. Colonel Herbert Fisher's second DSO was announced in the *London Gazette* of 16 September 1918 and with the following citation: 'For conspicuous gallantry and devotion to duty in handling his brigade. He conducted a retirement with masterly calm and determination, and on several occasions, by his prompt movement of batteries and by his reconnaissances and selection of positions, he inflicted heavy casualties on the enemy. Throughout the entire operations he set a magnificent example of cheerful optimism combined with a dogged and determined courage'. Similarly, Lt. Colonel Francis Sykes, received a bar to his DSO when in late 1918 he expertly: 'utilised four artillery brigades with great ability to crush counter-attacks'. Displays of superior organisational skills may be found in the records of the DSO; Lt. Colonel James Tapp who 'commanded a Field Artillery Group with great distinction' and on several occasions at very short notice during the first days of October 1918. Even though 'he only received his orders at 5:30pm on 2 October, his batteries then being some distance west of the Canal. He made a very skilful and daring reconnaissance, and by his excellent arrangement he was able to move his batteries two miles east of the canal, and took part in the opening barrage at 6.5am on 3 October'. Tapp obviously had good junior leaders to assist in carrying out his orders.

Good leaders demonstrated the following types of behaviour in battle; Major Arthur Bibby 'walked up and down behind his guns under heavy fire encouraging his men', with the result that, 'his example was an inspiration to all'. Lieutenant Colonel Edward Peel won a bar to his DSO when: 'Throughout the operations (of ten days) he kept the men together and cheerful, and they fought splendidly whilst the enemy was bearing close upon them' (*London Gazette* 16 September 1918). When his battery was under a heavy fire from gas, shrapnel and high explosive, Lieutenant Albert Kerby, 'constantly exposed himself, moving from gun to gun and encouraging the detachments.... it was mainly due to his gallantry and fine example that the battery maintained its rate of fire' (DSO, *London Gazette,* 24 September 1918).

In the first months of the war, prior to the institution of the MC, junior field officers were being awarded DSOs for acts which, later in the war, would have resulted in the award of an MC. For example, Lieutenant Edward Schreiber got the DSO on 14 September 1914 when he was involved in 'saving horses which had become entangled in a blocked road, and manhandling guns away from a position which had become untenable from a very heavy shell fire'. An early example of an officer operating as F.O.O. in the line is afforded by 2nd Lieutenant Colin Jardine who won a DSO in October 1914: 'For his fearlessness and enterprise in giving information from the firing line'. A late 1917 DSO won by 2nd Lieutenant Kenneth Wyn Maurice-Jones illustrates very well how the standard for a junior officer's DSO was made so much higher by the arrival of the MC; 'When his battery received an SOS call while it was being heavily bombarded with gas and high explosive shells, he got all the guns into action within 30 seconds. He moved about regardless of danger, encouraging his men while two ammunition dumps were blown up close beside him.... and continued to encourage his men and assist the wounded until he collapsed'. Even after that, he 'at once attempted to extinguish' an ammunition fire, only giving up when it exploded.

The DSO was still used to reward work as a Forward Observation Officer, but a far lower proportion of DSOs (18 per cent) than MCs (32 per cent), represents this task. Some DSOs state the places where officers established their FOP; in the case of Captain William Harrison it was his observation ladder which 'he moved to within 700 yards of the enemy trenches and remained up it all day'. Major Walter Johnston 'established himself, before dawn, on the remains of a tree' in order to direct his battery's fire in getting the German wire cut, and Captain Edward Boylan of the Royal Horse Artillery was successively knocked out of a railway truck by aimed shell fire and blown out of a haystack during March 1918.

DSOs were won in new ways in the final weeks of the war. In an effort to provide close infantry support on 9 October 1918, Major Spencer Strudwick 'personally led a gun forward…. and engaged enemy machine guns successfully over open sights…. and enabled our infantry to advance'. On 4 November at Flaque Farm, Major Geoffrey Holt showed 'inspiring leadership' by bringing his battery up to the front 'at full gallop over the crest, down the slope, through a hail of fire, losing several horses', and, getting into an excellent position out of sight of enemy machine guns and 77mm artillery pieces that were holding up the infantry, he destroyed them, allowing the advance to continue. Four days later, Major George Martin performed a similar feat when he 'led a gun at the gallop through the foremost infantry, coming into action at 700 yards, silencing several machine guns'. These acts demonstrate how close to the front line the artillery was operating in the mobile war of late 1918, and suggest the arrival of the self-propelled gun on the battlefields of subsequent wars.

# The Royal Engineers

The Corps of Royal Engineers performed a great many varied tasks on the battlefield and behind the lines. As engineers in the truest sense, they constructed and maintained fortifications, earthworks, railways, tramways, roads, water supplies and bridges. Some of this they did under heavy fire in the front line, but most of the time it was routine work behind the lines. As technical specialists there was weapon maintenance and repair to be carried out, they were in charge of the Army's surveying, signalling and telephonic communications and they constructed tunnels beneath enemy lines and filled them with tonnes of explosives. Engineers were in charge of releasing toxic gas from cylinders in front line positions, when the wind direction was right. They were also in the business of demolition – notably of bridges – and, later in the war, the tunnellers switched to de-fusing booby-trap devices in dug-outs, houses, cellars and at roadsides that had been left by the retreating German Army.

Whilst performing the duties outlined above, members of the Corps of Royal Engineers won nearly 8 per cent of all gallantry awards conferred during the First World War. Some of these awards were won with the infantry during attacks. For example, teams of Sappers were vital in the consolidation of newly won trenches, so they had to be there with the infantry when those trenches were captured. They assisted and coordinated the urgent repair, modification and fortification of West-facing trenches to become East-facing. Consolidation following capture had to turn those trenches around very quickly, before the counter-attack came – there was no fire step on the rear wall of a German trench, for example. Sappers carrying explosives took part in infantry trench raids, as they were sometimes required to destroy concrete emplacements, other fortifications and stores while the raiding party was over. Most significant in terms of gallantry awards was the job of the linesman – these men were charged with keeping communications open during all the most violent episodes of the battlefield, from attack to defence and bombardment. Men of the Royal Engineers signal companies laid, maintained and repaired telephonic cables which connected forward units to their headquarters units, artillery observation officers (spotters) to their batteries and the Generals to their operations. When communications failed, infantry runners had to be used, but when runners had to be relied upon, in very fluid battle situations, communications had already gone very wrong. Late in the war, during the more mobile periods of the Spring of 1918, awards for last-minute bridge demolition are encountered and in the second half of 1918, awards for bridge laying and pontoon erection appear. Both of these activities were carried out under impossible conditions of heavy fire.

With these tasks in mind, the Royal Engineers were divided up into specialist units or companies – Field, Signal, Tunnelling, Rail Operating (and Rail Construction) and Special (Gas) companies were the main divisions of the Corps. In addition, there were many other units, for example, men joined Forestry or Docks Companies, Army Workshops, Pontoon Parks (for bridging equipment), Advanced R.E. Parks (stores, dumps of equipment), Electrical and Mechanical companies and Anti-aircraft (searchlight) sections. There were also the Postal sections, Carrier Pigeon sections and Fortress Companies. Men's official service numbers and company numbers often betray their function within the Corps of Engineers, particularly as far as Field, Signal, Tunnelling, Rail and Gas companies are concerned. However, some of the other specialist units cannot easily be identified from a man's service number or his unit number. Some units gained large numbers of gallantry awards, others very few.

In the following pages, these units shall be dealt with according to their normal zone of operations, from the rear areas and moving up to the forward, front line, areas of the battlefields. In the rear areas were the Railway, Army Troops and various Depot Companies, for example the Pontoon Parks where bridging equipment was stored, constructed and serviced.

## Distinguished Conduct Medal, Royal Engineers, Categories

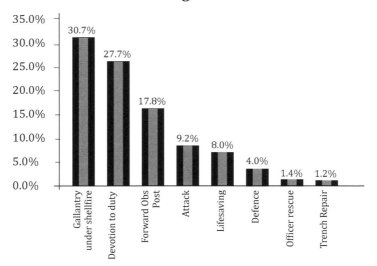

| Activity | % |
|---|---|
| Line Laying/Repair | 28.8 |
| Period of time | 25.7 |
| Working Party | 7.9 |
| Messages | 5.3 |
| Bridge Construction | 5.3 |
| Rescue from Galleries | 4.3 |
| Supporting Infantry | 3.6 |
| Consolidation | 3.4 |
| Laying Wire | 3.4 |
| Supplies Forward | 3.4 |
| Buried Men | 2.4 |
| Unexploded Ordnance | 2.4 |
| Rail Construction | 1.4 |
| Water Supply | 1.2 |
| Preserve Equipment | 0.7 |
| Tending Wounded | 0.7 |
| Cutting Wire | 0.2 |

| Unit | % |
|---|---|
| Signal | 40.4 |
| Field | 37.3 |
| Tunnelling | 11.3 |
| Rail | 2.8 |
| Survey | 2.3 |
| Special (Gas) | 1.7 |
| Army Troops | 0.8 |
| Waterways | 0.8 |
| Pontoon Park | 0.3 |
| Siege Coy | 0.3 |

| Rank | % |
|---|---|
| Sergeants | 44.0 |
| Privates/Corporals | 56.0 |

| | |
|---|---|
| Honours DCMs | 50.8% |

**Figure 11: Analysis of the Distinguished Conduct Medal, Royal Engineers**

*Results of a sample of 500 Immediate and Honours DCM Awards*

## Military Cross, Royal Engineers, Categories

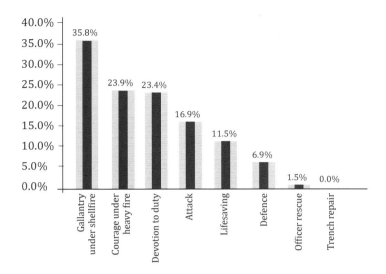

| Activity | % |
|---|---|
| Line Laying/Repair | 9.8 |
| Working Party | 15.7 |
| Bridge Construction | 12.8 |
| Consolidation | 11.6 |
| Supporting Infantry | 9.3 |
| Rescue from Galleries | 7.6 |
| Laying Wire | 5.8 |
| Supplies Forward | 4.7 |
| Unexploded Ordnance | 4.1 |
| Tending Wounded | 2.9 |
| Period of Time | 2.3 |
| Rail Construction | 2.3 |
| Cutting Wire | 2.3 |
| Buried Men | 1.7 |
| Water Supply | 0.6 |
| Preserve Equipment | 0.0 |
| Messages | 0.0 |

| Unit | % |
|---|---|
| Field | 48.8 |
| Signal | 14.9 |
| Tunnelling | 24.7 |
| Special (Gas) | 6.5 |
| Rail | 3.3 |
| Water | 1.4 |
| Fortress | 0.5 |

| Rank | % |
|---|---|
| Warrant Officer | 1.7 |
| 2nd Lieutenant | 44.8 |
| Lieutenant | 30.7 |
| Captain | 10.0 |
| Major | 2.5 |

| | |
|---|---|
| Honours MCs | 45.2% |

**Figure 12: Analysis of the Military Cross, Royal Engineers**
*Results of a sample of 241 Immediate Awards*

## Distinguished Service Order, Royal Engineers, Categories

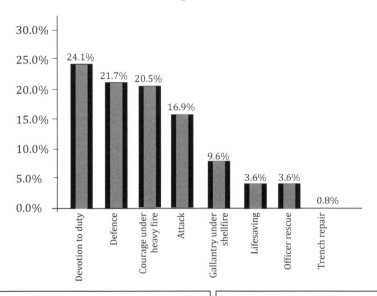

| Activity | % |
|---|---|
| Bridge Construction | 25.0 |
| Consolidation | 19.6 |
| Supporting Infantry | 12.5 |
| Working Party | 8.9 |
| Unexploded Ordnance | 8.9 |
| Period of Time | 5.4 |
| Line Laying/Repair | 3.6 |
| Supplies Forward | 3.6 |
| Messages | 3.6 |
| Rescue from Galleries | 1.8 |
| Laying Wire | 1.8 |
| Preserve Equipment | 1.8 |
| Rail Construction | 1.8 |
| Cutting Wire | 1.8 |
| Buried Men | 0.0 |
| Water Supply | 0.0 |
| Tending Wounded | 0.0 |

| Unit | % |
|---|---|
| Field | 61.9 |
| Signal | 7.1 |
| Tunnelling | 21.4 |
| Special (Gas) | 2.4 |
| Rail | 2.4 |
| Water | 0.0 |
| Fortress | 0.0 |

| Rank | % |
|---|---|
| 2nd Lieutenant | 2.4 |
| Lieutenant | 12.0 |
| Captain | 21.7 |
| Major | 43.4 |
| Lieut. Colonel | 18.1 |
| Brigadier General | 2.4 |

| | |
|---|---|
| Honours DSOs | 85.5% |

**Figure 13: Analysis of the Distinguished Service Order, Royal Engineers**
*Results of a sample of all 83 Immediate Awards*

## THE RAILWAY COMPANIES

Railway Companies provide a particularly interesting story; the best way of understanding what they did and how they won their gallantry awards is to follow one of the Companies through the war. For illustrative purposes, the 263rd Railway Company has been chosen. The fact is, a major network of railways, both standard and narrow gauge, as well as tramways, sprang up behind the lines during the war of 1914–18 in France and Flanders. Pre-existing railway lines acted as the nucleus, but many of these passed west to east through the front line and on into enemy territory. Thousands of miles of new rail track in sidings, stations, depots, rail yards and leading off to gun batteries and other dumps, was laid. The tonnage of men and material carried around the war zone was colossal and the contribution the Railway Companies made to the war effort was substantial.

Men of the 263rd Railway Company landed in France on 27 April 1917 and were set to work maintaining sections of railway track generally in the Ypres Salient. The full strength of the Company was a little over 200 men, fluctuating between 210 and 229. They were involved in the offensive known as Third Ypres, commencing 7 June 1917, and ending at Passchendaele in December of that year. As the infantry slogged slowly forward over the months, through the rain and mud of the Salient, the Railway Companies of the Royal Engineers were pushing forward rail and tram lines to the front, to supply dumps and to artillery gun positions. The network of interconnected rail routes multiplied in the back area during that time, but shelling and aerial bombing meant that repairs were always required. The Company constructed new lines, building embankments and bridges, track laying and ballasting as they went. They built railways and spurs to newly constructed gun positions under steady shell fire and bombing by aircraft, which resulted in casualties being evacuated weekly in ones and twos. The 263rd Railway Company at times lost as many men to shell shock as it did to wounds and deaths. Operating in conjunction with locomotive drivers of light railway train crew companies, their work took them right up into the forward areas allowing larger quantities of ammunition and supplies to be pushed forward far quicker than by any other means.

In the early part of December 1917, the Company was losing men to shell fire daily. It was a particularly unpleasant time for them. On the second of the month, one sapper was evacuated wounded to a Casualty Clearing Station (CCS); on the 5th, a 2.Lt. Robinson was evacuated with shell shock. Next day, Corporal MacKay was killed by a shell fragment; the following day 2.Lt. Farrin was mortally wounded, a Sapper was wounded in the head by an aerial bomb and another man was evacuated with shell shock. A third officer was struck off strength due to shell shock the following week and seventeen sappers were evacuated to a CCS on the 19 December. 21 December finds an entry in the unit war diary: 'Good progress made on construction of Y.6 Extension Line, despite frequent heavy shelling in clear vision of enemy'. This, then was the cause of the casualties, as so much of the work in the Ypres Salient was carried out in full view of the enemy who occupied surrounding ridges and hills. The Company received congratulations: 'on the progress made on the forward lines, the good finish to the work, and the good management shown in handling attached labour'. On the day after that note was received, 257391 Lance Corporal Baker was posted missing 'believed killed'. Two days later, his body was discovered in a shell hole, 'he having been killed by shrapnel'. On Christmas Eve 1917, 257211 Sapper A. Snow was 'mortally wounded by shrapnel and died in a Dressing Station'. Four other sappers were evacuated to a Casualty Clearing Station wounded.

In spite of the operational importance and danger of their tasks, the 263rd Railway Company won just one gallantry award for all their work in the Salient in 1917. It was a Military Medal and was awarded to 257206 Sapper Frank Jeffrey, 'for conspicuous gallantry on the day 2.Lt. Farrin was mortally wounded'. As is so often the case with the MM, further details are unavailable, but the award was certainly for gallantry under heavy shelling and possibly for attempting to save the life of his officer and other men who may have been partly buried by explosions in the forward area. The continual loss of men to shell shock illustrates the strain of working daily for relatively long periods in shelled areas. At least the infantry got regular respite from that.

In 1918 the 263rd Railway Company was moved to the Somme area and was caught up in the German Offensive starting on 21 March. The German Army came forward very rapidly as they broke down and penetrated the British front line. Events began on the 23 March as the enemy drew near, when a rail bridge in the Etricourt area was ordered to be prepared for demolition and 38 truck loads of stores were loaded up and evacuated. Most of the Company was ordered to retire, leaving observation posts out in front. Telephone lines from the rail terminal and stores dump were rigged up to the forward observation posts so that advance warning of enemy encroachment could be given. Timing of bridge demolition was crucial in allowing the last of the retreating British units to retire. The Etricourt railway bridge was demolished at midnight on the 23rd. The following day, trains were loaded and moved out of the area. Before the location was evacuated, a light engine proceeded forward to Trones Wood and pulled away two rail trucks bearing stores; another engine remained behind and pulled away two truck loads of ordnance stores. The Ancre bridge was demolished by the Company on the 25 March. On the 26th, a party under Lt. Edgar Penney, proceeded forward to Ancre Junction rail yards and succeeded, under heavy rifle and shell fire, to demolish a portion of them and all railway stores. For this action, and for bringing up a fresh lorry load of demolition charges along a shell-swept road next day, Penney was awarded the Military Cross. The 27 March saw the trains pull back further. Thirty hundredweight of explosives was received by the Company and used to demolish the Corbie rail yard while French soldiers prepared the Aubigny and Vecquemont bridge for demolition. It was blown on the 28th. Two tons of ammonal was used to blow the track from Corbie to Aubigny while another 30 hundredweight of ammonal was received. Rifles were distributed among the Company, with instructions that all men should be prepared to fight. However, by 30 March, it was clear that the German Somme offensive had petered out.

Three officers of the 263rd Railway Company won MCs and one Sapper the MM, 'in connection with demolition of bridges and railway track' during the March retirement. The citations for the Military Cross give further detail and put the MM award into context; the company was placed in charge of a rail station with adjoining supply dump and 12 howitzer positions. The area came under heavy shell fire as the Germans advanced, setting the R.E. dump on fire. The heavy artillery pieces were removed, with their ammunition and stores, from their positions and loaded onto rail trucks. One officer, Temporary Lieutenant George Campbell Newton, took charge of a locomotive and drew a howitzer out of the station and through the flames of the burning R.E. dump to safety. Captain F. G. Burgess supervised the removal of 'all howitzers from positions and then with two sappers, went personally, under heavy shelling, and fired the charges under a bridge'. Lieutenant Edgar Penney received the MC for blowing up railway material in a station yard under heavy shell fire. It is rather likely that the MM was awarded to one of the sappers involved in bridge demolition.

Among the Railway Companies, there were just a few tens of DCMs awarded in total. A few examples provide the flavour of those awards: Corporal E. W. Hallam's award was announced in the *London Gazette* of 26 April 1917. Hallam 'displayed great courage and determination in carrying out railway construction work under the most difficult conditions. He was frequently attacked by hostile aircraft'. In the same *Gazette* is Sergeant A. H. Kitchen's DCM award citation which states that 'he worked day and night' on arduous and important track-laying duties whilst under fire. During the second half of 1917, almost certainly in the Ypres Salient, Sergeant W. C. Burton had, 'rendered valuable service when in charge of working parties constructing tram lines in shelled areas, when his courage, energy and devotion to duty were very marked'. Corporal (Acting Sergeant) A. H. Furlonger of Wimbledon, received his DCM when he was in charge of trains evacuating wounded from an aid post. When the enemy commenced shelling of the line and 'cut it in seven places', Corporal Furlonger 'at once organised a party and had the line repaired under heavy fire. When one of the trucks was hit by a shell he transferred the wounded on it to another truck and got the train away to safety'.

## THE TRAIN DRIVER

Whilst track-laying parties were an obvious target for German gunners, so were trains, which were often driven by men who had been train drivers in their peace time occupation. The civilian rail companies of Great Britain supplied many qualified railwaymen, some of whom gave their lives in the service of their country, as the plaques in some railway stations to this day demonstrate. These men not only operated on the Western Front, they also operated in Palestine, as the DCM awarded to a locomotive driver from Inverness indicates. Corporal D. Grant was serving with the 98th Light Railway Company in 1918 when he won the DCM, 'For conspicuous good work and devotion to duty as a locomotive and tractor driver, many times under fire'. The award is a typical Honours award, for distinguished service over a period of time and was announced in the *London Gazette* of 1 January 1919 (citation printed in the *Gazette* of 3 September 1919). The citation concludes by commending him for setting 'a fine example to the younger sappers'. In the same *Gazette*, also for Egypt and having a similar 'New Year' character, Corporal T. S. Crawford of the 96th Light Railway Company received his DCM for 'devotion to duty at advance railhead and being very frequently under shell fire and working excessively long hours'. Men like these gave their all in the performance of their duty; it was right that they were rewarded.

## USE OF BEER IN AN AIR RAID

Like many Corps operating behind the lines, opportunities for winning gallantry decorations were relatively few and usually involved shell fire. But not always, sometimes it was an aerial bomb dropped by an aeroplane. William Pook, serving with the Royal Engineers Postal Section, won a Military Medal when 'An enemy aeroplane dropped a bomb which entered the room of a house in which C.S.M. Pook was sitting with three women and two children, whereupon he promptly threw a glass of beer over the burning fuse and picked the bomb up to take it away. Seeing what had happened, Sapper Rata rushed into the room and took the bomb from C.S.M. Pook, carried it outside to the street and emptied the contents of a kettle over it'. Pook's MM was announced in the *London Gazette* of 13 October 1916. Pook was later commissioned and joined an infantry battalion, winning a Military Cross in late 1918.

## AT STORES DUMPS

Less unexpected events, perhaps, overtook engineers working in stores and ammunition dumps. Here they faced life-threatening situations, particularly where ammunition was present. Corporal W. Graham of the 1st Northumbrian Field Company, R.E. was a pre-war volunteer of the Territorial Army. In early 1916 he was in charge of a bomb store when heavy shelling started. The enemy got sight of the dump and the store was set alight. Corporal Graham, 'went into the store regardless of the great danger and removed the gun-cotton primers. On his own initiative he then closed the roads to traffic and took every other necessary step'. His DCM was announced in the *London Gazette* of 30 March 1916.

## SHELLING OF TRANSPORT

From R.E. stores dumps to the forward areas, materials had to be transported and like all other units, the Royal Engineers had its own transport sections. Men worked daily on these transport routes, enduring whatever was thrown at them with no means of retaliation. Acting Corporal F. Lunn was a transport driver for the 77th Field Company. Over a long period of time he had distinguished himself as a determined and courageous driver of horse-drawn wagons. His DCM was a Birthday Honours award, announced in the *Gazette* of 3 June 1919 followed by the citation appearing in the 11 March 1920 edition. Lunn received the medal 'for conspicuous gallantry and devotion to duty on many occasions whilst in charge of wagons carrying R.E. material to the trenches. He has displayed great coolness and initiative, and has saved many casualties to his horses and wagons by his coolness and judgement in getting his transport through heavy shell fire'.

## AWARDS FOR THE TECHNICAL BRANCHES, ROYAL ENGINEERS

As the technical branch of the Army, the Royal Engineers provided field surveyors, cartographers, photographers and remote sensing specialists. One Sergeant even received the Distinguished Conduct Medal in the 1918 Birthday Honours list for his dedicated work experimenting with dangerous materials. The award was made to 11123 Sergeant S. P. Griffen 'for conspicuous gallantry and devotion to duty in carrying out many dangerous experiments with utter fearlessness. Most painstaking, his ingenuity has been invaluable, and the results of his work have been of the greatest importance'. A rare award of the DCM to a panoramic photographer appeared in the *London Gazette* dated 3 June 1918 (with the citation printed in the *Gazette* of 21 October 1918). Acting Corporal J. R. K. Dacre was from Freemantle, Australia, and his award was 'for conspicuous gallantry and devotion to duty. For the past eighteen months, while taking photographic panoramas on all parts of the Army front, he has shown coolness and judgement under fire, and has been most successful'. Engineers were also in charge of sound-ranging equipment which was used to 'listen' to the reports of enemy artillery fire, which might be concealed behind ridges or in camouflaged positions. From the readings of several devices, which included a directional component, the location of enemy guns could be plotted with reasonable accuracy. Their operators belonged to the Field Survey Companies of the Royal Engineers. Two examples, both from Birthday Honours lists, suffice to provide the flavour of their awards; the first, 188833 Corporal J. Keppie of the 5th Field Survey Battalion earned his DCM, 'for consistent good work as linesman and sound ranging forward observer. Between March and November 1918, he was in charge of a post and never failed to send accurate reports to headquarters. Especially at Badger Copse in September 1918, he maintained an exposed post with complete success, constantly repairing the line under fire'. Acting Sergeant T. W. Forster of Ashington, was a member of the 4th Field Survey Battalion when he won his DCM: 'As non-commissioned officer in charge of lines in a sound-ranging section, he has shown marked courage, energy and devotion to duty'. His work was considered critical to the overall success of the section, which depended so much on the linesmen. Another form of remote spying on the enemy was the use of listening sets, which by means of cabling laid in the front line area, were able to pick up telephonic transmissions made by the enemy. Sergeant A. G. Edwards of the Wireless Section, 'F' Corps Signalling Company, was awarded an Honours DCM, 'as N.C.O. in command Listening Sets of the Corps, he has set a wonderful example to all by his perseverance and energy in laying cable in the front line and beyond, under heavy hostile fire, thereby enabling valuable information on enemy movements to be obtained'. Many of the above technical fields were very much underdeveloped at the start of the war but were much advanced by the end of it, largely thanks to men of the Corps of Royal Engineers and inventors back in the United Kingdom.

## SERVICING AND REPAIR OF SCIENTIFIC EQUIPMENT

When delicate scientific equipment got broken, technical staff took on the job of repairing it. An example of a 'bravery' medal being conferred for instrument repair work is afforded by the DCM announced in the *Gazette* dated 29 August 1917 and awarded to Acting Staff Sergeant J. Keogh. The citation makes interesting reading: 'For distinguished service and ability as instrument repairer and as N.C.O. in charge of linesmen. He has shown untiring energy, and no task has been too difficult for him, no matter how trying the circumstances…. his work has been of the greatest value'.

## HAND GRENADE (BOMB) MANUFACTURE

Slightly less delicate, but just as 'tricky', was the fabrication of bombs during the early part of the war. At that time, the Mills bomb, the typical hand-grenade, had not been invented. In the 1 April 1915 *Gazette*, 12717 Corporal M. Gibbons' DCM was announced: 'for gallantry and good work in the fire trenches and for ability in the manufacture and use of bombs'. Some of these early bombs were no more than tin cans filled with explosive and with a fuse attached. They were not easy to use, or particularly reliable, so that anyone who really knew what they were doing with them had significant value to the soldiers who had to throw them in anger.

## ELECTRIC LIGHTING SPECIALISTS

Several awards were made for setting up lighting, for example in dug-outs. Number 572025, 2nd Corporal J. T. Bromley of Chiswick 'rendered very valuable service and displayed remarkable devotion to duty in installing and operating electric lighting in dug-outs and repairing damage caused by shell fire, often under circumstances of great danger and difficulty'. Other electrical work was performed in order to set up signalling equipment such as the lamp and buzzer systems described in 46497 Sapper H. Evans' DCM citation: 'This N.C.O. was in charge of the signalling detachment sent forward to establish communication at a forward report centre in the first objective line. All his men, except two orderlies, became casualties and he himself was wounded. Nevertheless he pushed forward and established communication to the front and rear by lamp and "buzzer". Under very heavy enemy fire he maintained his position throughout the day and did not close down the station until our troops had withdrawn'.

## BRIDGE DESTRUCTION

When, during the first half of 1918, the front line rolled backwards over the British Army's rear areas, many men of the Royal Engineers found themselves having to support the retreat. Their major contribution was in blowing up bridges at the last possible moment, but they also found themselves fighting as infantry in some desperate rearguard actions. Among the acts of gallantry performed at this time are some remarkably stirring examples. For instance, 55699 Corporal A. E. Harper of Cheltenham received a DCM, 'For conspicuous gallantry and devotion in assisting in the demolition of railway bridges under heavy fire. When one bridge was fired by electric exploder, only one charge went off. Accompanied by his officer he went to the bridge, under heavy fire and helped him to light the safety fuse again when the enemy were close to the bridge'. Harper had been 'under fire at other bridges for the past fourteen hours'. At about the same time, 397912 Acting Sergeant R. E. Crosley was in charge of a demolition party which had readied a bridge for destruction with explosive charges. His

DCM citation reveals that, 'the electric leads having been cut by rifle fire, he crawled out along the bridge under heavy machine-gun fire at close range and repaired them. He then demolished the bridge with the enemy only 50 yards away'. Thus, Crosley denied the enemy an important crossing point and cost the German Army time that it could ill afford to lose. His determination to deny the enemy the bridge, was a real contribution to the wider effort and his award of the DCM fully deserved.

Two of the most remarkable awards of the DCM for bridge destruction are those made to 470280 Sapper T. Maloney of South Shields and 548697 Sapper E. A. Staplehurst of Cuckfield in Sussex. These two were also caught up in the German Spring Offensives and their DCM citations, published in the *London Gazette* of 30 October 1918, are unusually detailed: They, 'accompanied the first wave of infantry during an attack. When the objective was reached, they attempted to demolish a masonry road bridge in full view of the enemy on the opposite bank'. At such close range, the two Sappers should have simply been shot down, if the German marksmanship was up to scratch. The Sappers knew the risk, they knew they were risking their lives, but the situation was such that they had little option because to fail to destroy the bridge would probably be disastrous for them anyway. What is truly remarkable is that they did not have the tools to successfully demolish the bridge, which turned out to be a far more resilient structure than anyone would have liked. Given that, 'during the whole time they were under heavy machine-gun fire from houses at close range', it is difficult not to wonder what kept them to their task, with bullets flying and ricocheting around their ears. After two failed attempts to blow the bridge down they identified the problem and, displaying an incredible determination not to be beaten, they, 'procured tools and proceeded to pick up the roadway, after which they laid their charge, and blowing a large gap in the bridge, rendered it impassable'. The citation contains an unusual tribute to the two men, it records that: 'their very gallant behaviour and disregard of danger was an impressive example to many who witnessed the occurrence'. It is a tribute originating from a wide body of men who were there to see it, and is a scarce example of such a testimony surviving into print in the *London Gazette*.

## CHIMNEY DESTRUCTION

The Engineers were asked to destroy many things in the war, including chimneys in no-mans-land which might house enemy observation posts. One such deed resulted in the award of the DCM to 2722 Sapper J. Dalziel of the 1st Lowland Field Company, when, during an enemy attack which threatened to capture a useful chimney, he 'worked under continuous shell fire' to demolish it. Back in 1914, number 5154 Acting Company Sergeant Major C. R. Foster of the 54th Field Company, Royal Engineers, received a DCM, 'For gallant conduct on 25 November 1914, when, in company with an officer, he succeeded in blowing up a house containing German snipers who were causing many casualties'.

## DEMOLITION PARTIES ON TRENCH RAIDS

Throughout the war, Sappers had accompanied infantry units on trench raids, typically as demolition parties. Raids were dangerous, but the Sappers had the benefit of a clear objective and infantry support whilst laying their charges and blowing up defences. Number 35773 Sapper N. Darroch's DCM was announced in the *London Gazette* of 25 August 1917. It is a trench raid award, the citation stating that it was for 'conspicuous gallantry and devotion to duty when in charge of an explosive party. During a raid upon enemy trenches he entered buildings and dug-outs which had not been cleared, and by his daring and coolness ensured the successful firing of all his charges. He set a very fine example to his party'. Another good example of the role of Engineers in trench raids is afforded by the award of the DCM to Pioneer W. Fryer, who already had the MM to his name. 'He was in charge of three men carrying charges to demolish dug-outs in a raid on the enemy's trenches. On arriving in the enemy's front line he became separated from the infantry, but located a dug-out full of the enemy. He descended into it, and captured a prisoner, and as the remainder refused to surrender, he blew up the dug-out'. Somewhat murderous perhaps, but the citation concludes with an incontestable truth, that 'he showed splendid courage and initiative'.

## CONSTRUCTION OF FORTIFICATIONS

So much for the destructiveness of the Corps. In terms of construction, the Engineers were usually hindered as much as possible by the enemy who attempted to destroy whatever they were constructing before the work was finished. Early in the war, in the Spring of 1915, Acting 2nd Corporal N. Byrne of the 12th Field Company was decorated for his gallantry and great ability on the night of 29–30 March at L'Epinette, when 'he made a machine gun emplacement in front of our trenches under the aimed fire of the enemy who were only 120 yards distant'. Concrete emplacements, known as 'pillboxes' were static fortifications that the Royal Engineers were tasked with building. Acting Sergeant A. T. Brooks was engaged in building pillboxes 'which were often under shell fire. He completed the works and maintained discipline throughout under trying conditions'. The work brought him the reward of a DCM in the Birthday Honours list of 1918 (citation published 21 October 1918). Lance-Corporal E. B. Esau won his DCM for the construction of an advanced Artillery observation station and for taking charge of the party when his N.C.O. was wounded whilst subjected to heavy rifle and machine-gun fire. His award was announced in the *London Gazette* of 11 March 1916.

## ROAD CONSTRUCTION PARTIES

Road construction parties were frequently subjected to heavy, targeted shelling; the citation for the New Year 1917 Honours DCM given to Corporal G. A. Glover states that, 'during a period of six months, when he was employed on roads in the forward area, his marked gallantry and coolness under heavy shell fire set a fine example to his men'. For the same work, Sergeant J. W. Harrison received a 1918 Birthday Honours DCM for displaying 'great gallantry…, particularly when engaged in the repair and maintenance under heavy shell fire of forward roads'. Harrison had been engaged on such work and had consistently displayed such qualities of leadership, for two years. Awards for work on roads include occasional examples for road clearance, for example, the DCM awarded to Second Corporal T. A. Daniell of the 1st Field Squadron related to an incident in which a tree fell across a road and, 'he at once went out under heavy shell fire and cleared it away, thereby enabling armoured cars to pass'.

**TELEPHONE LINE LAYING AND REPAIR: 'THE LINESMAN'**
We must now consider the work of the Royal Engineers Signal Companies, a group of men who shouldered some of the most hazardous and unending work of any Army unit on the Western Front. These were the linesmen, who laid, maintained and repaired telecommunications networks throughout the front area under all conditions of shell, rifle and machine-gun fire. Particularly in battle, they were required to repair breaks in cables that had been cut by shell fire. Their work took them across open ground as well as through communication trench systems that might be saturated by a defensive enemy barrage and almost impassable to living things. One of the annoying aspects of life in the trenches was the mass of cables that conspired to make movement along them difficult. Infantrymen often complained about tripping over or getting tangled up in wires that were not always at ankle height and were often at chest height. There were hundreds of thousands of cables, many of them were broken and irreparable, given up for lost or the object of salvage teams; but some were live and were key links in the communication chain. It was these latter that the Engineers of Signal Companies were primarily concerned with. Gallantry awards to linesmen for carrying out line laying or repair, comprise 29 per cent of all DCMs presented to the Corps, the largest medal winning act. Of the DCMs for which the type of unit is known, Signal Companies took 40 per cent of the total and Field Companies 37 per cent. These, of course, were the Companies that worked in the front line. Linesmen, like the Royal Army Medical Corps medics and stretcher bearers, earned the high respect of infantrymen who saw them out in the open, throughout heavy bombardments, attempting to keep up communications long after the infantry had taken cover

and were keeping their heads down. It was exactly the same for both sides, and it is the late 1917 tribute of a German infantry officer that shall be recorded here: '... in a ring of fire ... a couple of telephonists were laying their wires across a cabbage field. A shell landed right next to one of them; we saw him crumple, and thought he was done for. But then he picked himself up, and calmly continued laying his wire'.[4]

Here, then, are some remarkable and typical examples of the gallantry awards made to linesmen. Announced in the *London Gazette* of 4 March 1918, the DCM awarded to 311075 Corporal G. W. Hobson illustrates the supreme dedication of some linesmen to their tasks: 'He worked without ceasing for five days and nights under heavy machine gun and shell fire, relaying and maintaining telephone wires, until brought in in a delirious condition. His disregard of personal safety contributed largely to the successful maintenance of communications, and his example had a fine effect on the men under him'. Even Honours awards speak of the great efforts made by linesmen; 443934 Sapper H. Grundy of the 42nd (East Lancs) Divisional Signalling Company was attached to the 211th Brigade Royal Field Artillery to provide signals communication. His DCM citation reads: 'For consistent gallantry and devotion to duty whilst acting as signaller, particularly during the period 17 September to 11 November 1918. The splendid example he set his comrades by his fearlessness in always volunteering for dangerous work in the communications between brigade headquarters and batteries under the heaviest shell fire and most trying conditions was most praiseworthy'. What it meant to work under 'the heaviest shell fire' is suggested by the following example. During the Somme battle of 1916, 41324 Corporal T. L. Allen won the DCM: 'For conspicuous gallantry when mending telephone wires under heavy shell fire.... He was struck five times by pieces of shell, and was blown over three times by explosions. On one occasion, with the assistance of one man, he captured 23 of the enemy, though he was armed with only one single bomb'. The linesman's work might also bring him into direct contact with the enemy, he did not only work crouched over cables under shell fire. Operating with the infantry during an attack in the middle of 1917, Sapper G. Y. MacKay laid a telephone line from the advanced signal station forward to the attacking infantry. His citation reveals that, 'although the line was continually cut to pieces by heavy shell fire, he continued for four days and nights to mend it and keep up communication, passing twice through a hostile barrage without the slightest regard for his own personal safety'. The DCM was gazetted in the 25 August 1917 edition. Moving on to 1918, Lance-Corporal H. E. Drage received the DCM after 'he spent the whole night under persistent shell fire repairing the breaks in the telephone line from brigade to battalion. He also, with five linesmen under his charge at a linesman's post, mended lines for several hours under heavy gas shell bombardment, and though badly gassed, remained and worked the exchange single-handed after the rest of the men had been removed to hospital'. The conditions of his work are scarcely imaginable and his citation rightly concludes: 'He behaved splendidly'. A final example illustrates the spirit of the R.E. linesman nicely. On 1 October 1918, 109599 Acting Sergeant T. H. Giblett of the 41st Divisional Signalling Company, 'tied a line round his waist' and under heavy shell and machine-gun fire, 'running through the barrage, laid a line to the infantry. Though blown over by a shell bursting and badly shaken, he remained at work and maintained the line throughout the night'.

## SIGNALS VIA PIGEON, HELIOGRAPH AND FLASHLAMP

Other forms of signalling are worthy of mention, for pigeons were still being used late in the war alongside the heliograph and the flashing lamp for visual signalling using morse code. Motorcyclist Corporal S. F. Cross, of 'C' Corps Signal Company, was gazetted with the DCM in the 11 March 1920 edition: '... in charge of pigeons, he did fine work in keeping in touch with the infantry during the advance on the Somme'. Captain Owen Morshead received a DSO: 'For conspicuous gallantry and devotion to duty in making his way forward with a supply of pigeons to clear up a situation and sending back clear information. He also conveyed important orders to the leading battalions. It is impossible to speak too highly of his conduct'. In the last six weeks of the war, 20765 Sapper T. Brogan was commended for being: 'out at all hours of day and night in the laying and repairing of cables and the provision of visual signal stations'. His award appeared in the same *Gazette* edition as that to Motorcyclist Corporal Cross for his work with pigeons.

## BRIDGE CONSTRUCTION AND THE ASSAULT CROSSING

Up in the front line area, sappers of Field Companies were involved in the construction of trenches, fortifications, dug-outs for observation posts, headquarters and gun positions among many other tasks. They did not regularly participate in attacks alongside the infantry, as the awards distribution indicates (only 10 per cent of Royal Engineers DCMs was given for acts which may be categorised as part of an attack). But occasionally, men of Field Companies were at the spearhead of attacks, a spectacular example of which is the crossing of the Sambre-Oise canal near the village of Ors on 4 November 1918. There were many such crossings of rivers and canals towards the end of 1918 as the German Army was being pushed rapidly east, but that carried out at Ors holds a particular poignancy for many, as this was the action in which Wilfred Owen, the celebrated war poet, was killed with the 2nd Manchesters. The action was but a small component of the Battle of the Sambre and one of many crossings made that morning. German troops were dug in on the far bank, equipped with machine guns and rifles, their artillery also made conditions very unhealthy. The plan for the assault crossing was to advance to the canal, throw out pontoon bridges and floating bridges based on cork floats and to ferry storming parties of the 2nd Battalion Manchester Regiment and 16th Battalion, Lancashire Fusiliers by bridge and raft across the canal. Having already been tested during the bridging of the St. Quentin Canal on 29 September, the 218th Field Company, Royal Engineers was selected as the 'forlorn hope' to storm the Sambre-Oise canal on 4 November.

Their earlier crossing of the St Quentin Canal on 29 September had been a successful operation carried out in the face of relatively light resistance but significant shell fire. The work of 218th Field

Company involved construction of a heavy motor transport bridge. Both officers involved were awarded the MC (Lt Kilpatrick in charge and 2.Lt. Oates assisting) for ensuring that the Company completed the work in difficult conditions, which allowed heavy guns to be moved across the Canal. A batch of five MMs was announced in the *London Gazette* of 11 March 1919. Major Waters, in command of the Company, got his DSO for this action, to add to the two MCs and five MMs awarded to his men. It was a very fair clutch of awards considering the importance of their work and its successful completion.

The actual crossing of the Sambre-Oise Canal was a far more desperate affair, as the War Diary of 218 Field Company tersely records:

2 November: assembling necessary equipment and preparing for the operation.

3 November: carrying stores etc. up to the canal ready to build the floating bridges.

4 November: Sections 1, 3 and 4 (strength; 42) and 'A'-Company, 16th H.L.I. constructed two floating bridges across the Sambre-Oise Canal south of Ors at 05:45. R.E. casualties 30 including 2Lt Oates, Barker and 10 other ranks killed. HLI casualties about 30. No.2 Section constructing pontoon bridge at Ors. Company spent night at Bazeul'.

The diary entry indicates that forty-two men of 218 Field Company formed the storming party and were assisted in the actual bridging operations by 'A' Company of the 16th Battalion, Highland Light Infantry. Three quarters of the forty-two engineers sent into the battle became casualties. Twelve men were killed by heavy machine gun and rifle fire from very close range; four Victoria Crosses were won by various units at Ors, the citations for these awards state that enemy fire was coming 'from a few yards distance' and 'at point blank range'. Another eighteen men were wounded, making up a huge percentage of the storming party, whose casualties were as bad as the worst hit battalions on the 1 July 1916. Both bridges were completed successfully, this having a very significant impact on the success of the wider operation. Military success combined with individual 'heroism' always attracted a larger number of gallantry awards.

The crossing at Ors on the 4 November resulted in the award, to 218 Field Company, of two Victoria Crosses, three DCMs, a bar to the MM and thirteen MMs. Out of a force of forty-two, 45 per cent of those involved were decorated. In fact, two thirds of those left alive at the end were decorated. The dead were buried in a battlefield cemetery close to the canal called Ors British Cemetery and also in the Ors Communal Cemetery. Wilfred Owen was killed on the canal bank whilst gathering and preparing his men for the crossing.

## IMMEDIATE AWARDS OF THE M.C. TO THE ROYAL ENGINEERS, 1914-18: SAMPLE SUMMARY

| RANK | UNIT | LG Date | Category | Activity | Note |
|---|---|---|---|---|---|
| 2Lieut | Field | 3.7.15 | Defence | Supporting Infantry | Demolition |
| Lieut | Field | 24.7.15 | Devotion To Duty | | blowing a mine |
| 2Lieut | | 24.7.15 | Attack | | Gallipoli, excellent |
| 2Lieut | | 25.8.15 | Gallantry Under Shellfire | Line Laying/Repair | Gallipoli |
| Lieut | Tunnelling | 6.9.15 | Devotion To Duty | Unexploded Ordnance | Enemy mine |
| 2Lieut | Tunnelling | 15.9.15 | Devotion To Duty | Unexploded Ordnance | excellent |
| Captain | Field | 2.10.15 | Devotion To Duty | Period of Time | Remarkable, organisation of civilians |
| 2Lieut | Tunnelling | 29.10.15 | Lifesaving | Rescue From Mine Galleries | Failed |
| Lieut | Field | 4.11.15 | Defence | Erecting wire | excellent |
| Lieut | Field | 4.11.15 | Devotion To Duty | Supporting Infantry | excellent |
| 2Lieut | Tunnelling | 18.11.15 | Devotion To Duty | | A very peculiar award; there was no danger |
| 2Lieut | Field | 7.12.15 | Attack | Supporting Infantry | Gallipoli |
| Captain | Tunnelling | 23.12.15 | Devotion To Duty | Period of Time | Sneaky trick |
| Lieut | Tunnelling | 22.1.16 | Attack | | Raid |
| 2Lieut | Tunnelling | 22.1.16 | Devotion To Duty | | great mental tension |
| 2Lieut | Tunnelling | 15.3.16 | Lifesaving | Rescue From Mine Galleries | excellent |
| 2Lieut | Tunnelling | 15.3.16 | Officer rescue | Rescue From Mine Galleries | collapsing |
| 2Lieut | Field | 15.4.16 | Devotion To Duty | Consolidation | mine craters |
| 2Lieut | Tunnelling | 16.5.16 | Attack | Supporting Infantry | Also for mining |
| Lieut | Fortress | 16.5.16 | Gallantry Under Shellfire | | Reconnaissance prior to attack |
| 2Lieut | Tunnelling | 31.5.16 | Devotion To Duty | | Disarmed an enemy mine |
| 2Lieut | Field | 31.5.16 | Courage Under Heavy Fire | Consolidation | Battle for mine craters |
| Lieut | Field | 19.8.16 | Courage Under | Supplies forward | 1.7.16 awards this Gazette |
| 2Lieut | Tunnelling | 19.8.16 | Attack | Supporting Infantry | Trench Raid |
| Lieut | Tunnelling | 19.8.16 | Attack | Supporting Infantry | Led infantry 1.7.16 |
| Warrant Offr | Field | 19.8.16 | Lifesaving | Buried Men | Retrospective award to WO for May 1916. |
| 2Lieut | Field | 25.8.16 | Attack | | Raid, demolition |
| Lieut | Field | 25.8.16 | Courage Under Heavy Fire | Erecting wire | excellent |
| 2Lieut | Field | 25.8.16 | Courage Under Heavy Fire | Working Party | new trench |
| 2Lieut | Field | 25.8.16 | Courage Under Heavy Fire | Consolidation | mine crater |

# BATTLEFIELD ACTS – THE ROYAL ENGINEERS

| RANK | UNIT | LG Date | Category | Activity | Note |
|------|------|---------|----------|----------|------|
| Lieut | Field | 20.10.16 | Defence | Working Party | excellent |
| Lieut | Signal | 20.10.16 | Gallantry Under Shellfire | Line Laying/Repair | Wireless station |
| Captain | Field | 20.10.16 | Officer rescue | | Classic VC |
| Lieut | Field | 20.10.16 | Attack | Supporting Infantry | Sufficient for DSO; quota exceeded that month? |
| 2Lieut | Field | 20.10.16 | Gallantry Under Shellfire | Working Party | Strongpoint construction |
| 2Lieut | Field | 20.10.16 | Courage Under Heavy Fire | | demolition |
| 2Lieut | Gas Special | 20.10.16 | Gallantry Under Shellfire | | gas discharge |
| 2Lieut | Field | 21.12.16 | Courage Under Heavy Fire | Working Party | Consolidation |
| Lieut | Field | 10.1.17 | Attack | Consolidation | demolition |
| Lieut | Field | 10.1.17 | Gallantry Under Shellfire | Working Party | new trench |
| Lieut | Field | 10.1.17 | Courage Under Heavy Fire | Working Party | demolition |
| Captain | Tunnelling | 10.1.17 | Attack | | Sufficient for DSO; quota exceeded that month? |
| Lieut | Tunnelling | 17.4.17 | Attack | | demolition |
| 2Lieut | Field | 17.4.17 | Courage Under Heavy Fire | Working Party | Construct emplacements |
| 2Lieut | Field | 17.4.17 | Courage Under Heavy Fire | Erecting wire | Consolidation |
| Lieut | Field | 26.5.17 | Attack | Consolidation | Construct emplacements |
| 2Lieut | Signal | 26.5.17 | Gallantry Under Shellfire | Line Laying/Repair | For burying armoured cables |
| Captain | Gas Special | 26.5.17 | Devotion To Duty | | For his reconnaissance prior to an attack |
| Lieut | Field | 18.6.17 | Courage Under Heavy Fire | Bridge Construction | Erection of pontoons |
| Lieut | Field | 18.6.17 | Devotion To Duty | Consolidation | Wounded 3 times |
| Lieut | Field | 18.6.17 | Attack | Bridge Construction | Ferrying troops over a river |
| Lieut | Signal | 26.9.17 | Gallantry Under Shellfire | | Lamp & buzzer |
| 2Lieut | | 26.9.17 | Gallantry Under Shellfire | Working Party | Liaison officer |
| Lieut | | 26.9.17 | Gallantry Under Shellfire | | Organised signal posts |
| 2Lieut | Field | 26.9.17 | Gallantry Under Shellfire | Consolidation | Building strong points |
| 2Lieut | Field | 26.9.17 | Gallantry Under Shellfire | Consolidation | Constructing emplacements |
| Captain | | 26.9.17 | Gallantry Under Shellfire | | Taping out new trenches |
| 2Lieut | | 26.9.17 | Courage Under Heavy Fire | Erecting wire | During broad daylight |
| 2Lieut | Field | 26.9.17 | Gallantry Under Shellfire | Consolidation | Constructed strong points |
| 2Lieut | Field | 26.9.17 | Gallantry Under Shellfire | Bridge Construction | Made a ford |
| 2Lieut | Field | 26.9.17 | Gallantry Under Shellfire | Bridge Construction | Set an example to men |
| Captain | Signal | 26.9.17 | Gallantry Under Shellfire | Line Laying/Repair | Supervision thereof |
| Lieut | | 26.9.17 | Gallantry Under Shellfire | Supplies forward | Bridging supplies |
| Lieut | Field | 26.9.17 | Courage Under Heavy Fire | Bridge Construction | Boring for piles and charges |
| Captain | | 26.9.17 | Gallantry Under Shellfire | | Set an example to men |
| 2Lieut | | 26.9.17 | Attack | Cutting wire | Trench raid |
| 2Lieut | Field | 26.9.17 | Gallantry Under Shellfire | Bridge Construction | Bridge repair |
| Lieut | | 26.9.17 | Courage Under Heavy Fire | Working Party | Road construction; assumed command |
| Lieut | | 26.9.17 | Gallantry Under Shellfire | Line Laying/Repair | Was hit by a lump of concrete |
| 2Lieut | Field | 26.9.17 | Gallantry Under Shellfire | Working Party | Howitzer emplacement |
| Lieut | | 26.9.17 | Gallantry Under Shellfire | Line Laying/Repair | Organisational skills |
| Lieut | | 26.9.17 | Gallantry Under Shellfire | Tending Wounded | Road construction party |
| Major | Field | 26.9.17 | Defence | Supporting Infantry | Construct emplacements |
| 2Lieut | Signal | 26.9.17 | Attack | Line Laying/Repair | During a raid across a river |

| RANK | UNIT | LG Date | Category | Activity | Note |
|---|---|---|---|---|---|
| 2Lieut | Field | 26.9.17 | Courage Under Heavy Fire | Bridge Construction | Bridge repair |
| 2Lieut | | 26.9.17 | Courage Under Heavy Fire | Working Party | Laid tape for sap leading to a strong point |
| Captain | Rail | 26.9.17 | Gallantry Under Shellfire | Rail Construction | Survey route |
| 2Lieut | Rail | 26.9.17 | Gallantry Under Shellfire | Rail Construction | For determined leadership |
| 2Lieut | Field | 26.9.17 | Attack | | A Sapper's raid |
| 2Lieut | Gas Special | 26.9.17 | Gallantry Under Shellfire | | Getting mortars forward & for successful ops |
| Lieut | Field | 26.9.17 | Gallantry Under Shellfire | Bridge Construction | Bridge repair |
| Captain | | 26.9.17 | Gallantry Under Shellfire | Supplies forward | Guns by rail; line often broken |
| 2Lieut | Tunnelling | 26.9.17 | Gallantry Under Shellfire | | Searching mines, dug-outs and salvaging |
| Captain | Rail | 26.9.17 | Gallantry Under Shellfire | Rail Construction | Surveyed the route under fire |
| Lieut | | 26.9.17 | Attack | Cutting wire | Bangalore torpedo |
| 2Lieut | Field | 6.9.17 | Gallantry Under Shellfire | Working Party | MG emplacements |
| Captain | Signal | 22.6.18 | Devotion To Duty | Line Laying/Repair | Organised everything |
| Captain | Rail | 22.6.18 | Gallantry Under Shellfire | Bridge Construction | Rail bridge repair |
| 2Lieut | Field | 22.6.18 | Defence | | Bridge Destruction |
| Lieut | Signal | 22.6.18 | Defence | Line Laying/Repair | For initiative in setting up a report centre |
| Captain | Waterways | 22.6.18 | Lifesaving | | Searching for missing men |
| Lieut | Field | 22.6.18 | Courage Under Heavy Fire | Bridge Construction | During a raid |
| Captain | Rail | 22.6.18 | Gallantry Under Shellfire | | Cleared railhead rolling stock |
| Captain | Gas Special | 22.6.18 | Defence | | Discharging gas |
| 2Lieut | Signal | 22.6.18 | Devotion To Duty | | Electrical work for large force |
| 2Lieut | Waterways | 22.6.18 | Devotion To Duty | | Obstacle clearing, Scarpe River, March 1918 |
| Lieut | Field | 22.6.18 | Courage Under Heavy Fire | | Bridge Destruction |
| 2Lieut | Signal | 22.6.18 | Defence | | Exposed himself, encouraging men to defend |
| Lieut | Tunnelling | 22.6.18 | Courage Under Heavy Fire | | Bridge Destruction |
| 2Lieut | Waterways | 22.6.18 | Devotion To Duty | | Scarpe River |
| Captain | Tunnelling | 1.2.19 | Devotion To Duty | Unexploded Ordnance | Booby traps |
| Captain | Field | 1.2.19 | Gallantry Under Shellfire | Working Party | Road construction |
| 2Lieut | Gas Special | 1.2.19 | Gallantry Under Shellfire | Supplies forward | Stokes bombs. Took charge |
| Captain | Field | 1.2.19 | Gallantry Under Shellfire | Working Party | Surveying |
| Lieut | Signal | 1.2.19 | Attack | | Great initiative to capture MG |
| Major | Field | 1.2.19 | Gallantry Under Shellfire | Bridge Construction | Bridge erected in 7 hours in heavy gas & HE |
| 2Lieut | Signal | 1.2.19 | Courage Under Heavy Fire | Line Laying/Repair | Communication cable pushed fwd during attack |
| Lieut | Field | 1.2.19 | Courage Under Heavy Fire | Bridge Construction | Escaut Canal footbridge |
| Lieut | Field | 1.2.19 | Courage Under Heavy Fire | Water Supply | Removed explosive charges from a well |
| Major | Field | 1.2.19 | Courage Under Heavy Fire | | Recce for bridging ops |
| 2Lieut | Field | 1.2.19 | Devotion To Duty | Unexploded Ordnance | Landmines |

**Table 7: Variety of officer's awards, Royal Engineers, and the everyday tasks they represent**

Additional information concerning the nature of courage exhibited by the men of 218 Field Company at the Ors crossing can be gleaned from the various award citations. The two Victoria Crosses won by 218 Field Company went to Sapper Adam Archibald who received his award from George V in 1919: 'On 4 November 1918 near Ors, France, Sapper Archibald was with a party building a floating bridge across the canal. He was foremost in the work under a very heavy artillery barrage and machine-gun fire. The latter was directed at him from a few yards distance while he was working on the cork floats. Nevertheless he persevered in his task and his example and efforts were such that the bridge which was essential to the success of the operations was very quickly completed. Immediately afterwards Sapper Archibald collapsed from gas poisoning.'

Major A. H. S. Waters, DSO, MC, commanding officer of 218 Field Company, received the second of 218's VCs, adding it in front of his already distinguished array of gallantry decorations. The citation reads: 'For most conspicuous bravery and devotion to duty on 4 November 1918, near Ors, when bridging with his Field Company the Oise-Sambre canal. From the outset the task was under artillery and machine-gun fire at close range, the bridge being damaged and the building party suffering severe casualties. Major Waters, hearing that all his officers had been killed or wounded, at once went forward and personally supervised the completion of the bridge, working on cork floats while under fire at point-blank range. So intense was the fire that it seemed impossible that he could escape being killed. The success of the operation was due entirely to his valour and example'. Major Waters had in fact been recommended for a bar to his DSO, but this recommendation was upgraded to the Victoria Cross.

The medal for Distinguished Conduct was awarded to three Sappers; 183496 G. W. Quinton of Hadleigh, 514546 W. J. Elson of Plymouth and 277853 G. Frankland of Slights, Yorkshire. Sapper Quinton's citation indicates that he worked on the floating bridge 'notwithstanding very heavy machine-gun fire from the bank opposite'. Sappers Elson and Frankland share the same citation which tells us that both were working on the cork floats on the enemy held bank throughout the operation until the bridge was completed, again 'under very heavy machine-gun fire'. One of the MMs awarded to the party has been noted in a private collection, it is the award made to 305188 Sapper Allan Leo Dickinson and it is pictured with its British War Medal and Victory Medal, below. Allan Dickinson was from Grewelthorpe, Yorkshire and his civilian employment was in a factory as 'stationary engine man', responsible for the running of machinery. His pre-war employment was, without doubt, the reason for him being taken on the strength of the Royal Engineers. On the day he stepped into the storm of fire, his wife, Anne waited for him at home with their children while he likely wondered if he would live to see the sun go down.

Two infantry officers won the VC, their citations add to the wider picture of what happened. Second Lieutenant James Kirk, 2nd Battalion of the Manchester Regiment, was twenty-one years old and from Droylsden, Manchester. His citation for the Victoria Cross, published in the *London Gazette* of 3 January 1919, tells us how he materially assisted the bridging parties: 'To cover the bridging of the canal he took a Lewis gun, and, under intense machine-gun fire, paddled across the canal on a raft and, at a range of ten yards, expended all his ammunition. Further ammunition was paddled across to him and he continuously maintained a covering fire for the bridging party from a most exposed position till killed at his gun. The supreme contempt of danger and magnificent self-sacrifice displayed by this gallant officer prevented many casualties and enabled two platoons to cross the bridge before it was destroyed.'

A second infantry VC went to Lieutenant-Colonel James Neville Marshall (VC, MC and bar) of the 16th[h] Lancashire Fusiliers. He was aged just thirty-one and in command of a Battalion when he won the decoration. The citation captures this young man's vital contribution to the operation extremely well; 'when a partly constructed bridge came under concentrated fire and was broken before the advanced troops of his battalion could cross, Lt. Col. Marshall at once went forward and organised parties to repair the bridge. The first party were soon killed or wounded, but by personal example he inspired his command, and volunteers were instantly forthcoming. Under intense fire and with complete disregard of his own safety, he stood on the bank encouraging his men and assisting in the work, and when the bridge was repaired, attempted to rush across at the head of his battalion and was killed while so doing. The passage of the canal was of vital importance, and the gallantry displayed by all ranks was largely due to the inspiring example set by Lt. Col. Marshall'.

## CRITICAL LEADERSHIP ACTIVITIES OF ENGINEER OFFICERS

The Corps of Engineers only gained 83 Distinguished Service Orders during the First World War. Most of these awards were made for the performance of specific battlefield tasks to a high standard under difficult conditions; a continuance of the theme of 'just doing one's job' which dominates MC awards. These tasks include the direction of wiring parties in front of positions, assisting the infantry to consolidate captured trenches, destroying and constructing bridges and defusing enemy booby traps and unexploded ordnance. Nearly 30 per cent of DSOs were awarded to officers who were acting largely in the role of an infantry officer, either by leading men into the attack or by organising and participating in the defensive actions of Spring 1918. For example, it was Captain Arthur Penrice Sayer of 91 Field Company, Royal Engineers, who, on the morning of 26 September 1915, when subjected to a German gas attack, saw that men were retiring from Hill 70 in the vicinity of Loos, and he shouldered the responsibility for reorganising them and leading them back up the hill to hold their ground successfully. During the late summer of 1917, Second Lieutenant Alfred Best, whilst engaged on a reconnaissance, also left his allotted task to rally infantry; 'during an action he saw a large party of men, without officers, who had been driven from their position. He at once rallied the party, led them forward, and succeeded in re-establishing the position'. He accomplished this, 'by his example and good leadership'. Captain George Sim's DSO was announced in the *London Gazette* of 25 August 1916, the citation states; 'He led forward his company with great bravery in the assault on a wood, and then advanced himself under heavy fire of all kinds to locate strong points for the defence'. In the

Spring of 1918, Major Mark Whitwill was busy repairing telephone cables until an enemy attack required him to join in the defence. He 'assumed command of some troops, organised defences and held the posts until relieved. He constantly exposed himself to heavy fire, and by his coolness and example kept troops together when there was serious danger of their becoming disorganised'. Similarly, Major Frederick Mulqueen was able to assist the infantry: 'He was of the greatest assistance to the defence. His fearless bearing and gallantry stimulated all ranks and enabled the positions to be held for a long time, though repeatedly attacked by overwhelming numbers'. Lieutenant Colonel George Paton Pollitt, Royal Engineers, was attached to the 11th Battalion Lancashire Fusiliers when on 27 May 1918, during the fighting on the Aisne, he won a second bar to his DSO: 'Thanks to his example and leadership, his battalion put up a splendid defence when over 40 per cent of them had become casualties and the remainder were almost surrounded'.

**Figure 14: Military Medal and pair awarded to Sapper Allan Dickinson, Royal Engineers (Ors, 1918)**

## DEFUSING OF EXPLOSIVE DEVICES AND BOOBY TRAPS BY ENGINEER OFFICERS

Late war editions of the *London Gazette* contain DSO awards relating to the disarming of booby traps and charges. Major William Wilson of the 256th Tunnelling Company, R.E., won a DSO: 'For conspicuous devotion to duty at Bellenglise on 30 September 1918 when he supervised the clearance of mines and traps from the Bellenglise-Magny Tunnel'. Lieutenant Hugh Eddowes, 185th Tunnelling Company, 'located and fired' a delayed action mine at Flines railway station nine days after the armistice, which, according to German information, had been set to explode five days previously. Eddowes' citation further states that the work was, 'extremely dangerous, as the mine might have exploded at any moment'. His officer, Captain George Howatson, also won a DSO after 'he spent 36 hours in excavating a shaft and gallery approaching the large delay action mine in Douai station, due to explode on 7 November 1918'. Lieutenant Harry Fyers, 179th Tunnelling Company, did similar work in defusing acid delay mines on rail tracks and at rail stations between 25 October and 17 November 1918. He was working under Captain George Sale, of the same unit, who oversaw safe removal of 50 such devices, some of which were again overdue to explode. These awards of the DSO for acts that would later be made famous under the umbrella of bomb disposal, were not carried out in the face of the enemy and pre-date the institution of the George Cross and George Medal, which were used extensively to reward bomb disposal experts in the Second World War and in subsequent operations.

# The Machine Gun Corps

On the 1 July 1916, recalls an anonymous N.C.O. of the Machine Gun Corps, 'the whole of the Somme battlefield was ablaze with fire when our draft ... set off for the line in the last hour of daylight'. He remembers that 'our limbers went off at five-minute intervals straight up the metalled road to the line' and the men followed, eventually passing through the Artillery lines with 'guns banging away ear-splittingly to left and right'.[5] Thus, the machine gunners went into battle.

The Machine Gun Corps won nearly 5 per cent of all awards for gallantry. Its men fought machine guns in every battle from the institution of the Corps in October 1915 until the end of the war. Army Divisions had their machine-gun companies distributed around the infantry brigades until February 1918. After that, companies were all amalgamated to form single Divisional Machine Gun Battalions. Hence, post-February 1918 awards show the man's unit as an MG Battalion rather than an MG Company. The battalion number was taken from the parent division, whereas the old company number was taken from the parent brigade.

The Corps was not only composed of machine gunners; gun teams required support in the field and this was provided by men assigned within each unit to perform duty as signallers, runners, supply and transport as well as cooks. Moving in and out of the line, along rough roads and tracks with heavy guns and belts of ammunition required carts drawn most often by mules. When close to the front, the transport would be left behind and the remaining distance covered on foot, the guns and supplies being carried by hand. When moving out of the line, their transport often met them and carried their loads back to the rest camps. Like everyone moving to and from the line, they had to pass through the shelled back areas, where something could happen in an instant, or where certain points were being heavily shelled. Not all Machine Gun Corps awards were won in set-piece battles, but it is true that the vast majority were. It was in the front line, whether engaged in offensive or defensive operations, that the Machine Gunners earned most of their decorations for gallantry. In common with the other front line units such as infantry, tanks and medical corps, they gained just 25–30 per cent of their DCMs and less than 20 per cent of MCs in Honours gazettes.

Static machine guns operated as support points for defence and when mobile they provided anchor points from which suppressive and destructive fire could be poured as the infantry clawed its way forward. Not infrequently, the machine gunners were carrying their guns into action ahead of the infantry, searching for commanding positions from which to eliminate enemy resistance. In defence, machine gunners felt keenly their responsibility and many gallantry decorations were earned for holding out doggedly until the last possible moment before withdrawing. Many awards won in defence were for breaking up enemy attacks, often repeatedly, when the defenders were hard pressed over many hours and days. At all of these times, the supply of ammunition and water for the guns was critical to their effectiveness, and we must not forget that behind the guns were men with mules and horses struggling over rough ground, sometimes through shell explosions and bullets, with boxes of ammunition, fresh guns and water (not to mention rations and other necessary supplies). In the mud, 'the difficulties of keeping the guns cleaned and in action ... was seldom appreciated and certainly not understood'.6 But it was the gunners themselves, sat behind their spitting weapons, who made themselves the target for every calibre and type of ordnance that the enemy could throw at them, from infantry rifle bullets to explosive contrivances the size of dustbins.

## Distinguished Conduct Medal, Machine Gun Corps, Categories

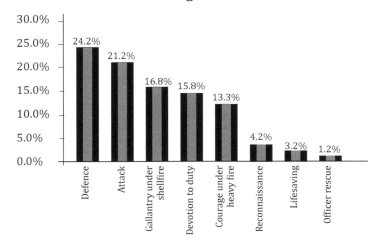

| Activity | % |
| --- | --- |
| Period of time | 15.8 |
| Break up enemy attacks | 13.5 |
| Dogged determination | 11.0 |
| Getting guns forward | 10.1 |
| Ammunition forward | 8.5 |
| Preserve guns | 7.6 |
| Supporting infantry | 7.3 |
| Eliminate enemy MG | 6.8 |
| Armoured cars | 2.8 |
| Consolidation | 2.8 |
| Tending wounded | 2.8 |
| Rations forward | 2.5 |
| Buried men | 2.3 |
| MG barrage | 2.0 |
| Messages | 1.7 |
| Hand-to-hand fighting | 1.78 |
| Explosion ammunition | 0.8 |

| Rank | % |
| --- | --- |
| Sergeants | 57.1 |
| Privates/Corporals | 42.9 |

| | % |
| --- | --- |
| Honours DCMs | 27.5% |

**Figure 15: Analysis of the Distinguished Conduct Medal, Machine Gun Corps**
*Results of a sample of 403 Immediate and Honours DCM Awards of the MGC*
*(50% of total)*

## Military Cross, Machine Gun Corps, Categories

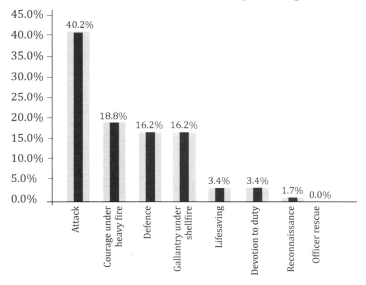

| Activity | % |
| --- | --- |
| Getting guns forward | 24.5 |
| Break up enemy attacks | 24.5 |
| Dogged determination | 9.8 |
| Consolidation | 7.8 |
| MG barrage | 6.9 |
| Supporting infantry | 5.9 |
| Eliminate enemy MG | 5.9 |
| Ammunition forward | 3.9 |
| Tending wounded | 2.9 |
| Messages | 2.0 |
| Hand-to-hand fighting | 1.0 |
| Armoured cars | 1.0 |
| Preserve guns | 1.0 |
| Buried men | 1.0 |
| Rations forward | 1.0 |
| Period of time | 1.0 |
| Explosion ammunition | 0.0 |

| Rank | % |
| --- | --- |
| Warrant Officer | 1.7 |
| 2nd Lieutenant | 53.8 |
| Lieutenant | 36.8 |
| Captain | 4.3 |
| Major | 3.4 |

| | |
| --- | --- |
| Honours MCs | 16.3% |

**Figure 16: Analysis of the Military Cross, Machine Gun Corps**
*Results of a sample of 117 Immediate Awards*

## Distinguished Service Order, Machine Gun Corps, Categories

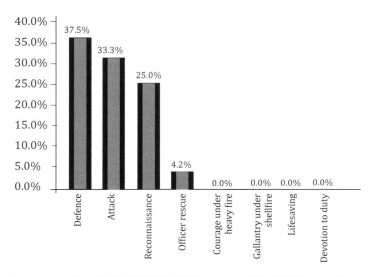

| Activity | % |
|---|---|
| Break up enemy attacks | 33.3 |
| Supporting infantry | 19.0 |
| Eliminate enemy MG | 14.3 |
| Armoured cars | 14.3 |
| Getting guns forward | 9.5 |
| Dogged determination | 4.8 |
| Consolidation | 4.8 |
| Ammunition forward | 0.0 |
| Tending wounded | 0.0 |
| Messages | 0.0 |
| Hand-to-hand fighting | 0.0 |
| MG barrage | 0.0 |
| Preserve guns | 0.0 |
| Buried men | 0.0 |
| Rations forward | 0.0 |
| Period of time | 0.0 |
| Explosion ammunition | 0.0 |

| Rank | % |
|---|---|
| 2nd Lieutenant | 25 |
| Lieutenant | 13 |
| Captain | 17 |
| Major | 33 |
| Lt Colonel | 13 |

| Honours DSOs | 72% |
|---|---|

**Figure 17: Analysis of the Distinguished Service Order, Machine Gun Corps**
*Results of a sample of all 24 Immediate Awards*

## INTO THE ATTACK

In the fighting at High Wood on the Somme, 15 July 1916, machine guns with their teams were pushed forward as support points for the infantry advance, engaging the Germans in the wood with heavy fire, followed forward by the infantry.[7] At this point, a Lance Corporal, Bradbury, made sufficient impression to earn the medal for distinguished conduct: 'He advanced single-handed with his gun to within 100 yards of the enemy posts, where he was severely wounded in three places. Despite his wounds, he continued in action until he had placed his gun under cover, when he collapsed from loss of blood'. It was a desperate undertaking against very heavy opposition; the attack on their right was destroyed and the flank of the Brigade left exposed. In these conditions in front of High Wood, the complete teams of six guns had become casualties. Remaining machine guns were gathered together and moved to form a battery guarding the flanks. Shell fire became so heavy overnight that a retirement and abandonment of the attack became necessary.

## THE MACHINE GUN BARRAGE

Machine gunners also served behind the front line during attacks and fired 'barrages' often consisting of hundreds of thousands of rounds – a bullet hailstorm – focussed on enemy trenches and other specified target areas some distance away and usually out of sight. On 24 August 1916, it is thought that the first machine-gun barrage was carried out, using a battery of ten Vickers machine guns.[8] The demand for ammunition and water was such that the whole Company, plus two further Companies of infantry, were employed to carry all day of 23 August and overnight into the 24th. Later in the war, barrages were put down by many more than six guns and the demand for ammunition was met by a long build-up of stocks and use of belt-filling machines to insert all of the rounds into ready-use belts. In the barrage of 24 August, the ten guns fired nearly a million rounds in 12 hours and Private Robertshaw and Artificer H. Bartlett manned the belt-filling machine for the whole of that time without a moment's rest. DCMs won by those taking part in these barrages are rather scarce, approximately 2 per cent of DCMs was made for this activity, and all of those were for gallantry under shell fire as might be expected. As a particularly good example, the DCM of Sergeant Henry Smith of the 38th Battalion, won in the closing fortnight of the war, will suffice: 'Near Englefonteine, on 4 November, whilst firing a machine gun barrage, his section officer and 15 men were wounded. Though under severe artillery fire, he reorganised the remainder of his men and maintained the fire of his guns. Later, he successfully led them to their objectives'. Most MG barrage DCMs were in fact Honours awards rather than immediate awards.

Members of the Machine Gun Corps did not only fight with their machine guns, they occasionally picked up other weapons. Being close to the enemy, they found themselves in situations similar to those of the infantry. Sergeant Aylmore (42nd Battalion MGC) was reconnoitring a position for his MG section when he encountered a party of 25 of the enemy. Aylmore immediately 'attacked them with the bayonet, shouting for his gun team to follow with bombs and took them prisoner'. His citation for the DCM states that he 'afforded a splendid example to his men'. Pte Aubrey of the 61st Battalion MGC gained his DCM on the 2 October 1918 when the attacking infantry were held up by an enemy machine gun during an advance on Bartlett Farm. Aubrey 'fixed his bayonet and dashed across the open at the gun, which he captured with its crew of four, thus enabling the infantry to advance'. Being without any kind of a weapon did not stop one machine gunner from capturing an enemy machine gun complete with its five crew; his name was Private Ryan, and he won his DCM for his gallantry and initiative when 'he held a piece of clay in his hand, pretending to throw it like a bomb. This caused the enemy team to surrender. He was at the time under heavy rifle fire'. Private P. Ryan would seem to have been, at this moment, free of fear and totally consumed by what he was doing, otherwise he would certainly have thought better of this foolhardy, cheeky escapade. The end of his existence was imminent, yet he managed to pull it off. Many others, there can be little doubt, perished while attempting similarly forlorn feats, but how many could honestly say they were unarmed at the time?

## THE RUNNER

Machine gun battalions needed runners for carrying messages like any other unit in action; Private J.W. Diskin gained his DCM 'when performing duties of a runner crossing again and again an area swept by bullets and heavily shelled. He showed absolute disregard of danger when working a gun single-handed in addition to his other duties'. These men also got involved in fighting as they moved forward with their officers ready to receive messages and carry them back. Private Stone of Everton was a runner accompanying his section officer during an attack. The pair of them encountered a hostile machine-gun position which they reconnoitred and rushed from different sides, 'Private Stone using a shovel to great effect'. His 'aptitude' for trench fighting may have been part of the reason he later transferred to the infantry, joining the Liverpool Regiment prior to the end of the war.

## THE TRENCH RAID

The trench raid was not out of bounds to the machine gunner either. The DCM awarded to Acting Sergeant Phillips was for one of the many raids carried out over the winter of 1916–17. His citation reads: 'For conspicuous gallantry and devotion to duty during a raid on the enemy's trenches. He handled two machine guns with great skill and inflicted many casualties on the enemy'. It was around this time that the size and ambitiousness of raids increased; this carrying of machine guns across no-mans-land at night and into the enemy trenches was certainly ambitious.

Other members of the Corps became unwillingly involved in trench raids. When Germans raided, anyone in the line would be swept up in the defence. Lance-Corporal Maund, again during the winter of 1916–17, showed conspicuous gallantry during an enemy raid when he 'threw bombs into a party of the enemy, thereby forcing them to retire'. A year later, Sergeant Mawbey was caught up in an enemy raid and he showed 'great skill in bringing his machine gun into action under heavy fire and inflicted casualties on the enemy'. These are unusual awards for the Machine Gun Corps.

## AMMUNITION, RATIONS AND WATER SUPPLY

Supply of ammunition and other necessary stores (including water for the operation of the guns and rations for the men) was as critical for MGC operations as for any other front line unit. Upon supply they thrived or perished. For this purpose each MGC Company or Battalion had a transport section. A machine gunner of the 17th Division recalled how 'rations were never certain to reach us and we were obliged to take cover, often for long periods, in mere grooves in the ground'.[9] It is rather surprising to note how few DCMs were awarded to men of the MGC Transport sections. One such example is that made to Sergeant T. Baker of the 46th Battalion. His citation was printed in the *London Gazette* in March 1920, being a late war award, it states: 'On several occasions during the operations from 29 September 1918 to 18 October 1918, he showed marked gallantry and coolness in taking up ammunition and supplies for his company under shell fire when in charge of transport. He was wounded, but remained at duty until sent down by an officer'. Company Sergeant Major Calletly distinguished himself in charge of pack mules during late 1917. He was getting ammunition, rations and water up to his gun teams: 'Despite the most difficult conditions', reads his citation, 'he brought the supplies through night after night, pushing further forward than any other train in the area'.

As in other Army units, the Quartermaster Sergeant was the man responsible for getting the necessary supplies and for distributing them in a timely fashion to his men. He tended to remain behind with Battalion HQ, rather than go into battle with the men. The Quartermaster Sergeant's opportunities for winning gallantry decorations were necessarily limited. However, C.Q.M.S. Smith of Acton, London, deservedly received his DCM in the 1919 New Year Honours list because he 'never failed to deliver ammunition and rations to all his gun teams. On one occasion, when a driver was wounded, he took the wounded man's place and delivered much needed ammunition'. During the Battle of the Somme in 1916, Private R. H. Bowles 'carried water and rations to his gun team in an exposed position close to the enemy's lines, across a bullet swept zone. While doing so he was severely wounded in both hands'. The value of his work was recognised by the announcement of the DCM in the *London Gazette* of 14 November 1916. Lance Corporal Wilson won his DCM for his part in keeping the supplies coming: 'for nine days he conducted carrying parties to the front line under heavy fire'. He was just doing the job assigned to him; his mates were relying on him. Furthermore, there was pressure on him to do his job. If he could not get supplies across the rear areas what would the men in the firing line, taking a pounding from shell fire, think of him? A man who'd helped his mates in hardship and danger could be proud. These were powerful motivators.

## THE TRANSPORT SECTIONS

Men of the MGC transport sections received DCMs for 'never failing to bring up the transport, often through heavy shell fire' (Sgt. C. Wells), for reconnoitring supply routes for the pack mules through heavily-shelled areas (Actg./Sgt R. McGill of Jamestown) and for 'taking charge of transport and pack animals, taking ammunition up to forward dumps for barrage work' (Sgt. C. H. Nixon of Wandsworth). This man Nixon: 'Notwithstanding heavy animal casualties... never failed to carry out whatever task was given to him'. A member of the 98th M.G. Company remembered his time on nightly ration fatigues: 'Animals were fed and watered in good time; various packs looked over; water jars filled up; post bags collected; and other seemingly small but nevertheless important jobs completed'. After being looked over by the Quarter Master Sergeant at 8pm, the order 'Walk march!' was given 'and we were on our way'.[10] The mules and men with their burdens made their way slowly over the shelled roads up as far as a sentry, where they unhitched their animals and made the remainder of the way on foot, over the duck-boards and up to the line where men were waiting on the deliveries up to their knees in water and frozen stiff. In the first half of 1917, in the aftermath of the Somme battles of the Summer and Autumn of 1916, the German Army fell back several miles, almost overnight, to prepared defensive positions on the so-called Hindenburg Line. Two men of the 100th M.G. Company transport section received the Military Medal for 'particular skill and daring' on the night of the 22 April

1917. They were Sergeant Keeble and Driver Messenger who drove the transport to within 300 yards of the new German lines, and deposited 12 heavy Vickers guns under the noses of the Germans, on high ground overlooking their positions. A flanking M.G. barrage was organised to coincide with an attack by this battery of 12 guns, situated well out in front of the British lines. Awards made to MGC transport sections are very unusual.

**THE SIGNALLING SECTIONS**
There were signalling and communications sections too. Sergeant Enoch, a native of Carmarthen, saw his DCM announced in the Birthday Honours list of June 1919. It was given for operations in September and October 1918, near Armentieres, when he 'showed great coolness and resource under fire. In the rapid and constant advance of units he maintained the communications under his charge. It was largely due to his work that communications were maintained during a critical period, and the ordered mobility of the machine guns with the advancing infantry was possible'.

**LIFESAVING AND STRETCHER PARTIES**
The Corps needed stretcher bearer parties as well, and it was in this role that Lance-Corporal Cannell won his DCM during the German Offensives of Spring 1918: 'When in charge of stretcher-bearers he brought in wounded under a heavy fire'. When gun teams and their support sections were moving around on the battlefield they became a target for artillery. On 30 October 1918, a machine gun battalion was ordered to unload its limbers in an orchard, where 'Jerry started shelling us... we raced for shelter behind the fallen trees in the orchard. Shrapnel knocked out two of our gunners. We had already taken away our guns and tripods, ammo and other items, but the limbers remained exposed and beside them lay our two chums'. A Sergeant then went out to rescue the wounded, two other men followed him, a dud shell landed right next to them, knocking the Sergeant about. 'He was so badly shaken that for a few moments he was unable to speak'. It was almost irresistible to go out and rescue wounded chums, no matter what the risk.[11]

144

Other forms of lifesaving attracted the DCM among MGC men. Whereas the Army Service Corps and artillery far more often got involved in the rescue of comrades from exploding ammunition dumps and fires, examples of this type of act in the MGC are very scarce. Acting Corporal C. Barrett was decorated with the DCM after 'he volunteered to extinguish a burning shell dump under very heavy shell fire'. Company Sergeant Major R. Woolmer earned his DCM when, in mid-1917, he 'organised a party and successfully extinguished a burning ammunition and ration dump. Afterwards he dug out an officer and his orderly who had been buried by a shell'.

Digging out buried comrades was something that machine gunners, being posted within range of German guns, sometimes had to do. On the Gallipoli Peninsula, on 17 and 18 April 1915, Sergeant S. Clarke was involved in an attack on 'Hill 60' and won the DCM for 'assisting to dig out guns and men who had been buried by shell fire'. It was not only guns and men that needed rescuing; 19171 Sergeant Jack Tate of Bradford felt compelled not to leave his gun tripod behind, even when the enemy had already forced all of his comrades to retreat. It was the Spring of 1918, his citation reads: 'For conspicuous gallantry and devotion to duty during an enemy attack. He kept his gun firing under heavy shell and machine-gun fire, inflicting very severe casualties on the advancing enemy. After covering the withdrawal of the infantry, he led his team back; he then went back through a hail of bullets to fetch his tripod, which had been left behind, and at once got his gun into action again. He displayed fine courage and determination'. It seems remarkable to risk one's life through a 'hail of bullets' simply for a tripod; acts of this sort rightly raise the question, what did these men think they were doing? However, there is a basic human urge to do things correctly and to persist until they are done correctly; this urge appears even in the most dangerous of undertakings to the extent that it may override that of self-preservation.

**THE DOGGED DETERMINATION OF THE MACHINE GUNNER**
Any description of MGC activities and decorations for gallantry would be incomplete without looking at some of the examples of

great determination that are recorded in DCM citations. A great majority of MGC DCMs were for hard fighting, the above awards for support roles and lifesaving are scarce. Roughly three times the number of DCMs were awarded to Machine Gun Corps men who carried ammunition up to the guns than for carrying rations and other supplies. Four times as many DCMs were awarded to men who carried fresh guns up to the firing line. The emphasis on actual fighting is clear from the awards distribution, yet rations and water had to be brought up every night, not just during the fighting. A great deal of courage was shown by men on ration parties that were not considered fit for a decoration. Again and again, everyday courage went unrewarded in the First World War.

The fighting spirit of some machine gunners is well exemplified by those who gained the DCM and a bar for a second award. Sergeant A. G. Lee of Rushington gained his DCM in late 1917 when, although wounded, he 'repaired a gun which had been temporarily put out of action, and carried on firing. Later, during a heavy barrage, he was blown off the parapet, sustaining fresh injuries, but again mounted his gun and kept it in action'. He won another DCM in the Spring of 1918 when in charge of a section of four guns: 'Though his position was attacked continuously by large bodies of the enemy, he used his guns on the larger masses and kept off small parties with his revolver and bombs. His fine courage and cheerfulness were a great support to his men'.

Perhaps the time when the machine gunners exhibited their greatest levels of dogged determination was in the dark days of the Spring Offensives of 1918. Sergeant Cowley was another who won two DCMs. He gained both while holding up the German onslaught of Spring 1918. Under great pressure from advancing enemy, and seeing his gun teams wounded and killed around him, Cowley 'remained alone with one gun covering the withdrawal of his men and the other gun, and then successfully brought his gun back with him'. Note that what he was doing was covering his men's escape; a very strong and quite a common motive in the performance of 'brave' deeds. Later that Spring, in similarly desperate circumstances, he performed an even more remarkable feat; 'during an enemy attack, and when the gun was damaged by shell fire, he got another into action through a determined enemy barrage. After inflicting heavy casualties on the enemy surrounding him, he finally got clear with his gun. His courage and cheerfulness were a splendid example to his men'. It is always puzzling to read the word 'cheerfulness' in these sorts of description, most particularly when he was surrounded by enemy who were very keen to kill him. He might yet have only moments to live. It is a simple fact that men did remain cheerful for they were doing their jobs among mates, and they knew they were doing it well. In the thick of it, fear did not play on their minds, there was too much to think about, and much of that was exciting.

Similarly, Acting Corporal George Mountain, originally from Cheriton, 'continued to inflict heavy casualties on the enemy until practically surrounded. When the enemy tried to bomb his gun he rushed forward with his revolver, and gave his gun time to withdraw and come into action further back. His courage and determination inspired his men to exceptionally good work throughout the operations'. Elsewhere along the line during the same phase of fighting, Sergeant George McHard was in charge of two guns in the front line: 'During the preliminary bombardment (*of 21 March 1918*) one of his gun teams was knocked out, but when the enemy attacked he immediately got the gun into action and continued to fire until he was surrounded and his gun destroyed by a bomb. He then drew his revolver and fought his way to his section officer to report what had happened. His courage and determination were magnificent'. Eighteen months earlier, during the Somme battle of 1916, Acting Corporal C. Loggey won his DCM when 'he fought his machine gun with great courage and determination, killing an enemy officer and five bombers at ten yards range'. In these citations, we have a record of those who stuck it out. There is no surviving record of those who retired unnecessarily, or buckled under the pressure of enemy attacks. The record we have is a distorted one, but the conditions faced by the Corps were as described; how each man reacted was different.

Corporal Thomas Baldwin's exploits whilst under heavy attack in Spring 1918 provide an illustration of the fighting of that time and indicate how so many men came to be taken prisoner of war; the German advance was very rapid and they came on in great numbers. Baldwin's citation for his award also shows how important setting an example of fearlessness was in providing a backbone to a solid defence. Promoted Sergeant later in the war, Corporal Baldwin received his DCM for 'conspicuous gallantry and devotion to duty in operations when he kept his machine gun in action under the most difficult conditions. Finally, when practically surrounded by the enemy, he rushed at the first man and shot him, being himself bayoneted by the next man, the thrust being broken by his box respirator. This man was also killed and, covering the retirement with his revolver, Corporal Baldwin enabled his team to successfully withdraw to another position. His splendid fearlessness throughout the battle was the means of inspiring his men with confidence'. Once again we learn that a display of bravery inspires others who see it and they are given confidence by the presence of the 'hero' in their midst. A display of heroism brings strength to others. Underlying the effect is the cause of the action; Baldwin fought this hard so that his mates could get away and he had no specific intent to survive his actions. A theme of self-sacrifice so that others might live is becoming clear.

## UNTIL THEY PHYSICALLY COLLAPSED

Men went on fighting their guns until they physically collapsed. Private Cottington's DCM award best illustrates men's willingness to fight until they dropped. The circumstances of his award are remarkable: 'When his section was shelled and practically wiped out on their way to the line, he rescued what guns he could from the confusion'. Again he witnessed men killed right next to him as a sniper claimed one of his section, quite likely shot through the head. He was undeterred by all of this, or perhaps motivated by losing so many colleagues and he persisted in his duty with selfless determination: 'When he lost much ammunition and had his gun buried by shell fire, he dug up the gun and got it into action again. When shelled out, and seriously wounded, he succeeded in selecting still another position before he collapsed'. During March 1918, Private Poole of Cambridge Heath 'volunteered to accompany some bombers to reconnoitre "pill-boxes" which had been rushed by the enemy the previous day and in which three machine guns had been left. He retrieved one of the guns under heavy fire, and was severely wounded by a sniper, but hung on to the gun and crawled back with it until he collapsed and was carried in'.

## LAST MAN STANDING

Some fought until they were the last man standing after all around them had been killed. The following example relates to an action carried out, once again, during the dark days of Spring 1918. Private W. Thomas of Everton was 'the sole survivor of a gun team' who showed conspicuous gallantry in continuing to fire his machine gun on the advancing enemy 'until the last round was expended, and then he brought his gun safely away'. A more poignant example of a soldier's devotion to duty than the next is difficult to find among the many hundreds of citations for bravery decorations. Sergeant Albert Jones of Stoke-under-Ham in Somerset received his DCM in the New Year Honours list of 1918 for 'conspicuous gallantry and devotion to duty. Although he had an arm and a leg blown off he remained at his post until relieved by the No.1 of the gun, and insisted on handing over his reports'. Albert Jones was an ex-infantryman. He arrived in France on 4 January 1915 with the Somerset Light Infantry and was terribly wounded in the incident just described. He was an old hand in 1917, one who had known the early stages of the war. Not to be stopped by having half the requisite number of limbs, he actually managed to gain a commission in the Army on the first of November 1918.

## IN ARMOURED CARS

The Heavy Branch of the MGC had been formed in 1916 and later converted into the Tank Corps. Its members, although originally machine gunners, became tank men and their awards do not appear among those of the MGC. Armoured cars, on the other hand, remained within the influence of the Machine Gun Corps, who supplied men as drivers and gun operators; they were particularly useful in Egypt, Iraq and Mesopotamia where open warfare allowed their use. Sergeant Tom V. Camm was in the vicinity of Anah in Mesopotamia (modern day Iraq, on the Euphrates river) when on 28 March 1918: 'He took his cars close up to an enemy stronghold and then approached on foot, accompanied by another man, although exposed to the fire of snipers. By his daring and determined action he induced the entire garrison to surrender', although it is not known exactly how he achieved that. Whereas Camm won his decoration on foot, Gunner Albert Milsom of Geneva, Switzerland, did so on a motorbike. Milsom became a member of the 'Motor Machine Gun Service' winning his DCM when 'he followed the armoured cars into action on his motorcycle, though under heavy fire at 800 yards from the enemy trenches, in order to maintain communication between the cars and headquarters. His great gallantry enabled early information of the enemy's dispositions to be sent back to headquarters'. Fighting actually inside an armoured car, Battery Sergeant Major Charles Unbeham 'manoeuvred his armoured car with great skill and opened fire on an enemy machine gun with great success'. He later gained a commission in the Royal Flying Corps on 12 December 1917.

Cars operated reconnaissance patrols and often came into early contact with the enemy, attracting heavy fire. Battery Sergeant Major Andrew Buchanan of Dumbarton was in Mesopotamia in late October 1918 when his patrol was 'suddenly attacked by the enemy'. He led one car to safety under heavy fire, and when another 'became stranded in a river he went to assist the crew in extricating it. He set a fine example under hazardous circumstances'. Armoured cars were softer targets than tanks, but nevertheless just as attractive to an enemy. They became the focus of fire and on occasion got into deadly situations. In Egypt, on the 19 September 1918, Gunner Saunders, 'after seeing to the evacuation of his wounded officer, took over command of the car and fought it most gallantly under heavy fire, inflicting heavy casualties on the enemy. Later, he rescued the battery commander and crew of a car which had been disabled by a direct hit. He also fired on a house containing enemy troops and a machine gun, and having caused them to surrender, brought them back to our lines as prisoners'. Albert Saunders was from Taunton, Somerset, and survived the war. His immediate award of the DCM was announced in the *London Gazette* of 25th February 1920.

## ON HORSEBACK

There were also machine gunners who went into action on horseback. Private W. G. Harris from Chertsey was awarded the DCM, 'For very conspicuous gallantry as a driver of a machine gun fighting limber during operations near Kwaadestraat on 22 October 1918. He drove his limber into action at the gallop over and down a crest for a distance of about 800 yards under intense machine-gun fire in order to enable his officer to get his guns into action quickly against hostile machine guns which were holding up the infantry advance and inflicting severe casualties. His splendid conduct made it possible for the gun teams to get forward unhampered and without serious casualties'. Thirteen days earlier, on 9 October 1918, Sergeant Harriott, 6th Squadron, Machine Gun Corps (Cavalry) performed the act for which his DCM was awarded: 'When several of the lead horses of which he was in charge were knocked out, he successfully saved a machine gun and ammunition pack under very heavy machine-gun fire. Later he carried ammunition to the guns which were in action, though the whole time exposed to close range hostile fire'. Harriott was one of those rare survivors of 1914, an 'Old Contemptible' who had proceeded to France on 31 October 1914 with the 3rd Dragoon Guards. He transferred to the MGC Cavalry in February 1916 and had sufficient experience of fighting not to take cover when the shooting started, but instead to take personal responsibility for what needed to be done. The spectacle of mounted machine-gun units being galloped into action in the last weeks of the war is a reflection of the increased mobility of the front at that time, when daily advances of the order of miles were being achieved. Even so, earlier in 1918, during the Spring offensives of the last week of March, Squadron Sergeant Major G. F. Wakefield of 1st Squadron MGC (Cavalry) showed marked courage when 'his squadron was repeatedly involved in rearguard actions in the neighbourhood of Bethencourt'. In all probability though, his DCM was earned whilst dismounted.

## SUPPORTING THE INFANTRY

Part of a machine gunner's job was to support and pave the way for the infantry's advance. In order to do this the gunners often had to advance in front of the attacking infantry, especially in the frame of late war tactics and continuous advance. Terence Lawler of East Ham received the Distinguished Conduct Medal for breaking the enemy's resistance ahead of an infantry attack, 'on the 25 October 1918, near Ooteghem. While advancing he was twice wounded. In spite of this he carried on, as an enemy strong point was checking our infantry advance. He took his gun out in front of the infantry under fire, and in doing so was again twice wounded; but his fire permitted the infantry to continue the advance, and contributed largely to the success of the attack. He set a splendid example of pluck'. Lawler also had the MM, showing that these exploits were not his first. It must be recorded here, that the four wounds mentioned above were serious enough for him to die on 28 October 1918, just a fortnight before the end of the war. He had sacrificed the rest of his life in the performance of his duties.

## A HUNTING WE SHALL GO

Another aspect of the machine gunner's or infantryman's job was to observe the enemy in action and to search for opportunities to outwit him. There are comparisons to be made with hunting, and the successful conclusion to a hunt is a deeply satisfying human experience. Therefore, supporting infantry attacks also required initiative – the spirit of the hunter – to identify and deal with problems as they occurred, often by getting up and moving to fresh positions, hunting the enemy down, outmanoeuvring and trapping him. This process of spotting, planning and executing is a game which, once started, has its own momentum, absorbs the intelligent mind and thus allows the soldier to carry on with a dangerous task whilst suppressing risk. When enemy machine guns and strongpoints held up the advance, the assistance of the machine gunners was appreciated by infantry units. On 18 September 1918, when infantry were held up and pinned down by heavy machine-gun fire, it was Sergeant Hopkins' two guns which turned the battle. 'He led his guns forward in spite of heavy machine-gun and artillery fire. Seeing the troops on his flanks held up... he got his guns into action, engaged and silenced several hostile guns, thereby enabling the troops to continue their advance. Throughout he showed great gallantry and initiative'. In this description we catch sight of one man who took the responsibility to help hundreds of others get out of a lethal position in the open. Had they lain there, surely enemy artillery fire would have dealt with them. With his powerful machine guns, he knew that it was his job to do what he could for the infantry. Engaged in helping others, the task he set himself consumed his thoughts and reduced his fear, perhaps to a minimum. Service to others can triumph over service to self.

## GROUP BEHAVIOUR AND INDIVIDUAL INITIATIVE

Leadership became especially critical when enemy fire pinned men down in shell holes. In the following example, the infantry attack came under heavy and accurate machine-gun and rifle fire from strongly held positions. From Private Victor Roberts' DCM citation, we can infer what happened. The attack stalled, no-one moved. Roberts' machine gun section was ordered forward to assist, his section commander was immediately shot and one gun destroyed in the maelstrom of fire. Roberts, 'although wounded, immediately assisted another man to bring the other gun into action, and kept it in action until another two guns were in position and the enemy finally overpowered. It was largely due to his courageous and gallant action that the remaining guns were able to get into position and the enemy's fire beaten down, thus enabling the infantry to continue the advance'. Of all those lying across the battlefield at that instant, two men, Roberts and one other, shouldered the responsibility, got up and did what was required. It is a characteristic of group behaviour, that when in a bad situation, many will sit tight and wait to see if someone else will take responsibility. It might be the survival instinct, a fear of getting up and being the only one to get up (a hundred rifles pointing at me), or it might be an expectation that it is indeed 'someone else's job' that makes men sit and wait. All wish to be able to do something, but none feels the moment is right. Those that got up and did something were immediately marked out as special, but their underlying motivation was usually rooted in simple and ordinary concerns. What typically happened in such situations was, however, something remarkable; once one or two took some particular action all those wishing to do something to assist took their cue. As if by magic, groups of men and then the whole line would rise and charge forward. From small courageous actions, large results may be obtained from men who all want to do their job or 'get it over with'.

## CRITICAL LEADERSHIP ACTIVITIES OF THE MACHINE GUN CORPS OFFICER

The role of officers (and senior NCOs) in the Machine Gun Corps was critically important for the success of most of the operations described above. Junior officers in charge of gun sections won the Military Cross for the skill with which they selected gun positions and organised the defence; for the skill, energy and rapidity with which they urged and led their teams forward (as we have seen, often in advance of the infantry) and for controlling the fire of the guns at critical moments. Just over 90 per cent of all MCs were won by junior field officers holding the rank of 2nd Lieutenant or Lieutenant. The numbers of Captains winning the MC was very much lower in the MGC than in any other unit (roughly 4 per cent, compared to 24 per cent in the Northumberland Fusiliers and 78 per cent in the Royal Army Medical Corps).

The determination of the junior leaders often made the difference between defeat and victory. Second Lieutenant Richard Northcote demonstrated how coolness in very challenging circumstances could save a position from defeat. Forming the flank of a successful divisional attack, Northcote's machine gun section was immediately counter-attacked in large numbers. The nearby infantry pushed off the position, and he was rapidly becoming surrounded. However, he kept his guns firing in all directions including to the rear, spotting for them and controlling their fire so that he, 'undoubtedly saved the situation by keeping his guns firing... His coolness in keeping the section steady and controlling the fire enabled the infantry to reform'. His will to fight on, to encourage his men to fight, by his own example, even in the most difficult of circumstances was rewarded with a Distinguished Service Order, a rare distinction for a junior field officer.

What Northcote did was to maintain a firm grip on command that created an ordered environment in which NCOs and men felt that the situation was not out of control. He kept responsibilities off their shoulders and firmly upon his. In other words, he maintained his team structure and hierarchy in an emergency; it is a good example of overcoming adversity in the role of group leader.

Northcote's methods were not the only way to mould an effective team. The junior leadership of the Machine Gun Corps was instrumental in keeping men's spirits up in 'the suicide club'. Lieutenant Colonel William Tillie took care that his men should feel that they were in good hands: 'His energy and fearlessness in going amongst his men at critical periods at great personal risk set a fine example and inspired great confidence'. The result of this paternalism was that his men would fight for him wholeheartedly when asked to do so: 'The determination with which he handled his machine guns was largely responsible for defeating many hostile attacks' and he was awarded the DSO for his courageous leadership. During late July 1917, Temporary 2nd Lieutenant Philip Alfred Durlacher's gun section was facing a determined attack, but 'he visited his guns which were in exposed positions and by his personal example under a heavy barrage encouraged his men to keep their guns in action'. On a second occasion he, 'assisted his men to carry ammunition across the open to their guns, which were in shell holes'. This was an officer whose men could rely on him to be there with them and to provide for them. More than that, it is obvious that he took personal responsibility for his men's emotional well-being by touring the isolated posts and encouraging them. With an officer in charge who could be relied upon to personally deliver ammunition to keep a threatening enemy at bay, we might also wonder whether this officer also did everything he could to ensure his boys received water, rations and bandages for their wounds. Durlocher was awarded the MC for his actions. Second Lieutenant Edward Field similarly impressed all around him when during the defensive actions of the Spring of 1918; 'His determination and fearlessness were magnetic. Throughout the day he fought magnificently'. The concept of a man's actions being 'magnetic' is a useful one in understanding how the example set by the group leader inspired those under him to resist manfully. These were ways in which junior officers won the confidence and absolute loyalty of their men, and maintained the fighting spirit of the British Army. There was more than an element of caring paternalism in such behaviour, the ultimate result of which was this:

Military Cross. Ypres, 31 July 1917
Temporary Lieutenant Gwynfryn Jenkins, Machine Gun Corps:

*'For conspicuous gallantry and devotion to duty. He led his four guns to their objective with the infantry assault and, in spite of heavy casualties, placed them in good defensive positions and made complete arrangements for the supply of ammunition, which had run short. He afterwards took charge of two more machine guns when their officer had been killed, and kept all six guns in action for three days in spite of continuous and severe shell fire, which reduced the teams to a minimum. But for his cheerfulness, gallantry and untiring efforts in going from gun to gun and encouraging the men, they could never have stood the strain'.*

# The Tank Corps

Tanks were an invention of the First World War, indeed, their very name stems from the secrecy surrounding their initial development and deployment. In the early days, the gun and machine gun armed tanks exerted a psychological blow on the enemy. Their small numbers and unreliability, particularly their habit of getting ditched while crossing trench systems, mechanical problems and vulnerability to shell fire, dictated that their effectiveness on the battlefields of 1916–1917 was not greatly above zero. Rather quickly, too, artillery and infantry soldiers of both sides realised that tanks could be defeated, and new weapons were drawn up against them; the armour piercing bullet and the anti-tank artillery shell. As long as infantry were experienced enough and had the support of small numbers of specialist weapons, they knew that tanks, although formidable and dangerous, could be stopped.

With origins in the Royal Naval Armoured Car sections, and another foot in the Machine Gun Corps (Heavy Branch), the Tank Corps may be said to have been revealed to the world on 15 September 1916 at the battle of Flers-Courcellette, part of the Somme battle. As they lumbered over rough, shell-holed country, the noise of their engines drowned by the noise of battle, the tank crews encountered that most Naval of problems; the moving gun platform. They found just how difficult it was to shoot accurately while on the move, particularly for the gun-equipped 'male' tanks, but this may have been less of a problem for the machine-gun equipped 'female'. So the pattern of tank action was very often drive, stop, fire.

But in most battles on the Western Front there were simply not enough tanks, they were neither sufficiently mobile nor invincible enough to do anything more than *support the infantry effectively*.

There are far more stories of tanks getting bogged down or being destroyed by shell fire than there are of tanks single-handedly rolling up trench systems and capturing entire villages full of Germans. They did achieve impressive results on occasion, but not as often as might be thought. Even in the greatest tank action of the war, the attack in front of Amiens in August 1918, when 414 tanks[12] took the field of battle, most broke down and so many were knocked out that the use of tanks on this scale was not attempted again during that war. From Amiens onwards, the tank was maintained in its ideal role of infantry support. It would take another major war before the tank achieved anything approaching a dominant role in warfare and by the end of that war, in 1944, the rocket-firing aircraft was already beginning to dominate.

That the Tank Corps was, for the most part, a small organisation we can see from the growth of its gallantry medal list. The first Tank Corps awards appeared in small handfuls for actions in 1916 and through most of 1917. The tank attack at Cambrai in late October 1917 brought about the largest haul of gallantry awards seen up to that point, but the Corps would have to wait for the Hundred Days – the last three months of the war in 1918 – to start accumulating rewards at anything like the rate of other Corps. The total of DCMs won by the Tank Corps in World War One is considered to be just 144 (and one bar), the number of MMs 604 with 23 bars. This represents approximately one third of the awards made to the Northumberland Fusiliers.

Members of the Tank Corps won approximately 0.3 per cent of all gallantry awards conferred during the war, and roughly 2.5 per cent of their personnel received an award. There were 17 tank battalions in total and these were supported by signals, supply, stores, workshop and headquarters units. Mechanical repairs were carried out at workshops out of the line and also by specialist mechanicians who went into action with the tanks and effected battlefield repairs as required. Two peculiarities of the Tank Corps awards lists are the high proportion of lifesaving DCMs (second highest of all units at 18 per cent) and the abundance of DCM awards made for actions outside of the tank. Considering the

Victoria Cross in relation to tank actions, M. C. Smith has noted that there were no VCs awarded to men who remained inside the tank, all were awarded for 'dismounted' acts such as fighting with the Lewis guns kept in the tank, for leading the tank on foot through obstacles and onto the objective, for running messages across the battlefield, for rescues from burning tanks and for salvage of broken down machines from the battlefield. Inside tanks, men won medals for their work as driver, for eliminating enemy strong points, for their dogged determination in attack and for providing critical support to infantry moving forward.

What men did to receive their rewards in action will now be considered with an analysis of the important components of these acts.

## PREPARATION FOR ATTACK: THE LAYING OF TAPES
Preparatory to an attack, tapes were laid out to mark the routes to be followed by the tanks. There was only one medal for distinguished conduct awarded to the Tank Corps for this dangerous task, and it was 200195 Pte C. S. Allen of Doncaster who received it. He laid out tapes in the run up to the Battle of Cambrai and his DCM was announced in the *London Gazette* of 6 February 1918: 'He twice marked out routes under heavy enemy barrages, though on the first occasion he was blown up and badly shaken. Later he accompanied the tanks into action on foot, showing magnificent courage and contempt of danger'. Some 3 per cent of awards of the Military Cross were made for laying out tapes, indicating that this was more of a field officer's task.

## LEADING THE TANK ATTACK, ON FOOT
Leading tanks into battle was done by men on foot out in front of the advance. It was spectacularly dangerous work. One NCO who led tanks forward and into the attack on foot was Corporal W. Bell of the 4th Support Company, Tank Corps. He did so on 22nd August 1918: 'When his sub-section commander had been killed he led his tank on foot through an extremely heavy barrage'. The situation became dire, when: 'Arriving at our front line, he endeavoured

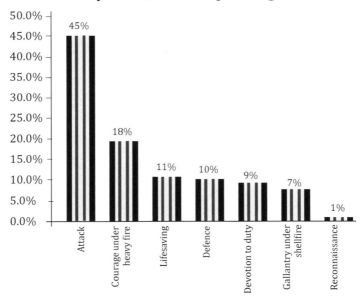

| Activity | % |
|---|---|
| Preserve tank | 14 |
| Outside tank | 14 |
| Dogged determination | 12 |
| Supporting infantry | 10 |
| Driver | 10 |
| Messages | 7 |
| Leading on foot | 7 |
| Crew rescue | 7 |
| Eliminate enemy MG | 7 |
| Tending wounded | 4 |
| Mechanic | 4 |
| Ammunition forward | 3 |
| Officer rescue | 1 |
| Rations forward | 1 |
| Organise infantry | 0 |
| Break up enemy attacks | 0 |
| Tape laying | 0 |

| Rank | % |
|---|---|
| Private | 33 |
| Gunner | 18 |
| L/Corporal & Corporal | 29 |
| Sergeant | 18 |
| QtrMr Sergeant | 0 |
| Warrant Officer | 2 |
| Privates & Corporals | 80 |
| Sgt and higher | 20 |

| Honours MMs | 0% |
|---|---|

**Figure 18: Analysis of the Military Medal, Tank Corps**

*Results represent the total of MMs award to the Tank Corps, i.e. approx. 164*

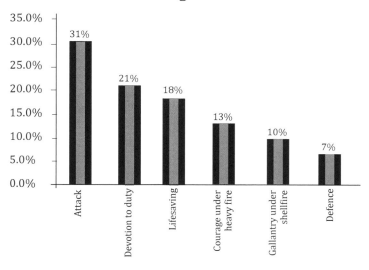

**Distinguished Conduct Medal, Tank Corps, Categories**

| Activity | % |
|---|---|
| Period of time | 14.1 |
| Crew rescue | 10.9 |
| Supporting infantry | 10.2 |
| Preserve tank | 10.2 |
| Outside tank | 10.2 |
| Eliminate enemy MG | 10.2 |
| Dogged determination | 9.4 |
| Drover | 5.5 |
| Mechanic | 4.7 |
| Messages | 3.9 |
| Leading on foot | 2.3 |
| Tending wounded | 2.3 |
| Rations forward | 2.3 |
| Ammunitions forward | 1.6 |
| Officer rescue | 1.6 |
| Tape laying | 0.8 |

| Rank | % |
|---|---|
| Private | 20 |
| Gunner | 6 |
| L/Corporal & Corporal | 27 |
| Sergeant | 34 |
| QtrMr Sergeant | 4 |
| Warrant Officer | 10 |
| Privates & Corporals | 80 |
| Sgt and higher | 20 |

| Honours DCMs | 34% |
|---|---|

**Figure 19: Analysis of the Distinguished Conduct Medal, Tank Corps**
*Results represent the total of Immediate DCMs, i.e. approx. 41*

## Military Cross, Tank Corps, Categories

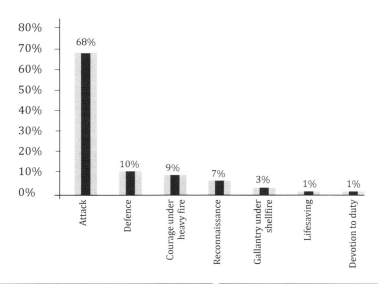

| Activity | % |
|---|---|
| Eliminate enemy MG | 20.0 |
| Leading on foot | 17.4 |
| Supporting infantry | 16.3 |
| Outside tank | 15.3 |
| Dogged determination | 6.3 |
| Organise infantry | 6.0 |
| Preserve tank | 4.7 |
| Tape laying | 3.2 |
| Break up enemy attack | 2.6 |
| Crew rescue | 2.6 |
| Mechanic | 2.1 |
| Ammunition forward | 1.1 |
| Period of time | 1.1 |
| Officer rescue | 0.5 |
| Tending wounded | 0.5 |
| Messages | 0.0 |
| Rations forward | 0.0 |
| Driver | 0.0 |

| Rank | % |
|---|---|
| 2nd Lieutenant | 43 |
| Lieutenant | 22 |
| Captain | 28 |
| Major | 6 |
| Chaplain Major | 0.5 |

| Honours MCs | 20% |
|---|---|

**Figure 20: Analysis of the Military Cross, Tank Corps**
*Results represent the total of Immediate MCs, i.e. approx. 134*

## Distinguished Service Order, Tank Corps, Categories

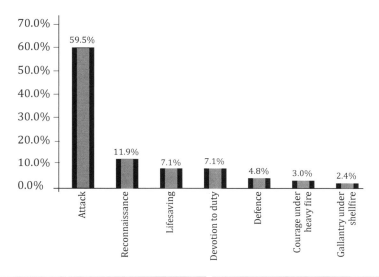

| Activity | % |
|---|---|
| Leading on foot | 27.8 |
| Supporting infantry | 19.4 |
| Outside tank | 16.7 |
| Organise infantry | 13.9 |
| Dogged determination | 8.3 |
| Eliminate enemy MG | 5.6 |
| Preserve tank | 2.8 |
| Messages | 2.8 |
| Period of time | 2.8 |
| Officer rescue | 0.0 |
| Crew rescue | 0.0 |
| Break up enemy attacks | 0.0 |
| Ammunition forward | 0.0 |
| Tape laying | 0.0 |
| Tending wounded | 0.0 |
| Rations forward | 0.0 |
| Driver | 0.0 |
| Mechanic | 0.0 |

| Rank | % |
|---|---|
| 2nd Lieutenant | 15 |
| Lieutenant | 5 |
| Captain | 24 |
| Major | 41 |
| Chaplain Major | 15 |

| | |
|---|---|
| Honours DSOs | 48% |

**Figure 21: Analysis of the Distinguished Service Order, Tank Corps**
*Results represent the total of Immediate DSOs, i.e. approx. 134*

to unload, but the infantry unloading party and three of his crew became casualties from the severe barrage. He endeavoured to collect a second party, but the infantry began to withdraw owing to the intense fire. He was unable to start his engine owing to half-unloaded supplies, but remained with his tank to the last until the enemy were within 50 yards of him, when he withdrew. He made several attempts later with volunteers to reach the tank, but the very severe machine-gun fire made it impossible'. The tank was lost, thanks to the weight of the enemy fire that was intended to make it impossible for anything to move. Acting Sergeant A. Pepper of the 19th Battalion, Tank Corps received a Birthday Honours DCM in the June 1919 list: 'For marked gallantry on 28th September 1918, at Raillencourt. He led his tank on foot and fought with such skill that two tanks cleared the whole village of the enemy, enabling the infantry to capture it. Later he was responsible for putting out of action two enemy machine guns, enabling the infantry to reach the Marcoing Line'. Corporal W. Prest, 'led his tank on foot under heavy machine-gun fire to ensure crossing over difficult places'. He later, 'rendered magnificent service' when he drove his tank to capture a battery of field guns and 200 prisoners.

**DISMOUNTED FIGHTING**

Awards for dismounted action include the DCM to Corporal W. Clark who, 'Leaving his tank, he ran across the open under heavy machine-gun fire and drove away the crew of an anti-tank gun which was preparing to fire. He brought back over 20 prisoners from rifle pits near the gun'. After a tank had been knocked out, the crews sometimes dismounted and carried on the fight on foot with the infantry. Such was the case when Lance Corporal W. Smye 'rushed forward and single-handed attacked an enemy machine gun, killed the crew and captured the gun'. After driving his tank for 13 hours in heavy fighting until it was eventually knocked out, number 427 Corporal W. Myleham 'went to the assistance of the infantry with a Lewis gun, and helped them to repel a counter-attack. He remained with them until he was wounded, displaying great coolness and gallantry throughout the day'. Men of the Tank Corps understood that their job was to support the infantry in combined operations rather than to drive forward heedless of the situation outside. For example, when Pte. W. M. Woodside's tank was moving forward in advance of the infantry, he noticed that the infantry were held up by an enemy machine gun post which had not been dealt with, so 'He at once left his tank, under machine-gun fire, and attacked the two gunners from behind, killing one and capturing the other. His prompt and courageous action allowed the infantry to continue the advance'. He couldn't leave the infantry to face machine-gun fire when it was his job to wipe out these enemy posts (a dereliction of his duty to let one exist) and he had the opportunity to assist the men on the ground, so he took it.

## TANK WARFARE

At the sharp end of tank warfare, in the attack, some stirring deeds are recorded in award citations. When the outside of a tank was hit by projectiles and shell splinters, metal shards and even melted drops of metal flew off the inside of the tank, spattering the crew and often temporarily blinding them. Sergeant H. Hibbert's DCM award provides an example of the perils facing the tank crews even inside their tanks: 'Although wounded in the neck by a bullet and in the face, thighs and arms and groin by splinters, he continued to command his tank, inflicting heavy casualties on the enemy. He only left his tank when ordered to do so by his section commander. His courage and fortitude were a splendid example to the remainder of his crew'. One member of a tank's crew recalled how it was a marvellous feeling hearing the bullets hitting the exterior of the tank, and how safe he felt inside, but the interior was not entirely free of flying metal and it was not 'bomb-proof'. 76226 Sergeant G. Drinkwater had been 'destroying several machine gun nests' with his Hotchkiss gun over a period of two days, 'when a shell struck his tank on one side, breaking his arm, he kept on firing from the other side until another shell crashed in the roof of the tank, disabling the crew. Wounded for a second time, he helped his officer to clear his wounded comrades and get the tank out of further danger'. The power of the tank in action, even the lumbering beasts of 1918, is well illustrated by the following award of the DCM to 201044 Sergeant W. E. Smith of the 2nd Battalion, Tank Corps: 'On the 8 and 9 August 1918, when in action, he showed most conspicuous gallantry and initiative as tank commander. On the 8 August, east of Villers-Bretonneux, he destroyed five machine guns and two trench mortars. Of these, four machine guns and one trench mortar were destroyed by the tank being driven over them. After having been fighting and working on the tank for 36 hours consecutively, he again went into action on the 9 August east of Harbonnieres. Here again he did excellent work'. In this case it was the Sergeant tank commander who received the DCM, perhaps his driver and other crew under his orders received MMs.

The dogged determination of some tank crews is shown by the following DCM citation relating to 201379 Sergeant H. Duddridge: 'For conspicuous gallantry during an attack. His tank successfully cleared the first objective, putting out of action several machine gun nests. He also put out of action a field gun before his tank was hit and set on fire. He then evacuated it under very heavy fire and took up Lewis gun posts in a trench in front, where he rendered great assistance and remained in place until infantry reinforcements arrived. Throughout the action he displayed great skill and courage'. A particularly good example of high determination is the award made to 301991 Sergeant G. W. Kerwood of the 14th Battalion, Tank Corps, published in the *London Gazette* of 5 December 1918: 'This non-commissioned officer fought his tank with great dash, being responsible for the capture of a considerable part of an important village. He knocked out a number of machine guns by his gun fire and, when his ammunition was exhausted, used his tank as a battering ram, causing havoc to houses and walls and driving the enemy out in confusion. Though three of his crew were wounded, he kept his tank in action over two hours'. When tank ammunition ran out, that did not stop tank crews from fighting, who usually kept stores of bombs and Lewis guns in the tank. However, Private W. G. King was awarded the DCM: 'For remarkable courage near Hallu, 10 August 1918. His tank, which became ditched, was riddled with armour-piercing bullets, wounding the whole crew. Pte. King, although wounded, continued to fire until all his ammunition was expended, and then assisted his officer to put up a desperate defence with revolvers. The enemy were forced to retire three-quarters of an hour later'. These men may have felt that surrender after such a hard defence would be a very unsafe course of action. His officer, 2nd Lieutenant Adam Robertson Fraser, was awarded the Military Cross and his actions are discussed in relation to the reward he received, later.

Every man in a tank's crew was exposed to the great stresses of this sort of fighting. Their home, with its hard shell, became the focus of heavy enemy machine gun and shell fire. One gunner, Pte. T. Suddaby received the DCM when: 'Although wounded, he worked his gun for two hours under very heavy machine-gun fire from close range. Later he was again wounded, but continued to fire until he fell unconscious'. Similarly, 40103 Pte. N. Wallace of Newcastle was a tank driver who: 'Though early wounded, he continued to drive his tank with skill and determination, so that the gunners were able to obtain the most effective fire on the enemy and cause them many casualties. After completing his duty he collapsed from loss of blood as he got out of his tank. He showed fine courage and determination'. Such determination was probably not altogether rare on the battlefield, and in the Tank Corps in particular, was enabled by the training, the tight bond of a small team and the expectation that no matter what, one could not let the other men down.

## TANKS AS SUPPLY VEHICLES

Tanks were used to get ammunition and rations forward, although all of the DCM awards for these activities were Honours awards. All three DCMs for getting rations forward went to Quartermaster Sergeants, who were in charge of supplies. An example DCM citation is that to Company Quartermaster Sergeant H. Jarvis of the 1st Battalion Tank Corps: 'For consistent gallantry and devotion to duty. During the March retreat, and again during the rapid advance, he never failed to supply rations and stores to his company. Owing to the continual change of locations his work necessitated great initiative and coolness, often under the most dangerous conditions'. This award was announced in the Birthday Honours list of 1919 and the citation published in the *Gazette* of 11 March 1920. Two DCMs were awarded for getting ammunition forward, both were Honours awards; 307575 Sergeant W. Siddle of the 3rd Carrying Company, Tank Corps, received the DCM 'For marked gallantry in front of Villers Bretonneux on 9 August 1918 and later at Joncourt on 7 October 1918. In spite of heavy hostile fire, he took his tank forward and succeeded in supplying our infantry with bombs and ammunition'. Sergeant J. Strang 'did marked good work with his tank in taking up supplies in action. He never failed under heavy shell fire in his duty of supplying the fighting tanks'.

## SERVICING AND REPAIR OF THE TANK

Battlefield repair was often necessary, being carried out by crew members or by qualified mechanicians and fitters who operated with the tanks in battle. Some 5 per cent of DCM awards went to mechanics. There were the highly qualified mechanics, for example, Acting Mechanic/Squadron Sergeant Major F. Sykes who received the DCM, 'For conspicuous gallantry and devotion to duty in an advanced position for two days and two nights, with very little rest, under very heavy shelling, repairing damaged tanks. His complete disregard of his own safety and unflagging energy set a splendid example to all who were with him, and his remarkable technical skill and resource very greatly helped the success of the salvage operations'. Displays such as this lifted the performance of all present, giving pride to be involved in such a good job and energised by the presence of the man in charge. There was also the mechanical training of the average Tank Corps soldier which came to the fore in difficult circumstances and resulted in the award of a decoration. During a defensive action in the Spring of 1918, 110075 Pte. G. W. Dickenson performed the following act for which he was awarded the DCM: 'For conspicuous gallantry and skill in repairing his tank after it had been set on fire, although closely surrounded by the enemy all the time. His officer had been killed and his first driver wounded, but he drove the tank through the enemy and brought in fifty prisoners'.

## THE SALVAGE OF DAMAGED AND BROKEN DOWN TANKS

Salvage of damaged and ditched tanks was an important activity and there were five DCMs awarded for this task. That awarded to Mechanist Staff Sergeant C. E. Wheelhouse is typical, it was, 'For conspicuous gallantry in March, August and September 1918. On 22 March, when several of his tanks were knocked out, he repaired some of these under heavy shell fire. Later, near Villers-Bretonneux, he followed up the attack on foot, and rendered valuable service under fire in salving knocked out tanks and getting them ready again for action'. This was a Birthday Honours DCM – for doing his job – announced in June 1919.

## COMMUNICATIONS IN THE TANK CORPS

Communications in the Tank Corps used all the normal means, including runner, wireless and the pigeons, which many tanks carried with them into battle. Awards for communications in the Tank Corps are very scarce, the DCM given to Pte. S. T. Griffiths is typical of a runner's award: 'For conspicuous gallantry and devotion to duty while acting as runner. He carried messages day and night for three days under close-range rifle and machine-gun fire. He showed great gallantry and determination and was of great service to his company commander'. A very unusual example is the award made to 69715 Sergeant F. Cuthbert in the *London Gazette* of 21 October 1918. Cuthbert was a tank driver who showed incredible, unquestioning devotion to his duties when he: 'As ordered, drove his tank across a bridge he knew to be damaged. When the bridge broke he rendered valuable assistance in extracting the crew from the canal'. Having lost his tank, through no fault of his own, he then, 'volunteered for and successfully, under fire, carried out the duties of a runner for the next twenty-four hours'. At the communications control centre of a tank formation, Lance Corporal V. J. Guiver was acting as chief wireless operator. 'After having erected the aerials, this non-commissioned officer remained at duty for 18 hours continuously under heavy shell fire. On several occasions the aerials and masts were shot away, but on each occasion he went out and repaired the damage under an intense bombardment. By his initiative, courage and perseverance the wireless station was kept open during the whole action'. His DCM appeared in the *Gazette* of 6 February 1918. A single DCM was awarded for an action involving a small component of pigeon handling. Lance Corporal T. Murdoch from Ayr in Scotland, had his award announced in late January 1918. When his tank was knocked out and several crew wounded, he evacuated the crew 'to a place of safety. Afterwards, under heavy shell and machine-gun fire, he returned to the derelict tank and fetched pigeons, by means of which a message regarding the position of the infantry was sent off. He then assisted two wounded men to the dressing station under very heavy shell fire'.

## THE TANK AS COFFIN, AND SUBSEQUENT LIFESAVING

When a tank was hit and knocked out by shell fire or by anti-tank rounds, men got into terrible and desperate situations as the fuel and ammunition burned and exploded, filling the tank with fire and black smoke. Men left alive inside risked being burned alive and it is perhaps this fear, as much as the frequency of tanks being hit, that resulted in the Tank Corps awarding such a high proportion of DCMs for rescuing crew members. Crew rescue from shot up and burning tanks was clearly a fairly common event, with nearly 20 per cent of DCMs being for lifesaving. The level of danger attached to the act combined with tanks being hit every time a unit went into action ensured that lifesaving in the Tank Corps was a common act of heroism. By contrast, just 11 per cent of MM awards was made for lifesaving, showing the danger and importance attached to this battlefield act. When 76697 Lance Corporal A. Budd's tank was successfully attacking an enemy trench system, 'his tank received a direct hit, which wounded all the crew save himself and another man. Without a moment's hesitation he collected bombs and bombed the enemy away from the tank. He then assisted to get all the wounded crew to a place of safety, thus preventing them from falling into the hands of the enemy'. Having a responsibility for their vehicles as well as towards their comrades, lifesaving sometimes went hand-in-hand with saving the tank from capture, as the following incident shows. Pte P.J. Perry, a native of Crewe, received the DCM as gunner, 'For conspicuous gallantry and devotion to duty. When his tank was "ditched" and on fire, he stayed with his officer and put out the fire, but they were eventually obliged to turn the tank homewards on bottom speed and walk in front of it, as the fumes of the phosphorous bombs made it impossible to stay inside. The enemy were all round, but Pte. Perry kept them at bay with his revolver, while he also supported his officer, who was quite exhausted and nearly collapsed. Eventually they all got back and the tank was saved'. Again, the actions of his officer, Lt. Rupert Walsh, are discussed later, as he received the DSO rather than the MC.

A small proportion of awards was made for the rescue of officers. Lance Corporal A. Pollard of South Shields, 'was in charge of the gun in a tank, and handled it with the greatest effect, destroying several hostile machine guns notwithstanding heavy enemy artillery fire. When the tank was put out of action by a direct hit, and filled with gas, he, assisted by another man, helped to carry his officer, who was heavily gassed, some 800 yards over ground swept by machine-gun fire to a place of safety. He then returned to his tank and blew it up, thus preventing it falling into the hands of the enemy'.

## THE TANK SOLDIER'S ROLE AND LEVEL OF REWARD

Most MM awards were for doing the job of fighting the tank. Surviving MM award recommendations often mention the job of the recipient. Of those for which a job is known, roughly 84 per cent of MMs was won by drivers and gunners (whether operating machine guns or 6-pounder guns). MM awards made to tank commanders are much more scarce. However, looking at the distribution of DCM awards among the tank crews, we can see that NCOs in command of tanks were much more likely to attract the award of the DCM, largely because they were in charge of the operation, they initiated, motivated and led; they were responsible for a tank's success. As previously stated, leaders received higher reward in part because they had to initiate events that might lead to their own destruction. The responsibility to initiate self-sacrifice lay with the leader, not with those who followed, and the awards committee was well aware of that particular heroic attribute.

An understanding of the differences between MM and DCM awards is made possible with reference to the Tank Corps, as this is the only unit for which all MM recommendations have survived. About half of DCM awards involved taking command when the leader was killed or injured, or involved shouldering the responsibility for a battlefield situation and winning the fight. Far fewer MMs involved taking on this sort of responsibility. It was the NCOs who had the experience and training to do that and who were expected to behave according to their rank and status. When there is an expectation of particular behaviour, individuals generally try to live up to it, and many do so. NCOs were also the best leaders, promoted for their ability into positions of responsibility. So it is no surprise that NCOs tended to receive a greater proportion of DCMs, when expectation, training and disposition all favoured the personal assumption of responsibility. Even so, whatever the man's rank, there was very often something extra present in the man's actions which merited the greater distinction of the DCM. Of the DCMs which did not involve taking responsibility, many show a level of determination, risk taking and success that is far beyond the average MM. Some MMs, however, have all the class of the DCM, and it may be the case that they ought to have been recommended for the DCM but were not, by mistake, or in order to keep the ratio of awards of DCM to MM in proportion. There is a great deal of overlap between DCM and MM and there are no hard rules.

The Military Medal was won by runners who took messages in the same way as infantry runners, over ground on foot. Their messages were sometimes of the utmost importance and their journeys perilous in the extreme. The runner put himself at greater risk than the man protected inside the tank and so stood a chance of a medal. Risk was proportional to reward. However, most runners gained MMs rather than the DCM; in fact there was only one Tank Corps DCM awarded to a runner. Mechanics seem to have stood a rather equal chance of gaining an MM or a DCM, although the DCM was more likely to be an Honours award than an immediate award (the MM being immediate awards only). The only award to a cook was an MM to 202076 Lance Corporal F. Fentem who 'although subjected to heavy shell fire at Velu Wood he worked unceasingly preparing hot meals, thereby greatly increasing the comfort of his comrades and indirectly contributing to the success of the operations' on 21 March to 24 March 1918. When the lantern of hope burned low, his extended wartime family had hot dinners.

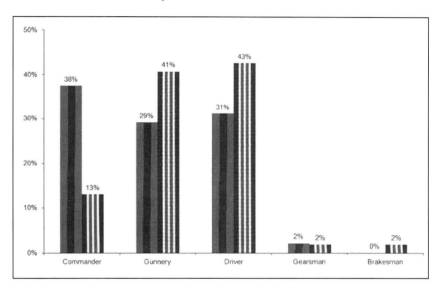

**Figure 22: Distribution of Awards Among Members of Tank Crews, by Role**

|                     | DCM     | MM      |
| ------------------- | ------- | ------- |
| Took Command        | 21%     | 9%      |
| Took Responsibility | 23%     | 5%      |
| Total               | **45%** | **14%** |

**Table 8: The Command and Leadership Component of the DCM, compared to the MM**

A typical tank driver's MM recommendation may be found in Private James Dickson's award for 8 August 1918: 'this man was acting as first driver... This tank engaged a hostile field battery at close range.

Pte. Dickson was wounded early in the engagement, but continued to drive his tank, which he manoeuvred with such skill that one gun of the battery was knocked out and many of the gunners killed or wounded before the tank received two direct hits which put it out of action. His courage and coolness on this occasion were worthy of the highest praise'. This is typical in that the MM was awarded for fighting the tank with particular determination. It was a successful and important fight, breaking through defences in order to ease the infantry's advance, but it lacked something critical. Similarly, 200259 Private Edward Weatherley was rewarded with the MM for his work as gunner in a tank: 'When a battery of small field guns were firing at close range and shells bursting around the tank he turned his 6-pdr on them, and kept the gunners down so effectively that the infantry captured them without a casualty. In this action and in previous ones he has shown himself to possess a splendid fighting spirit'. In spite of showing great courage and determination to see the job done, both Dickson and Weatherley did not leave their tanks, did not assume command and did not take responsibility on their shoulders. Their award citations lack the leadership required, they were not directly responsible for initiating actions that might lead to their own deaths; they were not in command. This is typical of MM awards.

But as this next example of an MM award shows, being a Sergeant and taking command to deliver a very successful result was not always enough to win a DCM: 'Early in the attack the officer in command of the tank was wounded. Sgt. Gibson then took command, and... by his personal example and powers of leadership, reached the final objective and was able to put at least five enemy machine guns out of action. He showed remarkable powers of leadership...'. He did not receive a DCM, and thus, 307230 Sergeant Walter Gibson was denied the more prestigious award, together with its gratuity of £20. In the following, Private J. B. Foster gained the DCM for very similar acts: 'His tank commander was severely wounded... Private Foster, in face of very heavy fire, drove the tank so skilfully as to bring a hail of fire on the enemy machine gun nests. When the tank was disabled he ran across the open and gained the assistance of another tank to clear up the situation'. Foster shouldered personal responsibility for the fighting, took the initiative where many others would have sheltered thinking they had done their bit and that was enough. In a number of cases, it appears that the difference between an MM and a DCM was the fact that a man was willing to get out of the tank and face greatly increased personal risk in order to press the operation to a conclusion. In this we sense the concept of ennoblement through Christian self-sacrifice on the battlefield. Those who chose the path of greatest danger received the higher honour.

## SYMBOLIC ACTS AND THE VICTORIAN HERO

Symbolic acts are rather rare in the Tank Corps, but these are considered throughout this work as they were an important component of the Victorian Hero of the mid-19th Century. Many symbolic acts were recognised with the Victoria Cross in the 1850s and 1860s, but it is a theme of this study that whilst symbolic acts were no longer rewarded by means of the VC, they continued to exist in battle and continued to be rewarded by means of lesser awards, such as the DCM and MM. 76481 Pte. Henry R. Deason, 2nd Battalion Tank Corps, won the MM when he: 'acted as orderly to his commanding officer during the attack on Harbonnieres on 8 August. At one point our infantry were held up by a machine gun post and he was sent to fetch a tank, which successfully dealt with the opposition. Later, he placed the Australian flag in Harbonnieres before either tanks or infantry had entered that part of the village. Throughout the action he displayed great bravery and cheerfulness'. We are reminded of those Victoria Crosses awarded to men who planted the British flag on the enemy ramparts as encouragement to those behind and as a symbolic and demoralising blow to the enemy.

## THE TANK COMMANDER

The Military Cross was awarded to field officers who were usually in command of their own tank and may have been in command of a section of tanks (typically four in number). These officers had limited battlefield responsibility and were not expected to direct wider operations, for example a complete tank battalion, or to take responsibility for higher level direction of combined infantry and tank operations. There are similarities with the MM, as most MCs were won for showing limited leadership, for directing fire at a local level and very often for service inside the tank only. There are also many MCs awarded for leading tanks into action on foot and for directing fire onto targets whilst outside of the tank. However, most Tank Corps MCs can be characterised as having been made for doing the job assigned to the officer very well and with determination and courage generally in a successful action. A very typical MC citation is this one to Lieutenant Winder for operations in Palestine (attacks on Gaza, 1917). 'This officer was in command of a tank operating against the Gaza defences. With conspicuous gallantry he attacked the Turkish positions, inflicting heavy casualties and, by rolling down the wire, let our infantry through, and afterwards patrolled the position while the infantry consolidated it.' On the Western Front, Lieutenant Rodney Watson Kerr demolished German defences by pouring 'a withering fire on the large number of enemy troops who were defending this place' and then returned to assist the infantry who 'were held up by flanking fire, and endeavoured to bring them forward'. His citation further suggests that the inspiration he provided to others was limited to his crew, a consequence of remaining inside the tank. To win recognition in the form of an MC required something in addition to the bare minimum of a man's duty. Those who took their tanks cautiously into action, stopped at or short of the objective, were deterred by difficulties and did no more than was necessary for the fulfilment of orders, could not expect recognition. 'After having done far more than the task allotted to him', 2nd Lieut. Thomas Cheeney Wilson then 'volunteered to stay with the infantry in case the enemy counter-attacked'. Infantry gained much comfort and confidence from the presence of a good solid tank among their number, with its machine gun or artillery battery mounted therein. This officer's action was calculated to have just such an effect. Earlier, he had exceeded his orders by pursuing the enemy 'half a mile beyond his objective, killing a great number and allowing the infantry to consolidate'. The latter had cause to thank him for his generous levels of support that day. Indeed, a number of MC recommendations make mention of the fact that the tanks enabled the infantry to capture their objectives without a single casualty. Thus, the success of the tank commander's actions was measured in infantry casualties. A good tank commander got his infantry through without a scratch. In that sense he was involved in lifesaving.

Very few MCs, however, were given for the physical act of lifesaving, in fact it was approximately 3 per cent. This is low compared to the 18 per cent of DCMs and 11 per cent of MMs for lifesaving. Arguably the best example of an officer rescuing wounded crews, if only for the level of determination and risk attached, is that to 2nd Lieutenant Mungo Tennant Archibald of C-Battalion, Tank Corps during the Cambrai battle of November 1917. On the 23rd of that month, he did 'great execution' of the enemy in the streets of Fontaine-Notre-Dame, but when another of his tanks was disabled by a direct hit, and 'in spite of being surrounded by the enemy and under heavy machine gun and sniper fire, he managed to rescue the whole of the crew and transfer them to his own tank. Whilst manoeuvring his tank out of the village, with 16 persons on board, himself and every one... being wounded with armour-piercing bullets, this tank was also set on fire by a direct hit. With complete disregard for his own safety, he got both crews out of the burning tank and back to the rallying point'. With the option of surrendering to the enemy who were close by, he chose the hard way out rather than give up the fight. This junior officer's citation further praises his 'courage, resource, and endurance... throughout a long and exhausting operation'. Each time we read, 'with complete disregard for his own safety', we may infer the old Christian heroic ideal of self-sacrifice on behalf of others.

Leading tanks on foot through heavy fire to the start lines and into battle was a common means of winning the MC; nearly one in five MCs related to such acts. Once in action, the tanks could be directed to targets by the same officers, still operating on foot. In many cases these men were far in advance of the infantry and presented a lone target to enemy rifles and machine guns. It was extremely dangerous work. Lieutenant Oliver Warren won an MC when he, 'although exposed to heavy artillery and machine-gun fire, led his section of tanks into action on foot, it being too dark to see from the tanks. He successfully guided them to their objectives, pointing out machine-gun nests and thus materially helping the attack'. Acting Major Maurice Miskin gained his second MC when 'he rallied a number of tanks and directed them to enemy machine guns which were holding up the infantry... he contributed largely to the success attending to those operations'.

Destruction of enemy machine gun and field gun positions was perhaps the primary task of the tanks in battle (support of the infantry advance, reduction of their casualties). Lieutenant Augustus Watkins was recommended for the MC after he; 'advanced eleven miles... finding many targets of both guns and infantry, showing great initiative... he ran over two machine-gun emplacements which were holding up the infantry, killing the gunners'. At this juncture we must wonder who showed the greater determination and self-sacrifice, the enemy machine gunners or the tank commander who steamrollered over them. That aside, Watkins' action continued as he looked around for ever more targets: 'he then got out of his tank, under heavy fire, to ascertain if he could be of further assistance, and stood on his tank to obtain a better view and locate more machine-gun positions'. He showed a keen desire to continue with his so far successful venture, and this may be said to be an ingredient of many MC awards; not being content with a measure of success, but pressing on until success and victory was complete.

Leadership was a key factor in other awards of the Military Cross. Acting Captain George Matthews already had an MC when he won his bar for the following: 'He commanded a section of tanks and led them towards their objective under very heavy machine-gun fire. He co-operated successfully with other crews, and to a very great extent was responsible for the splendid work done by his section'. Captain Ivan Glanville was also awarded a bar to his MC for 'skilful leadership' when he was operating on foot in the open, directing his section of four tanks onto their objective, a village held by the enemy. After three of his tanks received direct hits from the enemy and were put out of action, he organised the survivors and: 'pushed on with the only remaining tank through the enemy, held the village of Nauroy and, although wounded, carried on until the advance was complete'. When Captain Wilfred Baker was directing his tanks onto enemy positions, he received the MC for his 'gallant conduct and powers of leadership' which 'throughout a difficult operation were of the utmost value'. In these cases, the amount of responsibility was usually limited to single vehicles or a small number of tanks. Leadership, of course, was expected of all officers and MC citations reflect the level of responsibility.

Pressing an attack to a successful conclusion was also a characteristic of MC awards, with the ever-present act of initiating the action in spite of the risk to self. Lieutenant William Thorogood was engaged in the attack on the Canal du Nord on 27 September 1918, when he 'displayed conspicuous gallantry and initiative in organising an attack on an enemy strong point after his tank had been ditched'. The MC winning act was not to be found in the fighting of his tank in the face of heavy opposition, but after leaving the tank when 'having first engaged the enemy with rifles and revolvers and a machine gun obtained from the tank, Lieut. Thorogood, accompanied by two of his crew members and two infantrymen, rushed the strong point and was instrumental in the capture of 35 prisoners'. An important part of this act was initiating it; the officer was expected to plan, execute and lead the rush on the machine gun post knowing that the weapon would be pointing at him first. The officer had to initiate his own death, and this is why being an officer was such an onerous undertaking and why officers were a heavily decorated group. It was not because they were public school boys; the honours system was not a disgrace.

Fighting outside their tanks in the great retreat of Spring 1918, MCs were won for putting up solid defensive positions and breaking up enemy attacks with Lewis gun teams. Some of these awards strongly resemble those of the machine gun corps during the same period. For example, Captain Francis Hunnikin volunteered to cover the withdrawal of troops from Bray-sur-Somme on 26 March 1918. He 'continued using his Lewis guns and inflicting very severe casualties on the enemy, who had worked up very close to within 50 to 60 yards', until he was almost out of ammunition. Only when he had covered the withdrawal of all of his men and only he remained 'completely surrounded' by the enemy, did he succeed in 'cutting his way out'. Such dogged determination in defence is a characteristic of machine gun teams across the Army, who saw it as their duty to act as strong points in defence and to selflessly cover the withdrawal of others. When a duty is assigned to a group (by training and instruction), that group usually endeavours to perform the task expected of it, and generally with the aim of providing support to comrades of other units.

## THE OCCASIONAL TANK BATTLE

Tank battles were rare; the German Army failed to react to the appearance of the tank and build its own in large numbers. There were few occasions when these offensive weapons were launched into attacks at the same time and at the same place, so they rarely met. Some of the most interesting, in light of development of the tank later in the 20th Century, and yet the rarest awards of the MC were made for such chance encounters. At Cachy on 24 April 1918, Acting Captain John Brown of the 1st Tank Battalion led his section into action against enemy tanks on foot. He 'directed their movements, being the whole time exposed to heavy machine-gun fire and the enemy barrage' and, although two of his vehicles were knocked out by enemy gun fire, he helped a fellow officer successfully deal with the enemy. Inside a third British tank was 2nd Lieutenant Francis Mitchell, who 'fought his tank with great gallantry and manoeuvred it with much skill'. Whilst careful to offer as little of a target to the enemy as possible, Mitchell 'was able to register five direct hits on the enemy tank and put it out of action'. Captain Brown's recommendation mentions that this (Mitchell's) tank 'knocked out one enemy tank and put two others to flight'. It had been a determined piece of work. Late in the war, on 8 October 1918, another tank versus tank action developed when two enemy tanks appeared just after the New Zealand Rifle Brigade had captured a position. Before they had a chance to consolidate, these enemy tanks approached to within 150 yards of the infantry position, threatening their tenancy of the ground. Two British tank officers, seeing the imminent danger, quickly selected a position from which to attack and moved in. Second-Lieutenants Frank Clarke and Harold Sherratt moved into position behind a road and 'bombarded the two enemy tanks at a range of 300 yards, completely disabling the latter. The enemy crews, while attempting to escape, were shot down by our Lewis gunners'. It was described as 'a splendid action... full of daring and saved a difficult situation'. Both men received the MC for their quick thinking, although no doubt they would have insisted that they were only doing their jobs.

The Distinguished Service Order awarded to tank officers makes an interesting study too. An excellent example of the award made to a senior officer of the Tank Corps is provided by that to Acting Lieutenant-Colonel Edward Daniell Bryce, who in fact gained a DSO and a bar for second award during the war. His original DSO was won at the Third Battle of Ypres, 28–29 July 1917, when his company 'came under a heavy barrage... and being twice knocked over by shells bursting alongside him, continued to take charge and, walking in front, guided his tanks to their positions'. He later led his tanks into battle although gassed and nearly blinded himself. This, then, was a high level bravery award, for maintaining his power of command and seeing his allotted task through to a successful completion. His bar to the DSO was won later in the same year, at Cambrai, when in command of 'B' Battalion Tank Corps during the opening advance. The recommendation for the bar provides an example of a different type of award: 'This officer showed great gallantry and determination throughout the battle. Immediately after the capture of the Hindenburg support system Lieutenant-Colonel Bryce moved forward and established his battalion headquarters about three-quarters of a mile beyond the support system, about 600 yards west of Marcoing and in advance of the leading infantry. The battalion flag was erected in a prominent position and 16 tanks of the battalion were rallied at this spot and prepared to move forward again with the cavalry, while 14 tanks went ahead and attacked Marcoing. On the following morning this officer went forward with 12 tanks and personally launched them against Cantaing, which was successfully captured, heavy losses being inflicted on the enemy. The good judgement and tactical dispositions of Lieut-Col. Bryce were largely responsible for the success of the operations, while his coolness, total disregard of personal safety and determination were a great inspiration to the officers and men of his battalion'. This award shows much more of the requirement for leadership and professional dispositions of his force during the entire operations from advance, to operational control of his force in the field and pressing home a successful attack. These were the roles of the senior Tank Corps field officer and the reward of the DSO was for performing tasks assigned to him extremely well and for delivering a local victory.

**THE BATTLE LIAISON OFFICER**
Acting as the spear point of late war attacks, it was the Tank Corps field officer who found himself in the driving seat of battle. Being drawn from the infantry, the machine gun corps and other fighting arms, Tank Corps officers were often already trained and experienced in general battlefield tactics, combined operations (infantry, tanks, aircraft and cavalry) and organisational skills. They understood the battlefield and the needs of the infantry. Captain Frederick E. Hotblack received a bar to his DSO while acting as 'reconnaissance and battle liaison officer' during the Cambrai operations of November 1917. He: 'by his personal example and initiative, carried on the attack, reorganising the infantry, whose officers had become casualties, and collecting tanks. He had to pass through a heavy barrage and was continuously under machine-gun fire, but succeeded in launching a fresh attack with tanks and infantry'. Those around him found his energy and leadership 'an inspiration'. On 9 August 1918, Captain Fred Dawson of the 5th Tank Battalion was in charge of a section of four tanks when he 'directed operations during the clearing of the village' of Bouchoir by taking 'one tank and a platoon of infantry' to capture the place. He was on foot throughout and no doubt conspicuous by his movements in the open. Similarly, Acting Major Oswald Guy added a DSO to his MC and

bar when on 1 and 2 September 1918, his 'energy and cooperation with the infantry staffs gave them detailed information', which enabled combined infantry-tank operations to be organised 'with such complete detail that the success was great and the infantry enabled to enter two villages'. In these cases the action was a successful one, as indicated by the citations. In a very similar case, a Major Richard Clively won only a Military Cross for his conduct, when he 'held a conference with the infantry company commanders and, under heavy shell and machine-gun fire, organised a fresh attack to endeavour to reach the start line. Regardless of danger and personal safety, he distributed his tanks among the infantry, and by his coolness set a splendid example to all ranks'.

## COMPARISON OF AWARDS

The major difference between the MC and the DSO is the level of responsibility for organising the battle across a wider frontage using available resources. This difference can be largely explained by the rank and responsibilities handed to the officer. Recipients of the DSO were capable men in battle, and shouldered that wider responsibility. Not all officers were capable of doing so. In this sense it seems probable that the key leadership traits displayed by senior field officers who received DSOs for organisational duties and battlefield leadership, were charisma, a toughness, decisiveness, initiative and the confidence to take control of numbers of men in situations. These are personality traits which, although common to both junior and senior officers, are emphasised in the citations for the DSO.

DSO awards to junior tanks officers, as for other Army units, record acts of uncommon devotion to duty on the battlefield. After being shot in the face and twice in the body whilst inside his tank, 2nd Lieutenant William P. Whyte's tank suffered mechanical failure. He got out of the tank and, under 'intense machine-gun and heavy artillery fire' led and directed the remaining tanks of his section, setting a 'most conspicuous' example which had 'the greatest moral effect' on his men. This junior officer clearly displayed leadership and example beyond his rank; undoubtedly one of the decisive factors leading to his recommendation for the DSO rather than the more usual MC for one so junior. A second remarkable example is the DSO awarded to Lieutenant Rupert Walsh who, on 24 August 1918 was just doing his job as a junior field officer and did not display leadership far above his rank. His was purely for extreme determination to win through, whilst essentially at the point of defeat: 'While crossing a sunken road at dusk his engine gave out and he became stuck. Some 200 yards in front of our infantry he was surrounded by enemy, very many of whom were killed by fire from the tank. Enemy then shot phosphorous bombs at the tank, which made it impossible for crew to stay in it owing to fumes and all kit inside catching fire. Lieut. Walsh then ordered his crew to evacuate tank and remained behind with Gnr. Perry to put out the fire. He then got the engine started, put it into bottom speed, and turned the tank for home. He and Gnr. Perry then got out, the fumes being too bad for them, and walked away between the front horns of the tank. All this time they were surrounded by the enemy and were firing at them with their revolvers'. The two men then drove the tank home.

Tanks often found themselves stranded well ahead of the infantry and surrounded by enemy. It was 2nd Lieutenant Adam Robertson Fraser who won an MC for an act very similar to the DSO just described. On 10 August 1918, this officer's tank became ditched in one of the old Somme trenches, 600 yards ahead of the infantry: 'the enemy at once surrounded him and concentrated some 20 machine guns on the tank, which was pierced many times by armour-piercing bullets. 2nd Lieut. Fraser replied with machine-gun fire from the tank until all his guns were put out of action and all of his crew wounded. The enemy then called upon him to surrender, but he succeeded in keeping them off with his revolver until they were forced to retire by our infantry coming up three-quarters of an hour later. This officer remained with his tank under heavy rifle and machine-gun fire until all his wounded were dressed...'. The critical difference between the two acts is that Fraser waited for infantry support and remained inside his tank, thus winning the MC. Lieutenant Walsh secured his DSO in

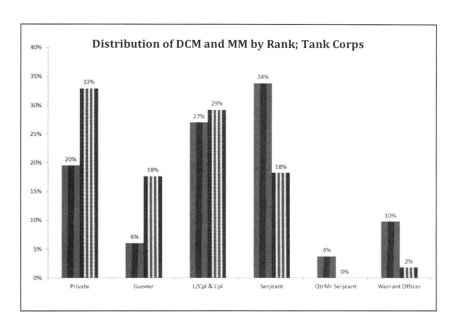

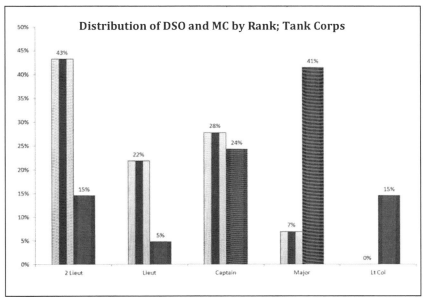

**Figure 23: Distribution of Awards by Rank**

very similar circumstances by leaving his tank and acting to save the tank from capture before morning came. Both did their job, however the situation was different and perhaps the level of direct risk was different. By leaving the tank to bring it back, it may have been considered that Walsh showed greater willing to sacrifice his life in the pursuit of duty, but Fraser had the well-being of his wounded men at heart when he remained with them until all were seen to.

For the junior officer, the nature of the act was more important than his rank in deciding which award would be granted. Generally speaking, for the bulk of officer's gallantry awards it is the man's rank which is linked to which award he received.

In the case of the MC, the award was generally granted for special acts associated with the officer's assigned job. Most awards were granted for attacking. For the DSO, either an extreme display of determination and leadership was expected of an officer below the rank of Captain, or the man's rank was such that he performed his assigned task of leading and organising operations extremely well, whilst engaged in a successful action. In most cases, a high level of determination to win against great odds is displayed.

Whereas most MMs were awarded for fighting inside the tank, a DCM became more probable when the man left the tank and exposed himself to increased danger outside. The DCM became more certain when the man, whatever his rank, showed leadership, took responsibility for a situation and won through. When it came to the Victoria Cross, this theme is amplified greatly. No tank VCs were won inside a tank. Acting Lieutenant Colonel Richard Annesley West sacrificed himself, as did Sampson the great hero of the ancients, in order to ensure victory against the enemy. He, a tanks officer, did it on horseback, showing 'brilliant leadership' and 'amazing self-sacrifice near Vaulx-Vraucourt on 2 September 1918'. Like a heroic officer of Waterloo, he 'had two horses shot from under him during the morning' whilst leading tanks and infantry into a successful battle. When the enemy counter-attacked an infantry position he: 'realising that there was a danger of the battalion giving way, at once rode out in front of them under extremely heavy machine-gun and rifle fire and rallied the men. In spite of the fact that the enemy were close upon him, he rode up and down in front of them in the face of certain death, encouraging the men and calling to them; "Stick it, men: show them fight, and for God's sake put up a good fight". He fell riddled by machine gun bullets'. No doubt the attacking German soldiers were astonished to see such an incredible occurrence in 1918; but they also recognised that he would be responsible for solidifying the defence by his example. His citation describes the effect of his action: 'The magnificent bravery of this very gallant officer at the critical moment inspired the infantry to redoubled efforts, and undoubtedly saved the situation. The hostile attack was defeated'. The citation tells of leadership, taking responsibility, an almost reckless display of courage throughout the day, turning imminent defeat into a victory, and it also implies the heroic Christian death by self-sacrifice. Richard Annesley West died a hero's death a long time ago now, but his self-sacrifice still sets the example to the Armed Forces today, and this is exactly the kind of act that the bronze cross was intended to reward; the one that would stand for all time.

# The Royal Army Medical Corps

S hining from the honours list of the Royal Army Medical Corps (RAMC) are both of the greatest accolades won by the British Army of all time. From their ranks emerged the two greatest heroes of the First World War: Captain Noel Chavasse and Lieutenant A. Martin-Leake, who both won second award bars to their Victoria Crosses. In addition, it should not go unnoticed that the most highly decorated soldier of World War One was a stretcher bearer with the North Staffordshire Regiment (L/Cpl W. H. Coltman). Although not a member of the RAMC, he was also assigned the task of lifesaving. His Victoria Cross was won: 'on... hearing that wounded had been left behind during a retirement, went forward alone in the face of fierce enfilade fire, found the casualties, dressed them and on three successive occasions, carried comrades on his back to safety, thus saving their lives'. He received the DCM and bar for: 'evacuating wounded from the front line at great personal risk under shell fire' and for 'taking no heed of either shell or machine-gun fire, and never resting until he was positive that our sector was clear of wounded'. His MM was for the rescue of a wounded officer in February 1917 and he received a bar to the MM for his conduct behind the lines in June 1917. That the only two bars to the VC and the most highly decorated soldier of the war, within an environment of industrialised killing, were lifesavers, suggests that there was a political requirement to produce these three exceptional heroes. The idea that the greatest heroes of the Empire should be lifesavers rather than life takers, when killing was the primary aim of the war, is doubly ironic, because the Victoria Cross, from Spring 1917 onwards, became increasingly a life taker's award.[13] Carrying a wounded man off the field of battle was increasingly considered an unsuitable act for the bestowal of a Victoria Cross.[14]

There is no Corps in the British Army for which the concept of receiving reward for doing one's duty is more obvious than the Royal Army Medical Corps. Consideration of RAMC awards weakens the argument that bravery medals were issued for acts 'above and beyond the call of duty' between 1914 and 1918. The duty of the Corps was to rescue and treat the wounded, under fire and during battle. The Corps' Victoria Crosses were all won while doing the job of lifesaving; indeed almost all of their medals were presented for lifesaving acts. Behind the spectacular VCs and bar, there lies the vast bulk of RAMC awards considered in this chapter. The RAMC won 3.6 per cent of the British Army's medals for gallantry. The men who won them were assigned across Army units and to field ambulance units (each of which consisted of nine officers and 224 other ranks at full establishment). The medical services were spread right across the area of operations, from hospitals in the rear areas to stretcher bearers and medical officers working in no-mans-land. Of the Corps, the Royal Army Medical Corps lends itself very well to a study of where men were in relation to the front line trenches when they won their awards. From the front line trenches and no-mans-land rearwards, the number of medals won declines rapidly, thereby reflecting the risks taken to rescue and treat the wounded. Half of all medals were won in the front line or in no-mans-land and another 20 per cent were won by the Corps within a few tens of metres of the front line at Regimental Aid Posts. The Advanced Dressing Station was positioned between half a mile and several miles from the front line. Over this ground the ambulances and wheeled stretchers plied their trade, passing the artillery gun lines. From the advanced dressing stations rearwards to well-equipped dressing stations and casualty clearing stations, horse drawn and motor ambulances moved, sometimes also miniature railways. At the large Casualty Clearing Stations, some five to 15 miles behind the lines, there might be a rail terminal which was visited by ambulance trains, taking patients back to large general hospitals, such as that at Rouen, or to the Channel ports for evacuation to England. Figure 24 illustrates the abundance of frontline lifesaving awards as well as the scarcity of medals won in the back areas and even in ambulance convoys. It will be recalled that many Army Service Corps awards were won in ambulance convoys, under shell fire, and so these men fill in the obvious gap in medals won when transporting patients. The graph is generally applicable to the entire Army; 70 per cent or more of decorations were won in or close to the front line; far fewer medals were won in rear areas.

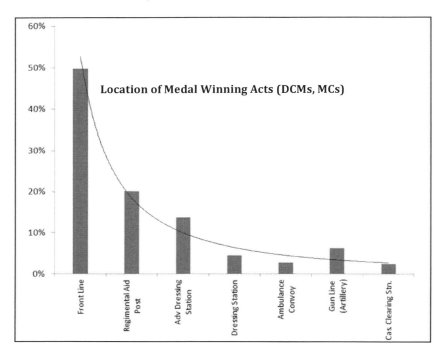

**Figure 24: Location of Award Winning Actions, relative to the front line**

Whereas a minor proportion of other branches of the Army performed lifesaving tasks, the RAMC did so almost exclusively. They earned decorations in a range of different ways, the most frequent 'rescues' being of wounded men from the front line by means of stretchers, or carrying them on their backs, whether under shell fire or during a major battle. Over half of all DCMs were awarded for getting wounded men out of danger. The next most common task for which awards were made was tending wounded whilst under

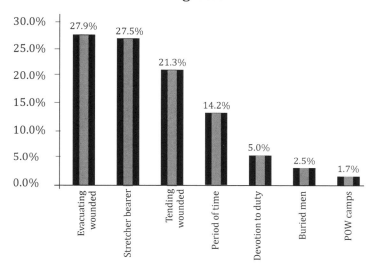

## Distinguished Conduct Medal, Medical Corps, Categories

| Activity | % |
|---|---|
| Under Shell Fire | 41.0 |
| Front Line (no-man's-land) | 23.8 |
| Regtl Aid Post | 9.2 |
| Adv. Dressing Station | 8.4 |
| Dressing Station | 4.2 |
| Ambulance Convoy | 2.5 |
| Gun Line (Arty) | 2.5 |
| Cas. Clearing Station | 1.7 |
| Treating Epidemics | 1.7 |
| Protect Wounded (own body) | 1.3 |
| Organisational | 1.3 |
| Sanitary Section | 0.8 |
| High Risk Disease | 0.8 |
| Water Supply | 0.4 |
| Clerk | 0.4 |

| Rank | % |
|---|---|
| Private | 35 |
| Corporal | 15 |
| Sergeant | 36 |
| QtrMr Sergeant | 3 |
| Warrant Officer | 11 |

| Honours DCMs | 30% |
|---|---|

**Figure 25: Analysis of the Distinguished Conduct Medal, Royal Army Medical Corps**

*Results of a sample of 240 out of a total of 438 Honours & Immediate DCMs to the RAMC*

## Military Cross, Medical Corps, Categories

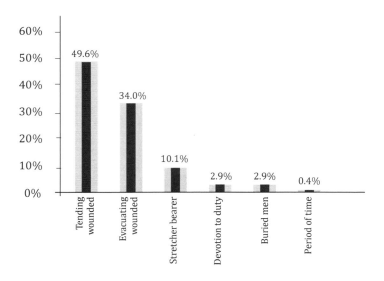

| Activity/Location | % |
|---|---|
| Front Line (no-man's-land) | 39.6 |
| Under Shell Fire | 23.6 |
| Regtl Aid Post | 17.0 |
| Adv. Dressing Station | 9.4 |
| Gun Line (Arty) | 5.7 |
| Dressing Station | 2.4 |
| Cas. Clearing Station | 1.4 |
| Ambulance Convoy | 0.9 |
| Protect Wounded (own body) | 0.0 |
| High Risk Disease | 0.0 |
| Organisational | 0.0 |
| Treating Epidemics | 0.0 |
| Water Supply | 0.0 |
| Sanitary Section | 0.0 |
| Clerk | 0.0 |

| Rank | % |
|---|---|
| Warrant Officer | 1 |
| Lieutenant | 18 |
| Captain | 78 |
| Major | 3 |

| | |
|---|---|
| Honours MCs | 32% |

**Figure 26: Analysis of the Military Cross, Royal Army Medical Corps**
*Results of a sample of 239 Royal Army Medical Corps Immediate MCs*

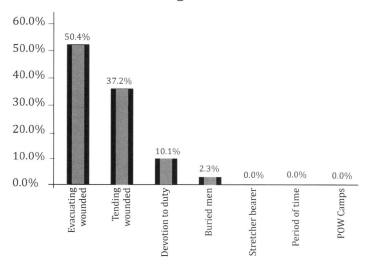

## Distinguished Service Order, Medical Corps, Categories

| Activity/Location | % |
| --- | --- |
| Front Line (no-man's-land) | 38.5 |
| Organisational | 13.1 |
| Adv. Dressing Station | 12.3 |
| Under Shell Fire | 11.5 |
| Regtl Aid Post | 9.0 |
| Cas. Clearing Station | 4.1 |
| Dressing Station | 3.3 |
| Treating Epidemics | 3.3 |
| Gun Line (Arty) | 2.5 |
| Ambulance Convoy | 2.5 |
| Protect Wounded (own body) | 0.0 |
| High Risk Disease | 0.0 |
| Water Supply | 0.0 |
| Sanitary Section | 0.0 |
| Clerk | 0.0 |

| Rank | % |
| --- | --- |
| Lieutenant | 6 |
| Captain | 50 |
| Major | 14 |
| Lt. Colonel | 30 |

| Honours DSOs | 77% |
| --- | --- |

**Figure 27: Analysis of the Distinguished Service Order,
Royal Army Medical Corps**

*Results of a sample of all 129 Royal Army Medical Corps Immediate DSOs*

heavy shell fire. Often the wounded men were lying out in the open and the medics went out to administer aid prior to evacuation of the casualty, crouching over them or lying next to them. Wounds were dressed as best as possible and water was administered. There was usually a choice of casualties to deal with; which one got dealt with first depended on a brief assessment of his chances. Medics at work were often static targets if anyone chose to shoot them, but the armbands they wore were designed to identify them for what they were. The best thing a medic could do was concentrate on the task in hand and get on with it, whilst trying to put fear out of his mind. They moved about the battlefield whilst others took cover. Infantrymen were often able to watch stretcher bearers go about their work under fire and, having nothing better to look at, were often deeply impressed by their apparent courage. There was a feeling that the best of the stretcher bearers were 'like angels of the battlefield' although in soldier's memoirs, the cry 'where are the stretcher bearers when you need them?' is frequently found. On occasion, there was simply too much work for them; for example in the first days of July 1916. Another reason was that they could not get through the communication trenches or over the top to where they were needed as a result of a heavy 'defensive barrage'.

## IN THE REAR AREAS

Men of the Corps were busy not only where there was fighting, but across the entire battle zone right back to the large hospitals in major towns where they were well out of range of German artillery. They were at the camps on the northern coasts of France where the hospital ships came in and took their broken loads back to England. It is to these back areas that we shall turn our attention first, before moving into the line to discover how doctors and stretcher bearers treated, evacuated and saved the lives of their wounded comrades. Awards made to men very far behind the lines are rare; Staff Sergeant Mattison of Balham, London, received a DCM in the New Year Honours list of 1916; 'For conspicuous gallantry and devotion to duty throughout the campaign when in a field unit. Later he has shown remarkable powers as a register clerk in the office of the DGMS'. Whilst his service in the back areas is mentioned in his citation for the award, Mattison had a distinguished war career, having entered France on 20 August 1914 with the 15th Field Ambulance and had been mentioned in despatches in mid-1915.

Also announced in the New Year Honours list of 1916 was the DCM awarded to Sergeant H. Russell: 'For conspicuous gallantry during the period; he kept open two advanced offices, both of which were heavily shelled, and the offices demolished. In spite of this, he kept up constant communication with the DADMS, and through him orders were conveyed with promptness and accuracy'. Later in the war, there still appear some awards of the DCM for organisational work, for example that made to Quarter Master Sergeant J. E. Pritchard for 'valuable service in connection with the formation of an amalgamated field ambulance, the success of which was largely due to his good work'. This award was announced in the *London Gazette* of 18th February,1918. Another example of this type of award illustrates the importance of supplies; Quarter Master Sergeant H. E. Bevans received a DCM whilst he was the Regimental Sergeant Major in charge of the 'supply of medical stores to the forward area and in controlling the transport for the evacuation of wounded'. The citation further indicates that this man was not easily put off his duties by heavy shell fire.

## ENSURING WATER SUPPLY AND THE SANITARY SECTIONS

Water supply was important to the Corps as wounds needed to be washed in uncontaminated water. Reflecting its importance, within the RAMC units there were men assigned the duty of obtaining clean water. A single award of the DCM has been uncovered for one of these men; his name was W. Fowler of the 6th (London) Field Ambulance and was earned whilst he was attached to the 21st London Regiment. It was a New Year Honours award of 1 January 1919 (announced in the *London Gazette* of 3 September 1919) and the citation reads: 'For outstanding services as water corporal since February 1918. The water supply has frequently been assured by his resource and determination, notably at Bouzincourt in April last, when the source of supply was constantly under heavy shell fire; and near Bois des Tailles, when he was blown over by a shell which killed the horses of the water cart and wounded the driver. On the latter occasion he showed particular gallantry, although severely shaken, refusing to go down to the transport lines though a relief was sent for'.

Sanitary sections were specifically tasked with ensuring clean water supplies, cooking facilities and billets and a section was attached to each Division. It was a small unit which usually operated at some distance from the fighting. A very small handful of awards was made to sanitary sections during the war, including the DCM to Lance Corporal W. Lamplugh in the Birthday Honours Gazette of June 1916, and this was 'for exceptionally good work in regard to the sanitary requirements of the Army'. Another identified award of the DCM made to a member of a sanitary section was made for tending wounded under shell fire rather than for his sanitary duties.

These awards stand out as some of the rarest, yet most interesting, of all RAMC awards, simply because these were daily duties in every unit that did not attract decorations for gallantry. Men were out performing these sorts of task on a daily basis in the Medical Corps and the importance of their tasks is largely forgotten.

## TENDING THOSE WITH CONTAGIOUS DISEASES

Other rare awards include those conferred upon men who courageously dealt with dangerous diseases in hospitals and Prisoner-of-War camps. Private F. Bennison received a DCM in the 1916 New Year Honours 'For gallant conduct and devotion in volunteering for isolation with cerebro-spinal fever patients and nursing them devotedly for many weeks'. Here, perhaps, we have an example of great courage when not in the face of the enemy. After 1916, he would not have been made an award of the DCM; instead, it would have been a Meritorious Service Medal (MSM) which was instituted in 1916 just for such purposes. However, Sergeant W. E. S. Taylor, the senior medical NCO with the 10th Cavalry Brigade Field Ambulance in the Jordan Valley, gained a DCM in late 1918 for outstanding organisational work over three months. In this period, 'casualties from sickness were extremely heavy' and he 'showed great devotion and unflagging zeal in carrying out the organisation of the field ambulance'. We may assume that the distinction between DCM and MSM must have been made on the grounds that he performed his duties while subjected to enemy action, but that is by no means clear from the citation.

Several men of the 22nd Field Ambulance received DCMs 'For devotion to duty and eminent services rendered by them, when prisoners of war, during epidemics of cholera and typhus fever at the Prisoner of War Camps in Gottingen and Ohrdruf'. For their devotion to duty at the Gardelegen POW Camp, Germany, Captains Arthur James Brown and Augustus Scott Williams received DSOs in the *Gazette* of 2 November 1916, presumably also for treatment of disease. Similarly, at the camp at Wittenberg, Germany, Captains Alan Cunliffe Vidal and James La Fayette Lauder received DSOs for treatment of typhus outbreaks between February to June 1915 (*London Gazette*, 18 April 1916).

**SELF-SACRIFICE**

Humans, if assigned the task of lifesaving and rescue, will generally perform the task well. It is easier to set out with rescue in mind than it is to set out to kill other men. Such acts are rendered particularly poignant when the rescuer has used his own body as a shield to the helpless victim. However common this particular act may have been on the battlefields, awards are rare. In late 1917, Private R. Wilson of Durham and Private C. D. Ayre of Gateshead were working as part of a stretcher squad and, 'while bringing in a wounded stretcher case they were heavily shelled. In conjunction with the others he lowered the stretcher, and with an absolute disregard of danger to himself protected the wounded man with his body. Though wounded himself, he with great determination and pluck, helped to carry the wounded man to safety'. It would appear that both Wilson and Ayre shared not only a citation but wounds received at the same moment, and the incident alludes to the stretcher-bearer's intense disappointment he felt when a man he had carried out of the line, his prize, was killed on the stretcher on the way.

Another example is that of 49086 Private F. Hudson who received a DCM during the battle of the Somme, 1916; 'For conspicuous gallantry when carrying a wounded man through an area full of gas from shells. The man had no gas helmet and Private Hudson, knowing the risk, put his own helmet on the wounded man and, although suffering himself from the gas, managed to carry him in'. A stretcher bearer's prize for risking his life was getting the casualty safely to an aid post; to lose a rescued man meant a failed rescue and there would be no momentary rest in the relative safety of an aid post either. Each rescued man had the devotion of his bearer for as long as it took to get him to safety. Such awards are similarly rarely found within the infantry: the only example of such selflessness recorded in the long awards list of the Northumberland Fusiliers is the DCM awarded to Corporal T. W. Allison of Choppington Station, Northumberland. He was an infantry soldier for whom 'no praise can be too great for... (his) splendid act of devotion'. The relevant DCM citation further states how, when out on a patrol, 'He accompanied his officer on a difficult reconnaissance and, when the latter was severely wounded and lying under fire, he went back and sheltered him with his body at great personal risk, remaining with him until it was possible to move him to a place of safety'. Perhaps, there were many examples like this but if so then most of them went unrewarded.

Other hazards for which DCMs were awarded include bombing by aeroplanes and the detonation of booby-trap devices left by the retreating Germans. The former may be illustrated by the award made to Pte. R. B. McCoy of Maidstone, when he assisted the wounded during a bomb and machine-gun attack made by German aircraft on the RAF Base to which he was attached. Although 'badly wounded in the thigh by the first bomb that fell and, although he could only walk with great difficulty, he struggled towards the other casualties and attended to them while bombs were still dropping...'. According to his citation, 'his splendid courage and self-sacrifice saved the life of a man who would have died had he not been attended to immediately'. Similar self-sacrifice was exhibited by 75074 Private W. N. Warren who, whilst attached to the No.2

Water Tank Company, Royal Army Service Corps, saved the lives of wounded and gassed men near Douai in late October 1918. An enemy mine perhaps fitted with a long-action delay time fuse and 'lined with gas shells', exploded, causing many casualties. Private Warren 'immediately proceeded to dress the wounded, which work he continued without a gas helmet for no less than three hours until finally overcome by gas'.

Many medical corps men honoured with decorations for gallantry were not simply displaying selfless devotion to duty, some acts were truly remarkable and most of these were performed in the arduous conditions of the battlefield where seriously hurt men lay out under fire. Corporal R. McKenna of the 37th Field Ambulance won a DCM and bar during 1916. His DCM citation provides an illustration of the determination needed and risks undertaken to get the wounded in: 'For conspicuous gallantry and devotion to duty. When several attempts had failed to rescue a wounded man from a crater, he succeeded in doing so single-handed. He was heavily bombed in the sap, and for over an hour was unable to move the wounded man. He eventually got him to safety. He returned to the crater and rescued a second wounded man. During the performance of this action he was hit by a bomb. He at once buried it in the mud and it failed to explode. He showed great endurance in carrying these wounded men long distances under most difficult circumstances'. It was commonplace that under heavy fire, stretchers could not be used and men had to be carried in. Another man of the 37th Field Ambulance to gain a DCM during the same fighting was Private S. A. Smith whose DCM citation records that due to the severity of the shelling, stretchers could not be used and 'Pte. Smith assisted in carrying wounded men to places of safety'. McKenna's bar to the DCM was awarded for his services during the Somme battle later in 1916; it was 'for conspicuous gallantry and devotion in attending to and carrying in under heavy fire large numbers of wounded, who had been lying in the open. He repeatedly led stretcher parties to the front line, and refused rest and food while he knew wounded were lying about'. In the absence of stretchers, any improvised means of carrying was employed: Private H. Tallon 'remained all night in "No-Man's-Land" with 17 wounded and was responsible for the recovery of these men, dragging them by means of blankets and waterproof sheets along the ground. He then returned for more…'.

## RESCUES FROM NO-MAN'S-LAND

Over 40 per cent of DCMs awarded to the Royal Army Medical Corps were for acts of gallantry in or in advance of the front line. One of the best examples is that to 120082 Private W. E. Spradbery from Walthamstow, who found himself working with the 36th Field Ambulance recovering the wounded of an infantry battalion who were under heavy fire (and taking cover in trenches). Spradbery received his award 'For conspicuous gallantry and devotion to duty near Mametz on 26 August 1918. He accompanied an officer when rescuing one officer and three men of an infantry regiment under very heavy machine-gun fire. One of the party was killed, two were wounded and two other men got bullets through their clothing. Notwithstanding this, he, with his squad, after bringing in the first party of wounded, returned under heavy machine-gun fire and brought in an NCO who was wounded'. Private W. M. Wallace of Manchester gained his DCM for going 'out over the top' with three other bearers to locate a wounded man lying in "No-Man's-Land"'. By going 'out over the top' it is implied that he and his party did not go via a trench, they got up and went over the open. Sometimes this was the quickest way to get to urgent cases and bearers certainly took such risks to get the wounded in. Wallace's citation refers to his 'courage and endurance' as a bearer. Many of those who received decorations for gallantry did show considerable endurance over long hours and sometimes days of hard, load-bearing work. Such a case is that of Private A. P. Inglis, a Territorial soldier of the 1/3rd Lowland Field Ambulance. On 29 June 1915 on the Gallipoli Peninsula: 'Though himself wounded in the leg and tired out by almost continuous duty for three days, he continued to attend and carry back the wounded under shell and rifle fire'. Similarly, we may look to Acting Lance-Corporal F. Rowlands, who already had an MM at the time he was awarded the DCM for his unceasing work.

During an enemy attack in the Spring of 1918, Rowlands: 'showed great courage and determination in leading bearer squads to the assistance of wounded men. He worked continually for two days from the front line to the dressing station and, in spite of machine-gun fire and heavy shelling, was most successful in getting his cases through. His example was such that the men would follow him anywhere'. Throughout the British Army, setting an example was of great value in steadying men under fire and leading them to their objective, whether the objective was an enemy position, a wounded man or a dressing station beyond a heavy barrage. Sergeant G. Jacobs' DCM was announced in the *London Gazette* of 26 September 1916 and was a Somme award. The citation states: 'For conspicuous gallantry during operations. When his stretcher bearers were dazed by the intense shell fire he jumped on the parapet and with the assistance of an orderly carried the first case through the barrage. The other bearers at once followed his lead'.

Stretcher bearers collected wounded from no-man's-land and from the front line but their passage rearwards to dressing stations often took them through the enemy barrage, which, during a British attack, was laid down by German artillery to disrupt the forward movement of men and supplies. During the Third Battle of Ypres, 1917, a prelude to the Autumn battle of Passchendaele, Staff Sergeant Wakeling was in charge of reserve stretcher bearers who were on call in case required. Of course, they were required and he led his party 'up to the forward trenches under heavy shell fire and brought them back through the enemy barrage with the utmost coolness. His indifference to danger kept his bearers together and brought them safely through the barrage'. These men did not only move patients about the battlefield, they also ran for medical supplies, as illustrated by the DCM award to Private W. Herd, whilst attached to the 8th Battalion of the Royal Scots: 'For conspicuous devotion to duty on 26 January 1915 when he left his trench and went to the rear across the open, at great personal risk in order to obtain some morphia for a wounded man'. The urgency of the case compelled Private Herd to cast his own life to one side in order to save that of another man, and yet his single urge was to get morphia; he may not have considered that he was risking his life. In the heat of action, such risk is often forgotten.

## TENDING THE WOUNDED IN NO-MAN'S-LAND

While working under fire in no-man's-land, first aid had often to be administered in order to stabilise a man before he was moved. Very often several wounded might be patched up in preparation for a bearer party to remove them. One in five DCMs were won whilst tending the wounded rather than in the act of moving them to safety. On the second day of the landings at Gallipoli, 26 April 1915, 1369 Corporal J. W. Jones, a pre-war Territorial volunteer, was on the beach at Cape Helles when he won his DCM: 'for conspicuous bravery in attending wounded and supplying them with water under heavy fire'. In even more desperate conditions, Staff-Sergeant G. Prince was attached to a small force which had been completely surrounded by the enemy, who were naturally trying to eliminate them. He 'attended to our casualties with absolute indifference to his own safety, remaining exposed to heavy fire for two hours'. Such bravery was an inspiration and an encouragement to those who saw it, but to the man who actually did it, it was 'simply his job'. So too at the Regimental Aid Post, positioned a short distance behind the firing line, where 20478 Staff Sergeant J. W. Hastings gained his bar to the DCM that he had won on the Somme two years earlier; 'He helped a Medical Officer to establish a walking wounded post and frequently brought in casualties caused by heavy hostile barrage. Though frequently under shell fire he was untiring in attending the wounded, and set a splendid example to all'. Further back, at an advanced dressing station, Sergeant W. M. Allan of Aberdeen was wounded but refused to leave his post even when a withdrawal placed his post in the front line: 'When the officers and men were ordered to leave the advanced dressing station he remained behind dressing wounded who were brought to him'. At a Casualty Clearing Station (CCS) in the Autumn of 1917, Quarter Master Sergeant B. L. Aldhous was decorated 'for conspicuous gallantry and devotion to duty. When a dressing station was being shelled he supervised and helped with the evacuation of all the wounded, visiting all the tents and huts to see that they were clear under heavy fire. It was largely due to his initiative that 500 cases were removed without a single casualty'. The rapid advances of the German Spring offensives of 1918 meant that dressing stations and casualty clearing stations, normally behind the lines, had to be evacuated rapidly. During 'several days of intense fighting', Staff Sergeant F. B. Challis was decorated for his remarkably successful 'evacuation of patients and stores from a casualty clearing station. Subsequently he rallied men during bombing and machine-gun fire from enemy aircraft and got all ranks working at high pressure erecting and striking a casualty clearing station, and attending to large numbers of the patients, although he and his men had had little rest for several days and nights'.

## AT THE GUN LINE

Those medics who were attached to artillery batteries saw up close the effects of enemy counter-battery shooting and, when hits were obtained on British gun positions, the wounded gunners needed to be extracted and attended to. Some 2.5 per cent of RAMC DCMs was won with the artillery on the 'gun line'. Corporal J. H. Barber was in the vicinity of the artillery positions when the call for medical aid was heard; 'he volunteered to accompany an officer of the RAMC to assist in the dressing and removal of numerous wounded from an allied field battery which was being heavily shelled, the ammunition dump also being on fire and exploding'. In late 1917, Private M. F. A. Brooke, a native of Nottingham, was attached to an artillery battery when 'during a heavy hostile shelling... he displayed the utmost promptness and gallantry in attending wounded men... and, in fact, on numerous occasions he has displayed exceptional gallantry and devotion in going into battery positions which were being heavily shelled to attend to wounded men'. During a heavy bombardment of gas and high explosive shells, Sergeant A. Blandford 'led a party of stretcher bearers to the rescue of some gunners whose dugouts had been blown in. At great personal risk they succeeded in digging them out and rescued three alive. It was due to his courage, initiative and energy that three lives were saved'. Some 3 per cent of Medical Corps DCM awards was made for the rescue of buried men, this being one act that attracted decorations across all of the branches of the Army, and at roughly the same rate (2–3 per cent of DCMs). Sergeant A. G. Cripps was in charge of a relay post for stretcher bearers. At a relay post, a team of bearers operating in the forward zone would hand over the carrying duty of stretcher cases to fresh squads who would take the wounded back to the dressing station, while the original team went back out to fetch more casualties from the battlefield. Sergeant Cripps, 'Hearing of wounded men lying under fire, made four journeys through the barrage, being blown up on the first journey but bringing four men in on his back. Later, a shell burst at his post, killing and burying 11 men. He restored order, organised a rescue party, and brought out the 11 men'. When a heavy artillery barrage hit his Regimental Aid Post in the forward area and a direct hit blew it in and buried three men, 446012 Sergeant E. Honey, 'went to their assistance and at great personal risk succeeded in digging them out and attending to them under continual shell fire'. Sometimes these sorts of rescues occurred in towns being violently shelled by the enemy. Men inside houses risked being buried by falling brickwork. Sergeant J. Ingram organised parties to search for wounded men 'who had been buried in the debris of a house. He dug out two men and assisted in digging out others under very heavy shell fire, and then dressed their wounds'. Throughout, the published citation states, he 'showed great courage'.

## IN AMBULANCE CONVOYS

Ambulance convoys were always active in the shelled zone behind the lines. In one typical incident, Private J. G. Bruce of the 1st Highland Field Ambulance was 'in charge of an ambulance wagon and two horses. One horse was killed and the other, which he was riding, wounded, he himself being struck by a fragment of the shell. The ambulance was full of wounded at the time, Private Bruce unhooked his wounded horse, rode it, returned with a fresh pair, and continued his duties under shell fire until all the wounded had been brought in'. Bruce was awarded his DCM in the New Year Honours list of 1916, and his citation appeared in the *London Gazette* of 11 March 1916. In the same *Gazette* edition, we find the DCM award made to Private H. Wallis of the 1st Home Counties Field Ambulance; 'he brought a motor ambulance into position for receiving wounded and, in spite of heavy shelling all round, continued, with great bravery, to perform his duties until all the wounded had been removed'. Under similar conditions of heavy shell fire in the summer of 1917, Acting Lance-Corporal T. Pinkney was engaged in 'loading wounded on a motor ambulance'. What happened next forms an isolated scene of a great many desperate scenes from the Great War: 'Coming under heavy shell fire, he continued to attend to the wounded with great gallantry and coolness, although twice men were killed beside him and the driver of the car was wounded. The car was also damaged, but he procured assistance in loading it up and then drove it himself under heavy fire to the Main Dressing Station, though his experience of driving cars was very slight'. Rightly, the published citation, which appeared in the *London Gazette* of 17 September 1917, concluded, 'his conduct was magnificent throughout'.

There was always a danger of being shelled on the roads. Where there were incidents, there were men whose devotion to duty was exemplary. When 'heavy shelling had caused severe casualties among artillery men and transport on a road', Sergeant T. G. Hopkins 'went to the aid of the wounded, extricating them from a tangle of kicking animals, and carried them to the comparative safety of shell-holes. He carried four wounded men one after the other on his back. On another occasion he brought many wounded from an area heavily swept by machine-gun fire. He was twice blown up by shells, but managed to reach the Advanced Dressing Station and notify where the wounded were collected before he collapsed. His gallantry and self-sacrificing devotion to duty were peculiarly admirable'. During the retreat of Spring 1918, when the ambulances were sent back, medical posts had to be evacuated. The scenes of those days are not always captured, but even in one DCM citation, the desperate situation and one man's response are. It was Private (Acting Corporal) H. W. Jordan who, when the time came, remained with the rearguard dressing the wounded, then, 'evacuated wounded on led horses, wheelbarrows and other emergency transport until all had been removed, and then guided the last stretcher squads over the ridge under intense shell and machine-gun fire'. His action, it is stated, prevented many wounded from falling into the enemy's hands. Those wounded, bloodied men had cause to thank Private Jordan.

## THE MEDICAL OFFICER

Within the environments described above, medical officers were busy tending wounds, stabilising the patients and, if necessary, performing minor operations prior to having them moved further back down the line to Casualty Clearing Stations and major hospitals even further to the rear. Only 10 per cent of Military Crosses were awarded to officers who assisted with stretcher bearing work. Most medical officers were given the rank of Captain, so as to have seniority over the majority of junior officers they were likely to meet in the line. Gallantry awards to Lieutenants of the Royal Army Medical Corps constitute just 18 per cent of MCs, compared to other units in which one finds 60–80 per cent of MCs awarded to 2nd Lieutenants and Lieutenants.

Almost exactly half of MCs were awarded for tending the wounded under fire, and another 35 per cent for organising or actually carrying out the evacuation of the wounded from the battle area. Typical examples of these types of officer awards are firstly the MC award to Lt. Bernard Score Brown who was attached to the 2nd Battalion of the Cheshire Regiment near Vermelles in early October 1915. This officer spent, 'the whole night... searching for and carrying back wounded who were lying between our own and the enemy's lines, which were only 200 yards apart. The enemy were firing and the ground was lit up by flares. After daybreak he carried back three more men under a very heavy fire'. In common with many battlefield lifesaving awards, his persistence set him apart from the usual: 'By his courage and ceaseless work all the wounded in his area were brought in'. The officers' tasks included supervision of stretcher bearers, as shown by the example of Captain Jerome O'Sullivan, who 'supervised the collection of many wounded in front of our lines and got them into dug-outs in our front line. He then conducted the bearers himself round these dug-outs, continuing to do so until all the cases had been cleared'. Captain Herbert Francis Wilson received his MC when he 'repeatedly led stretcher bearers under heavy fire, and succeeded in evacuating all the wounded on his front'. On the Salonika front, Captain Henry L. Messenger won his second MC for leading 'a party of stretcher bearers some 400 yards across the open through a heavy barrage, and succeeded in rescuing and bringing in a large number of casualties to his advanced post'. An officer's leadership and example was of great assistance to the men, as in the case of Captain John Stephenson, who was in charge of stretcher bearers at his Regimental Aid Post near Bellewaarde Ridge between 1–13 August 1917: 'He remained in charge of his sector for 13 days, refusing to be relieved... His personal example and gallant leadership were largely responsible for the way in which his bearers stuck to their duty'. Such an officer could get far more out of his men than many other officers, without having to threaten them. Higher ranking medical officers took on more of the responsibility for organising matters; Acting Major William Russell received a bar to his MC in the *London Gazette* of 1 February 1919. He was in command of bearers and numerous Aid Posts in the front line area during the period 22–24 August 1918, which 'he constantly visited by day and by night, often under considerable shell and machine-gun fire, and disposed his bearers and ambulance cars with such skill that all wounded were collected and placed in the most favourable conditions for recovery with the utmost celerity'. Most MC awards made to medical officers were for performing the tasks assigned to them as part of their role on the battlefield. Some exhibited leadership and organisational abilities, some inspired others by their energetic and courageous example under heavy fire.

Awards of the DSO to medical officers reflect the increased responsibilities of more senior ranks. The number of posts and dressing stations, as well as the number of men for whom officers of the rank of Captain and higher were responsible, grew rapidly. Whereas the MC may be thought of as an award for doctors performing their duty in the firing line, the DSO often shows management skills applied to more men over a greater area of operations. Nearly one in five DSOs shows a strong component of organisational ability, for example the citation relating to Lt. Colonel Montgomery-Smith's DSO illustrates some of the senior officer's responsibilities: 'By a systematic study of the ground, clever selection of aid and relay posts and routes, he evacuated a large number of casualties during the operations'. Two second awards of the DSO to Lt. Colonels Blackwood and Harty were published in the *London Gazette* of 16 September 1918; both of these illustrate the importance of the senior officer's work in touring scattered posts. In the case of Harty, he: 'frequently visited (the forward area) during heavy shelling to see that his orders were being executed properly, and also to inspire confidence'. During a long period of operations, Lt. Colonel Blackwood, 'visited the forward area daily, and his indefatigable energy and exceptional organising ability were invaluable to the division'. Senior medical officers were not rewarded for singular acts of bravery, but for their untiring and efficient contribution to the mechanics of treating and evacuating wounded over a wide frontage and for maintaining the morale of the men under their command. This work was absolutely vital in maintaining medical services at the highest possible standard.

Among lower ranking officers, Captains received the DSO for working under heavy fire, in much the same way as the MC was won. One officer who gained a DSO and bar is worth mentioning as this records a long standing willingness to get on with the job in any conditions of personal danger for the sake of the wounded. As a Lieutenant, Hugh Hughes won his DSO in the 1916 Somme battle for tending the wounded under shell fire in the front line area, 'in the open'. His bar to the DSO, this time as Captain in the Autumn of 1916, tells us that he showed 'utter contempt of danger' whilst performing his duties.

Self-sacrifice was undoubtedly a component of many RAMC awards; for example, while Temporary Lieutenant John Hammond was busy evacuating wounded men of the Devonshire Regiment early in 1917, he was suddenly seriously wounded: 'although both his feet were practically blown off he ordered his stretcher bearers to carry away another wounded man first'. Returning to Noel Chavasse, VC and bar, MC, in his three awards we see his habit of going into no-man's-land, no matter what the danger to himself, to look for and rescue wounded men. His MC was earned for doing this after the battle of Hooge in June 1915. He received his first Victoria Cross for the rescue of wounded from the battlefield over a period of 48 hours on 9 and 10 August 1916, on the Somme. His second VC was won during the Third Battle of Ypres, when, after he was wounded in the head and in much pain, he refused to be evacuated and selflessly went out time and time again in terrible weather into the morass of mud and shell holes to attend to and rescue his men. Three days into the battle, when he was resting in an aid post, a shell struck and mortally wounded him. But still he crawled with smashed body, face unrecognisable due to wounds, for half a mile to get help for others. A remarkable example of heroism is afforded by Captain Ralph Eminson's deeds in the Spring of 1918. He received high distinction in the form of the DSO: 'When two companies who had made a counter-attack and reached a village, were obliged to fall back 150 yards, suffering heavy casualties, whom it was impossible to rescue owing to the accurate machine-gun and rifle fire from the village, this officer went himself, regardless of fire, and in full view of the enemy, across "No-Man's-Land" many times, and carried and assisted back the wounded, who would otherwise have been left'. How much courage must these displays of heroism have given those who saw them? With such medical officers at hand, the men saw that they would not be left out there to die alone. There was limited value in the rescues themselves (a handful of wounded men were of very little value to subsequent operations), but there was far greater military value in the psychological effects such acts had on the ordinary soldier; seeing these acts carried out gave him the expectation of rescue and survival and the sensation that never would he be left alone. Thus fortified, Tommy could continue, he could go on to the end. Throughout preceding chapters, the value of giving courage to others has been recognised and emphasised. Setting a good example, maintaining a fine cheery bearing in battle, paternalism, going out to rescue wounded souls and displays of incredible 'bravery' are all, in fact, linked at a higher level – they spread courage among others, fortifying the group. This is something that goes beyond the superficial act itself; the honours and awards committees, the generals and the King all knew this very well. Official rewards for battlefield bravery are much more about the provision of courage to others by means of distinguished services, battlefield leadership and the encouragement of ordinary men to win through. Setting an example to others, of whatever kind, is contagious. Such is the true function of heroism in wartime and its official reward recognises this importance. The significance of the medical personnel who 'only did their duty' was in giving men the confidence to endure and survive, to fight and to win. The Army thus fortified, was ready to endure, with hope and with courage.

# The Army Service Corps

P erhaps the least understood of the Corps, the Army Service Corps (ASC) was a large organisation performing a a great range of tasks mostly behind the lines, was paid better than most and did not normally have to sleep rough. The ASC won 2 per cent of all gallantry awards between 1914 and 1918. In general terms, they were in charge of supplying the Army with everything they needed – animals, ammunition, food, weapons, wire, water and wood among many other things. Within the Army Service Corps were horse (or mule) transport sections which operated with carts. There were motorised transport sections operating with buses for the men, lorries for supplies and gun tractors for moving heavy artillery. Men having the rank of driver either worked with horses in the traditional sense of the word, or drove motor ambulances, lorries and buses on supply lines between railhead depots, the forward dumps and right across the militarised zone. Some ASC motor transport drivers were attached to front line units and went into battle in armoured cars and even in tanks, or got caught up in shelling of artillery lines as they moved the guns about. Quite a number of cavalrymen who arrived in the early parts of the war, between 1914 and 1915, ended up in the Army Service Corps as the British Army's supply arm grew in size and the demand for equestrian specialists increased. The good pay was a major attraction. So there was, in fact, plenty of scope for ASC men to perform courageous acts in a great range of circumstances.

If the Great War was a clash of developed economies, the Army Service Corps was the means of delivering the industrial strength of the British economy to the war zone. Usually overlooked, its contribution to winning that war was as great as that of the infantry. An overview of the decorations won by the men of the Army Service Corps allows their interesting and diverse stories to be told, and diverse they certainly were.

## THE LORRY DRIVER BRINGS PICKS AND SHOVELS

We shall begin with a scene from the front line that was re-written many times in later wars, in which Pte. R. Sharples was a driver with a motorised transport section. He won a DCM during the Spring Offensives, 1918, when the British Army had its 'backs to the wall' as the German Army ploughed forward, breaking through the line and overrunning rear positions. The award citation reads: 'For conspicuous gallantry and devotion to duty. In order to re-establish our line, which had been penetrated by the enemy, this man volunteered to take machine guns and their crews up to the spot in the motor lorry he was driving. He eventually succeeded in also bringing two companies to within a few hundred yards of where the enemy were advancing, though he was exposed to very heavy rifle and machine-gun fire at the time. The energy and promptitude with which he then fetched up picks and shovels, wire and necessary materials, enabled the line, which at one time was held only by the machine gunners he had conveyed, to be solidly re-established. His cheerful courage as he performed his duties under heavy fire never faltered'. This was a man with great presence of mind and a strong sense of duty to his own.

## THE MASTER BAKER AND THE CHIEF CLERK

Far behind the lines in 1915, Staff Sergeant A. J. Steele was 'Master Baker during the early part of the campaign at Boulogne' and received the medal for distinguished conduct. He was, according to the published citation: 'Working under the greatest difficulties in the open and exposed to all weathers, (and) successfully carried out the work of the First Bakery, never failing to turn out the maximum output from the ovens'. At this point in time, the only appropriate decoration for such services was the DCM, the Meritorious Service Medal (MSM) not being instituted until 1916. However, even after 1917, rare awards of the DCM for such 'meritorious services' behind the lines still appear: the published citation of Temporary Staff Sergeant Major C. R. Ormes of Folkestone describes a gallant assault on the paperwork: 'For conspicuous gallantry and devotion to duty and the highly efficient manner he has carried out his duties as Chief Clerk at force headquarters. Although short staffed and often single-handed, he has, through untiring energy, kept the heavy work most thoroughly up to date under most trying and adverse circumstances. He has worked for two years without being a day off duty'. Whilst front line infantrymen without a doubt scoffed at this kind of award, and whilst such awards may have contributed to the undermining of confidence in the entire awards system, it is important to remember that supporting the award was a detailed recommendation which may have given much more information about this man's gallantry under more dangerous circumstances. In particular, this was not a periodic (Honours) award, it was an immediate award of the DCM and, as such, during 1918 the guidelines were clear; the DCM could only be awarded for services in action with the enemy or for gallant services in areas affected by enemy action. Very often, recommendations were stripped of specific place names and events prior to publishing in the *London Gazette*, so it may be that specific detail of his 'conspicuous gallantry' was present in the original recommendation.

A total of 454 immediate plus honours MCs was granted to the Army Service Corps. There were just five immediate awards of the DSO to the Army Service Corps and so a similar analysis has not been possible.

Most of the awards relating to the Army Service Corps were made for work somewhere between the quiet rear areas and the front line itself. Whilst there were no awards of the DCM specifically for getting bread up the line to the troops, there were three awards for getting water forward. Two of these were for deeds in Mesopotamia and in Palestine, where water was more scarce than in France and Flanders. The immediate award for Mesopotamia was made to a Private S. Shepherd who was operating with a motor transport section: 'He carried water to the front line trenches under heavy fire'. A Birthday Honours award of the DCM was made in 1919 for Palestine to Company Quartermaster Sergeant J. S. Beerman, attached Camel Transport Corps. His published citation, which appears in the *London Gazette* of 11 March 1920, states: 'For gallantry and devotion to duty in charge of brigade canals... he

# Distinguished Service Order, Army Services Corps, Categories

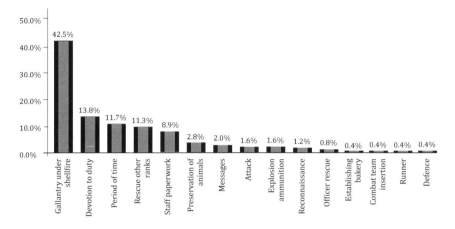

| Activity | % |
|---|---|
| Ambulance convoy | 21.8 |
| Zeal | 16.6 |
| Supply convoy | 6.2 |
| Ammunition convoy | 5.7 |
| Transport | 5.7 |
| Gun tractor | 4.1 |
| Extricate guns (gun tractor) | 4.1 |
| Anti-aircraft unit | 3.6 |
| Bakeries | 3.1 |
| Rations forward | 2.6 |
| Armoured car patrols | 2.6 |
| Supply gun battery | 2.6 |
| Motorcycle despatch rider | 2.1 |
| Stables | 2.1 |
| Stores forward | 2.1 |
| Motor mechanic | 2.1 |
| Water supply | 1.6 |
| Depot | 1.6 |
| Care for horses | 1.6 |
| With RAMC | 1.0 |
| Shelldump | 1.0 |
| Stretcher bearer | 1.0 |
| Tank driver | 1.0 |
| Ambulance wagons | 0.5 |
| Aerial bombing | 0.5 |
| Motorcycle scout | 0.5 |
| Railways (Supply) | 0.5 |
| With Artillery | 0.5 |
| Cyclist | 0.5 |
| Escaper | 0.5 |
| Farrier | 0.5 |

| Unit | No. | % |
|---|---|---|
| Mechanical Transport, New Army (M1, M2 prefix) | 108 | 44 |
| Supply, Old Army (S prefix) | 39 | 16 |
| Horse Transport, Old Army (T prefix) | 31 | 13 |
| Horse Transport, New Army (T1, 2, 3, 4 prefix) | 19 | 3 |
| Supply, New Army, (S2, S4 prefix) | 13 | 5 |
| Mechanical Transport Specials, Old Army (MS prefix) | 8 | 3 |
| Mechanical Transport (DM, DM2 prefix) | 8 | 3 |
| Supply, Old Army Specials (SS prefix) | 3 | 1 |
| Horse Transport, Special Reserve (T1ST, T2SR) | 2 | 1 |
| Horse Transport, Old Army Specials (TS prefix) | 2 | 1 |
| Old Army (C, CMT prefix) | 2 | 1 |

| Rank | % |
|---|---|
| Private/Driver | 52 |
| L/Corporal and Corporal | |
| Sergeant | |
| Warrant Officer | |
| Privates and Corporals | 52 |
| Sergeants and Warrant Officers | 48 |
| Honours DCMs | 60 |

## Figure 28: Analysis of the Distinguished Conduct Medal, Army Service Corps

*Results of a sample of all 247 Immediate and Honours DCMs to the ASC*

## Military Cross, Army Services Corps, Categories

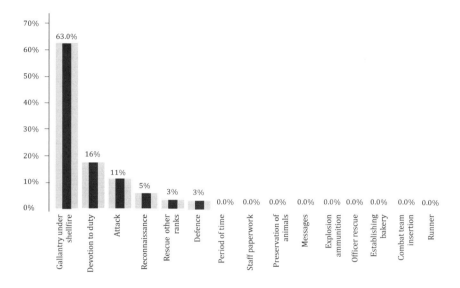

| Activity | % |
|---|---|
| Supply convoy | 26.7 |
| Ammunition convoy | 20.0 |
| With Artillery | 13.3 |
| Rations forward | 13.3 |
| Aerial bombing | 10.0 |
| Transport | 3.3 |
| Gun tractor | 3.3 |
| Shelldump | 3.3 |
| Armoured car patrols | 3.3 |
| Stores forward | 3.3 |

| Rank | % |
|---|---|
| Warrant Officer | 3 |
| 2nd Lieutenant | 26 |
| Lieutenant | 45 |
| Captain | 26 |
| Major | 0 |

| | |
|---|---|
| Honours MCs | 60% |

**Figure 29: Analysis of the Military Cross, Army Service Corps**

*Results of a sample of 38 Immediate MCs of a total of approximately 180 to the ASC*

stationed himself as close as possible to the firing line, and supplied his brigade with water as soon as fighting ceased'. This occurred in September 1918 when the heat in Palestine is likely to have been unbearable. On the Western Front, Pte. Humphreys of Pontypool was a motor transport driver who: 'assisted by another private, he continued to carry water the whole day through a heavy barrage and a burning ammunition dump. He did not cease work, although wounded, until all the tanks were filled'. His persistence in getting water to the men who needed his help warranted an immediate award of the DCM.

## TRANSPORT BY HORSE AND MULE

We have seen so far that Army Service Corps personnel operated motor vehicles, but a great deal of transportation was carried out using horses and mules. The importance of animals to all sides cannot be overstated and this is reflected in the award of 10 DCMs during the war (4 per cent of ASC total) for the preservation of animals and care for horses in dangerous conditions. In his book *Tommy*, Professor Richard Holmes has described the attachment many men developed to their horses and other animals in their care. It may be difficult to imagine that Sergeant Blaylock (attached Camel Transport Corps whilst in Palestine) experienced much love for his animals when he got his DCM for going out under fire to successfully recover a battalion's camels. No doubt Troop Sergeant Major Bleach of the 4th Cavalry Division's Motor Transport Company had to exert all of his skills in animal husbandry when his column was attacked by enemy aeroplanes: 'he rendered great assistance in recovering stampeded teams' while the aircraft, bombs and machine gun bullets were buzzing around and thumping into the soil all about. We can imagine the sadness felt by Farrier Sergeant T. Cussens when his horses' stables were hit by a shell and he had to go in and rescue the animals. He was assisted by Driver A. G. Hardesty and both received the DCM for 'conspicuous gallantry and coolness on 5 November 1914', their awards being gazetted on 1 April 1915. Another example is that of T/22211 Farrier Staff Sergeant J. Sayer who received a DCM in the

11 March 1916 edition of the *London Gazette* with the citation: 'By his devotion many valuable animals have been saved, and his duties frequently necessitated his being left behind with animals after the enemy was pressing forward'. The citation further notes his 'great energy and cheerfulness' in carrying out his work with the animals. Driver F. Liversedge used his skill with his horses when he 'was in charge of a pair of horses and a wagon which was being unloaded when the place was suddenly heavily shelled. Whilst others sought shelter in dug-outs he remained at his horses' heads and with difficulty prevented their bolting'. In November 1914, Driver H. J. Vickers faced a similar situation when his horse-drawn ambulance wagon came under fire, frightening the horses. His experience and ability with horses, 'enabled the remainder of the wounded to be conveyed to a place of safety'. Later in the war, Staff Sergeant Major C. Wassell earned a DCM when in charge of horse lines:'Amidst violent explosions caused by a burning ammunition dump he remained with the horses for three hours without any assistance, preventing them from straying and keeping them under control, thereby saving many valuable animals. His fearlessness and cool persistence in a most perilous situation were most marked'. Both humans and horses respond positively to a calm example; different species were comrades together within a shared experience.

All four of the DCMs awarded to the Corps for getting rations up to the line relate to horse-drawn transport (known as General Service wagons); all four were Honours awards and three of these are in the 11 March 1916 *London Gazette*, which also contains a number of ASC 'paperwork' DCMs. In this *Gazette*, Sergeant J. Barber won his DCM 'whilst taking up reserve rations under heavy fire', Driver C. T. Bold of the 50th (Northumbrian) Division 'displayed great bravery in taking rations through nightly for Brigade Headquarters' and Driver C. M. Lovell received his for 'taking up rations under continual shell fire to advanced headquarters of the division'. Whilst under shell fire, there is a theme of getting food and drink to the officers in headquarters in these citations. In contrast, the only other DCM awarded for getting rations through came much later, in the Birthday Honours gazette of 1918, and this one reads differently; 'during heavy shelling he frequently volunteered to take rations forward'. This was in relation to the German 1918 Spring Offensives and was won by Driver D. T. Williams of Llantrissant, Wales, who is further stated to have 'displayed a fine example of courage and greatly inspired his comrades'. Royal Engineer's stores (wood, wire, electrical cable etc.) were also taken up by general service wagon. Under heavy shell fire, it required great courage in order to 'stick to it', as the DCM citation for Driver J. Cairns of Edinburgh put it, when he had to get his wagon up the road under fire, unload and harness up fresh horses, to make up for those freshly killed. In doing so, 'a bursting shell knocked him over'. It would appear that motorised transport tended to be reserved for the heavier loads (ammunition, towing guns) and urgent medical evacuations (motor ambulances). Troops were moved about using buses on occasion, and these vehicles were driven by the Corps.

## Heavy Gun Tractors

Members of the Corps drove steam traction engines when operating with the heavy artillery. Heavy guns needed towing to and from their emplacements and only a traction engine had the power to do so effectively. Known as 'gun tractors', these contrivances offered a new way of 'saving the guns', traditionally carried out under fire by the horses and drivers of the artillery units. During this war, however, heavy artillery pieces were extracted under heavy enemy counter-battery fire and particularly during the German 1918 Offensives when infantry penetrated British lines and overran back areas. A typical example of a DCM citation relating to this work is that of Sergeant George T. E. Hockaday who was attached to the 79th Siege Battery, Royal Garrison Artillery: 'He was in charge of Caterpillars belonging to the Battery. On 10 April 1918, he succeeded in bringing away all guns and platforms from the position behind Wytschaete, under very heavy bombardment. A section of the battery was in position near Westoutre, and on 25 April came under such a heavy fire that it had to be removed. By his splendid example of coolness and absolute disregard of danger he enabled the guns to be got out'. Sergeant Hockaday had been in France since 26 September 1915, where he arrived as a Private with a motor transport section, and was also mentioned in despatches late in the war. Private Hugh Newick was tasked with saving the guns in late 1917, 'in spite of the enemy advancing to within 500 yards of the position, which was being subjected to very heavy fire'. His DCM citation paid tribute to his 'presence of mind and devotion to duty'. During the German Spring Offensives, Acting Sergeant J. W. Pearce performed a similar act which resulted in a DCM award when, with four caterpillars, he managed to, 'pull six guns out of action just in time to save them from the enemy', all the time being subjected to heavy fire. Pearce was attached to the 227th Siege Battery, Royal Garrison Artillery ammunition column, at the time of these actions. His ordinary role was to supply the heavy ammunition to the batteries. An indication of the difficulty of moving heavy guns and equipment is provided by the following DCM citation relating to Acting Sergeant George Talmey, a native of Brighton. Once again during the German Spring Offensives: 'This NCO was in charge of tractors, and worked unceasingly under gas and heavy shell fire of all descriptions, over ground which was a shell-torn morass, into which they sank repeatedly up to the driver's platforms. It was largely due to him that a great portion of the armament and stores was successfully retired. On completion of this work he assisted in pulling out under heavy shell fire some heavy howitzers belonging to another battery'. The gunners he was working with belonged to the 2nd (Australian) Siege Battery.

## DRIVER OF TANKS AND ARMOURED CARS

As qualified drivers, men occasionally operated on attachment to the Heavy Branch, Machine Gun Corps (which later became the Tank Corps) and found themselves involved in an attack. Two DCMs were awarded to ASC tank drivers; the first relates to the second half of 1916 and was awarded to Private (Actg. Cpl.) George B. Shepherd. He drove his tank throughout an action, which may have been one of the first tank attacks in mid-September, but what is remarkable is that, 'it was entirely due to Pte. Shepherd's skill and courage that it reached its objective, and was successfully withdrawn'. Most of the tanks involved in these attacks broke down; only a small handful made it onto the objectives and returned. Whilst this was an immediate award of the DCM, there is a distinct lack of anything other than determined driving evident in the citation. The first uses of tanks may have attracted awards in recognition of their arrival on the battlefield rather than for outstanding bravery. The second award of a DCM to an Army Service Corps driver is found in the *London Gazette* of 26 January 1918. Private G. Kirkbright of Birmingham was involved in an attack through sand dunes on the northern coast of Belgium near Nieuport in the summer of 1917. The objectives were some enemy coastal defences which were abundant along this stretch of the coast, along with barbed wire and machine gun emplacements: 'after the enemy redoubts had been attacked in succession, he was instrumental in bringing the tank back to safety in spite of the severe injuries which he sustained from shell fire, and that the remaining members of the crew were wounded. His coolness and gallantry deserve the highest praise'. The scarcity of awards for tank driving may be explained by the fact that although tank drivers were drawn from the Army Service Corps, it was normal for them to officially transfer to the Tank Corps and so their awards are far more numerous but appear among those of the Tank Corps itself. Occasionally, drivers never officially transferred and fought as Army Service Corps drivers on attachment.

In addition to driving tanks, five ASC drivers gained DCMs during the war as drivers of armoured cars. Two of these awards were given for devotion to duty during operations, two were awarded for conspicuous gallantry during attacks (one of these was in Mesopotamia) and the fifth award was for bravery on a reconnaissance patrol. It will be remembered that the armoured car sections came within the organisation of the Machine Gun Corps and that their gunners and many of their drivers were MGC men. As in the Tank Corps, ASC drivers served on attachment to armoured car sections. Private J. Summers won his DCM during the Spring of 1918 when: 'he three times drove his armoured car over difficult country to within 300 yards of the enemy's trenches under heavy fire. He showed great daring and coolness on this and many other occasions'. Summers was lucky to get away unhurt, for the armoured car was not impenetrable, and crews could find themselves in terribly difficult situations. Private A. R. Wilkes of Llangyfi, Wales, found himself in the kind of situation that has been repeated many times since: 'he was wounded while driving an armoured car during a reconnaissance. In spite of considerable pain he remained at his post, and when the car was temporarily disabled and for twenty minutes was the target of very heavy and accurate close range fire, he assisted in getting the gun into action and helped to observe the fire'. In Mesopotamia, the 8th Light Armoured Motor Battery of the Machine Gun Corps set out in its armoured cars on 'a daring raid into the enemy's territory' west of Anah on 28 March 1918. One of the car drivers was Corporal R. V. Thorne, a native of Sunningdale, Surrey, who won a DCM when: 'As driver of the leading armoured car… he displayed exceptional coolness and skill in handling it under fire and over unknown ground'. Operating in advance of the armoured cars, a motorcycle scout of the Corps won a DCM during the summer of 1917. This was M2/13163 Private B. Bourke, whose DCM citation was published in the *London Gazette* of 29 August 1917: 'As motor cyclist scout he has been invaluable in tracking and bringing the cars into action by the shortest and best routes, whereby many casualties have been inflicted upon the enemy. On many occasions he has gone forward under heavy fire to discover the best route by which to come into action'. This is the only such example of a motor cyclist operating in conjunction with armoured car sections winning a gallantry award with the Army Service Corps.

**HORSE-DRAWN AND MOTOR AMBULANCE DRIVERS**
Whereas awards to tank and armoured car drivers are very scarce, almost one in five of ASC DCMs were awarded to ambulance drivers. Ambulances were either animal-drawn or they were motor ambulances and operated to-and-fro between the medical posts and casualty clearing stations. Similarly, the ASC moved ammunition wagons between dumps and gun positions but awards made for this type of work constitute only a little over 4 per cent of DCMs won by the Corps. Much ammunition was shifted by artillerymen

of the Divisional Ammunition Columns. As may be guessed, most of these awards were made for gallantry under shell fire, often on congested roads leading up to the front. This is consistent with the environment they were operating in, some distance behind the front line. A few examples of ambulance driver's and ammunition wagon driver's awards follow, which should serve to illustrate the main characteristics of their war and their courage.

Early in the war, ambulances were horse-drawn wagons and their drivers were horsemen. At Neuve Chappelle in early 1915, Driver H. T. Cox drove his horse-drawn wagon 'in front of the German lines and thereby enabled his section to remove our wounded, who would otherwise have been left in the enemy's hands'. It took him two trips to complete the task, right under the German's noses. Another early war example is the DCM awarded to Sergeant J. Bean, who came to notice for his 'gallantry and devotion to duty in collecting wounded with his ambulance wagons under heavy fire, particularly at L'Epinette, where his conduct and resource were most commendable'.

Post-1916, most DCM awards for ambulance work involved motor ambulances rather than horse-drawn. During the Third Battle of Ypres, 1917, Sergeant E. M. Hatchell of New Brighton 'attempted to drive a car, under heavy shell fire, to the rescue of a motor ambulance which had been hit and disabled. His car was smashed and he then crawled along to the motor ambulance, temporarily repaired the extensive damage, and was able to drive it back to the dressing station'. The citation for his DCM is testimony to 'his great courage and exceptional resource under extremely trying circumstances'. During the Spring Offensives of 1918, Private A. Williams of Carrog, Wales, was working at a Field Ambulance post when the place was heavily shelled. 'He was severely wounded in the leg and foot', reads his published DCM citation, which continues: 'In spite of the fact that his leg was useless and that he was bleeding, Private Williams, who was in charge of a motor ambulance car, insisted on driving another wounded man to the Advanced Dressing Station though the road was being heavily shelled at the time and he was suffering severely from shock and haemorrhage'. One of the best DCM citations relating to motor ambulance convoys is this one, also from the Spring of 1918, a tribute to the courage of Private J. A. Dawson of Dundee: 'For conspicuous gallantry and devotion to duty. He behaved with great gallantry when clearing wounded from advanced positions under heavy shell fire. On several occasions he brought away as many as six men at a time. Once he drove his car (an unarmoured Ford) through a very intense barrage to the rescue of wounded men – the bursts of the shells at times lifting the car, which was riddled with fragments, right off the roadway. He was frequently under machine-gun fire during the performance of his duties in a retirement, and took his car into the rearguard to pick up wounded men. During one successful counter-attack, he was well in front of the armoured motor cars to bring back wounded left by the roadside until they could be got away. He continued at his duty with conspicuous courage until he was severely wounded'. This citation, loaded with self-sacrifice in the service of others, was published in the *London Gazette* of 3 September 1918.

A very typical ambulance driver's DCM citation is represented by that to Private L. Sell who was attached to No. 14 Field Ambulance: 'With an utter disregard of danger when roads have been under heavy shell and aircraft fire, this private has on many occasions shown marked courage in clearing cases by Ford ambulance from rear ambulance posts or from in front of those posts back to the collection posts. He has shown a complete disregard for his own safety, and a cheerfulness and willingness beyond all praise'. Driving an ambulance among the enemy was a rare feat of daring achieved by Private B. H. Sermon, who 'without being asked, drove his (ambulance) car through enemy outposts and evacuated all the wounded from an aid post, returning under heavy fire' in the Spring of 1918. Furthermore, he had evacuated wounded 'in full view of the enemy' for a period of 48 hours. That Sermon did not need to be asked, was certainly a point in favour of his DCM recommendation, which was duly authorised for the award of the medal.

## DRIVING AMMUNITION WAGONS
Those in charge of ammunition wagons knew their loads were dangerous and that their routes were fixed, with no possibility of

avoiding heavily shelled roads. Private (Acting Corporal) F. J. Greenall of Waltham Abbey was an Army Service Corps driver, 'in charge of four lorries with ammunition for a Siege Battery in a forward position'. Seeing that the road ahead was being heavily shelled, Greenall chose to leave two of his lorries behind and try to get through with the other two. His citation continues the story: 'One of these (lorries) was hit and disabled by a shell and the driver severely wounded. Corporal Greenall pushed on under heavy fire, and eventually arrived at the position, where he unloaded the ammunition himself, as there was no unloading party available at the time'. Pressing onward into a barrage with a load of heavy shells was carried out many times by ordinary men who could not help but consider their fate if their load suffered a direct hit. When an ammunition lorry was hit, it did not always blow up catastrophically, and so there were awards of the DCM made to the ASC for dealing with exploding ammunition. Sergeant P. A. Bush succeeded in moving ammunition from a wagon after one of the other wagons in his convoy had been hit and was burning fiercely. Private H. Wallace was driving an ammunition lorry in the early summer of 1917 when it was hit, 'His lorry, which was loaded with shells, caught fire'. Not tempted to run for it, 'He got inside the lorry, and succeeded in putting out the flames. His coolness and prompt action saved the lorry and a very serious explosion'. The medal for distinguished conduct issued to M2/082632 Sergeant R. Thompson was a New Year Honours award, appearing in the 1 January 1919 *Gazette*. His good services covered a number of dangerous acts involving ammunition over a period of time, but a portion of his published citation, which appeared in the *London Gazette* of 3 September 1919, relates to his actions at a gun battery under heavy shell fire:'On 19 May 1918, at Sailly Labourse, he pulled away burning camouflage, extinguished burning cartridges and saved a whole dump'.

## ON TWO WHEELS
Bicycles and motorcycles accompanied Army Service Corps men during their courageous actions only rarely, but two examples provide additional insight into the nature of ASC gallantry. Not always spectacular, their acts had consequences for the localised

continuance and success of the operations. Driver E. W. Halliday was in the habit of riding a bicycle alongside a convoy of horse-drawn supply wagons each night, probably in the capacity of a messenger. He won his DCM for clearing away dead horses and smashed limbers under heavy shell fire which enabled the convoy to proceed to its destination. The motorcycle despatch rider was of considerable importance during this war in which communications so often broke down. A great many runners won MMs for their work in the fighting arms, yet there are just four examples of DCMs won by the ASC for such activities as despatch riders. Three of these were periodic (Honours) awards, an example being that won by Private J. J. Hawker of Reading: 'For conspicuous gallantry and devotion to duty while acting as despatch rider throughout active operations. He has shown absolute contempt of danger while carrying despatches on heavily shelled roads both day and night'. Acting Lance-Corporal O. Dufour-Clark was attached to the 12th Brigade Ammunition Column, Royal Garrison Artillery as a motorcycle despatch rider and his immediate DCM was gazetted on 21June 1918: 'For consistent good and gallant work as a motor cyclist. He has never failed to deliver messages even when riding through shell fire. His motor cycle has twice been hit'.

## OFFICERS' REWARDS

Having now reviewed the awards of other ranks, we may now turn to officer's rewards for gallantry. Most of these were announced in Honours gazettes for good services over a period of time; the immediate award of the MC and DSO to Army Service Corps officers being quite scarce to rare.

The officers of the Army Service Corps gained rather few immediate awards of the MC and most of these were for acts similar to those resulting in the award of the DCM. Some MCs were made for displays of leadership but the story of the DCM is largely applicable also to the immediate MC. A small sample of 27 immediate MCs has been extracted from the *London Gazettes* which shows that one third (nine) were earned on attachment to the fighting arms (infantry, Machine Gun Corps, Tank Corps). Of the remainder, just four involved setting an example and encouraging the men around them; the remainder were awarded for what we might term 'routine acts of gallantry', for example fire fighting at ammunition dumps or for continuing an assigned task under shell fire. One that is worth quoting is the citation for the MC presented to Temporary 2nd Lieutenant Thomas Sharp Riley for his paternalistic behaviour towards his lorry drivers on roads near Observatory Ridge, 26 September 1917. Second Lieutenant Riley's lorries ran into heavy shell fire whilst engaged in getting supplies up to a dumping point. One of his drivers was wounded. 'With utter disregard for his personal safety, he carried the wounded man to a ditch, helped to dress his wounds, and then personally helped him to the nearest Aid Post. His coolness and devotion to duty not only ensured the delivery of valuable material, but also encouraged all the lorry drivers.' With such a figure looking after them, they had less to worry about. The danger seemed to them reduced as a result of Riley's care towards his men; they were encouraged to continue the work and to follow his example. This was a form of leadership that ordinary men really appreciated; with such men in charge of them, they found the strength to endure.

The Corps received only five immediate DSOs during the First World War; one of these was for work in supplying petrol, ammunition, rations and water to armoured car units in the early part of 1917 (Major Arthur Pereira). Another was for driving ammunition up to troops who had run out of ammunition (Major Vernon Conlan). Lieutenant Colonel Thomas Edwin Bennett received the DSO when he took charge of Brigade mule transport whilst they were moving 'ammunition, food and material to the front line, and suffering heavy casualties in doing so. He personally reconnoitred the ground and led the mules over the most dangerous and difficult parts of the track, at times wading thigh deep in water, and removing pack saddles from mules which had fallen into shell holes. He set a splendid example of coolness and devotion to duty'. This man's rank of Lt. Colonel assured him of the DSO, rather than the MC, yet there is no recognisable difference in the act for which more junior officers would receive the MC or for which NCOs might receive the DCM. There is just one immediate award of the DSO for large scale organisational skills; Major Henry Neville Watson was gazetted on 15 July 1919 for North Russia, being 'responsible for the organisation of all transport operating over a very large area during the operations 20 February to 4 April, Pinega area. He personally took charge of the transport column in the most forward area, and it was owing to him that its withdrawal under fire was uniformly successful'. This, then, represents a reward for organisational skill and power of command which remained undiminished when under enemy fire. Many DSO awardees across all units display similar characteristics.

In officers' awards, we therefore see a continuance of the general theme of doing one's assigned job under adverse conditions. There are not sufficient immediate awards of the DSO to gain any sense of whether it was about the recipients and their wider responsibilities that led to the award. These general aspects of officers' awards are brought out better by the study of other Army units.

The diversity of situations in which the Army Service Corps won its decorations for gallantry is far greater than for most other units. The only unit showing a comparably diverse set of awards is the Army Cyclist Corps, who fulfilled numerous roles other than as mobile infantry and scouting formations (a function largely denied to them by the nature of the static war on the Western Front).

# The Cavalry

Some of the grandest, most evocative, military paintings of all time have captured the cavalry in full charge, whether at the battle of Waterloo in 1815, on the Crimean Peninsula during 1854 or during the Boer War of 1899–1902. The British cavalry are imagined to be a throwback to battles of the nineteenth century and earlier, but they produced some typically Victorian heroes right up to the end of the 1914–18 war. But this was Victorian heroic imagery and the lot of the cavalry as a poorly utilised arm during the Great War was sealed in the last months of 1914. However, the flexibility, utility and, moreover, the value of the cavalry on the battlefields of the Great War are brought out when their medals for gallantry are reviewed. In particular, some of the awards made to cavalry officers illustrate the importance of a classical education when combined with a hunting background and a total belief in what it was they were fighting for; their country and our way of government.

In this chapter the mounted operations of British cavalry in 1914 will be reviewed followed by those of 1918. Then, the cavalry's dismounted operations, acting as 'emergency infantry' in certain actions of late 1914, during 1915 and during the Spring and early Summer of 1918 will be examined. The important work of the cavalry in Summer–Autumn 1918, in patrol work and in attack, will be reviewed. Finally, a review of the nature and importance of leadership will complete the chapter. In the analysis of awards, only the regular cavalry is included, the territorial and volunteer Yeomanry units are excluded from the statistics. However, the story of the Northumberland Hussars Yeomanry is included as a detailed example of cavalry activities in 1918.

The story of battlefield bravery preserved in cavalrymen's gallantry awards is quite distinct from other arms and is very revealing. The pre-1914 cavalryman's experience was largely one of small colonial wars against relatively poorly-equipped enemies. The fairly recent war against the Boers pointed the way to any future conflict against a well-equipped European enemy. It has been said that modern weapons almost permanently knocked the cavalry off their horses, sending them crawling in to the earthen trenches that their infantry brethren already knew well. But David Kenyon has argued that this is a fundamental misunderstanding of the utility of cavalry in the Great War. [15] In fact, the cavalry had adapted and prepared extremely well in the machine-gun age. Their mobility on the battlefield was greater than any other unit and it had already been noted in the Boer War that horsemen moving fast were very difficult to hit; that casualties from machine-gun fire would occur, but that those casualties would probably be lighter than those of slower moving infantrymen. (That moving targets are very difficult to hit was well displayed in the Second World War by naval anti-aircraft gunners, who expended vast amounts of ammunition in return for very few hits on incoming aircraft). Very rapidly, cavalry could ride over enemy positions, giving an enemy very little time to develop a stiff resistance. There was certainly scope for greater use of cavalry on the Western Front than was actually achieved, but even in the conditions of the western front, horsemen successfully charged the machine guns and artillery batteries of a modern army.

## THE CAVALRY CHARGE AND THE FLASH OF STEEL

In the defensive actions of March 1918, Albert Turp, a Farrier Sergeant with the 1st Dragoon Guards, was involved in a charge against German infantry at Villeselve, about 12 miles SW of St. Quentin: 'We took the Germans quite by surprise and they faced us as best they could, for there can't be anything more frightening to an infantryman than the site of a line of cavalry charging at full gallop with swords drawn... As our line overrode the Germans I made a regulation point at a man on my offside and my sword went through his neck and out the other side. The pace of my horse carried my sword clear and then I took a German on my nearside, and I remember the jar as my point took him in the collar bone and knocked him over ... as we galloped on, the enemy broke and ran'.

## Distinguished Conduct Medal, Cavalry, Categories

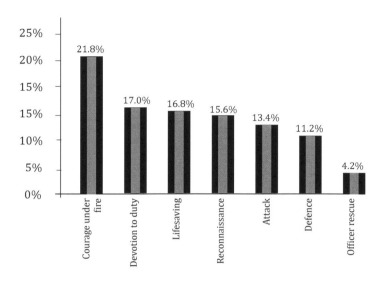

| Activity | % |
|---|---|
| In Trenches | 23.4 |
| Messages | 19.3 |
| Period of Time | 18.8 |
| Machine Gun | 10.4 |
| Stretcher Bearer | 5.7 |
| Bombing Squad | 4.7 |
| Supporting Infantry | 2.6 |
| Sniper | 2.6 |
| Raid | 2.6 |
| Organisation of Horses | 2.08 |
| Sword | 1.56 |
| Bayonet | 1.56 |
| Buried Men | 1.56 |
| Guide | 1.04 |
| Dressing Horses Wounds | 1.04 |
| Armoured Cars | 1.04 |

| Rank | % |
|---|---|
| Pte/Tpr/Bdsmn/Trptr | 23 |
| Corporal | 28 |
| Sergeant | 42 |
| Warrant Officer | 6 |
| Ptes etc. & Corporals | 51 |
| Sergeants & Warrant Offs | 49 |
| NCOs | 77 |
| Mounted | 46% |
| Honours DCMs | ?% |

**Figure 31: Analysis of the Distinguished Conduct Medal, Regular Cavalry**

*Results of a sample of 358 Cavalry DCM – Yeomanry awards excluded*

## Military Cross, Cavalry, Categories

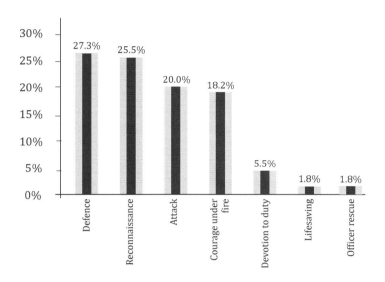

| Activity | % |
|---|---|
| In Trenches | 38.1 |
| Supporting Infantry | 16.7 |
| Messages | 11.9 |
| Machine Gun | 11.9 |
| Bombing Squad | 9.5 |
| Period of Time | 7.1 |
| Sword | 2.4 |
| Raid | 2.4 |
| Stretcher Bearer | 0.0 |
| Sniper | 0.0 |
| Organisation of Horses | 0.0 |
| Bayonet | 0.0 |
| Buried Men | 0.0 |
| Guide | 0.0 |
| Dressing Horses Wounds | 0.0 |
| Armoured Cars | 0.0 |

| Rank | % |
|---|---|
| Warrant Officer | 11 |
| 2nd Lieutenant | 22 |
| Lieutenant | 38 |
| Captain | 29 |
| Major | 0 |

| Mounted | 24% |
|---|---|

| Honours MCs | ?% |
|---|---|

**Figure 32: Analysis of the Military Cross, Regular Cavalry**

*Results of a sample of 55 Cavalry MCs – Yeomanry excluded*

## Distinguished Service Order, Cavalry, Categories

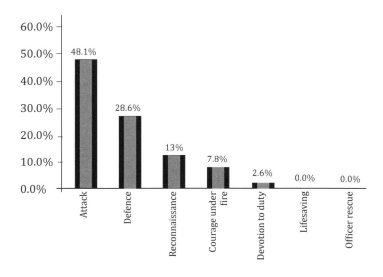

| Activity | % |
|---|---|
| In Trenches | 68.1 |
| Supporting Infantry | 8.5 |
| Machine Gun | 4.3 |
| Period of Time | 4.3 |
| Armoured Cars | 4.3 |
| Raid | 4.3 |
| Sword | 2.1 |
| Messages | 2.1 |
| Bombing Squad | 2.1 |
| Stretcher Bearer | 0.0 |
| Sniper | 0.0 |
| Organisation of Horses | 0.0 |
| Bayonet | 0.0 |
| Buried Men | 0.0 |
| Guide | 0.0 |
| Dressing Horses Wounds | 0.0 |

| Rank | % |
|---|---|
| 2nd Lieutenant | 5 |
| Lieutenant | 6 |
| Captain | 21 |
| Major | 21 |
| Lt. Colonel | 39 |
| Brigadier General | 6 |

| Mounted | 24% |
|---|---|

| Honours DSOs | 60% |
|---|---|

**Figure 33: Analysis of the Distinguished Service Order, Regular Cavalry**

*Results of a sample of all 77 Cavalry DSOs – Yeomanry excluded*

Of the 150 men involved, in spite of encountering machine-gun fire, only six were killed (although over 60 were slightly wounded).[16]

'Those who have never felt the sensation of a really good horse bounding and stretching away under them, and the consequent elation, the wonder as to 'what could stop us?' cannot grasp what a cavalry soldier's feelings are in the 'Charge'. So said Major General Rimington in his book, *Our Cavalry*, published in 1912.[17] The cavalry ideal, then, was to ride knee-to-knee in close formation, charge at the enemy from an unexpected direction, from cover of ground, and to 'ride over him' crashing like a wall of great beasts and flashing steel. Rimington again: 'It cannot be too often repeated that the main thing is to carry out the mission at any price. If possible this should be done mounted and with the arm blanche...'.[18] Rimington tells of the joy of battle in the following: '...though they must know some cannot come back, still they like to be deceived, to die, or to be maimed, fierce, high-hearted, happy and elated'.[19]

Well executed cavalry actions usually suffered relatively light casualties, particularly when in the moments before impact, a panicked enemy made wild shooting at a rapidly moving target. If performed correctly, the charge (shock action) ought to be relatively safe as well as decisive. However, the opportunities for shock action were, according to Kenyon, severely limited by the command structure of the cavalry divisions during the Great War.

The above emphasis on shock action and the moral effect of charging as a body of determined men, and using cold steel, explains the similar emphasis placed upon the use of the bayonet in the infantry.

**BRAVERY IN THE SADDLE**

*There's something poignant about a riderless horse coming out of battle.*

Although it is difficult to assess exactly how gallantry awards of the cavalry regiments were won, in the saddle or dismounted, an assessment has been made which suggests that approximately half of all DCMs were awarded for mounted service, much of which involved mounted reconnaissance and patrol work. One of the most important functions, in practice, of the cavalry in the Great War, was in patrol work. Small parties of fast-moving horsemen were, like Nelson's frigates, 'the eyes and ears' of the Army. A good patrol leader was self-reliant, full of cunning, took risks and stalked the enemy like a fox using the cover of the land. He often worked at night when things could be done that were impossible in daytime. Cavalry scouting patrols routinely encountered a well-armed enemy in superior numbers. Those who persisted in looking closer, in moving further into enemy territory, to establish a fuller picture, rather than being prudent and turning for safety early, would soon come to notice. When there seemed only the chance of getting a bullet, the audacious cavalry scout – sometimes alone – could find strength in his sense of duty to comrades, in his training and from the expectations and spirit of his officers and his unit. There were many such awards for scouting up to and among enemy positions throughout the war, and these represent some of the most courageous actions of the cavalryman in the Great War.

Early war awards from 1914 document a period of fluid fighting and in particular record encounters with machine guns. Private A. C. Barnes of the 5th Dragoon Guards was presented with a DCM when, 'during an attack... he was in charge of his section doing advance guard to his squadron and rode unwaveringly through heavy machine-gun fire to his objective. Single-handed he attacked a small group of enemy non-commissioned officers who were trying to organise the defence, and killed three and took three prisoners. He displayed splendid courage and dash throughout'. Also of the 5th Dragoon Guards, Sergeant F. Langford won his DCM, 'For handling his troop with great coolness and determination, killing one officer, nine Uhlans and 16 horses, and by getting round the enemy's flank brought a well-directed hit to bear on the hostile supports'. With a mounted patrol, Private E. Bush of the 3rd (King's Own) Hussars received his DCM, 'For the gallantry and coolness displayed at Longueil on 30 August 1914, when on patrol duty he successfully ambushed 10 German cavalrymen'. Very soon after the beginning of the war on the Western Front in 1914, cavalry actions became more infrequent and the cavalry lost men to other units and generally suffered a slow reduction in strength as the war went on.

During the second half of 1918, the cavalry were able to make a renewed and valuable contribution, amongst tanks and against field gun and machine gun batteries. Exhibiting remarkable courage and determination in a mounted attack on enemy positions, Corporal W. Reardon of the 9th Lancers won the DCM as follows: 'After his horse had been shot in a charge he took a Hotchkiss gun from a derelict tank and fired it with great skill and effect until a withdrawal was ordered. He then ran across the open to another tank and directed its fire on the enemy machine guns at close range, he himself sitting on the outside of the tank under very heavy fire'. Captain Nigel Kennedy Worthington was attached to the 3rd Dragoon Guards on 9 October 1918 when, in the aftermath of the German collapse and retreat from Cambrai, he led the advanced squadron in a charge to capture Honnechy. The citation for the bar to his Military Cross states: 'By his dash, the regiment gained its objective under very heavy artillery and machine-gun fire, with comparatively slight loss. Later in the day he took command of two squadrons, and then of the regiment when his commanding officer was wounded. Throughout the operations his courage and leading were beyond praise'. Similarly, Lieutenant Richard Twopenny won the second of his Military Crosses near Ypres on 31 July 1917, when his mounted squadron was suddenly caught by machine-gun fire. After his squadron leader and the second in command were both hit, Lt. Twopenny immediately had the men dismount, 'took command of the squadron and led them under heavy machine-gun fire to their objective, which he held until relieved on the following day'. His calmness under fire and quick positive action undoubtedly steadied the men, allowing him to lead them forward, and secured his prestigious bar to the MC.

Pte J. Sheehan, 17th Lancers, gained his DCM in Egypt, for an attack near the Jordan River on 23 September 1918. 'He assisted in the capture of a position from which seven machine guns and about 200 infantry were harassing the outflanking movement of the detachment. With conspicuous gallantry he charged right up to the machine guns under very heavy fire, and assisted in their capture. During this fight his horse was shot under him'.

Sergeant H. N. Watts of the 19th Hussars attacked not machine guns but, far more unusually, an artillery battery, in an act strongly reminiscent of the Victorian era: 'For conspicuous gallantry and able leadership on 8 October 1918, between Braucourt and Bohain. He led his troop in a charge against a battery which was firing at point-blank range, personally shooting five of the gunners with his revolver. When he had passed through the position he coolly rallied what remained of the troop and brought them back to the squadron'.

The cavalry still charged 'into the Valley of Death' in World War One (as they did at Balaklava in 1854), and still helped to save the guns (as some of them did in the South African war at Colenso, 1900); mounted soldiers still dashed out and rescued comrades from under the noses of the enemy and still received awards for being 'first into the enemy positions'. These were all classically Victorian heroic acts for which the Victoria Cross might have been awarded in earlier conflicts. In his very useful study of the Victoria Cross, M. C. Smith has highlighted how the First World War forced the concept of gallantry to evolve rapidly away from the Victorian heroic ideal and move to a much more modern concept, in which the hero would in future have to kill the enemy in order to be considered for a Victoria Cross. While this certainly appears to be true of the Victoria Cross, the Victorian hero lived on in the more abundant awards, the DSO, MC, DCM and MM. Not only that, but more than any other unit of the British Army, it was the cavalry regiments which provided the Victorian hero with his last and most enduring refuge, as the following rewards show.

Sergeant S. W. Roshier was 'first into the breach' at the storming of an enemy position when, 'He advanced with his unarmoured car and machine gun... and was actually first into the enemy's gun position'. We are left to imagine the storm of fire, for there is no more substance to this citation, which was sufficient to gain a cavalryman a DCM. Sergeant W. H. Tetheridge of the 13th Hussars took extraordinary risks to retrieve one of the Regiment's machine guns which disappeared off the back of a horse in 1914: 'During a mounted attack a horse carrying a machine gun broke loose. After several attempts he succeeded in catching it among the trenches occupied by the enemy and brought it in under heavy fire. He showed splendid coolness and resource'. The event is close to comical, a sensation that cannot have been lost on the Germans as they watched with some incredulity a man chasing a horse within and behind their lines. Whether carried out mounted or dismounted we do not know, but it may be the case that the decisive factor in the award of a DCM was not, what happened, but the presence of a valuable machine gun on the horse's back. In that sense, the award may be viewed as denying the enemy a symbolic prize, or as a 'saving the guns' DCM. It is comparable to one of those 'Boy's Own' deeds that thrilled the Empire.

True, 'saving the guns' DCMs are typically found among the awards made to the Royal Field and Royal Horse Artillery during the first months of the war in 1914. Yet, two were won by Sergeants of the 9th Lancers, who got involved with saving the guns of the 119th Battery, Royal Field Artillery, near Doube, on the 24 August. Sergeants G. Davids and A. W. Turner assisted 'by manhandling them into shelter, only three gunners of the Battery being left alive'.

## THE CAVALRY SWORD

On the Western Front, there was still opportunity for the cavalry sword to be used in anger, too. On a reconnaissance patrol, Corporal Bodman of the 2nd Dragoon Guards gained his DCM when, 'he penetrated behind the enemy line and entered a village, capturing many prisoners. Although under heavy machine-gun fire from the flanks practically the whole time, he pushed forward, using his sword, and obtained much valuable information. He did very fine work'. Sergeant A. Ford of the same regiment got the DCM for similar actions, 'while in charge of a patrol during an attack. He kept close touch with the advancing infantry, and sent back valuable information. Later, he pushed forward through the infantry, using his sword with great determination, regardless of machine-gun fire, and co-operated with an officer commanding another patrol and captured 70 prisoners'. Perhaps the best example of swordsmanship to be preserved in the records of the Distinguished Conduct Medal is the award made to 3999 Squadron Sergeant Major W. Wright of the 6th Dragoon Guards. His citation reads: 'For conspicuous gallantry near Messines on 1 November 1914. When taking a message to an advanced troop he was attacked by Germans, through whom he cut his way, killing five of them, and then delivered his message. Two days previously he acted in a similarly gallant manner'. Whilst the 4th Cavalry Brigade, which included the 6th Dragoon Guards and was defending the Wytschaete-Messines Ridge in the last days of October and into early November 1914, was already acting in a dismounted capacity, it seems most likely that Sqn. Sgt. Mjr. Wright was indeed mounted for the purposes of delivering messages and that he used his sword deftly. Officers too, used their swords in action, even in late 1918. For example, Lieutenant Frederick William Byass (19th Hussars) was honoured with the Military Cross (*London Gazette* of 1 February 1919) for his actions on the 8 October 1918, between Brancourt and Bohain; 'He led his troop in a charge against two of the enemy's battery positions, which were supported by infantry and machine guns. He killed several of the enemy himself with his sword and revolver… His coolness was beyond praise'. This officer was involved in the same action for which Sgt. Watts got his DCM (page 233).

## LIFESAVING ON HORSEBACK

In the cavalry, the rescue of an officer was between three and five times more likely to be rewarded with a DCM than in any other unit. Just over 4 per cent of cavalry DCMs was made for rescuing the officers, who were often members of the British aristocracy; the cavalry was more aristocratic than other units and so England had more to gain by preserving these officers and the cavalry knew it. There are many classic Victorian 'officer rescues', often carried out on horseback, and the cavalry were still doing this and being rewarded for it in 1918. Whilst in previous wars they might have won the Victoria Cross, the act of officer rescue was not considered suitable for the award of the prestigious bronze cross after the Boer War. But the act lived on in the DCMs awarded to, for example, 8390 L/Cpl J. Bowstead of the 4th Hussars, 'For bringing in a wounded officer under heavy fire' and to three men of the 14th Hussars who 'assisted to carry (their) Troop Officer a distance of 1,000 yards under intense fire'. Two men of the 19th (Queen Alexandra's Own Royal) Hussars received the DCM 'in trying to rescue Major McClure who was wounded, under a heavy close range fire'. One of the most impressive for its Victorian flavour, is the award made to 861 Lance Corporal R. A. Ballard of the 21st (Empress of India's) Lancers on the North West Frontier of India, who 'endeavoured to save his commanding officer, whose horse had been shot, and afterwards kept the enemy away from his body until he could secure help to bring it in'. This, in a former conflict, was sufficient for a Victoria Cross, but Ballard got the DCM.

The 21st Lancers only gained three DCMs between 1914 and 1919; all were for lifesaving up on the North West Frontier of India and all three men were classic Victorian heroes. Regimental Sergeant-Major E. N. Ryder, 'picked up a comrade who was hanging by his foot from the stirrup, placed him on his own horse, and charged through the enemy, by whom he was surrounded'. Saddler Staff-Sergeant W. A. Simpson, 'dismounted and rescued a comrade by shooting a tribesman, and then went on foot to the assistance of an officer of his regiment and held off the enemy with his revolver. The officer was mortally wounded, and Sergeant Simpson was hit in the shoulder and badly hacked about by swordsmen, before he was rescued by some other men of the regiment'. As is evident, the 21st Lancers were isolated from the changes to heroic ideals that were occurring on the Western Front in France and Flanders. Even there, there was still room for Sergeant B. D. Hull of the 14th Hussars to show his mettle when, during a withdrawal, he 'returned under heavy fire and rescued a Sergeant who had been shot through the head, placing him on his own horse and bringing him out of action'. Sergeant Hull was also recommended for good mounted reconnaissance work as Troop leader.

Lifesaving was a theme in the cavalry. The abundance of lifesaving

DCMs among cavalry recipients is second only to the Royal Army Medical Corps, whose speciality was lifesaving. It is a remarkable feature of the cavalry of 1914–18 that 21 per cent of DCMs were awarded for lifesaving acts, compared to between 3 and 13 per cent in most other units. Aside from the RAMC, the nearest to the cavalry with 18 per cent lifesaving awards was, perhaps not surprisingly, the Tank Corps; the new, armoured, cavalry.

## TENDING WOUNDED HORSES

Losing the wounded, or losing comrades, has always been a painful experience. Those who worked with horses in that war became very attached to their animals and painfully felt their wounding and passing away. We have already touched on this aspect in relation to the Army Service Corps. Gallantry awards made to cavalrymen in charge of the horses' welfare are very scarce, there being just six DCM awards spread across all regular cavalry regiments during the First World War. In overall charge of the regiment's horses was the Farrier Staff Sergeant, and it was he who often looked after them when the regiment rode up to the line, dismounted and went into action as infantry. When the 5th Lancers went into action against enemy machine guns in a house on 10 November 1918, Guernsey-born Sergeant C. Baudains, 'showed great coolness in moving led horses of the troop out of heavy shell fire' before getting around the flank of the houses and thus 'forced the enemy to withdraw'. Farrier Quartermaster Sergeant C. Landgraff of the 6th (Inniskilling) Dragoons got his DCM for exemplary devotion to duty: 'Whenever the regiment has been in action he has shown great gallantry attending to horses under heavy fire, and showing absolute disregard for danger'. Similarly, in the 4th (Royal Irish) Dragoon Guards, it was Squadron Sergeant Major H. Rowlatt who 'has invariably been the greatest help to his squadron commander, and has shown great initiative and foresight in the placement of his squadron's led horses when all officers have been absent in dismounted action. By his skilful choosing of cover he has undoubtedly saved many horses, and by his complete disregard of personal danger he has at all times in action given a fine example to the men of his squadron'.

In the 7th Dragoon Guards, Farrier Staff-Sergeant L. Keating earned his DCM when: 'At Le Cateau, on 10 October 1918, he was severely wounded by two shells whilst attending to wounded horses, one of which was killed whilst he was dressing its wounds. On several other occasions he has undoubtedly been the cause of saving many good horses which have been badly wounded. By his fine example and cheerfulness under very trying circumstances he has gained the admiration of all ranks'.

## RECONNAISSANCE WORK

During 1918, one of the primary functions of the cavalry was as the reconnaissance arm of the Army. Operating in advance of friendly forces, or sometimes behind enemy lines, many were the scrapes. Sergeant F. Walkington, 8th Hussars, gained a DCM, 'when with a patrol which had been completely cut off. In the dash for escape he steadied the leading men, whilst the officer brought up the rear, and although exposed to fire at 150 yards, he successfully extracted the patrol'. Corporal W. A. Singer of the 12th Lancers received his DCM, 'For conspicuous gallantry and valuable service at Hestrud on 10 November 1918, in command of the leading section of the advanced troop. Having been stopped by heavy machine-gun fire, he got his horses under cover and took up a very exposed forward position, whence he observed and sent back most excellent reports as to the enemy's positions. Meanwhile the enemy put down a very heavy artillery and machine gun barrage between his post and the infantry. Having located two machine guns, he personally took the information back, and successfully gave his information to the leading company commander'. Private C. E. V. MacDonald of Fort Rose (Ross-shire) was perhaps less lucky, but made the most of his situation all the same: 'While he was lying on the ground, stunned by the fall of his horse, which had been shot under him, the enemy came up and commenced to kick him. He feigned death, was able to note the hostile positions, and crawled in after dark with very valuable information'.

## BRAVERY OUT OF THE SADDLE

When the shooting started, the cavalry often dismounted. In

the difficult conditions of static trench warfare the cavalry was prevented, by Army Generals as much as by conditions, from operating in the mobile manner to which it was accustomed. Instead, cavalrymen operated as infantry on many occasions, starting in late 1914 and continuing at various times throughout 1915, 1916 and 1917. In these conditions, cavalry officers received gallantry medals for battlefield leadership. A Military Cross was presented to Captain Stewart Graham Menzies, DSO, 2nd Life Guards for a dismounted action in front of Ypres on 13 May 1915; 'after his commanding officer had been wounded, (he) displayed conspicuous ability, coolness and resource in controlling the action of his regiment and rallying the men'. His DSO was won on 7 November 1914 when he was involved in an attack (almost certainly another dismounted action) against a German position. During early 1916, 2nd Lieutenant Derek Stuart-Saville of the 12th Lancers gained an MC, 'when in charge of bombers' on 2 to 3 February. He 'led his men with great coolness' into a recently exploded mine crater, which he held 'under heavy fire'. Second Lt. Frank Moxon Stout of the 20th Hussars was rewarded with an MC for a technically dismounted action, which was nonetheless remarkable for this officer's obvious comfort sat upon any creature's back. When Stout discovered an enemy working party in his vicinity during the night of the 25 January 1916, he took a corporal and a light machine gun with him and made off down a sap, when: 'mounted on the corporal's back, Lieutenant Stout opened fire.... Next morning 14 dead enemy were counted, and more must have been wounded'. Both Stout's and Stuart-Saville's MCs were announced in the *London Gazette* of 15 March 1916. Acting Captain James K. McConnel, also of the 20th Hussars had won a DSO as a Lieutenant in 1914 (dismounted, at Messines in late October to early November 1914) and won his MC on 9 October 1917, near Boesinghe for organising the Brigade in their forming up position and later undertaking a dangerous reconnaissance of enemy positions after the attack had concluded successfully. The citation states: 'His brilliant staff work contributed largely to the success of the brigade', illustrating nicely the dual roles that some officers undertook; that of traditional field officer gathering intelligence and leading men into battle, but also as the planners and executors of large-scale operations. Crouching in an isolated position and getting heavily fired on was no fun, but an officer's cheerful bearing and fearless example could be relied upon to help get men through, and so it was for Lieutenant Francis Collingwood Drake of the 10th Hussars at Monchy on 11 April 1917: 'He organised and defended a detached post with great resource and ability, despite heavy casualties. His cheerfulness and example under very heavy fire were most marked'. More typical of an infantry NCO's award, the DCM awarded to Corporal of Horse H. T. Bishop, Household Cavalry illustrates the nature of trench fighting that the cavalry had to endure for several years: 'With five men he captured an enemy "pill-box" and over 20 prisoners. He held it with two men until his ammunition gave out, and was then captured by two of the enemy'. Not willing to admit defeat, however, Bishop remarkably 'managed to lead them into our lines, and so received them both as prisoners'.

## DEFENSIVE ACTIONS OF THE CAVALRY
During the Spring Offensives of March to May 1918, the cavalry and dismounted Yeomanry units assisted very ably in the defence, often equipped with the French light machine gun, the Hotchkiss. These guns, equivalent to the infantry Lewis gun, but slightly shorter and lighter, supported the hard-pressed infantry and provided anchor points in the line in the same way as the machine gun corps. The machine guns carried by the cavalry made them more of a potent force than at first might be suspected. Early in the war each regiment carried Maxim or Vickers heavy machine guns, whereas later in the war, many units were equipped with the Hotchkiss. Lance Corporal A. H. Smart, 5th Lancers won a DCM in an action very reminiscent of many of the machine gun corps at this time: 'For very great gallantry on 30 October near Hollebeeke, when he continued to serve his machine gun with great bravery although shot in the mouth and shoulder'. During fighting in the trenches, Squadron Sergeant-Major E. Percival of the Dragoon Guards was present when an enemy bombing attack was launched against his

men: 'he rallied his men and, by moving up and down the line, set a splendid example'. Private R. G. Larkin of the 16th Lancers defended his section of trench against an enemy incursion: 'For... holding the corner of a traverse single-handed for one hour, thereby enabling the erection of a barricade which prevented any further advance of the enemy'.

In the defence of Spring 1918, there are awards that could have been made to almost any of the fighting arms, for example Sergeant W. Martin of the 5th Lancers won his DCM: 'For conspicuous gallantry and devotion to duty in rallying the remnants of his troop and encouraging them to continue fighting. When ordered to retire he remained to the last, and was for some time alone in the trench with the enemy, but succeeded in getting away after covering the retirement of his men'. In that great defensive action, many grand tales of the cavalry's Hotchkiss guns were recorded. Sergeant W. McHardy was one of the few cavalrymen who already had a Military Medal to his credit when he carried out this act of gallantry with the 2nd Dragoons (Royal Scots Greys): 'For conspicuous gallantry and devotion to duty while in charge of a post of 40 men and two Hotchkiss guns. The troops on his flanks had withdrawn, but, having received no orders to retire, he held his post for six hours against vastly superior numbers of the enemy, until nearly surrounded, when he fought his way back over a canal, bringing all his party with him. He was severely wounded early in the engagement, but his coolness and courage did much to maintain the steadiness of his men in an action against overwhelming odds'.

## CAVALRYMEN IN TRENCH RAIDS

Some tasks allotted to the cavalry appear to have been a little specialised, for example when involved in trench raids, normally the domain of the infantry and a couple of Royal Engineers demolition experts. A pair of DCMs was awarded to two privates of the 5th Dragoon Guards for their contribution to a raid when they boldly attempted to blow a gap in the enemy wire through which the raiding party would pass. However, after Corporal F. A. Chiselton had placed, and successfully fired, one of the charges, the enemy immediately opened up a heavy fire with two machine guns at 20 yards range, killing and injuring some of the raiding party. It was then that Private D. Bisset stood up and 'regardless of danger' tried to place a second charge in position. Meanwhile, Chiselton was continuing 'for some time to cut the wire by hand, until ordered to withdraw'.

## SNIPING

Several awards were made to cavalry operating as snipers in the trenches, for example Corporal of Horse. P.A. Macintosh of the Life Guards, gained his DCM when he 'did good work as sniper on various occasions'. Another Corporal of Horse, W. H. E. Briton of the Dragoon Guards, got his medal 'when acting as sniping corporal. He showed total disregard of personal danger in lying out in front of the line in isolated and dangerous positions for long periods, and thereby collecting much valuable information'. Private Slater, also of the Dragoon Guards, 'invariably volunteered for the most dangerous duties, and on one occasion he remained in front of the trenches for three days, sniping'. On occasion, those with the aptitude for dangerous tasks volunteered for them because it was better than the terrible boredom of kicking one's heels in the trenches.

Other tasks were assigned to the cavalry, much as miscellaneous tasks were assigned to any unit on the Western Front. Cavalrymen won bravery medals under fire in back areas, whilst engaged in the transport of stores up the line, for guiding infantry units to their new positions in or out of the line and for running messages. The flavour of awards relating to these types of act are well covered elsewhere so are not repeated here.

## THE NORTHUMBERLAND HUSSARS YEOMANRY

The experience of the Northumberland Hussars (a mounted regiment of the Territorial Army) in 1918 was quite typical of many cavalry units; a brief review of their awards for the final year of war serves to illustrate how their role changed in that year as well as some of the scrapes they got into. Early in 1918, the order came through that all Territorial cavalry regiments not in a Brigade should

245

be permanently dismounted. Further, they were to take up bicycles and become a cyclist battalion. The horses of the Northumberland Hussars Yeomanry were separated off and sent elsewhere, saddlery was handed in and the Hotchkiss guns were loaded up on lorries to be given to other units. This was ongoing on 20 March 1918, the day before the first day of the German offensives. When the warning order 'Prepare for Attack' came through, the machine guns were quickly recovered from the lorries and re-issued. As a result, 13 Hotchkiss guns loaded on limbers and with ample small arms ammunition, were ready with their dismounted teams to face the massive German assault over the following days. At 08:30am on the 21st, these gun teams marched out to cover the crossings of the Croizat Canal, Somme region, and were split up to cover different positions. In the mist, visual signalling was impossible and communications had to be made solely by means of runners, who were found from the regiment's signal section. The regimental history was published by Howard Pease after the war and in it he states that the signallers 'had to move about all day in very heavy shell fire, and their devotion to duty was magnificent'. Notwithstanding this praise, not one of these men received a bravery decoration. The honours went to the men in charge of the Hotchkiss gun teams who skilfully engaged and delayed the German advance, even though they were outflanked, until all of their guns were put out of action. The Hussars' gun teams, 'by their gallantry and knowledge of the country and open warfare' enabled an infantry Brigade to escape to safety after being surrounded, and from a situation which seemed to be 'certain disaster'.[20] In an action of this sort, it was necessary to move the gun positions frequently in order to keep a step ahead of the enemy and to avoid being sighted and destroyed.

For their rearguard action of 21–23 March 1918, the Northumberland Hussars were awarded one Military Cross, two DCMs and four Military Medals. The MC was awarded to a Lieutenant A. E. V. Brumell for his organisation and control of the defence and the positioning of the guns. His skilful work was viewed as having been critical to the success of the operation: 'he showed great initiative, devotion to duty and skill in the placing and handling of these guns, and... by the way they were placed and moved at intervals, undoubtedly barred the way to the Germans and caused much delay, besides inflicting very severe casualties'. Two of the Squadron Sergeant-Majors received DCMs; one was Frederick W. Peacock of Sunderland and the other was Edgar Nicholson. The gun teams under these men's charge were sent to different positions, but both men 'kept the men in hand' under severe enemy fire. Peacock personally kept in touch with his teams, and 'all the time showed remarkable coolness and bravery, having to be continuously moving through severe enemy fire of all sorts'. Nicholson was severely wounded in the fighting, and at the end of the action was the only survivor of three gun teams. Both men, once the Hotchkiss guns were knocked out, kept their men firing with their rifles 'until the end came'. The DCMs therefore went to the men who kept the more junior ranks fighting against overwhelming odds and in the face of death; it was no mean feat. The four MMs went to a Sergeant, a Lance-Corporal and two Privates; the Sergeant was, like Peacock and Nicholson, in command of a Hotchkiss gun detachment, and his MM citation is indistinguishable from the DCM citations. We must conclude that three DCMs were considered one too many and that the awards list would be 'unbalanced' if three DCMs and three MMs were to be allowed. Further, we may conclude that Sergeant Peter McMillan had been ranked third in order of merit. His acts were the same as those of the more senior NCOs, but his more junior rank and the fact of acting under the wings of Squadron Sergeant Majors was against him in the final judgement. The MM citations for Lance-Corporal John W. Robson and Corporal Alfred W. Fisher reveal that these two were in charge of individual gun teams, and that they were probably the two most successful of the teams involved in the fighting. Corporal Fisher, 'stuck to his gun and kept it working in most praiseworthy style, and, when his flanks were turned, remained with his gun, mowing down the enemy masses until his gun was knocked out. He then kept the remnants of his section together and fought a rearguard action with the nearest troops until they were withdrawn, and finally arrived at Noyon, having been in action for four days'. Lance-Corporal Robson was watching the situation in his area develop, when he saw the enemy getting into their positions. Seeing the infantry counter-attack to recover the lost positions, and without receiving any orders, Robson quickly 'brought his gun and team forward to a flank and, by opening fire as the infantry advanced and doing much damage, greatly contributed to the delay of the enemy on this part of the line. Soon afterwards his gun was knocked out, but he continued fighting with his rifles for four days (with the nearest troops) and rejoined at Noyon'. Private J. L. Anderson's MM citation indicates that he did similar work until he was the only survivor and his gun was damaged. He then carried the damaged gun around with him rather than abandon it, and continued to fight with rifle alongside other troops, even though he was the only man of his unit, rejoining the regiment several days later. Anderson showed, 'not only great bravery during this strenuous rearguard action, but, in dragging along a damaged gun and fighting for several days, he displayed great devotion to duty', concludes the citation. Comparing the DCM awards with the MM awards, we may conclude that the MMs were arguably the more pure 'fighting awards'. The two DCMs were expressly for the leadership and example set by the senior NCOs, whose presence and paternalism alone was sufficient to bolster the defence along hundreds of metres of the front line. Had those NCOs been absent, the defence might have crumbled and the MMs absent from the final reckoning.

Once the German Spring offensives had exhausted themselves one after the other, the Northumberland Hussars once again became a mounted cavalry unit. On 8 August 1918, the first great blow to the German Army was launched by combined British and Canadian Divisions in front of Amiens with the backing of massed tanks, many of which were of new types. Mobile cavalry rapidly showed their worth, for example when a mounted patrol of the Northumberland Hussars, on the evening of the 9 August, 'proved once again the value of good cavalry well used; the information obtained (by the patrol) was in great measure responsible for the Division's attack on the following day'.[21] Two Military Medals went to the members of this patrol, for their work which had such a great influence on the military operations at Divisional scale. Lance-Corporal Robert Ord: 'was sent out with a patrol north-east of Bois-des-Celestins, in front of the infantry. Though fired on from one point, he went to another in order to try and find out the extent of the line, and, though he and his patrol were under continuous fire, he was able to hand in a most exact location of the enemy's line, which proved to be of very great value'. Private Thomas Gurwen Watson's MM award citation is not a little spectacular for its display of courage: 'This man, when fired on, went on with great dash, right up to the German position, and by this means obtained the exact location of the enemy, thereby being of great assistance to the patrol leader'. Given the daring nature of the patrol and its far-reaching military consequences, one wonders why a DCM was not given to either of these men.

Many of the Northumberland Hussars' gallantry awards of the last six months of war were for gallantry on patrol work, which was mostly carried out mounted. However, the regiment's 'finest moment' came on the 22 August 1918, near Bray-sur-Somme, when in combination with fast, new whippet tanks and with aircraft support, both unimaginable in 1914, they were ordered to charge enemy positions on high ground to the front. It is not known whether such cooperation had been tried before, but it must rank as one of the first and last such combined operations. The Northumberland Hussars mounted and trotted off for action; ahead, an enemy reportedly demoralised and retiring rapidly; behind, cheering infantry and the dust kicked up by the forward squadron, on a still, misty and warm summer's morning. The Hussars' pace quickened, forward over a railway line, across slight undulations of ground, meeting sporadic rifle fire, but there was not a sign of the tanks in support. The objective, a rise to the front, lay across a main road where enemy shelling was heavy. With friendly aircraft buzzing the enemy, they 'pressed on, dashing over the Bray-Meaulte road at full gallop, over the bend in the railway, down the steep slopes of the valley, and so up the other side on to the flat – there to be met by the most terrible fire imaginable from every weapon and from all sides. In front were a huge wire entanglement and a sunken road... machine-gun fire was coming from behind the wire; there was enfilade fire from the north and south... bombs were falling from the sky, the German guns firing with open sights'. Squadron Sergeant Major J. E. Dickinson, of Ashington, Northumberland, was leading the charge when his horse was shot under him, 'close to the enemy machine guns'. Major Rea was one of many who were hit close to the German wire, at point-blank range. Seeing the Major was wounded, his orderly, Private Arthur Oliver, and the Squadron's trumpeter, Cherrington, whose horses had also been shot under them, attempted to get him away on foot. Cherrington was severely wounded by the explosion of a shell in their midsts, yet Oliver carried his officer unaided, on his back and through heavy machine-gun and shell fire, a distance of three miles over trenches and stretches of wire entanglement, to safety.[22] The Major survived. Trumpeter F. Cherrington died where he fell but Private Oliver was awarded the Military Medal for an act that was typical of certain Victoria Cross awards of previous wars, illustrating how the DCM and MM took some of the Victorian heroic acts away from the VC.

During the charge, Private Nicholas was carrying the flag of the Commanding Officer attached to a lance. After he was wounded and had to leave his horse behind, he 'struggled on, still bearing his lance, with the flag. Weak as he was, the weapon became too heavy for him, but he would not part with the flag. Tearing it from the lance, he took it with him, and, in the end, he brought it home'.[23] Here is another 'symbolic' act, typical of Victorian heroism and reminiscent of the Napoleonic era when the regimental standard was a symbol of a regiment's honour. Private Nicholas knew that his pennant must not be captured by the enemy, could not be left on the battlefield, for he knew how that would be interpreted by his comrades and enjoyed by the enemy. Once again, in previous wars, men had got the VC for such symbolic acts, yet in 1918, Nicholas received no medals. Even so, the symbolic importance of this rather inconsequential, almost irrelevant military act warranted a permanent record in the pages of the regimental history published in 1924.

During the last fortnight of the war the Northumberland Hussars gained several Military Medals and other decorations which serve to illustrate the role of the cavalryman in the closing days of the Great War. There were abundant mounted reconnaissance parties out and there was dismounted fighting. The widely-scattered patrols needed rations and large volumes of forage for the horses. Lance Corporal Patrick Loftus was in charge of a mounted patrol whose task was to establish communication with a battalion of the Queen's Regiment who had been held up by heavy fire during the advance on Robersart. It was 24 October when Loftus 'succeeded in finding the battalion and brought back most accurate and important information which resulted in the capture of the village during the afternoon'. He performed this work 'in spite of heavy machine-gun and shell fire'. During the period 4–6 November, patrols were reconnoitring the enemy positions and got into many heavy contacts. Second Lieutenant R. J. Hawley won the Military Cross and two of his men the MM when he led patrols through a 'heavy enemy barrage' and through heavy machine-gun fire. He assisted in mopping up enemy parties during which Private Frederick J. Green 'went forward alone to mop up an enemy post, bayoneting part of the garrison who attempted treachery'. Private Fred Dixon 'pushed on amidst great danger' to reconnoitre the enemy positions, 'showing a fine example and determination to finish his work, and thereby assisted in gaining most valuable information' about the enemy dispositions. He also braved aimed machine-gun and rifle fire from the enemy line which was very close by, as he took badges from German dead in order to obtain identification of enemy units, which he had been asked to obtain. These patrols also managed to clear up 'an obscure situation', resulting in a gap between two British Divisions being closed. Private William Anderson distinguished himself on the night of 4–5 November as limber driver, 'in safely bringing up rations and forage to several detached parties in the Foret de Mormal. Despite the heavy shelling and danger, this man stuck to his work amid great difficulty, in the darkness, with the result that the men of his unit got their rations and forage, owing to the bravery of this man, where so many others had failed'.

**CRITICAL LEADERSHIP ACTIVITIES OF THE CAVALRY OFFICER**
Cavalry officers led the men whose awards are detailed above. The nature and importance of battlefield leadership is a theme which runs throughout this work. In particular, a review of the cavalry DSO allows several important aspects to be highlighted. Good, determined leadership could result in spectacular successes for mounted cavalry units, as the bar to the DSO won by Lt. Colonel Charles Russell Terrot of the Inniskilling Dragoons for the summer of 1918 indicates: 'When sent forward to exploit the infantry success, he led his regiment rapidly through the attacking waves and beyond the final objective. When checked by heavy machine-gun fire from a village, and unable to manoeuvre on account of wire, he dismounted and fought his way forward with two squadrons, so enabling his flank squadron to gallop round and operate to the rear of the village. Many enemy were killed, five guns and 700 prisoners captured, and the success of the operation was entirely due to the daring and splendid leadership of this officer' (*London Gazette*, 15 October 1918).

When dismounted, a determined cavalryman, Major Ing of the 2nd Dragoon Guards, possessed the strength of character to turn a group of defeated infantrymen into a solid defence: 'At Ypres on 13 May 1915, when the line was broken beyond the right flank of his regiment, he came out of his trench in the front line, stood on the road in the open under heavy shell fire, stopped the retirement of 40 men of another unit, and turned them into his section of the defence. The good results of this gallant action were far reaching'. Lieutenant Colonel Alfred Burt of the Dragoon Guards solidified his defence when: 'by his personal courage and example, he so cheered and inspired his men, that he was able to keep his portion of the defence intact' in spite of having been outflanked by an enemy breakthrough on his left. In these rewards we see how a single officer's determination could form the backbone of a defence and galvanise the men's resolve to fight rather than retire. Any man who could do that had enormous value in the front line. This ability largely arises from the individual officer's character.

Similarly, in attack, the importance of leaders cannot be overstated; Lt. Colonel Stewart's role in developing his regiment's will to fight is mentioned in the citation for his DSO: 'He led his battalion with great skill in an attack, capturing all the objectives and holding them against several counter-attacks. By his example and training he inspired all ranks in his battalion with a very fine fighting spirit'. It was this fighting spirit, the will to fight and win, which characterised the British Army throughout most of the war and which was eroded in the German Army as the war dragged on.[24] The role of the British officer in maintaining the will to fight must be acknowledged as a major factor in final victory. One of the ultimate sources of this strength is indicated in the following DSO citation published in the *London Gazette* of 6 April 1918 (originally announced without citation in the *Gazette* of 26 November 1917): Lt Col Wyndham Raymond Portal of the Life Guards, 'When, during an attack, a village in the rear of the attacking troops was discovered to be still occupied by the enemy, he successfully organised a defensive flank and personally led forward a company, who had lost most of their officers, to fill a gap. The splendid behaviour of his battalion, which suffered heavily in a critical position, was largely due to his personality'. This citation illustrates the critical importance of the quality of leadership available to an army when engaged in a major conflict. With this in mind, we may understand more clearly the following extracts from citations: Brigadier General Lionel Sadleir-Jackson, Lancers, was described as 'a bold leader of men, and under all conditions full of energy and fine fighting spirit'. He gained a bar to his Boer War DSO for personally organising and leading very successful counter-attacks. In the Spring of 1918, Lt. Colonel Richard Sparrow received the following accolade: 'Under heavy fire his decisions were masterly and decisive, and showed the qualities of a brilliant leader'. Brigadier General McCulloch, 7th Dragoon Guards, and in command of 64th Infantry Brigade received a second bar to his DSO, 'For conspicuous gallantry and ability to command' when he personally led a brigade 4,500 yards into enemy lines at night, and 'over the worst country'. His award citation further states that: 'success was entirely due to his magnificent leadership, moving at the head of his brigade'. Upon the morale and motivation of these key leaders, rested the fate of ordinary men and ultimately of the nation.

Germany struggled to maintain the required quality of their leaders in the field, and many of these men struggled to maintain their motivation to fight on against increasingly overwhelming odds.[25]

When a key leader takes the initiative in a fight, the significance of surprise is demonstrated, from which dramatic results were sometimes obtained. During Spring 1918, when in one location British infantry had retired, Major Evelyn Williams of the Hussars shouldered personal responsibility for the situation and, 'led a mounted charge along the hostile line... and in the face of the heaviest machine-gun fire, he carried out the manoeuvre successfully, sabring nearly 100 of the enemy, and taking 100 prisoners, although his own troop was only 150. His fine action rallied the infantry, who advanced, and recovered over 3,000 yards in depth of the whole line'. Similarly, Lt. Colonel Glyn Mason, when in command of the Dorsetshire Yeomanry in Egypt on 27 September 1918, was able to turn defeat into victory by saddling up and charging: 'Whilst his regiment was holding a position west of the village (Er Remte), it was strongly counter-attacked... his advanced firing line was steadily forced back by superior enemy machine-gun fire, but he at the right moment seized the opportunity to mount his retiring firing line and charge the counter-attacking enemy. The latter were entirely surprised and routed. This action was almost entirely responsible for the rapid capitulation of the enemy holding the village'. With bold, courageous leadership and decisive action, both Williams and Mason showed that even in 1918, cavalry charges could be used to excellent effect and even inspire infantry (who were often in awe of the cavalry) to offer their mounted comrades the most determined support. Making oneself conspicuous on the battlefield by one's courage, often causes men to offer their utmost support. Once a leader shows the way, men will generally follow in support, rather than watch him die.

The value of an officer's emotional support has been mentioned in previous chapters. One such example from the cavalry is the award of the DSO to Major Ernest Wriothesley Denny of the Hussars who, during a week's heavy fighting and retreat in the Spring of 1918, 'visited every company in the front line... His personality did much to encourage the young soldiers during a trying time for officers and men who had only just been sent to the division, and the majority of whom had not been under fire before'. An officer who ignored the needs of his men, particularly the new and inexperienced, might be repaid for his oversight with a weak performance from them when events took a turn for the worse. Good officers were no doubt very conscious of the fact that every enemy soldier would gain strength from seeing his opponent capitulate and flee, and so encouraging men to manfully resist, in fact represented everyone's best chance of survival.

Some officers were able to put their sporting background to good use on the battlefield; occasionally we sense the value of horsemanship in the cavalry officer's pre-war experience. Captain Archibald Winterbottom of the Dragoon Guards was the son of millionaire William Dickson Winterbottom. Archibald's father was, according to the obituary in *The Times* of Friday, 25 April 1924, 'a keen sportsman, being especially fond of hunting and polo' and was also Master of the High Peak Harriers, a hunting club in Derbyshire from 1894 to 1896.[26] Archibald was born in 1885 and must have been heavily involved. Bearing in mind young Archibald's pre-war sporting background (as well as his Eton education), the following DSO citation makes interesting reading as it contains many elements of that hunting background: 'For conspicuous gallantry and dash in an attack. This officer led his squadron over a most difficult country with the greatest skill and ability. He judged the pace for a four mile gallop to a nicety, disregarded all rifle and machine-gun fire, made straight for his objective, and rode over several hundred of the enemy, killing a good number, and subsequently making the rest prisoners. Later in the day, he took command of the regiment when his commanding officer was wounded, and carried out his duties most successfully. He did brilliantly' (*London Gazette*, 15 October 1918). That we may view the run in to the objective in terms of Derbyshire stone walls and rough country, and the enemy as the huntsman's quarry, is perhaps no surprise, but we may also acknowledge his Eton education which allowed him to take command of the regiment with such ease and ability, whilst in his early thirties. Having some family background to hand, elements of some citations may be understood more clearly. An officer's background, his public school education and long training in life and martial skills by means of sport, had a marked effect on his behaviour on the battlefield.

# An Infantry Regiment:
# The Northumberland Fusiliers

The infantry was by far the numerically strongest arm of the British Army between 1914 and 1918, having typically more than 400,000 men in France and Flanders, in other words about half of the entire force. The next strongest arm was the Artillery with about 150,000 men.[27] To keep the work manageable and representative, a single unit of infantry, the Northumberland Fusiliers, has been chosen as a suitable example because of its large size and its diverse composition. Twenty-five Battalions were fielded by the Northumberland Fusiliers; two regular Army, four Territorial Army, a Railway Pioneer Battalion, three Ordinary Pioneer Battalions and the remainder were Service Battalions of the New Armies. Its composition was one of the most diverse of all infantry regiments. The regiment was also one of the largest present on the Western Front, supplying approximately 100,000 men for overseas service between 1914 and 1918 (the number of Medal Index Cards showing service in the Northumberland Fusiliers minus those for gallantry awards etc). These men suffered over 17,700 fatalities (Commonwealth War Graves Commission) and came out with approximately 2,290 bravery medals having gone through all the hardest battles of the Western Front with their rifles, bayonets, machine guns, hand grenades, fists, rolls of barbed wire, shovels, their bodies and their minds. All were battered into pieces.

The first and second battalions of the Northumberland Fusiliers were part of the standing Army and as such had a long history of campaigning prior to 1914. Originally the first battalion was the 5th Regiment of Foot, and believed it was the first to introduce a medal to be awarded for long service and good conduct in the ranks in

1767. It is claimed that this award, the 'Regimental Order of Merit', was the forerunner of the formally introduced Army Long Service and Good Conduct medal. The Regimental Order of Merit came in three classes; bronze for seven years, silver for 14 years and another class of silver for 21 years. Only the latter was engraved with the recipient's name. The association of the regiment with Northumberland began in 1782 but its recruiting area was only formalised as the County of Northumberland in 1881 and the name was changed to the Northumberland Fusiliers.

Two battalions of the 5th Foot served with distinction in the Peninsula (Spain and Portugal, 1808–1814) during the retreat from Corunna and later with Wellington at most of his major battles, greatly distinguishing themselves as part of the 'forlorn hope' – the first wave of assault at the storming of Badajoz. The regiment missed Waterloo on account of being in North America. Spending much time in Ireland during the 1820s and 1830s, the battalion was moved to India in the 1850s, thus missing the Crimean War of 1854–55. This in itself gave cause to wonder when the regiment would next see action, as it had been 30 years since it had fired a shot in anger. However, the regiment gained three Victoria Crosses during the Indian Mutiny of 1857–58, particularly during the first Relief of Lucknow and subsequent defence of that place.

The 5th next found themselves in Afghanistan 1878–80 and whilst they took part in none of the major battles that occurred on the marches to Kabul and Kandahar, they still found plenty of hard fighting to be done. Again, being largely based in India, the regiment missed the Egypt and Sudan campaigns of 1882–89, including the failed attempt to relieve General Gordon in Khartoum. The first campaign involving the 2nd Battalion was the 'Black Mountain Expedition' or the Hazara campaign of 1888, during which the battalion stormed the mountain top position of Chela Crag at 14,000 feet above sea level. Men involved in this expedition were almost all too old for service in the First World War, but that did not stop some of them trying to re-enlist in 1914. The first battalion had to wait until Crete 1897 and the battle of Omdurman in the Sudan in 1898, for its next spell of action, and many of these men would in due course find themselves in France as some of the most experienced soldiers in the ranks of the battalion. Their experience was in fact vital to the battalion during the war of 1914–18 in spite of the differences in soldiering encountered in France and Flanders. The other 27 battalions of the regiment generally did not receive these men who, if they weren't still serving, came through the Militia and 3rd (Reserve) Battalions of the regiment to rejoin the first battalion in France as reinforcements during late 1914 and 1915.

Both the first and second battalions served during the very difficult Boer War of 1899–1900, through its reverses of 1899 to its victories of 1900 and the long slog to the finish through 1901 and 1902. This was a war of trenches, mobile warfare in wide open country and of modern rifle and machine-gun fire. However, the firepower revolution of the artillery and machine gun was still in the future and so its lessons still had to be learned. After the Boer War, the first battalion served on what was known as the Mohmand Expedition of 1908, more informatively known as the North West Frontier of India. This was another campaign that ended with medal ribbons placed upon the chests of its participants; ribbons that marked the men out as old campaigners during the war of 1914–18. These ribbons commanded the respect of the inexperienced, as is shown by Wilfred Cook in his recently published memoirs from his time with the first battalion 1915–17.

It is noteworthy that even though the regiment had 'adopted' Northumberland as its county affiliation, as a result of large amounts of time spent in Colchester and Ireland, it was never a regiment composed of men from Northumberland in particular. Like all the county regiments, it recruited from a number of centres, of which Newcastle and the North-East was but one. There was, however, always a significant proportion of Geordies and Northumbrians in its ranks. It was in the first two years of the First World War that the Northumberland Fusiliers was at its most Northumbrian, with close to 4,000 men local to the North-East, serving with the four territorial battalions and many thousands more newly enlisted in the service and pioneer battalions including the Tyneside Scottish and Irish Brigades.

The Northumberland Fusiliers, like almost all other infantry regiments, was a mix of a core of old campaigners and enormous drafts of inexperienced recruits. They were volunteers at first and conscripted civilians from late 1916 to the end.

## COMPOSITION OF THE REGIMENT

Officially, the strength of an infantry Battalion in early 1916 was 30 officers and 977 men, or 3 per cent officers. The Northumberland Fusiliers fielded the following 25 Battalions:

Regular Battalions: 1st and 2nd (the professional volunteer soldiers)

Territorial Battalions: 4th, 5th, 6th and 7th (part-time volunteer soldiers, originally raised in 1908 as a reserve force for the defence of the United Kingdom, and subject to an annual training commitment).

The regular and territorial battalions were in existence and were mobilised on the outbreak of war on the 4 August 1914.

Between August of 1914 and January of 1915, Kitchener oversaw the formation of the so-called 'New Armies'. To these, the Northumberland Fusiliers were able to contribute 19 new battalions filled largely with untrained but enthusiastic volunteers:-

The 8th, 9th, 10th, 11th, 12th and 13th 'Service' Battalions and the 16th (Newcastle Commercials) Battalions plus the 20th, 21st, 22nd and 23rd 'Tyneside Scottish' and the 24th, 25th, 26th and 27th 'Tyneside Irish'. There was a 3rd Battalion, but this was a reserve unit, supplying drafts of men to other battalions throughout the war. It never saw active service in its own right. A 15th Battalion was never formed.    In addition to the traditional front line infantry battalions above, four pioneer battalions were formed, these being the 14th, the 17th (North Eastern Railway Pioneers also known as the 'Newcastle Railway Pals'), the 18th (1st Tyneside Pioneers) and 19th (2nd Tyneside Pioneers) battalions. No other regiment had as many pioneer battalions.

During the war, some of the above battalions were amalgamated and others disbanded leading to a reduced number of battalions operating during the later part of the war:

- Amalgamation of the 12th and 13th Battalions occurred on 10 August 1917, to become the 12/13th Battalion
- Amalgamation of the 24th and 27th Battalions of the Tyneside Irish Brigade to create the 24th/27th Battalion also occurred on 10 August 1917.
- Disbandment of the 16th Battalion occurred in February 1918, its members going to the Territorial Battalions, the 4th, 5th, 6th and 7th. Also in February 1918, the 20th and 21st (Tyneside Scottish) Battalions were disbanded and the 24th/27th and the 26th (Tyneside Irish) Battalions were also disbanded.
- Conversion of the 7th Battalion to pioneers also occurred in February 1918.
- During the Spring Offensives of March to June 1918, the 4th, 5th and 6th Territorial Battalions were very heavily engaged, part destroyed and part taken prisoner. These battalions were all so far below strength and the survivors so exhausted at the end of May that they had virtually ceased to exist. Only small cadres remained until very late in the war and none of the battalions took any further significant part in operations. The 7th (Territorial) battalion largely escaped this fate as a result of its conversion to pioneers.
- Further, the German Offensives also succeeded in largely destroying or capturing the remaining Tyneside Scottish and Irish Battalions, who were similarly hard pressed in those dark days. By mid-May 1918, the 22nd and 23rd Tyneside Scottish were reduced to cadre strength, their remaining men being transferred to Depot for reassignment to other units before the battalions were rebuilt later in the year. The 25th Tyneside Irish suffered the same fate, but all three of these battalions were reborn and took part in actions late in the war, winning additional gallantry medals for their work.

Thus, from August 1917 the regiment went from fielding 25 battalions on active service overseas to just 17 in the field. The regiment lost three of its four Territorial Battalions, two Service Battalions and five of the eight Tyneside Scottish and Irish Battalions. None of the pioneer battalions was lost, rather a new one was created (7th). At the end of the German Offensives in early June

1918, the regiment was at its lowest strength of just 14 battalions; four of which were pioneers. Reduced from 25 to 17 battalions, it may be supposed that the regiment's capacity for winning gallantry medals was reduced by approximately one third. The only gain was the late arrival of the 36th Battalion, and in a short time this unit contributed a Victoria Cross to the Regiment's laurels.

## DISTRIBUTION OF MEDALS IN THE INFANTRY

In previous chapters, we have seen that gallantry medals were scarce among privates and increasingly abundant with greater rank. We have argued that this is a reflection of the greater responsibility and leadership displayed by (and required of) the more senior other ranks and officers. It was these men, we have so far argued, who had to plan and initiate actions that would see them singled out as particular targets, but who influenced the outcome of battles and who solidified any defence. If these assertions are correct, then we should expect to find abundant evidence within the honours lists of the infantry. With that object in mind, the distribution of gallantry medals in the Northumberland Fusiliers and the acts for which they were awarded, are described in the following pages.

Officers of the Northumberland Fusiliers received approximately 77 Distinguished Service Orders and nine bars plus 449 Military Crosses, 42 bars and three second bars for services during the First World War. Of these awards, half the DSOs and almost a quarter of the MCs were periodic awards announced in the King's Birthday or New Year Honours Lists (3 June and 1 January respectively each year). The remainder were immediate awards. The breakdown of awards by officer rank shows that the DSO was largely a Captain's and Major's award, these two ranks earning 70 per cent of all DSOs. Some of the DSOs won by junior field officers after the introduction of the MC were made for exceptional acts of gallantry on the battlefield. The MC by contrast was very much a company commander's award; 85 per cent of all MCs being awarded to captains and junior officers (company commanders and below). Other ranks of the Northumberland Fusiliers received 258 DCMs and nine bars for second awards as well as approximately 1,428

MMs, 82 bars and one second bar. Analysis of these awards reveals that just 23 per cent of DCMs was won by privates, the remaining 77 per cent by NCOs. Of the NCOs, Sergeants carried away 145 (55 per cent) of these medals. The splits between different ranks highlight that the DSO was a senior officer's award, the MC was a junior officer's award, the DCM was more of a senior NCO's award and the MM was more of a junior NCO's and private's award. This very strongly suggests that the hierarchy of so-called Level 1 gallantry (VC), through Level 2 and Level 3 gallantry that is in place today, was not as well established during the First World War.

Other factors were at work. The medal a man received depended on his rank, more so than it did during the Second World War and far more than it does today. With the attainment of rank came an increase in responsibility and an increased leadership role as well as the requirement to plan and initiate dangerous operations, so it can be argued that the First World War division of medals based on rank was absolutely correct. In the post-World War Two era, there has been a fairly clear hierarchy of awards, within which the VC is awarded for the most spectacular and significant acts of battlefield bravery irrespective of rank, with 'Level 2' awards (DCM) for marginally lesser acts of gallantry, the 'Level 3' award being the MM and Level 4 being a Mention in Despatches. During World War One, it would appear to be incorrect to think in terms of a simple award hierarchy with the DCM sat beneath the VC and the MM beneath the DCM. The DCM did not always require a greater bravery than that required for an MM during the war of 1914–19, it was mainly an NCO's award requiring leadership responsibility and status within a unit, a man who set an inspiring example to others. Many of those who won the DCM formed the backbone of their units.

Whilst DCMs could be presented for devotion to duty over a long period, even for establishing a field bakery, soldiers who attacked and overcame machine gun positions were more often awarded the MM rather than the VC.

**GALLANT ACTS OF AN INFANTRY REGIMENT**
Having reviewed the acts for which men received awards in the

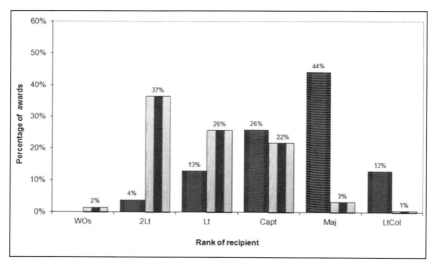

**Figure 34: DSOs and MCs won by different ranks, Northumberland Fusiliers**

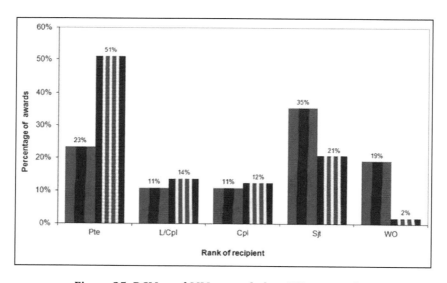

**Figure 35: DCMs and MMs awarded to different ranks,
Northumberland Fusiliers**

various corps and in the cavalry, it is the infantry which remains to be considered. Table 9 shows the types of action for which each gallantry award was made. These numbers relate to the Northumberland Fusiliers, a complete regiment, but are limited to those awards which we know something about. In the final row are the periodic awards (announced in New Year and King's Birthday Honours gazettes), which, although it is not known what they were awarded for, can be categorised as honours awards.

| Type of Action | DSO | MC | DCM | MM |
|---|---|---|---|---|
| Large Scale Attacks | 23.1 | 27.5 | 26.7 | 22.8 |
| Defensive actions | 19.2 | 15.9 | 18.0 | 23.7 |
| Raids | 2.6 | 7.6 | 5.6 | 14.6 |
| Patrols & reconnaissance | 2.6 | 10.6 | 4.5 | 7.6 |
| Gallantry under shellfire | 1.3 | 5.3 | 9.0 | 6.6 |
| Lifesaving | 1.3 | 2.5 | 10.5 | 12.7 |
| Runner | 0.0 | 0.2 | 4.9 | 5.4 |
| Working party | 0.0 | 2.1 | 1.1 | 2.8 |
| Periodic Awards | 50.0 | 24.9 | 23.7 | 0.0 |

**Table 9: Types of Action for which Gallantry Medals Were Awarded:
Northumberland Fusiliers**
*Values given represent the percentage of the total*

That the fractions of honours awards were 50 per cent, 25 per cent and close to 25 per cent, suggests some form of quota applied to honours awards. However no evidence has been found by the authors to prove this.

The total number of DSOs in the above sample is 78 (of 86 awarded to the regiment during World War One), the number of MCs is 473 (of 494 awarded), of DCMs 266 (of 267 awarded) and MMs 316 (of 1,511 awarded). Results strongly reflect the allotted tasks of officers and men in the field, and support the concept that most gallantry medals were won in the performance of duty and not 'above and beyond the call of duty' as is often suggested.

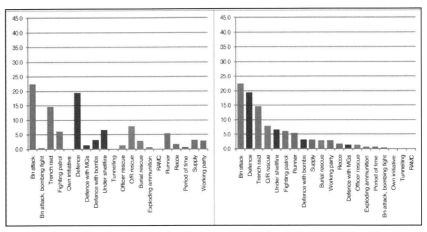

**Figure 36: Awards of the Military Medal by Activity (left) and ranked (right).**

The following points may be made concerning this tabulation:

Those DSOs having citations, clearly show that this medal was mainly awarded for the organisation and execution of battalion scale operations, with over 40 per cent of all awards made to the regiment being specifically for attacks and defensive operations. A further 50 per cent of the regiment's DSOs were periodic awards for which no citation survives. Many DSOs were awarded for work over the duration of a major action and this is particularly true of the defensive actions of the German Spring Offensives in 1918, when senior officers were engaged in planning and execution of defensive positions and withdrawals over days and weeks. Very few DSOs were awarded for undertaking the typical duties of the field officer; patrol work or leading trench raids for example. In fact, most of the DSOs awarded for these kinds of action went to junior officers and some of these were downgraded Victoria Cross recommendations.

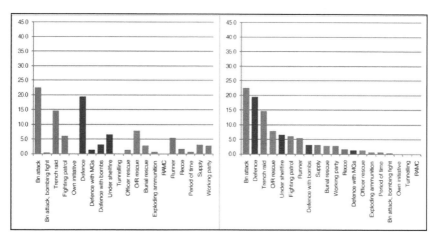

**Figure 37: Awards of the Distinguished Conduct Medal by Activity (left) and ranked (right). Both immediate and periodic awards.**

About one quarter to one third of all gallantry awards was made for large scale attacks (larger operations than the trench raid). The proportion is fairly consistent across all of the decorations, from DSO to MM. Other activities, including trench raids, defensive and lifesaving actions make up the remainder of the regiment's honours list.

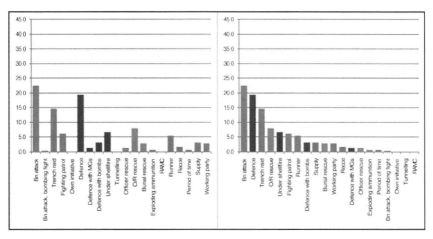

**Figure 38: Immediate Awards of the Military Cross by Activity (left) and Ranked (right).**

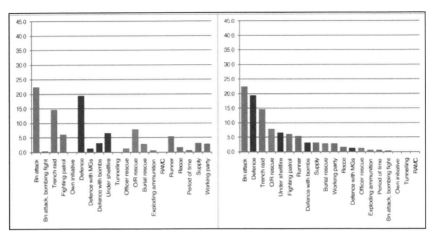

**Figure 39: Immediate Awards of the Distinguished Service Order by Activity (left) and Ranked (right).**

## THE RESCUE OF OFFICERS AND THE MOVE AWAY FROM LIFESAVING

During the Victorian period, recommendations for gallantry awards had been regularly received by the War Office, relating to soldiers who had carried their wounded officer from the battlefield to safety. Some of these resulted in the award of the Victoria Cross. During the Boer War, a steady flow of such recommendations was received, particularly for the VC, but started to be rejected. The act of lifesaving on the battlefield was particularly 'class-conscious', as the following illustrates: In the case of DCMs awarded to the Northumberlands in World War One, just five 'officer rescue' awards were made to other ranks, four for 1915 and one only during 1916. No such awards were made in the second half of the war. Another nine DCMs were won for the rescue of other ranks, making 14 lifesaving DCMs in total. Of the 29 lifesaving MMs for which we have details of the action, 25 were for the rescue of other ranks and only four were for rescue of officers. Whereas one third of the regiment's lifesaving DCMs was awarded for officer rescues, less than one fifth of lifesaving MMs was made for the rescue of officers. Whilst equal numbers of DCMs and MMs were given for officer rescue, three times as many MMs were given for non-officer rescues. These numbers suggest that whilst awards for officer rescue were infrequently made, a man was more likely to get a DCM for rescuing an officer and he was far more likely to get an MM for rescuing a private or NCO. This was an entirely practical reality because the value in war of one very good officer was much higher than others who did not lead, organise or inspire. An infantry battalion was nothing without its leadership. With approximately 3–5 per cent of a battalion being officers, all of the rescue award statistics seem to indicate a greater level of reward provided for men who rescued officers, than for rescuing their non-commissioned colleagues. Further to the above, the numbers of lifesaving DCM awards made to infantrymen declines spectacularly during the war, confirming the observations made by M. C. Smith concerning the Victoria Cross:[28]

| Lifesaving | 1914 | 1915 | 1916 | 1917 | 1918 |
|---|---|---|---|---|---|
| Northumb. Fusiliers | 20% | 28% | 9% | 1% | 1% |
| **% of that year's DCMs** | | | | | |

Whereas there can be no doubt that the same numbers of lifesaving acts were being carried out on the battlefield in 1917 and 1918, this tabulation shows that medals were no longer being awarded for this form of battlefield bravery. They were made for particular acts. The move away from lifesaving as an act worthy of a Victoria Cross is also seen in awards of the Distinguished Conduct Medal.

## GALLANTRY IN THE REGULAR INFANTRY BATTALIONS

On the outbreak of the First World War, the second battalion was doing its share of the alternating tours of duty in India, but the first battalion was immediately sent out to France and met the relatively enormous and powerful German Army head on, in open warfare. Whilst the outcome of the famous 'retreat from Mons' by that Army was undeniably a defeat for the German Army, it was scarcely a victory for the British, who had been very much caught on the back foot and fighting a desperate rearguard. The whole episode was bumbled and tactically weak. The men themselves were unprepared for the force of a European land war and were shocked to the point that some units submitted to mass surrender.[29] Had the BEF worked out its tactical approach to a major European land war prior to its outbreak, there might have been much less retreat in the retreat from Mons. However, conjecture and criticism of this sort has little real value, particularly in this study, as halt the enemy advance they did, eventually, and the actions they fought were punctuated by several notable feats of gallantry. At this stage of the war, the nature of the awards is interesting, as there were clear changes from 1914 going on into 1915 and 1916. This was a period when the recognition of gallantry began to change, permanently, moving away from the award of medals for acts of a Victorian character and evolving into something more recognisably modern. This is not at all surprising as the nature of war itself was changing into something more recognisably modern at the same time.

Arguably, the honours and awards system lagged behind the evolution of warfare, such that, rewards still had a whiff of the Victorian right up to late 1915. The launch of the major British offensives in the Summer of 1916 gave the honours and awards committees hugely increased choice in terms of what acts to honour, and they chose, increasingly, fighting and distinguished leadership above lifesaving and symbolic.

Returning to 1914, the Northumberland Fusiliers first encountered the German Army on 23 August, at the Mons-Conde Canal. Skirmishes resulted. The next day there was a fight at Frameries and a few days later the Battalion counter-attacked at Pont du Hem. It was over a five-week period between 13 October and 21 November that the Battalion was heavily engaged almost daily, at Bout de Ville, Pont du Hem, Horlies, Neuve Chappelle, Wijtschaete village and finally in the area around Hooge. With their backs to Ypres, the first Battalion finally dug in on a static line and licked its wounds, worn out and weakened from continuous fighting and prolonged retreat. In this period, 331 men had been killed and a great many of the remainder had been wounded to a greater or lesser extent. Those physically unscathed by the fighting were very much in the minority.

| Type of Battalion | Btn | Awards per Btn | Awards total | Mean per Btn |
|---|---|---|---|---|
| Regular Battalions | 1st 2nd | 226 86 | 312 | 156 |
| Territorial Battalions | 4th 5th 6th 7th | 88 78 75 71 | 312 | 78 |
| Service Battalions | 8th 9th 10th 11th 12th 13th 12/13 16th | 88 133 115 139 41 27 72 36 | 651 | 93 |
| Pioneer Battalions | 14th 17th 18th 19th | 44 15 34 52 | 145 | 36 |
| Tyneside Scottish Brigade | 20th 21st 22nd 23rd 24th | 85 52 99 105 36 | 341 | 85 |
| Tyneside Irish Brigade | 24/27 25th 26th 27th | 8 74 53 41 | 212 | 53 |

**Table 11: Northumberland Fusiliers; Total Gallantry Awards by Battalion**

Having taken a lead role in depriving Germany of her ultimate goals (permanently, so it turned out), the honours and awards list for this period is remarkably short. Just seven men were decorated for their gallant conduct in these desperate days and the family of one of these men, killed at Hooge on 15 November 1914, had to wait until December 1918 for an award to be announced in the *London Gazette* (probably because he was killed on the same day as the action for which he was recommended for an award, but at that time, and throughout the First World War, posthumous awards of the DCM were not allowed).

One cannot doubt the determination of the men to hold out at all costs during the Autumn of 1914; that is evidenced by the huge casualty lists and, in the face of those growing casualty lists, it is remarkable that the spirit of the men was not catastrophically broken whilst on the field of battle. Later in the war it is true that some battalions of the regiment, composed of too many inexperienced conscript soldiers and lacking staunchly determined and experienced leaders, would certainly have buckled under the pressure exerted by the enemy long before the 1st Battalion ever did. In spite of the turnover of men, the 1st Battalion remained as a wall in defence and as a spearhead in attack. They formed, in short, an elite unit of the BEF throughout the First World War who could be relied upon to deliver in almost any circumstances. How they achieved that and why other battalions could not, is dealt with later.

The scarcity of awards for 1914 continues throughout 1915 and into the Spring of 1916. Only 20 awards for bravery on the battlefield were made to the 1st Battalion during the first 21 months of the war, at a price of 740 dead. The statistic is shocking; a man was 35 times more likely to be killed during this period than to receive a gallantry medal, and there were many more wounded and disabled who have not been counted. It is not simply a function of the lack of the Military Medal as an available reward; this has far more to do with the inactivity of the British Army during that period. The battalion spent much of 1915 in the line being daily shelled, taking hits from rifle grenades and from the big shells of trench mortars, as well as taking casualties from sniper's bullets.

Very wearing indeed, the strain on the men and turnover of men was tremendous. That they continued to do their duty, that they remained at their posts, is astonishing to the casual observer of the 21st century. The names on the battalion muster list changed almost completely, twice in less than two years with very little to show for the human cost, least of all ground gained, but also a very slim honours list. This situation was true of the entire British Army, not just the Northumberland Fusiliers.

Turning to the 2nd Battalion, the situation was even worse. Between their arrival in France on 17 January and 16 October 1915 when they left for Egypt, only five gallantry medals were awarded for a loss of 520 dead. Given that the battalion had landed in Le Havre with a strength of 970 men and 25 officers, the scale of the death is apparent, not to mention the woundings and psychological strain. In these nine months, the 2nd Battalion had participated in the successful attacks at Wittepoort Farm and Bellewarde Farm during the Second Battle of Ypres, May 1915. Later in the war, such a successful battle would have attracted more gallantry awards, but the awards process was both cramped by the quota system and overwhelmed by recommendations coming in from the front. Heavily shelled in the line and subjected to repeated break-ins by German bombing parties, the battalion continually suffered badly in the trenches. Considering the frequency of these enemy break-ins, which occurred several times at gaps left between battalions, one must conclude that something was not quite right in the 2nd Battalion (and other units in that brigade). Leaving gaps and allowing the enemy to sneak in quietly during the night, in strength, and then to roll up a flank by bombing up the trench, indicates inherent weaknesses in sentry duties and communication with neighbouring units in the line.

The record of the 2nd Battalion during 1915 is not as solid as that of the 1st, not least because they suffered such heavy casualties for avoidable reasons. The five awards received for nine months of lethal operations seem to be not only a testimony to the bravery of a few, but also something of an indictment of the performance of the battalion in trench warfare. Perhaps marked as a brigade not to be entrusted with line holding, they were shipped out to Egypt, a far quieter front, not to return to France until late 1918. With three years of open warfare soldiering under its belt and having taken relatively few casualties (98 dead in the three years), the 2nd returned to France with its now experienced old-timers, where once again open warfare was being conducted, and pulled off 'one of the most brilliant episodes in the history of the Fifth'.[30] This event was the successful attack at Le Catelet, during which a strongly fortified and heavily defended position was charged, leading to the capture of 250 prisoners and 18 machine guns. For this and the operations around Le Catelet in October and successful operations in the Foret du Mormal in early November, the 2nd Battalion received 68 medals for bravery in a little over four weeks.

During 1915, the awards system was not functioning as well as it ought, it needed changing; this is a large part of the reason why the MM was established in early 1916 and why, once it was established, a review of previously submitted recommendations was carried out with a view to identifying men who missed out on a DCM, but who now ought to receive retrospectively the MM. There were, in the end, rather few who were lucky enough to be so honoured, but that it was done is a sign that the War Office recognised the seriousness of the problem and the oversight that now had to be corrected.

Recognising that the majority of the graph in Figure 40 represents awards made to the 1st Battalion, whose total of 264 bravery medals is more than double that of any other battalion of the regiment, several aspects stand out. Firstly, the low award rate for 1914 to Spring 1916 is obvious, contrasting starkly with July 1916 onward. A minor step up occurs at April–May 1916; these are the awards for the battle of St Eloi, 27 March 1916; a model attack, the significance of which ought to have been disseminated widely across the Armies in France at the time, as the techniques used at St Eloi could have helped to minimise the disaster of the First of July on the Somme. The attack at St Eloi, 27 March 1916, was a minor battle of 'line-straightening', but one that showed the way forward in attack, already well beyond the worst tactics of the First of July. A demonstration of all-arms coordination and surprise assault was provided by the 1st Battalion. Before dawn that morning, the attackers had assembled secretly; there was no preliminary artillery bombardment, but instead the artillery's fire was timed to coincide with the explosion of several mines at exactly zero hour. The Northumberlands went into the attack at the earliest possible moment, barely 30 seconds after the explosion of the mines, and hugged the artillery barrage as closely as they dared, reaching the German wire with just one fatality. Other units which had not gone over the top so quick off the mark, were caught by German artillerymen who responded very fast; less than a minute after the last of the Northumberlands left the front line, shells began to fall on the British trenches, no-man's-land and the mine craters, catching the reserves who were trying to get up in support. This was at once a lesson in the power of defensive artillery fire and the importance of surprise attack, without an extended preliminary bombardment, the utility of mines in the offensive and the importance of hugging one's own artillery barrage as closely as possible. St. Eloi was recorded as a disaster overall but it was a great success for the 1st Battalion. All were lessons that had been learned from the French, by observing the Germans and from first-hand experience. They were lessons digested and regurgitated in 'field manual' form at Divisional, Corps and Army level by 1917, but which had already been worked out, practiced and proven on a smaller scale, during attacks and raids in the first half of 1916 and into early 1917.

Key tactical lessons had been learned by the 1st Battalion and its supporting services up to a year earlier than in the majority of the British Army, and the result was reduced casualties in exchange for greater military success plus an abundance of military honours and awards. The Major leading the battalion at St. Eloi won a DSO; five MCs went to officers for successful leadership against enemy machine guns, against enemy bombing parties and for defeating a counter-attack; four DCMs were awarded to stretcher bearers, runners and for leading men across the enemy wire and into their trenches; seven of the newly-instituted MMs were also won that day (no citations available). A large total of 17 awards were received in return for escaping relatively lightly with 49 dead. The ratio of one medal for every three killed is low for the Western Front 1914–18, and is the mark of a very successful action.

The first major step upward in the award rate comes with the *London Gazettes* of October 1916, and these awards were for the battles of July 1916 on the Somme, particularly the successful attacks on Bazentin-le-Grand (13 July, 33 dead), Delville Wood and Longueval Village (23 July, 34 dead) and again at Delville Wood (18 August, 13 dead). These attacks were remarkable for their relatively low casualties considering the notoriety of the Somme, Delville Wood and Longueval in particular. One may wonder what the casualty figures might have been had the 2nd Battalion been tasked with these jobs, as it is clear that each battalion's tactical approach to operations had a material effect on the casualties it sustained. What is of interest with regard to the awards made for this period of operations on the Somme, is that there were 37 MMs and one DCM only. No immediate awards to junior or senior officers were made, although certain officers appearing in the New Year Honours List for 1917 may have been rewards for the Somme battles. It is suggested that this is evidence for the importance of the ordinary soldiers and non-commissioned junior leaders in driving these actions to a victorious conclusion. Certainly the officers writing recommendations, felt that the honour belonged to the men rather than to themselves, and this in itself may be a key to understanding the morale and trust that developed between the ordinary 1st[t] Battalion soldier and his junior leadership. Of 38 medals awarded, 17 went to privates, three were lance-corporals or corporals, but 16 were sergeants of one sort or another. The key leadership in the 1st Battalion on the Somme, seems to have been provided by the sergeants, many of whom were tremendously experienced having pre-war campaign service on the North-West Frontier of India, in South Africa and some even in the Sudan in 1898. The significance of these men for the 1st Battalion, and the likely tactical reasons for the success of other ranks during the Somme battle, are explored in a later chapter (refer Section III).

After the Somme, life for the 1st Battalion was fairly quiet, although they were involved in three actions during 1917. The first was a successful trench raid on the night of 21 March. Raid objectives were limited to obtaining an identification, and, as soon as that had been achieved, the party was to extract itself and in any case not linger any more than 10 minutes under any circumstances. Composition of the 30-man raid party was simple, being a directing party consisting of 2/Lt Passingham and four men; a right, centre and left blocking party each of one NCO and four men; and finally two 'Souvenir' parties whose sole concern was to obtain the identification. The party crept out into no-mans-land at 1:10am and made slow progress over towards the enemy wire. They were a little late in arriving on a very dark night, so that when the planned artillery barrage opened up, they were still 20 yards away. However, the light from the explosions showed them the way and the objective 'was immediately rushed'. They got over the two-foot high dense wire with some difficulty and had to face of an enemy, already alerted and throwing bombs at them. A sergeant and another man were hit and killed on the wire. Their bodies could not be brought in, but they would not have been wearing any badges so that the enemy could not itself obtain an identification.

According to the battalion war diary report, 'the enemy fought well' in their own trenches and here, in hand-to-hand fighting, one NCO and one man were wounded, believed killed. It was estimated that 11 or 12 Germans were killed, indicating that the Fusiliers fought rather better. Their 'souvenir' was discovered pretending to be dead, but 'came willingly' once his game was discovered. He turned out to be an NCO of the German 107th Reserve Infantry Regiment, thus an identification was successfully obtained. The raid resulted in heavy retaliatory shelling by the German artillery that killed six men in addition to the two killed on the raid itself. One MC and two MMs were awarded for this minor action on the Western Front. It was 2/Lieutenant Edward Passingham who was awarded the Military Cross, his citation reads: 'For conspicuous gallantry and devotion to duty. He led a raiding party with great courage and determination through uncut wire and succeeded in entering the enemy's front line trenches, where he personally shot three of the enemy'. Passingham was killed in action barely six weeks later on 3 May 1917, near Monchy (Arras sector). He was fairly typical of junior officers at that stage of the war, in that he was not long out of public school and just 21 years old; arguably too young to be leading a party such as this one on such a perilous, murderous mission.

Bearing in mind the limited raid objectives, the small size of the party (30 men) and its successful outcome, the total of three gallantry medals awarded seems very reasonable, being 10 per cent of the raiding party decorated. However, this contrasts strongly with the few medals awarded in the first 18 months of the war in exchange for so many dead.

Not allowing the enemy to gain an identification during raids and patrols was important, because identifications allowed friend and foe to gain an understanding of the behaviour and tactics of different units in the line. Later in 1917 a patrol officer received the MC when his patrol was spotted in no-mans-land and came under very heavy fire from rifles, machine guns and artillery. Two men being suddenly wounded, he recognised the risk and sought to get both men back to his lines through a hail of fire. The citation states: 'When in charge of patrols sent to reconnoitre the enemy wire, across a distance of 800 yards, on reaching the wire the patrol was heavily fired on and retired after sending a volley of bombs (*by this we understand rifle grenades*) into the enemy posts. He carried one wounded man to a shell hole 100 yards away, and another from the shell hole 600 yards to his own lines, being all the time under heavy artillery, machine gun and rifle fire. His gallant behaviour undoubtedly prevented an identification being obtained by the enemy'. In contrast to the raid, his was the only decoration for this dangerous patrol, so what we learn from this is that this award was made for a quite specific tactical reason; it was for denying the enemy an identification. It was made as much for its military value as for the man's 'bravery'.

The year 1918 was when the 1st Battalion really showed its class in comparison to others in the Regiment. This is represented firstly by the large number of awards announced in the *London Gazette* of July to early August 1918 and then by an ongoing high award rate right through to the end of the war.

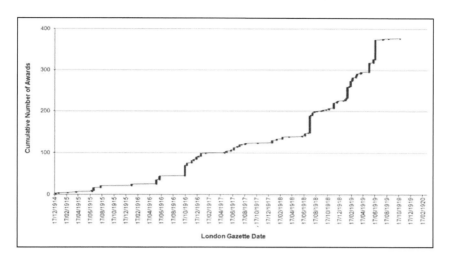

**Figure 40: Awards Growth, 1st and 2nd (Regular Army) Battalions, Northumberland Fusiliers, 1914-1920.**

## GALLANTRY IN THE TERRITORIAL BATTALIONS

The Territorial Battalions of the Northumberland Fusiliers, in common with the entire Territorial Army, came into being in 1908. With a part-time annual training commitment and tasked generally with the defence of the Kingdom, the territorial battalions were not the equivalent of regular soldiers. Whereas some territorial battalions performed some extraordinary feats on the Western Front, for example the 1/1 Cambridgeshire Regiment who captured the 'impregnable' Schwaben Redoubt on 14 October 1916, the territorial battalions of the Northumberland Fusiliers never performed similar feats of arms. The four territorial battalions of the Northumberland Fusiliers (4th, 5th, 6th and 7th Battalions) were grouped into one brigade, 149 Brigade of the 50th (Northumbrian) infantry division. They were solid enough units, recruited from mining and farming communities of the Tyne Valley, Newcastle and northward up the North-East coast to Alnwick. However, their war record is far short of that of the 1st Battalion. Landing in France on 20 April 1915, they were thrown straight into the fierce battle to hold the German attacks around Ypres. At St. Julien, five

279

days after landing, they received their horrible baptism of fire on open ground, pinned down all day, and were machine-gunned and shelled. The 7th Battalion history makes much of the difficulties. Of three battalions committed, there were, however, relatively light casualties of up to 189 killed, dying of wounds during five days fighting. A complete list of decorations received for this baptism of fire is not available, but up to six DCMs have been identified and perhaps a single immediate MC. If other decorations were awarded, they may be hidden in Honours gazettes or as retrospective MMs gazetted in late 1916. This difficult action is now buried in history. Whilst the 1st Battalion was used as a fighting force throughout 1915 and the first half of 1916, after their performance at St. Julien, the Northumberland Territorial Brigade was only used for line holding, mainly in the Ypres Salient. They were not committed to the Somme battle until the battle of Flers-Courcelette on the 15 September 1916, which turned out to be 149 Brigade's 'First of July' although not quite as catastrophic (with the 5th in support, the other three battalions suffered 366 dead on the opening day). Another year of minor operations and line holding followed; this was a brigade which was, perhaps, labelled as not entirely reliable. Their next major attack was on South Houtholst Forest in the north Ypres Salient, 26 October 1917, which was, like much of the fighting in that area towards the end of the Third Battle of Ypres, bogged down in mud and shell holes. The brigade suffered 385 dead in what was largely an unsuccessful attack that failed to reach its objectives. However, in contrast to the honours list for St. Julien, the action at Houtholst Forest generated a bar to a DSO, five MCs, five DCMs and as many as 40 MMs for the Brigade as a whole. This is a slim honours list when considered that these rewards were divided between four battalions suffering about 400 killed.

In terms of raiding, the four battalions only managed two in the entire war, one carried out by the 5th Battalion and one by the 7th, in spite of pressure from High Command placed on all infantry units to raid the enemy regularly.

The war record of the Northumberland Territorials up to the end of 1917 is therefore a depressing picture of line holding and working parties interrupted by occasional days of slaughter in no-man's-land. Several minor attacks designed to bite off small features of ground, characterised the remaining activities of these battalions; these were attacks with limited objectives which were variably successful (although holding ground gained in the face of counter-attack proved problematic). Ball (2006) has shown how they received less training, less rest, and were asked to perform more labouring and line holding than the 1st Battalion. Their casualties show long periods of 'attrition' in horrible parts of the line, where they suffered an average of 45 dead per month just line holding in 1916.

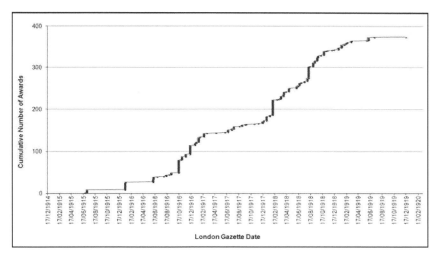

**Figure 41: Awards Growth, 4th, 5th, 6th and 7th (Territorial Army) Battalions, Northumberland Fusiliers, 1914-20.**

Comparing the activities of the territorial battalions with those of the 1st shows that whilst the 1st were committed to 17 attacks (resulting in 16 successful), the average for the territorials was only four attacks each during the whole course of the war (only one of which was successful). In 12 defensive actions, only one is considered successful whereas seven out of 10 defensive actions of the 1st Battalion resulted in the enemy being held and defeated.

The territorials struggled to deliver the goods in attack, struggled to halt German advances whilst they and flanking units tended to retire.

The territorials were able to show themselves in their best light in the Spring of 1918, during many difficult rearguard actions. The 7th Battalion was at this time detached as a pioneer unit and were no longer part of 149 Brigade, leaving the 4th, 5th and 6th Battalions fighting as infantry. It was the brigade's lot to be caught up in the Somme battle of March 1918, being posted for rest in the Aisne sector just in time to bear the brunt of the German attack there in April, and then being posted to the Lys area in late May where they were once again heavily attacked. At the end of all of this, the men were worn out, had suffered 708 fatalities, as well as losing many more men as prisoners of war and wounded. On 27 May 1918, whilst attempting to hold their ground, the 4th Battalion was surrounded and the 5th and 6th so weakened by fighting that the Brigade was reduced to cadre strength. Fighting alongside 149 Brigade, the 5th Battalion of the Durham Light Infantry was captured in heavy fighting the next day. Only a very few men of the 4th Battalion and of five DLI escaped over bridges, the remainder was either taken prisoner or sold their lives dearly.

The awards associated with this phase of the fighting bear looking at in some detail, as they tell the story of a great many infantry units caught up in these great retreats. The 149 Brigade first contacted the enemy on 22 March 1918, the day after the offensive began. The 4th Battalion was holding the line at Caulaincourt on the Somme, and won a DSO, three MCs and five MMs on 21–23 March. Second Lieutenant G. Davies gained the MC the day before they first contacted the German Army, 'when he volunteered to go forward and locate the enemy's position, returning with valuable information'. Later in the battle, on 27 March, near Vauvillers, Davies 'again showed great gallantry, fearlessly exposing himself and encouraging his men under heavy fire, afterwards leading a counter-attack with great dash and holding on until compelled to withdraw for want of ammunition'. Lieutenant Thomas Alexander Lacy Thompson gained a junior field officer's DSO: 'From the 22 March to 28 March

1918, after his Commanding Officer was wounded, he commanded the Battalion with the greatest courage. On the 27 March 1918, near Harbonnieres, the enemy having captured a village ..., he led his Battalion with conspicuous gallantry in a house-to-house counter-attack, and by his example his Battalion cleared the greater part of the village and re-established the line. On the 28 March 1918, in spite of two gunshot wounds in the leg, after the units on his flanks had been driven back, he held his ground for over an hour until the counter-attack restored the situation. By holding his ground he made a counter-attack possible, and inflicted the heaviest losses on the retreating enemy'.

Lacy Thompson received the able assistance of Second Lieutenant William Anderson who formed a nucleus of resistance: 'on 21 March 1918, near Caulaincourt... he showed great initiative in reorganising his company after a withdrawal, fearlessly exposing himself under heavy fire. On 27 March 1918, he again showed great gallantry near Vauvillers in organising and leading a counter-attack; and though his right arm was broken by a gunshot wound, he remained in the line encouraging his men until compelled to withdraw for want of ammunition'.

Although alone, Lieutenant William Barry Hicks showed great determination when, 'the company commanded by this officer was separated from the remainder of the battalion by a river. He covered the retirement of the battalion and held the position for five hours afterwards, although completely isolated, and sustaining many casualties. He afterwards extricated his company in a most able manner, and rejoined his battalion two days later. The bridge by which the river was crossed was blown up as soon as the rear of the company crossed. On 26 March 1918, near Framerville he showed the utmost gallantry when leading a counter-attack. He did splendid service'.

The defence came down to a handful of surviving officers who organised the men to defend. In many instances, men without leadership tended to run for it, rearwards.

While the 4th were thus engaged, the 5th Battalion held the advancing enemy from a ridge position on 22 March, but were forced to retreat the following day. On 23 March the 6th Battalion was heavily attacked whilst attempting to hold shallow trenches, and had to beat a hasty retreat under heavy shell fire from untenable positions that offered the troops almost no protection.

The defence in the Aisne area commencing 9 April was a harder affair in terms of fatalities, the brigade incurring almost twice as many as in March on the Somme, 319 versus 175. For these losses, the awards list was shorter, containing approximately nine MMs, three DCMs and just one award to an officer, a bar to the MC. This honour fell to Captain J. V. Gregory, in command of the battalion.

In terms of 4th Battalion awards for 27 May, the day the battalion ceased to exist, there are only five; one DCM and four MMs. It is unlikely that the battalion did not put up a fight, but the fact they were taken prisoner of war after surrendering voluntarily may have sealed the question, because POWs could only receive awards if they had been taken prisoner 'through no fault of their own'.[31, 32] No doubt, some very defiant acts were unrewarded. The single DCM was awarded to one of the few who was not taken prisoner, 200490 Sergeant J. Kelly, who 'On 27 May 1918, near Revillon... assisted in organising Lewis gun teams for the purposes of retarding the enemy's advance on Fismes. He displayed the utmost coolness under fire, and his example and leadership on several occasions prevented premature retirement on the part of young and inexperienced soldiers. Later in the day, near Glennes, he took up a position with two Lewis guns in a wood commanding the enemy's approach, and though twice slightly wounded he held this position until almost surrounded, inflicting heavy loss on the enemy and considerably delaying its advance. The courage and tenacity shown by this NCO was beyond praise, and rendered great service in difficult circumstances'. This is the only gallantry award made to a man who actually fought in the front line that day, the remainder being killed or captured. The four MMs were all won by men operating behind the front line as runners, on Battalion Transport or attempting to get ammunition to the fighting line. For example, Private John Knott was rewarded with the MM when, 'On the 27 May 1918, on the road between La Fait Farm and Ventelay

Village, the transport was being heavily and accurately shelled. One shell landed on a limber and the driver and mules were all wounded and the rear half of the limber destroyed. Pte Knott salved the rear half of another damaged limber and hitched it on. He mounted the wounded mules and drove them through Ventelay, still under heavy shell fire, until they collapsed'. The most important conclusion to be drawn here is that nearly all of the fighting went unseen and was unrewarded. None of the returning prisoners of war received decorations retrospectively for these actions in the *POW Gazette* of 30 January 1920.

We don't have comparable figures for the 4th Battalion on 27 May, but casualties of the 5th DLI for 28 May are stated to be '33 Officers and 650 Other Ranks', many of whom must, in reality, have been taken prisoner. The unit war diaries for Spring 1918, appear to camouflage mass surrenders under the heading 'casualties'. That many hundreds of men of 149 Brigade were taken prisoner is shown by the fact that 162 are noted simply as 'died' between June and December 1918 by the Commonwealth War Graves Commission. It is thought that most of these died in captivity and represent a substantial proportion of those who were interned as POWs.

During the same period, 21 March to 27 May, the 1st Battalion had held their position four times against mass attacks, knowing that the positions they selected were good and that the steadfastness of their men was more than a match for the Germans. They showed that British infantry could hold off these attacks and resulted in 71 awards to the 1st Battalion (203 dead) compared to 63 awards of all types split between three battalions of Territorials (710 dead). Whereas the 1st Battalion had survived by standing firm, it is noteworthy that 149 Brigade had been destroyed in the retreat and by getting surrounded. Retreat is far more dangerous than standing firm in entrenched positions, but to resist requires a determined and steadfast leadership.

Within the history of the Territorial Battalions we find an infantry brigade which shouldered some of the most unrewarding work of the war in some thoroughly unpleasant parts of the line, who were shot to pieces in shell holes several times, and who had little military success to show for their sacrifice. They took part in some of the hard fighting in the later stages of the Battle of the Somme and went forward in the first tank attack on 15 September 1916. Back home in the Tyne Valley and Newcastle area, certain towns and villages received notification of the death of many of their young men, rather few of whom gained any special military distinction.

## Gallantry in the Pioneer Battalions

Most infantry regiments had one or more pioneer battalions as a part of their strength in the First World War. Most of the gallantry awards made to the pioneer battalions between their arrival in France and March 1918 relate to the activities of working parties of various kinds. The war diaries of pioneer battalions record a great deal of labouring both behind the lines and in (or in advance of) the front line. Behind the lines much sweat was expended on road repairs, for example filling shell holes, levelling and widening roads, digging sunken roads to hide traffic from view and also the camouflaging of roads using poles, netting and material. Some pioneer battalions were railway specialists and worked on the standard and narrow gauge railways, a particular feature of the Ypres Salient. Railway construction companies of the Royal Engineers, infantry pioneer battalions and miscellaneous labour units were combined to perform duties such as track repair, building embankments and cuttings, as well as laying the rails. Various small branch lines of the railways were built, with sidings at artillery positions (for delivery of shells by rail rather than by the congested and heavily shelled roads). War diaries of pioneer battalions record much dangerous work in the front line digging and improving trenches (for example deepening, revetment, construction of fire steps, bays and dugouts). The digging and improvement of communication trenches and saps was a common activity in the front line. Work of this sort might be carried out in daylight but a great deal was done at night, particularly in the Salient where the ridges to the East were occupied by the enemy and his artillery. Constantly overlooked, the British Army was subjected to an almost ceaseless, searching, shelling as they did their best to keep their activities from view.

Work carried out by infantry pioneers in advance of front line trenches was almost exclusively a nocturnal activity, and included erection, repair and strengthening of the barbed wire, it included the digging of saps out towards the enemy lines and repairing, deepening and draining of these. At sap heads, out in front and close to German rifles, sentry outposts were constructed. Occasionally, lines of shell holes or isolated outposts had to be joined up to create a single new front line trench, some distance in front of the existing front line. The Pioneer Battalions had all of these activities to perform, whilst always subjected to actual or threatened enemy shooting.

Working parties in no-man's-land were given an infantry guard consisting of Lewis gun outposts stationed at intervals in front of the working party. Everyone needed to know where other units were, what they were doing and when. Unexpected encounters in no-man's-land at night sometimes resulted in friendly fire casualties at worst, nasty frights at best. When the work of the pioneers was complete, the working party quietly moved off and finally the Lewis gun outposts were brought back in.

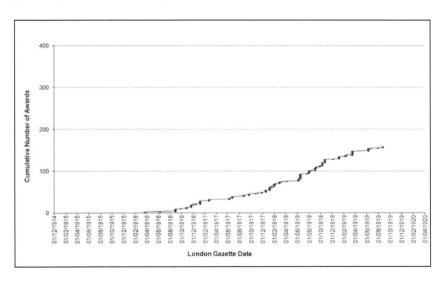

**Figure 42: Awards Growth, 14th, 17th, 18th and 19th (Pioneer) Battalions, Northumberland Fusiliers, 1914-20.**

The pioneers were still infantry battalions and some of their awards emphasise this fact. During the attacks of the 1–3 July 1916 on the Somme, a party of the 17th Pioneer Battalion, Northumberland Fusiliers, was detailed to dig a sap from our lines to the enemy lines, commencing immediately the attack went over. The objective was to provide a communication trench up to the captured German positions which could be used to get reserves forward without needing to go over the top. Critical work, the sap was dug, but owing to the difficulties encountered by the attacking troops, the Germans were close by when the work was completed. An enemy bombing party launched a savage attack on the working party, but was beaten off with bombs and bayonets. Well out in front of the lines in Copse Valley on the Somme on 16 July 1916, Captain Arthur Muir of the 19th Pioneer Battalion led a party of W-Company digging a connecting trench between several advanced posts. Once dug, the defence of the new front line trench became the, perhaps unwanted, responsibility of Muir and his men. Germany was not best pleased with their work and the pioneers were heavily shelled for their impetuous digging. Captain Muir was decorated with the MC; he would continue his daring work over the next years as indicated by his DSO with the 2nd Battalion of the Northumberlands and a bar to his MC with the 16th (Pioneer) Battalion of the same regiment.

Consolidation of positions was a key activity for the pioneers. After ground had been captured, either the re-use of old positions or the construction of new, defensible positions was often required. Communication trenches had to be dug across what had recently been no-man's-land. Before the digging could start, the location of the new trenches had to be taped out by someone. Captain John Fawcett of the 19th (Pioneer) Battalion Northumberland Fusiliers was required to mark out the lines for new trenches that would be dug by his company. He carried out his work successfully under heavy shell fire and was decorated with the MC, the citation reads: 'For conspicuous gallantry and devotion to duty. During a heavy bombardment, and while the situation was obscure after an enemy counter-attack, he taped out over 500 yards of trench up to the captured position. The work was carried out under heavy fire and his company was thereby enabled to begin the work of consolidation without delay'.

Lance-Sergeant Freeman of the 17th Battalion was part of a working party shelled by Germans after being spotted; a shell landed in a communication trench causing five to be killed. 'He behaved so well on this occasion that he was granted the Military Medal'.

The demolition of a factory chimney by the 19th Battalion Pioneers on the 24 September 1916, was an unusual task that resulted in the award of several medals. Captain Herbert Dawson blew up the chimney which was only 30 yards from the enemy trenches, working inside the chimney for over three hours. Sergeant I. Jackson displayed courage, coolness and ingenuity throughout the task. Work was delayed on two occasions by the close proximity of enemy patrols. They received the award of the MC and DCM respectively.

Transport of materials to the front line was of vital importance to the pioneer battalions, who needed supplies in order to be able to carry out their work digging and improving trenches and saps, laying duckboards, constructing dugouts and gun positions or as wiring parties. A clutch of awards was earned by the Regimental Quartermaster Sergeant of the 19th Pioneer Battalion and two of his men when, in late 1917, urgent construction supplies were got up to the line in spite of extremely heavy shelling of the battalion transport. Such supplies enabled captured, and frequently heavily damaged positions, to be consolidated and capable of holding in the event of a counter-attack. Pioneer units were often sent up in the immediate aftermath of a battle to assist in the consolidation process, and it was at such times that some of the awards to the pioneers were gained.

Similarly underlining the importance of the supply sections to the work of pioneers, it was Sergeant Laing of South Shields, 19th (Pioneer) Battalion, who gained a periodic award of the DCM in the New Year's Honours gazette of 1 January 1919: 'As Transport Sergeant since January 1916, he has shown great devotion to duty throughout. In charge of convoys carrying RE stores to positions under heavy shell fire he has shown coolness, initiative and resource. Throughout the period he has never lost an animal killed by enemy shell fire, and the prompt delivery of stores in most difficult circumstances has been of invaluable assistance in operations'. Further information on this remarkable award may be found in the published Battalion history. The DCM was probably for operations in the Salient near Boeschepe during July and August 1918 when the battalion transport did fine work getting rations and RE stores up nightly on shelled roads from the base at Godewaersvelde, with the loss of not a single man or animal. The book offers the following tribute: 'coolness, judgment and dash were called for, and all ranks of the Transport came up smiling'.

MMs were often won at night when working out in the open in no-man's-land putting wire up. Out in the open, under the constant threat of discovery, working parties were expected to continue with their work, digging, wiring or constructing outposts, whatever fire might be put down upon them. Regularly, flares were sent up from the enemy lines, during which the sometimes large parties of several hundred men would stand absolutely still in the eerie light. An occasional machine gun would splutter into action, spitting a stream of bullets out over the open country, searching for victims. If sighted by the enemy, of course the working parties faced getting caught in shell, machine gun and trench mortar fire. Discovery of their activities occurred in the light of flares, by the clank of metal against metal, a shovel hitting something hard, the flash of bright metal in moonlight or when an enemy patrol, lurking around in no-man's-land bumped into them. On the night of 12‑13 July 1917, a working party of the Northumberland Fusiliers was out when a German raid was launched. The raiding party encountered the working party by surprise, a deadly firefight developed in no-man's-land, and the raid was repulsed before it had got into its primary objective, the British trenches.

The 17th (Newcastle Railway Pals) Battalion of the Northumberland Fusiliers provides a very interesting example of a specialist pioneer battalion at work. Arriving in France on 22 November 1915, the battalion was engaged in typical pioneer work. Through January and February 1916 the battalion supplied working parties road building, making dugouts, revetting trenches, wiring, constructing iron shelters and laying a tramway. At the beginning of July 1916 they were engaged in digging saps forward to captured enemy positions, carrying mountains of supplies up to forward positions in support of the offensive and even some tunnelling work. However, their railway work began in November 1916 when they were officially converted to a Railway Pioneer Battalion. The standard and light gauge railways were an especial target for German artillerymen, and so it was on their first rail work at Pozieres, when two men were killed by shell fire. In conjunction with the 119th and 277th Rail Construction Companies, Royal Engineers, they worked on light rail repair and construction throughout the winter of 1916–17. By 3 April 1917, the battalion had been moved to the Salient area where they began work on the Great Midland Railway in the Ypres sector, as a unit of 'Railway Construction Engineers'. Despite being regularly shelled, no gallantry medals had been conferred. During the summer offensives in the Salient, the battalion was tasked with running the light railway lines forward as fast as possible, to keep up with the advancing troops and maintain supplies. At this time, the rail construction parties and the line itself were constantly shelled and broken. The battalion was almost continuously engaged in light rail construction in the Salient until the German Spring Offensives of 1918. There were only two possible medals for bravery on rail construction work awarded in mid-1917 to Private G. S. Aldis (MM) and Major G. Stamp Taylor (MC). Unfortunately no citations were published so the circumstances of these interesting awards cannot be stated. Later in 1918, the battalion was mainly involved in road construction and repair, with some gallantry awards being awarded for bravery under shell fire.

One award of the MM may have been made when a heavy shell hit a major ammunition dump in the Salient on 30 November 1917, causing over 150 casualties among Labour and Ordnance Corps troops. Those of the 17th (Newcastle Railway Pioneers) working nearby, assisted with the fire fighting and rescue work; Lt. McKay and his platoon came in for special mention. It is possible that Private Serginson of the battalion may have been awarded his MM for this event, which was seen and heard by every soldier anywhere near the Salient at that time; there was a devastating explosion and shock wave followed by a veritable fireworks display. Many desperate deeds were performed by those working in and close to this inferno.

The German Spring Offensives of March to June 1918 was a period of desperate rearguard fighting in which many of the pioneer battalions had to assist with the defence. They were additionally used in the defence of bridgeheads across watercourses and in the demolition of those bridges once the last British troops had passed back over them. A good example of this work is afforded by that of the 18th (Pioneer) Battalion, Northumberland Fusiliers. When the second of the German Spring Offensives was launched on 9 April 1918, the battalion fell back towards the River Lys and the bridges at Erquingham. The pioneers were ordered to defend the bridgehead and destroy the bridges once the last remains of tired, shocked and depleted British battalions retreated over the bridge and the German Army drew ever nearer. On 10 April, the enemy came within rifle shot of the bridge. Positioned on a defensive outer perimeter, Corporal J. R. F. Welsh of Newcastle handled his Lewis guns with such effect that: 'although half his men became casualties from the intense fire, he succeeded in carrying on until the enemy's advance was stopped. By his pluck he prevented what might have resulted in an awkward situation'. At the last possible moment, most of the men and weapons were extracted and got back across the bridge, leaving only a handful of pioneers between the British and German Armies and two bridges to destroy. At this point, the situation became typically desperate, but Captain James W. Vasey was with a small party detailed to provide covering fire for the destruction of the bridges: 'He held the enemy at bay, with eight men and two Lewis guns, while the infantry withdrew across a river. It was not until he was nearly surrounded that he retired'. In charge of a second party was Lieutenant Frank Webb whose 'conspicuous gallantry and devotion to duty' aided his party to destroy 'two foot bridges while the enemy was firing on his party continuously. At the second bridge he organised a party of Lewis guns and so obtained covering fire while the bridge was cut away. It was owing to his coolness that the task was accomplished, as he was nearly surrounded and losing men fast'. Private T. Wainman of Leeds was one of those men ready with an axe; 'he was one of a party of four detailed to destroy a footbridge across a river after the troops had all crossed. They began chopping, but owing to the hail of bullets three of the men left the bridge and lay on the bank. He, however, continued working alone until he had cut the bridge completely in two, thus enabling the pontoon to be liberated and floated downstream'. All the while, the battalion's seven Lewis guns were barking away at the enemy, who provided plentiful targets. The men then took to their heels to clear the area and, according to the published battalion history; 'despite the fact that there were bullets whizzing around, everybody started to laugh very heartily, apparently at the hiding which we all considered we had given the Boche'.[33]

During the German offensives the pioneer battalions of the Northumberland Fusiliers gained gallantry awards at a greater rate than at any time before or after. The 18th (Pioneer) Battalion gained two MCs, two DCMs and five MMs in the single defensive action described above. Between 26 March and 28 March 1918, the 19th (Pioneer) Battalion, Northumberland Fusiliers had successfully defended a position at Montauban against overwhelming enemy fire and violent infantry attacks for which they reaped a substantial reward in decorations: 10 MMs, five MCs and a DCM. It was, for these pioneers, a departure from the routine work of the previous years as well as a marvellous affirmation of their dual role as regular infantry. When really up against it, they showed that they were able to outperform some of their fellow battalions in stubborn defensive fighting.

In spite of all the important work, the pioneer battalions carried out over more than three years at war, work that always required courage (and bravery); the awards lists are much shorter than those of other battalions. The pioneers of the Northumberland Fusiliers gained approximately one third of the total number of gallantry awards compared to Territorial and Service Battalions and one tenth of the total awards gained by the 1st Battalion (regulars). It should be said at this point that the pioneer battalions suffered an average of one third of the fatalities of the average fighting infantry battalion, meaning that their awards list remains very much in proportion to the number of deaths they suffered.

## Gallantry in the 'Kitchener' Battalions

Packed with ardent volunteers, these units formed the New Armies raised in 1914 and early 1915. They proceeded overseas in the main during the summer and autumn of 1915 but some were shipped to France in January 1916. The Kitchener battalions of the Northumberland Fusiliers were heavily involved in a mixed series of engagements including the disaster of the 1 July 1916, trench raiding and one of the most successful battles around Ypres, 1917; the Battle of the Menin Road in September. Their activities and record of bravery are therefore pertinent to the study of infantry on the Western Front.

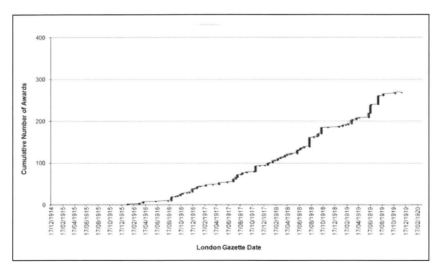

**Figure 43: Awards Growth, 8th and 9th Battalions, Northumberland Fusiliers, 1914-20.**

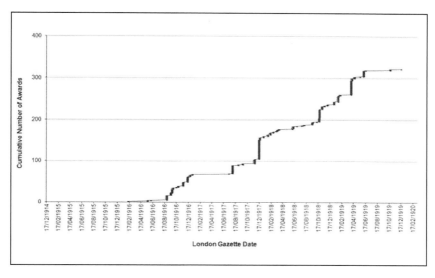

**Figure 44: Awards Growth, 10th and 11th Battalions, Northumberland Fusiliers, 1914-20.**

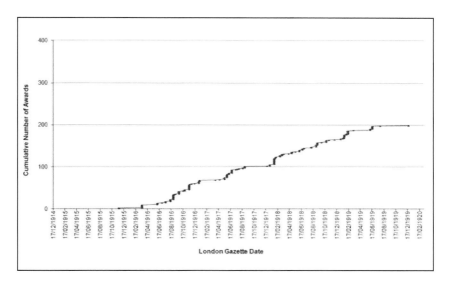

**Figure 45: Awards Growth, 12, 13 and 12/13th Battalions, Northumberland Fusiliers, 1914-20.**

## AN INFANTRY DISASTER: KITCHENER BATTALIONS AND THE FIRST OF JULY, 1916

Considered the greatest British military disaster of all time, the 1 July 1916 saw 10 battalions of the Northumberland Fusiliers committed to battle near the village of La Boisselle. Masses of Tyneside men got out of their trenches that morning at 7:30am, some with 'entrenching tools in tunics to protect their bellies'[34], after a seven-day bombardment of enemy positions had finished and two large mines were exploded. They were played across no-man's-land by their pipers, until the German machine guns and rifles opened up on them. 'It was real red blistering hell hot and make no mistake' reported one Tyneside Scottish Corporal to a Newcastle newspaper.[35] Private Elliott of the 20th (Tyneside Scottish) Battalion, Northumberland Fusiliers, wrote of this attack that he saw a Battalion Piper, 'riddled with bullets, writhing and screaming. Another lad was just kneeling, his head thrown back. Bullets were just slapping into him knocking great bloody chunks off his body'.[36] From the other side of the wire, German machine gunners plainly saw British soldiers hit by their bullets whose pocketed hand grenades exploded, ripping their bodies to pieces and flinging the splintered bone and blasted flesh into the air.

A little to the south, the men of the Tyneside Irish Brigade had gone forward into the same storm. Their Pipers also played the men over the top, one of these, Pte J. Brown, told his family that, 'I played the "Minstrel Boy" because the words seemed the most appropriate that I could think of'.[37] The song opens with, *The Minstrel Boy to the war is gone, In the ranks of death you will find him*. He was playing for his comrades, but just as much for himself and his dire predicament.

The attack by men of the hardest hit Tyneside Scottish and Irish Brigades is very well described, from the British perspective, in the two books written by John Sheen and Graham Stewart. Since these books were published, a German account of the fighting to the south of La Boisselle has also appeared.[38] As the British attack unfolded, recalled Oberleutnant Kienitz of the 110th Reserve Infantry Regiment's Machine Gun Company, 'Silently our machine guns and the infantrymen waited until our opponents came closer'. According to Kienitz, the British were allowed to get very close indeed, 'only a few metres' away, before they were 'sprayed with a hurricane of defensive fire'. As the attackers dropped to ground, the battle seemed to die away, until German grenades were thrown into the masses of huddled men, machine guns searched them out, discovered them and destroyed them. What happened next is not recorded in British accounts, '…initially in small groups, but later in huge masses, the enemy began to pull back' continued Kienitz, '…it seemed as though every man in the entire field was attempting to flee'. He notes that they had been firing ceaselessly for two hours when the battle died away in Sausage Valley, making this about 9:30am. With a reasonable field of view up and down Sausage Valley, any fleeing British would have been seen by many on both sides, even through the dust and smoke of battle. British accounts emphasise the various relatively small bodies of men who had made it into the German lines and continued fighting until the next day, but it seems these were very much a minority and had no effect on the outcome of this fight. The major outcome of the battle in Sausage Valley was recorded by Germans, not by British.

A possible intimation of events may be found in an account written by Captain Rigby of the 27th (Tyneside Irish) Battalion, Northumberland Fusiliers, who crossed Sausage Valley itself. He stated that: 'The advance was inspiring but the sights and sounds of the return journey are not pleasant and are better omitted'.[39] This could be a veiled reference to men fleeing the field of battle, but he may only have been referring to his own difficult return journey over cut up corpses and the sounds of dying, whilst he himself was wounded. Whatever the events he was referring to, he was notably keen not to tell the story.

Of his journey out of Sausage Valley to safety, the wounded Private James Tunney of the 26th (Tyneside Irish) Battalion, admitted that he lost his nerve after being hit out in the open, 'I was a bit lost in No-Mans-Land. I pulled myself together a bit by drinking my water, then found my way out'.[40]

A Tyneside Irish Lance Corporal, Michael Manley of the 25th

Battalion Northumberland Fusiliers, summed up the emotional experience of those who made it back: 'I sat totally stunned. Young lads were all around me, some were sobbing hysterically, they'd seen things no one should have to see'.[41]

None of the Tyneside Scottish and Irish survivors mentioned above earned bravery awards, in spite of the courage they had shown and emotional trauma they suffered.

South of La Boisselle, the initial attacks were beaten off, almost certainly in view of officers watching the progress through binoculars. It is a possibility that the reputation of the Tyneside Irish Brigade suffered for the nature of the failure in this part of the battle, as they won just 17 gallantry awards for the action of 1 July 1916, compared to the 44 of the Tyneside Scottish. The Tyneside Irish won two DCMs both of which were for the 26th Battalion which was operating to the north with the Tyneside Scottish. In terms of fatalities per MM award, the Tyneside Irish were rewarded with one medal per 50 fatalities, compared to one MM per 23 fatalities in the Tyneside Scottish. Fifty fatalities per MM is by far the highest MM to fatality ratio uncovered during this study and the only available explanation is one that British participants may have failed to record. If the scale and nature of the defeat is not the reason, then perhaps the Tyneside Irish Brigade submitted fewer award recommendations.

| | **Battalion** | **DSO** | **MC** | **DCM** | **MM** |
|---|---|---|---|---|---|
| Pioneers | 18th | 0 | 0 | 0 | 5 |
| Tyneside Scottish Brigade | 20th | 0 | 2 | 1 | 10 |
| | 21st | 0 | 2 | 1 | 9 |
| | 22nd | 0 | 1 | 1 | 9 |
| | 23rd | 0 | 2 | 0 | 7 |
| Tyneside Irish Brigade | 24th | 0 | 1 | 0 | 1 |
| | 25th | 0 | 1 | 0 | 3 |
| | 26th | 1 | 0 | 2 | 3 |
| | 27th | 1 | 0 | 0 | 5 |

**Table 12: Immediate Awards made to Battalions of the Northumberland Fusiliers for the First of July, 1916**

This then, the 1 of July 1916, was the worst of all failed attacks. One thousand three hundred and ninety five Tyneside Scots and Tyneside Irish, killed on the 1 July. Altogether, the regiment lost 1,556 killed in action; the heaviest price paid by any regiment that terrible day. The Northumberland Fusiliers battalions experienced many failed attacks in the war, but no other on such a scale.

## RAIDING BY THE TYNESIDE SCOTS AND IRISH

After the debacle of the First of July, the Tyneside Scottish and Irish Brigades took no further part in the Somme battle and instead spent their time taking in reinforcement drafts and training on quiet areas of the front. In the Winter of 1916–17, the brigade developed a reputation for raiding, which they carried out with all the accoutrements of close-quarter fighting. Whereas the apparatus of the raid was fearsome, the raids carried out by these two brigades were not particularly dangerous affairs; the average number of dead was three per raid and half of their raids incurred no dead at all. In fact, a man who participated in one of these raids was twice as likely to get a bravery medal than get killed. There are no recorded raids during which a man was more likely to be killed than to win a medal. By way of contrast, the large scale attacks in which the men took part resulted in an average of 13 times more dead than medals, and a maximum of 50 dead per medal. Greater bravery, one might assume, should be found where there is the greatest risk of death, but the distribution of bravery medals does not follow that logic. Typically, about 15 per cent of the raiding party would be decorated but there were two raids, one carried out by 33 men of the 20th Battalion on 12 October 1916 and a 34-man raid by the 23rd Battalion on 30 September 1916, which resulted in a quarter of participants receiving a decoration – a proportion rarely achieved in successful, large scale attacks. Even after one of the most successful attacks on the Western Front, the Battle of the Menin Road on 20 September 1917, in which the 10th and 11th Battalions took part, some 73 medals were distributed among approximately 1,600 to 2,000 men, representing only 4 per cent of the attacking force.

A successful raid always attracted more awards than an unsuccessful one. Considering the Tyneside Scottish and Tyneside Irish raids of 1916–1917, raids that went wrong got few or no gallantry awards because they failed to inflict casualties upon the enemy, bring back prisoners or materiel. The most successful raid, that of 23rd (Tyneside Scottish) Battalion on the night of 11–12 February 1917, attracted two DSOs, five MCs, a bar to the DCM, three DCMs, a bar to the MM and 12 MMs, which was a very rich haul by a raid party of 265 men. Nine per cent of participants received a decoration for gallantry, i.e., approximately five times the whole-war average award rate for the regiment.

## THE JOB OF THE INFANTRY IS TO BE SHELLED

Shelling has always required the greatest of courage to endure; this is clear from veteran's accounts from 1914 right through to the Falklands in 1982. However, bravery medals were rarely awarded to those who went through the heavy bombardments of the First World War. During the middle of October 1917, the Tyneside Scottish Brigade moved into the line in the Salient, relieving the Tyneside Irish of their duty. The conditions in the line were described as 'horrendous, the whole area was a vast sea of deep mud' and the so-called front line was 'really a series of defended pill boxes and shell holes'.[42] For over a week the men were shelled and gassed without respite. Rations and water could not be obtained and sleep was denied to them. In this relatively short period of line holding, the worst hit units suffered nearly 50 per cent loss of strength due to casualties and sickness. The strain of shelling, the conditions and deprivation was as potent a force as direct contact with the enemy. Having lost 127 dead, the Tyneside Scottish Brigade received a total of 17 medals for gallantry. It is thought that these were made to ration parties as well as officers and NCOs who toured the positions by going from shell hole to shell hole in order to keep up the morale of the men. Dealing with enemy snipers was also a means of winning a medal in such periods of line holding. Simply having the courage to endure the beating without being able to retaliate, was never enough to win a medal. Men had to achieve something in those conditions and it may be wondered whether the busy men did not experience less fear than the man sat in a shell hole with nothing to do but press his face into the mud.

Over a longer period, the four Territorial Battalions of 149 Brigade lost 231 dead whilst holding some of the most unpleasant parts of the line in the Ypres Salient during the first half of 1916. Daily casualties occurred during this time as a result of enemy trench mortar attacks, artillery fire and snipers. The brigade only won approximately 10 medals for acts of bravery carried out under shell fire in these six wearing months.

## AN INFANTRY TRIUMPH: THE BATTLE OF THE MENIN ROAD, 20 SEPTEMBER 1917

Order number 32 was distributed to the Commanding Officer of the 11th Battalion, Northumberland Fusiliers, to each company commander, to the battalion medical and signal officers and to Brigade Headquarters by runner, at 11am on 11 September 1917. It had been prepared and signed by Captain and Adjutant Robert C. Mayall. It opened with:

*The enemy is occupying a position running North and South through Inverness Copse and Dumbarton Lakes. His troops are distributed in depth, the foremost line consisting of a series of Strong Points, fortified shell holes and portions of destroyed trenches. 68th Brigade will attack the enemy's position on the front from Java Avenue J.19.b.6.1/2 to junction Jasper Drive and Green Jacket Ride J.19.b.7.7. with X Brigade (41st Division) on its right and the 69th Brigade on its left.*

The Menin Road led from Ypres more or less eastward towards Menin, over the Passchendaele Ridge. Here, nature had been shattered already and the shell-ploughed, sodden landscape exists already in our collective imagination. There was little reason to suspect that those tasked with advance were in anything other than a serious predicament. An enemy distributed 'in depth' meant his defensive line was deep and consisted of a series of interlocking, and mutually supporting, strong points and infantry positions. A concentrated artillery barrage could not destroy a diffuse target; the enemy line had strength in-built. All previous assaults in this area had met with limited success, or none at all. Objectives for the planned battle were firstly the Red Line, to be captured by A and C Companies of the 11th Northumberlands; next was the Blue Line to be taken by the 10th Battalion who would pass through the 11th as the attack progressed. Finally the 13th Battalion of the Durham Light Infantry would pass through the captured Blue Line to take the Green Line. Heavy Vickers machine guns would move up and occupy strong points to be constructed during the battle by D Company 11NF with help from Royal Engineers and Infantry Pioneers. The 11th Battalion Company Commanders for the infantry attack were Lieutenant C. S. Bowman (A-Coy), Captain H. M. P. West (B-Coy), Captain C. J. H. Adamson (C-Coy) and Captain J. W. Hunter (D-Coy). Not one of these men won a medal for their work on the 20th – other officers won the medals – but half of them were killed (West and Adamson) and the other half were wounded, leaving them unable to contribute to the fighting and the results. No officer above the rank of captain went into action; this was a company officer's, NCO's and private's battle.

The men were well organised. It was ordered that 'each Platoon and Section must be given a special task, a special objective and special work to do on reaching it'. The attack was particularly clearly organised, right down to the establishment and marking of 'runner routes' under the responsibility of the battalion signals officer. 'These will be marked by sticks, three feet long, painted red and white'. In addition, runner routes to the rear from Battalion HQ to Brigade HQ were marked with 'flags two feet square, half white, half yellow'. Artillery was primarily concerned with targeted barrage work, but one battery was available 'to deal with any special object' which the infantry needed help to eliminate. The creeping barrage would move forward at a rate of between four minutes and eight minutes per 100 yards, and would stop and pause shortly beyond each of the Red, Blue and Green Line objectives. The infantry would be notified by means of smoke shells fired with the barrage, when the barrage had reached each of these objectives. Visual cues were therefore built into the barrage to provide information about the location of the objectives, which were being monitored by aircraft observation and artillery forward observation posts. Specific instructions regarding the cooperation with aircraft were given; when the aircraft fired a white flare and sounded a klaxon horn, then the infantry should light a red flare to show their positions, and so progress on the ground could be monitored. These flares were distributed amply around the fighting men. The aircraft would also be 'up all day for the purpose of looking out for counter-attacks and for transmitting infantry messages calling for barrage'. At a large scale, it was a coordinated operation involving infantry, machine guns on barrage work, flexible artillery support and aircraft. Homing pigeons were, nevertheless, still carried into battle.

At platoon and section level, it was not simply to be a blind advance, of throwing men against gunfire. The techniques outlined in Army pamphlet S.S.143 (the vitally important 'Instructions for the Training of Platoons for Offensive Action', War Department Document number 613 of 1917, emanating from the Office of the Adjutant General) were to be fully employed. Extracts from this pamphlet, given below, provide a clear picture of how the infantry operated and allow us to imagine what the officers and men were actually doing on the field of battle that day.

Each platoon was divided into sections of riflemen (both marksmen and bayonet men) with specialist bombers, rifle grenadiers and Lewis gunners operating in mutually supportive roles. Extracts from S.S.143:

*Characteristics and Uses of the Various Weapons.*
(a) *The rifle and bayonet, being the most efficient offensive weapons of the soldier, are for assault, for repelling attack, or for obtaining superiority of fire. Every NCO and man in the platoon must be proficient in their use.*
(b) *The bomb is the second weapon of every NCO and man, and is used either for dislodging the enemy from behind cover or killing him below ground.*

*(c) The rifle bomb is the 'howitzer' of the infantry and used to dislodge the enemy from behind cover and to obtain superiority of fire by driving him underground.*

*(d) The Lewis gun is the weapon of opportunity. Its chief uses are to kill the enemy above ground and to obtain superiority of fire. Its mobility and the small target it and its team present, render it peculiarly suitable for working round an enemy's flank or for guarding one's own flank.*

The use of the Stokes mortar as an infantry weapon is not described in this pamphlet but is mentioned in the operational orders for this action. The rapid and heavy fire of this small, portable weapon was best utilised to lay down a part of the artillery barrage, presumably hitting near and visible targets with direct fire as they appeared.

S.S.143 continues with descriptions of the duties of the specialist heavy weapons and of the junior battlefield leadership:

*The section of rifle bombers should open a hurricane bombardment on the point of resistance from the nearest cover available. The section of Lewis gunners should in the first instance open traversing fire on the point of resistance from the nearest cover available. At a later stage it may be desirable to work round a flank.*

The action of the various sections and commanders should be as follows:
*The section of riflemen should, without halting, gain a position on a flank from which to attack both with fire and with the bayonet. The section of bombers should, without halting, gain a position on a flank and attack under cover of the bombardment of rifle bombs. The section of rifle bombers should open a hurricane bombardment on the point of resistance from the nearest cover available. The section of Lewis gunners should in the first instance open traversing fire on the point of resistance from the nearest cover available. At a later stage it may be desirable to work round a flank. Section commanders control and lead their sections, keeping touch with the platoon commander. The platoon commander controls and*

*directs the sections and sends back information to the company commander.*

At 3:30 am on the morning of the 20th, the battalion was ready. They were in position on a taped line in front of Dumbarton Lakes, ESE of Ypres. At 5:40am a combined artillery, machine gun and Stokes mortar barrage was opened and the battalion, with A and C companies in the firing line, B-Coy in close support and D-Coy in reserve, moved to the attack of the Red Line, the first objective. There was no preliminary bombardment, the infantry attack started with the artillery support. Very heavy opposition was met with at first from machine-gun fire, especially from one enemy post which held out for a long time causing many casualties. It seems likely that it was 45940 Pte. E. Allen of Fenton, Staffs who dealt with this machine gun: 'Single-handed he attacked an enemy strong point, which was causing heavy casualties and captured a machine gun and accounted for the whole garrison. He set a magnificent example of fearlessness and initiative' (DCM). In addition, Sergeant E. Lightowler of Bradford, Yorks won another: 'When all the NCOs had become casualties he did valuable work in collecting the men of his company and assisting to organise the attack. He took six prisoners single-handed. As a platoon commander he displayed great coolness and determination, and was directly responsible for much of the success of the attack'. Lightowler was moving over the battlefield, speaking to his men, signalling to them, organising the plan of approach, but leaving the initiative and details of approach to his men. Rifles, bombers, Lewis guns and rifle grenade teams were all in touch and working together.

But it was far from an easy fight, as the war diary indicates: 'After heavy hand-to-hand fighting, A and C Companies reinforced by B Company reached their objective and dug in'. At the head of the fighting, MCs were won by 2nd Lt. Hugh Mellor and 2nd Lt. Edmund Smith. The former, Hugh Mellor, 'collected the men and pushed on and captured the objective allotted after heavy fighting. He displayed great gallantry in going through the barrage and capturing a strong point which was giving considerable trouble'. Edmund

Smith gained his MC when: 'On reaching his objective after heavy fighting he collected the men of his company and took command when the company commander was wounded. Throughout the following 36 hours, by his coolness and disregard of danger, he set a magnificent example to his men'. 2nd Lt. Andrew Stewart's citation for the Military Cross contains some indications of the platoon tactics employed right across the battlefield that day: 'Under heavy machine-gun fire he crawled up to within five yards of an enemy strong point and opened fire with a Lewis gun to cover his platoon's attack on the strong point'. The only decoration won by a Company Commander was that conferred upon Captain Thomas Lindsley Browne of the 10th Battalion: 'Although most of his company were heavily engaged on the first objective, he collected men from his own and other units and, after heavy fighting, secured his ultimate objective. He set a fine example of courage and devotion to duty'. This officer's awards are illustrated at the end of this section.

Almost nothing is known of how the MMs were won, and there were some 54 in total spread between the 10th and 11th Battalions. We have to assume that they went to individual privates and junior NCOs for actually doing the fighting, clearing resistance, pushing forward and for getting ammunition and supplies up. One of them, we do know something about; 2nd Lt. Hugh Mellor had a young lad at his side acting as his runner. It is probable that his name was Stephen Forrest, who: 'During operations... was platoon runner to the only surviving officer of his Company. He unceasingly carried messages under heavy shell fire, and also collected many stragglers and brought them back to the main body, and so assisted greatly in the capturing of their objective, i.e. Tower Hamlets and Passchendaele Ridge'. It is noted in archives that Pte. Forrest had been wounded three times and whilst home on leave, is reported to have said that: 'I tried to do my duty'. Doubtless, most of the men thought exactly the same.

The 10th Battalion war diary speaks only briefly of the battle: *5:40am. Battalion advanced to the attack, keeping closely in rear of the 11th Northumberland Fusiliers. All objectives were gained'.*

And the 11th Battalion diary continues: *'Enemy shelled captured position intermittently throughout the day but owing to the success of the 10th NF and 13th DLI in capturing the Blue and Green Line our battalion position became support'.* In this note we first sense the scale of the successes achieved, the front line had moved so far forward as to make casual movement in the open basically safe. Men walked about kicking their heels, talking to mates, with only the occasional sniper round, fired from a long way off, clipping the ground around them. In the Ypres Salient, such a result was highly unusual.

The following day the band marched the companies out of the line and congratulations were received from the Divisional Commander who emphasised that: 'the marked success which attended your efforts is largely due to the excellent relations which exist between all ranks, arms and services of the Division, and to that readiness to cooperate with one another'. It was one of the first of many successful combined operations battles that would follow, fully employing the new methods of inter-service cooperation and platoon and section based tactics.

Not only those who did the actual fighting but also, and rightly, those acting in support of this battle received awards. Lieutenant Sidney Brewin was 'in command of a carrying party and although severely wounded he completed his task', allowing the construction of strong points and consolidation to occur and 'set a wonderful example to his men'. Two MCs and a DCM were won by men who organised the operation; Captain Robert C. Mayall, HQ Company, won an MC for working 'untiringly for three days and nights continuously, setting a magnificent example to all'. 2nd Lt. James Moffatt also of HQ Coy 'superintended the marking out of the position on which the Battalion assembled for the attack'. Quartermaster Sergeant R. L. Parker of Dewsbury, Yorkshire received the DCM for getting the ration supply right: 'which largely contributed to the success of the operations'.

What about success, then? Two battalions had committed some 1,500 to 1,700 men to the battle, and a relatively slight 124 were killed. In reward they received a bravery award for every two dead. They had got off lightly compared to the First of July 1916 when the Tynesiders had advanced in long lines without the creeping barrage and without the benefit of the 'all-arms' platoon tactics and combined operations support. These men died en-masse facing massed machine guns and shell fire, and received just one medal per 50 dead.

Whilst it may be thought that bravery medals were awarded for acts of bravery in the most fearful, dangerous and life-threatening circumstances, this was clearly not so. When men were experiencing the most fear, they could generally not expect to receive a medal. When men were busy doing something – organising, turning the enemy out – then they started to receive commendation and medals. The contrasting award patterns versus casualties, from the relatively safe trench raids showered with medals to the desperately dangerous undertaking of the First of July 1916, and the relatively dangerous periods of line holding under artillery bombardment, show that medals were not awarded for the most dangerous actions. As we have repeatedly seen, medals were heaped upon the junior and senior leadership for delivering success; the more responsibility a man took for operations, the more likely he was to receive medallic recognition and a pecuniary reward at some stage. The trench raid was certainly something of an exception, for it is well documented that both British and German Generals adopted a policy of encouraging raids and of rewarding handsomely those 'volunteers' who took part in them.

## VICTORIA CROSSES

Men of the Northumberland Fusiliers won only five Victoria Crosses during the First World War, which is surprising given that they were the largest regiment present. This underlines the rarity of the VC; that over 100,000 infantry soldiers could be fielded by a regiment in one of the hardest infantry wars the world has ever seen, and only five would come away with the nation's highest decoration for gallantry. Of these five, two were awarded to the Tyneside Irish Brigade less than nine months after they had suffered over 600 dead on the First of July 1916. Just one was awarded to a man from the North East of England, and that to an officer (2nd Lt. Johnson of Widdrington, Northumberland).

After fighting for two and a half years on the Western Front, the Northumberland Fusiliers finally got their first VC on 9 April 1917, on the opening day of the Battle of Arras. It was won by 22040 Lance Corporal Thomas Bryan, 25th (Tyneside Irish) Battalion, from Stourbridge: 'For most conspicuous gallantry during an attack. Although wounded, this Non-commissioned Officer went forward alone with a view to silencing a machine gun which was inflicting much damage. He worked up most skilfully along a communication trench, approached the gun from behind, disabled it and killed two of the team as they were abandoning the gun. As the machine gun had been a serious obstacle in the advance to the second objective, the results obtained by Lance Corporal Bryan's gallant action were very far-reaching'. Thomas Bryan was born at Stourbridge, Worcestershire, in 1882, and was a Castleford miner before he enlisted into the Northumberland Fusiliers. On the 9 April 1917, the first day of the Arras offensive, he took part in the attack on the German positions on the southern slopes of the Vimy Ridge. Operating to the right of the Canadians who were assaulting the main ridge, the 34th Division was held up early in the attack by a well placed German machine gun: 'It had a wonderful field of fire, and had held up the Brigades on our right and left. It had caught our people as they came over the ridge, about 300 yards in front of the machine-gun position. Our men and the men of the Scottish Division were lying dead almost in a line just on the ridge. But for Bryan the Division would never have reached its objective that day.'[43] The Victoria Cross was presented by the King at St James's Park, Newcastle, on the 17 June 1917.

40989 Private Ernest Sykes from Mossley in Yorkshire also won the Victoria Cross on 9 April 1917, with the 27th (Tyneside Irish) Battalion: 'For most conspicuous bravery and devotion to duty when his battalion in attack was held up about 350 yards in advance of our lines by intense fire from front and flank, and suffered heavy casualties. Private Sykes, despite this heavy fire, went forward and brought back four wounded – he made a fifth journey and remained out under conditions which appeared to be certain death, until he had bandaged all those who were too badly wounded to be moved. These gallant actions, performed under incessant machine-gun and rifle fire showed an utter contempt for danger'. The Empire Theatre, Newcastle was the location used for a presentation ceremony in July 1917, at which Sykes and his wife were given £100 of war bonds, a timepiece and a wallet of notes. At another ceremony in Yorkshire, he received a gold watch. King George V pinned the Victoria Cross on his chest at Buckingham Palace on 21 July 1917. Ernest Sykes died on 3 August 1949, aged 64, from the effects of a wound received on the Gallipoli Peninsula in 1915.

The next man to win the VC for the Northumberlands was Lieutenant John Scott Youll of the 11th Battalion: 'On 15 June 1918 south west of Asiago, Italy, Second Lieutenant Youll was commanding a patrol which came under heavy enemy fire. Sending his men back to safety he remained to watch the situation and then, unable to rejoin his company, he reported to a neighbouring unit where he took command of a party of men from different units, holding his position against enemy attack until a machine gun opened fire behind him. He rushed and captured the gun, killing most of the team and opened fire, inflicting heavy casualties. He then carried out three separate counterattacks, driving the enemy back each time'.

Performing remarkable work, equivalent perhaps to that of an entire infantry company, 1325 Private Wilfred Wood, a native of Hazel Grove, Stockport, won the VC with the 10th Battalion on the day after the costly crossing of the river Piave, when Lt John Scott Youll, VC, was killed by a shell exploding: 'On 28 October 1918 near Casa Vana, Italy, when the advance was being held up by hostile machine guns and snipers, Private Wood on his own initiative worked forward with his Lewis gun, enfiladed the enemy machine-gun nest and caused 140 men to surrender. Later, when a hidden machine gun opened fire at point-blank range, Private Wood charged the gun, firing his Lewis gun from the hip at the same time. He killed the machine-gun crew and, without further orders, pushed on and enfiladed a ditch from which three officers and 160 men subsequently surrendered'. At this time on the Italian Front, the Austro-Hungarian Army had been very short of food, supplies and ammunition for many months, and large parts of that Army were in the mood for surrendering. In fact the entire Hapsburg Army surrendered just one week after Private Wood's 'plucky' actions.

Second Lieutenant James Bulmer Johnson of Widdrington in Northumberland won the Regiment's final VC of the war whilst serving with the 36th Battalion on the Western Front at Wez Macquart on 14 October 1918: 'During operations by strong patrols, Second Lieutenant Johnson repelled frequent counter-attacks and for six hours, under heavy fire, he held back the enemy. When at length he was ordered to retire he was the last to leave the advanced position carrying a wounded man. Three times subsequently this officer returned and brought in badly wounded men under intense enemy machine-gun fire'.

Between the commencement of hostilities on 4 August 1914, and the winning of the regiment's first VC, 8,297 fatalities had been suffered. For five VCs, the regiment suffered 16,091 dead, indicating that a man was 3,200 times more likely to be killed than win a VC. Given the nature of the award citations above, which are not incomparable to many of the citations for other decorations provided in previous chapters, and considering the death toll, one is forced to wonder how representative the Victoria Cross is of bravery on the Western Front between 1914 and 1918. There are so few of them that it is difficult to make any analysis for the largest infantry regiment fielded in the war. One senses that had these five awards not been raised to a Victoria Cross recommendation and supported all the way to the King, that they could so easily have been DSOs or DCMs and lost to view in the main mass of the regiment's record of gallantry.

The Victoria Cross, when considered as a whole, does document some remarkable feats in battle against all odds, but it is not in the least representative of the bravery displayed by the ordinary man in war. That record is found within the lists of the awards of the more abundantly conferred decorations which are the main focus of this work.

# CASE STUDY 1

**2101 Company Sergeant Major Arthur Burness Rose, XVth Corps Cyclist Battalion, Army Cyclist Corps, received the Distinguished Conduct Medal and French Croix de Guerre.**

Born in 1882 and brought up at Kilravock Castle, Scotland.

**The Distinguished Conduct Medal:** 'From 25 July 1918, to 16 September 1918, by his consistent devotion to duty he has contributed to the efficiency of the company to an extent it would be impossible to exaggerate. His conduct during the enemy attack in April, 1918, and again when the company were in the line, from 15 July until 1 August, near Vieux Berquin, was excellent. Not only did his remarkable efficiency and thoroughness in handling his work add materially to the men's comfort, but his coolness and courage under fire were admirable. He set an excellent example to all ranks on all occasions'. A New Year Honours DCM, *London Gazette,* 1 January, 1919.

CSM Rose's medals, L to R: the MBE (for his work as Captain of the Home Guard, Lewisham), DCM, the 1914 Star trio, WW2 Defence Medal, the French Croix de Guerre and finally the King Albert Medal (1914–1918) awarded for humanitarian or charity work on behalf of the Belgian population. This last award is consistent with the Rose family's strong Christian faith. The badges are cap and collar, Army Cyclist Corps.

**Croix de Guerre:** 'During the operations from 16 to 20 October 1918 this Warrant Officer showed courage and marked ability in dealing with isolated enemy machine guns. On 19 October at Petite Audenarde his company was held up by heavy machine-gun fire. He took charge of a few men and crawled around the flank and engaged the enemy, killing one and taking one prisoner. This action enabled his company to push forward and demoralised enemy machine guns on the flanks'.

The Croix de Guerre was given in recognition of an act which the British state had elevated to a position of highest bravery, and which was dominating the awards of the Victoria Cross; that of capturing and putting out of action enemy machine guns. It is both remarkable that the DCM was given for the less spectacular long period of distinguished service and that it is the modest foreign decoration which hides the more readily appreciated act of battlefield bravery. The difficulty of obtaining a second award bar to a British decoration is implied.

# CASE STUDY 2

**Captain Thomas Lindsay Browne won the Military Cross on 20 September 1917, for the most successful battle of the war up until that point, the Battle of the Menin Road. He was aged just twenty. The 10th and 11th Battalions, Northumberland Fusiliers won an exceptional 73 medals for bravery in one day.** Born in 1897 in Newcastle Upon Tyne, He was educated at Durham University. Commissioned into the Northumberland Fusiliers in 1915, he transferred to the 1/5th Lancashire Fusiliers and served on the Gallipoli Peninsula until December 1915. He was then transferred to the 10th Battalion North'd Fus and served in FRANCE, BELGIUM and ITALY from May 1916 until the end of the war.

**Military Cross:** 'For conspicuous gallantry and good leadership while in charge of his company during operations. Although most of his company were seriously involved on first objective, he and very few others managed to get on, and collecting and encouraging men of his own and the units on his right after heavy fighting arrived at his ultimate objective, throughout showing a very fine example to those under him'.

**Captain Browne's medals, including the Military Cross, left, and the Italian Al Valore Militare, far right.**

**Al Valore Militare:** 'On 27 October 1918 when this officer's Company was crossing the bridge over the River Piave, under heavy shell fire a shell burst on the bridge breaking it. Captain Browne remained standing amongst the shell fire until the bridge was repaired, steadying his men and setting a fine example of gallantry. On 29 October when leading his company in an attack near Cascina Milanese this officer was always foremost in the attack, exposing himself fearlessly. On 30 October near Ramera Captain Browne led his company in a night advance, capturing or killing 50-60 of the enemy. For 56 hours without rest this officer shewed immense energy, determination and devotion to duty. His exceptional personal courage and marked powers of leadership were a great factor in the successful operations'.

The Al Valore Militare shows all the characteristics of his MC. It is thought that a foreign decoration, when given as a second award, in some cases may suggest the reluctance to award a bar to the original British decoration.

# CASE STUDY 3

**Temporary 2nd Lieutenant Arthur Augustus Morris, a jeweller's manager from Shrewsbury, who won the Military Cross near Arras between April 9–11 1917, and a Mention-in-Despatches when taken prisoner at the chemical works, Roeux, 29 April, 1917.**

Born on 10 May 1884, Shrewsbury, Shropshire and attended Durham University.

**Military Cross:** 'For conspicuous gallantry and devotion to duty. He patrolled for several hundred yards beyond the final objective and sent back most valuable information. This patrol was carried out under heavy artillery barrage'.

**Arthur Morris's MC is beautifully engraved on the reverse, consistent with employment as jeweller.**

**Taken Prisoner:** 'My battalion was ordered to attack and capture the chemical works. I led my company against heavy machine-gun fire and after bombing the front line got through to the objective where we commenced digging in. We numbered about 30 men and three officers. I went to get in touch with the other battalions but found we were the only one. I sent back two runners but no reinforcements arrived. 2nd Lt Jamieson who was then wounded took a party back into the village to bomb out a machine gun and later I received a message from him that the village was strongly held. I decided, rather than lose my men in the open, to reach Jamieson and fight it out in the village, so divided my men into two sections. I reached Jamieson with eight men. Later Jamieson was wounded for a third time and was still fighting when he was again hit and killed. Things were becoming too hot so I decided to charge them. In carrying this out I was wounded and taken prisoner together with the men who were left, most of them being wounded also'.

In cases such as this, the desperate, futile, actions resulting in his being taken POW are almost more heroic than those which resulted in the award of his MC, in that he elected to attack the enemy relentlessly rather than attempt to get back to safety. Yet, being taken prisoner almost eliminated a man's chances of receiving a decoration for bravery.

Morris's Mention in Despatches resulted from an attempted escape from captivity but probably also took account of the circumstances of his capture.

# SECTION III:
# IN THE MIND

# Finding The Courage

A major aim of this work is to examine not only the distribution of gallantry awards over time, types of act, differences between units and the distribution by rank, but also how men found themselves capable of performing what appear to be spectacularly brave acts in the particular conditions of the Western Front. It is hoped that the foregoing chapters have provided an adequate survey of the variety of roles each Army unit carried out and the services for which they won awards. In the following chapters, the psychological aspects of battlefield gallantry and the experience of those who won the medals is surveyed, in an attempt to understand battlefield gallantry from the point of view of the hero and how it occurs.

The 'Poor Bloody Infantry' received the lion's share of gallantry medals during World War One. This is no surprise because the infantry was at the sharp end for over four years. How professional soldiers and, increasingly as the war went on, large numbers of ordinary individuals recently plucked from civilian life, managed to do that is a major point of focus of this work.

## FEAR AND HORROR

It is very easy to imagine that many soldiers might have been overcome at times by a sense of doom when they arrived at the front. The evidence all around them of familiar objects, from shell-ploughed fields to things that hung about their own person, forcibly smashed and bent, such as rifles, water bottles and helmets, must have brought home the unstoppable force of flying lumps of metal. Metal was not the only material to fly around the battlefield – soil, rock, lengths of barbed wire, splintered wood, lumps of human body, flesh and splintered bone also knocked the living daylights out of men. In towns and villages, stone lintels, tiles, bicycles, rafters, fireplaces, tin baths, furniture and crockery also took to the air, spinning amidst the smoke, dust and airborne shrapnel balls. At the front, ordinary items were thrown up and turned inside-out – trappings of civilisation, households, human and animal bodies were torn open and eviscerated by explosives. A traumatic vision of one's own body exploding crept into the imagination, which itself was unprotected.[1] This was one basis of fear.

In contrast, the press at home shielded the population from the full horrors of modern war; the publishing of photographs and the exhibition of paintings showing corpses was banned,[2] but few could have failed to notice the growing list of dead as the early battles raged in 1914 and 1915. It was much easier for civilians to continue their belief in the Glory of War. Even so, all but the most naïve must have been apprehensive about what the trenches and the fighting would be like. A first experience in the trenches encouraged Pte. Thomas Smith of the 22nd (Tyneside Scottish) Battalion, Northumberland Fusiliers to write home: '…we have a nice big fire in our dugout and there is plenty of food'. Thus encouraging his mother not to worry (he did, after all, have the most important of home comforts), he continued his message by stating: 'So you see there are worse places than the trenches'.[3] His words do not only reveal his desire to reassure his parents, but he had also obliquely admitted that his first period in the line had worried him and he was relieved that events had turned out better than they might have.

A typical experience, one may imagine, was that thoughts of glory lingering in soldier's minds would have been initially dimmed by news reports from the Front, largely extinguished on arrival at the front and permanently eliminated during a man's first battle. A great many of those arriving from 1916 to 1918 must have been psychologically crushed by the overwhelming mechanised force brought randomly and suddenly to bear on tiny mortal men. If a man didn't want to die, he might have made a very serious mistake in coming to the war.

The Great War demanded that soldiers endure things outside of normal experience. Letters and diaries regularly indicate that fear was at its most intense when waiting for battle to begin or when being shelled. Horror was reserved for different occasions; some found that the greatest horror was experienced when encountering corpses[4], or parts of corpses. In Mametz Wood in July 1916, scene of prolonged and brutal fighting, Captain Llewellyn Wyn Griffith thought that 'there were worse sights than corpses. Limbs and mutilated trunks, here and there a detached head, forming splashes of red against the green leaves'. He further tells us that 'there were more corpses than men'.[5] Other soldiers describe how living among dead became normal and had no great effect on them, but even in these cases, insensitive treatment of the dead could be disturbing. Gunner Aubrey Wade, Royal Artillery, recalled how he, with his battery, had to cross a bridge over a stream east of Ypres in 1917 that was composed of 'a compact mass of human bodies... I was not at all squeamish, the sight of dead men having lost its terror for me, but making use of corpses... seemed the limit of callousness'. After a long spell on the firing line with his artillery battery, Gunner Wade wrote that the men were infested with lice, unwashed, unshaved, stinking of mud, gas and cordite, but more significantly were 'desperately tired, haggard with fear and nervous with kittens from incessant shell fire'.[6] He and his battery did not have to go over the top in attack, but they were nevertheless in the front line and subjected to great psychological and physical stress. We may recall how the frequently shelled Rail Construction Company of the Royal Engineers lost as many men to shell shock as it did to actual injury and death. Thus, shelling ground men down to the point that any form of action was better than inaction; that attack was something of a relief, a chance to get back at the foe rather than cowering impotently.

## ENTRAPMENT AND RESIGNATION

Whilst it may seem obvious that in taking these risks for a higher purpose, every man was brave, it is worth asking whether going into a battle was made possible by an incredible heroic courage? Perhaps, but there are other conditions that made it possible for the most ordinary and sometimes terrified young men to carry on and carry out acts that appear heroic in the face of frightfulness.

The first such conditions were joining an Army and receiving the training. On enlistment, recruits were given a uniform with its martial glory to live up to, and were told to act in unison and without question. Almost all humans, when asked to perform to expected standards, will try to do so. Much time was spent inculcating men with an aggressive fighting spirit by means of bayonet training. Sergeants and officers provided orders to them which they were expected to obey. The power of the recruits to think and act individually was, necessarily, removed. When an order was given, all moved as one; and so they proceeded overseas, as a unit, dedicated to each other and with high expectations of giving the Hun a whipping. Training, as 2nd Lieutenant John Bellerby related: 'It is impossible to continue for months, training with one specific aim in view to which all have implicitly committed their whole being, without becoming seized with eagerness to put the training to the final test'. From the point of view of a bored Private Gadsby of the 100th Machine Gun Company: 'the only thing one existed for was to lug boxes of ammunition here, there, and any old where.... what it was all about, no one seemed to know or care. Just "muckin us abat" I think, to make us fit, and eager to do anything to ease the monotony'.[7] Endless monotony served to make men crave 'anything' in the way of excitement, even if it might be deadly. Expectation of a future battle encouraged men to want to get it over with, and so, a desire to do the job arose within them. Danger was a worry, but waiting was worse.

It was possible, too, to suffer greatly from depression and anxiety. The only way out appeared to be death or injury. Thinking men sat down and calculated that in order to reach only the Rhine river, at the war's current rate of progress, 180 years would be needed.[8] Some concluded that the war would take all of them and several future generations down with it, and would never end. There was no reason to think otherwise; nobody could see an end, nobody could see how the deadlock could be broken or how an end to the slaughter would come about; it was 'the suicide of nations'. This is how men lost their battle with fate. The war would have them, devour them, yet this realisation helped men to go on, as dazed automatons waiting to be torn to pieces and scattered about rather than as thriving human souls.

## SUBMISSION

It is often heard that these were brave young lads, the like of which we might never see again. It is not easy for us to understand how, after waiting in a trench, through whose walls were transmitted the violent shocks of heavy shell bursts, men climbed up the ladders and out of a relatively protected place into the teeth of a 'storm of steel'. However, once an infantry soldier in King George V's Army, a man's journey to this moment was unstoppable; with tin hat on, heavy rifle weighing on shoulder and belt tight around the waist, they witnessed men cracking open boxes of live grenades, thrusting them into eager hands, shoving them into pockets, bandoliers stuffed with shiny coppery and brassy ammunition. At the moment of attack, there was the Corporal shouting at his men to affix bayonets, 'Fix 'em! Fix 'em!' amid the roar of shells passing overhead and the continuous din of blasts and explosions coming from out there, somewhere unseen beyond the confines of the trench walls. These sights and sounds were frightening, extraordinary, yet mindlessly exciting and they were vividly and intensely experienced by our forefathers in the last minutes of their lives (whether they were right about the imminence of their fate or not).

Were they all brave or were they merely swept up in events? There was no getting out of it; the uniform, the command structure, being there in a trench among thousands of other soldiers, all kitted up, with sergeant majors and officers in control, the giant machine of war barking its music in expectation of one thing only; for the individual to go over the top with the rest. Everything was funnelled towards that one act, control over one's destiny was irretrievably relinquished; in such circumstances the soldiers submitted themselves to the enormous events, to their fate. Who among us would not go? There was no way out but to scramble up the parapet, mindful not to be seen to waver in one's duty or to delay the man pressing from behind. So up and out from the narrow trench into a new and awesome world they all went, their lives, families, homes, mothers and self-worth discarded somewhere behind the lines. Most felt that their fate would soon be decided, one way or the other and many became completely resigned to death or mutilation; it was just a matter of at what moment and how it would happen. It was this very resignation to fate which helped men deal with their fear of going over the top; it was not going over the top that they feared the most, it was certainly not death they feared the most. Indeed, many accounts suggest that men felt much better doing something once the fearful waiting was over.

Going to war, enduring and participating in war was neither a question of bravery nor of heroics; a great many men were quite simply victims of circumstance, that such a war had broken out in their lifetimes and that their friends and acquaintances had joined up at the same time. The threat of receiving a white feather from a young lady and the famous Kitchener recruiting poster served as a push, but enlistment with mates was a major pull. The Australian Edward Lynch noted that all the men in his unit said they joined up with their mates, they enlisted because their mates were enlisting. Grander social considerations also played a role in nudging men to enlist, such as God, Empire, duty, honour, concerns about the safety of the mother country and of their families, but these were probably not the primary reasons for enlisting in most men's cases. Later in the war, call-up papers were a primary reason for getting involved; they became obliged to go to war as conscripts. However a man got himself into the Army, for those in the infantry, going over the top in attack was an unpreventable climax, the act was the culmination of patriotic fervour, enlistment, training and circumstances rather than individual heroics. For others the climax was on the gun line as an artilleryman, or on the churned up roads getting supplies up the line and damaged men back down. The great majority of soldiers on the Western Front were just doing their duty and just doing the job that was expected of them, for their mates rather than for any grander cause.

## GETTING THROUGH IT ALL

Richard Holmes, in his book *Tommy*, summarised what did and did not contribute to men's ability to get through it all. It was neither patriotic fervour, so prevalent in the civilian population back in Blighty, nor was it military discipline (the threat of being shot for desertion) that got men through and allowed them to push forward on the battlefield. It was instead a combination of 'mateship', having good leaders, a desire to finish a job that needed finishing, a spirit of endurance, dogged determination and Tommy's sense of humour.[9] The importance of and components of good leadership are discussed throughout this book. These attributes came to the fore in the trenches, but were not a product of the military system, they were brought to the Army by the civilians who were recruited into it. If the British Army did well, that it did not mutiny, that its morale remained generally intact, is the single finest tribute to our ancestors, those ordinary men who saw it through whatever the cost. The achievement of ordinary civilians temporarily converted into soldiers is remarkable.

What it was that imparted men with the ability to endure is not straightforward to describe, for it was a great many things. Voluntary services established themselves behind the lines on the Western Front; the Red Cross, Salvation Army and YMCA for example provided havens where men could receive all kinds of help and recreation, from cooked food to free writing paper and games. These institutions and others helped measurably to keep soldiers from depression. Men kept themselves 'in the pink' in other ways too. The infantry officer H. E. L. Mellersh iterated what many soldiers experienced: 'One of the curious things about a nation at war – one of the tragedies too – is that life is intensified. There is much happiness in wartime, much that is spirited, much that is admirable, much that is just jolly...'.[10]

And battle itself was not always an experience without joy. Colonel David Campbell, a Grand National winner and Commanding Officer of the 9th Lancers, actually charged twice with his men in 1914. His attitude to war was perhaps typical of the Victorian officer, or of the sportsman, for he was found by the medical officer lying wounded on the field of battle, who said to Colonel Campbell, 'I am sorry to find you like this, Sir'. But the Colonel replied, 'Not at all, my boy! Not at all! I've just had the best quarter of an hour I've ever had in my life!'.[11] Early in the war, a spirit of sportsmanship existed that even the Germans noticed (and found perplexing). In this regard, the DCM awarded to 290763 Private A Stubbs of the Cheshire Regiment is notable for its sports field flavour: 'Throughout the advance against an enemy position, he was always well in front of his section and at the final "run in", he raced his company commander to the enemy trench. His splendid example greatly assisted in maintaining the advance'. His is not the only example of, 'I'll race you to the enemy machine guns, sir'; there were many such reports being printed in newspapers in the early days. On the morning of the 1 July 1916, there are the stories of the battalion rugby or football player, often an ex-professional, kicking a ball far out into no-man's-land as they went over the top. But war as an extension of the playing fields of Eton, as an attitude, does not seem to have survived intact on the Western Front beyond the summer of 1916.

It is obvious too that given an array of explosive devices, many young men had great fun blowing things up and destroying them. Yet not all of the fun was violent, as men found themselves detached from the confines of English society and were very ready for mischief. From stealing the pig destined for the Sergeant's mess, to raiding a neighbouring Battalion's chickens or ensuring that water filled trenches drained into those of the enemy, there was a great deal of mirth behind the lines as well as at the front. Soldier's memoirs are full of examples of men having tremendous fun at war. Wilfred Cook of the Northumberlands describes how, on a long, slow train ride, French civilians had British Army rations donated to them: 'Opening the van doors to full extent the "bombers" would stand, poised... on reaching the target (the level crossing) over went a shower of Bully Beef in unopened tins, jam and biscuits which flew like cardboard in the wind... Amongst the missiles was a 7lb tin of Fray Bentos, which hurtled like a trench mortar to drop on an old man'.[12]

Training, mateship, pranks and humour couldn't eliminate fear, stress and unease, however. Norman Gladden recalled his arrival in France, 'during the months ahead fear was hardly ever to leave me and there were moments of terror. I do not believe this was unusual'.[13] Private Albert Bullock, lying in a shell hole with others of his regiment, saw a man 'daft with fear' take off his pack and make a run for the rear. Bullock himself endured the shelling but found himself 'shaking from head to foot through concussion of so many shells'.[14] Here is evidence of the effect concussion could have on the human nervous system. Fear, terror and stress could not be trained out of men by the Army system, all men felt these emotions to a greater or lesser degree and so they had to be dealt with when they arose, dismissed or endured in the long term. Unless a man could do this he would break up under their immense, debilitating weight, and the debris of the war included plenty of the broken cases. Sensory shut-down sometimes developed in situations of extreme stress and fear. Some suffered this acutely in the form of extended periods of amnesia; Bombardier Ronald Skirth lost three to four months of memory, a blank period in his life that he could never fill.[15] Very much a thinking man, Skirth reacted to the stresses dealt out to him by becoming a pacifist during the war, as well as by undergoing a complete mental collapse. Men remembered that 'we all reached that physical state of weariness where we would have welcomed a Blighty one with gratitude'.[16]

## BATTLEFIELD PSYCHOLOGY

The psychology of soldiering in the conditions of trench fighting was dealt with not by Army organisations, but in an informal way among the soldiers themselves. Private Edward Lynch mentioned the disturbing outstretched hand of a buried corpse that was sticking out of the trench wall. An experienced Corporal, an old hand, offered him the following advice: 'Look here, lad... you give up thinking too much or this war will get you down. It will beat you. I've been in it since Gallipoli and I know. The man who thinks is done'.[17] These words were spoken in the trenches by a man who was there, who had seen and who knew. They summarise quite clearly one way in which men were able to perform acts that appear to be outstandingly brave in what appear (to civilians) to be extremely frightening circumstances. Give up thinking, perform one's duty as if it were just a job.

There is another consideration with regard to battlefield psychology; the workings of chance. Chance events proved to men that cogitating over past and future was not a good idea. On the battlefields of the First World War, it was the high explosive shell and the shrapnel shell, fired by artillery or the trench mortar, which did most of the damage. It was an imprecise weapon, in a way that a rifle bullet aimed by an infantryman was not. Soldiers had death by chance and survival by chance demonstrated to them time and time again. Several examples of how luck appeared to seal his personal fate are recorded by Ernst Junger, who was shelled twice on one day. The first time he sheltered in an old farmhouse because it was raining, the second he remained outside because it was not, and the farmhouse was completely destroyed. He states: 'That's the role of chance in war. More than elsewhere, small causes can have a vast effect'.[18] No two shells fell in the same spot, suggesting that the safest place to be in a bombardment might be the freshly created shell hole. Men often tried, or felt compelled to try, to beat chance. By way of contrast, there were innumerable tales of the most miraculous escapes. There was no rule that any man could follow in order to ensure his own survival, which led men to consider Fate. This is what was depicted in the famous Bairnsfather cartoon of two Tommies in a shell hole in the pouring rain and an enemy barrage: 'If you knows of a better 'ole...' then go to it. The cartoon's great popularity arose from the fact that it captured the real soldier's dilemma and implied the real soldier's resignation to Fate. This thinking, which pervaded the soldier's unofficial newspaper, *The Wiper's Times*, had a basis not in superstition but in fact, and may have been the single most important piece of self-administered psychology going round the ranks between 1914 and 1918.

A belief in fate certainly contributed to the erosion of the self-preservation instinct, but being with a group of mates in a fight also contributed to the warrior's vigour. Edward Lynch thought that: 'although a man doesn't go into a stunt with the deliberate intention of killing his fellow man, yet put a bayonet or bomb into his hand and he'll do as his mates are doing and use them to the full'[19]. Soldiers who, in addition to the above, also had a reason to 'get their own back' could be inspired to immense displays of aggression. In practice, it was not heroism it was base aggression; a function of mob psychology.

Edward Lynch felt strongly that it was humour and mateship that got men through; in short, a strong community and the support of fellow beings rather than a man's individual emotional robustness or heroism. The sage Australian veteran of Gallipoli continued to advise Lynch: 'Try to see the funny side of everything as you will see enough that hasn't any funny side... Take my tip, bring yourself to treat danger as a humorous episode and not as a narrowly averted tragedy, and although I can't say you'll live longer, you'll live happier'.[20] Lynch, among others in his unit, appears to have been able to live up to that advice, given to him early in his time in France.

There were other forms of psychological treatment handed around on the battlefield; the officers who famously stood upright and walked about in a hail of fire demonstrated to all under them that: 'if he can stand up there and live then so can we'. The average soldier preferred to be optimistic about the level of danger he faced, and such displays by those he respected were very encouraging indeed.

These were some of the ways in which men survived day to day in the First World War; their mates got them through it with their simple yet potent, and daily administered psychiatric help. Soldiers, in a group, gave each other the emotional tools to deal with fear and horror, gave the group greater fighting power and courage than they would have as individuals, and so gave their units the ability to defeat the enemy in violent battles. The presence of good, wise characters in a unit could strengthen it more than any Army training, for these men altered the mood of a group, keeping spirits up.

Some men received gallantry medals for their actions, but it is not straightforward to understand what gave men the courage to do what they did in the face of death. To the average reader, it may seem amazing that men even went to fight that war. Yet, Wilfred Cook of the Northumberland Fusiliers relates in his memoirs how: 'My parents said that when I left to go back to France (at the end of leave) it was as if I was going on holiday with not a care in the world. I loved my parents and my brothers and sisters as they did me, but I had no regrets about my service as a volunteer. I was looking forward to going back to my friends who had a duty to do and where I would be happy in spite of the hardships. To me it was the right place to be at that time'. 'Cooky' made sure he had some clay pipes and some twist tobacco 'for Smiler, Harry and others' who were delighted when he produced them from his pack.[21] Those who have not known war may not understand how men were keen to return to the front.

Not everyone was paralysed with fear, some found the war 'wasn't so bad as all that'. There were men who discovered that they were less frightened than others, and 'everyone likes the thing that he finds he does a bit better than the other fellow'.[22] The less frightened got into the habit of being at the front, of getting involved rather than hanging back, bringing a further reward – respect from their comrades. This was a powerful motive when there was little else to be truly proud of.

Religious men in the line were sometimes of great assistance. In Cook's battalion, a new man named McAlpine who sat reading a bible in the corner of a dugout asked, 'Is there anyone here who is afraid to die?' After a silence, one man replied that he was afraid, 'I confess that I live in fear of being killed. I think of my wife and kiddies in York and feel as if I shall never see them again'. There was a discussion about faith, at the end of which McAlpine suggested that they would show the fearful man that 'the bullets he heard had already become the bullets that had missed'.[23] A fine observation, as it was well known that the dead man never hears the sound of the bullet that kills him. A check of the 'Soldiers Died in the Great War' database has revealed that the man from York lasted no more than six months; he died from wounds received at the front on 31 October 1917, and therefore never did see his wife and kiddies again.

Tommy's self-administered psychological treatments didn't work for everyone. Plenty did not survive the crushing external and internal torments of the fighting and their minds. What was for some a happy-go-lucky game of chance, was for others a physical and mental torture that did not recede in their post-war years.

## FATHERS AND SONS

One of the most important factors that allowed men to perform in these situations was unit cohesion. Difficult to define precisely, this was a dynamic phenomenon occurring between friends, between larger groups of mates, at section, company, battalion and greater scales. Charles Carrington, who published two volumes about his experiences of the war, felt that 'we were banded together by a unity of experience that had shaken off every kind of illusion, and which was utterly unpretentious'.[24] The components were the men, with their individual concerns, but the cement was provided at various scales by friendships, by men who commanded authority, by officers and NCOs possessing an authority born not of fear but of respect and even of love. Whilst some NCOs were despised, others were the backbone of unit cohesiveness such that where they went, others would follow. This ability to lead men into dire situations and win, to take control of a lost rabble of individuals and move them on to the objective, had war-winning value in the battles of World War One, but the foundation for these relationships was often laid down long before the fighting started in earnest.

Relationships between men developed not only in situations of fear and stress in the front line, but began during men's earliest days with their units. The wartime memoirs of Private Wilfred Cook of the 1st Battalion Northumberland Fusiliers were published for the first time in 2009.[25] His account was written retrospectively, some decades after the event, yet his book is dedicated to Company Sergeant Major Drayson. Years after the events, Cook was able to speak with love about the men he met, and particularly about some of the men who led him. CSM Drayson was a man who went on to be awarded the MC as a Warrant Officer 2nd Class, but his award was not made for astonishing gallantry in the front line, it was a periodic award made in the New Year's Honours list of 1 January 1917. Drayson went to France with the 1st Battalion on 13 August 1914 and was one of the 'Old Contemptibles' who held up the German invasion of Belgium that Autumn. He was mentioned in despatches (*London Gazette* 15 June 1915), his obituary appears in the Regimental Journal the *St George's Gazette* and his medals now reside in the regimental museum at Alnwick Castle. This man was already an old campaigner in 1914, with experience on the North West Frontier of India during 1908, he had the 1914 (Mons) star medal that marked him out clearly as one of the few. Sadly he was killed in action in June 1918, but one of his men, Wilfred Cook, dedicated his memoirs to him many years later. Cook states that his narrative: 'is mostly about men, individual men whom I have no desire ever to forget'.[26]

On enlisting, Cook met the old timers who were returning to the colours after previous military service. They commanded Cook's respect, for they knew the Army system and were able to offer the young men a helping hand; getting the hang of putting their putties on, on the parade ground, in training and later offered them their wisdom in the trenches, lifesaving wisdom very often. In the Army they were fathers, who had lots of sons. 'The old soldiers must have been a great help to the staff in knocking us civvies into shape', Cook states. In the 1st Battalion of the Northumberland Fusiliers were men like George Brown who had fought in the Sudan in 1898, at the nearly disastrous and desperate action at Nooitgedacht in the Second South African (Boer) War when the fighting devolved into a confused hand-to-hand struggle on the cliff tops and half the battalion were taken prisoner. Brown was from Hebburn on the banks of the River Tyne, where mining, shipbuilding, chemical works and docks were familiar and demanding industries. Men like Brown sported the medal ribbons from these past campaigns and, as ex-regulars, having a relationship with their old battalions, they often found themselves back in those battalions with their experience of soldiering. Wilfred Cook described the instructors that he first encountered on joining the Army as 'excellent... they certainly went the right way about it' and gave credit to the man in charge, Colonel Friend, a man who 'rode a horse magnificently and to see him taking a full parade was a proud sight'. Cook speaks of his platoon Sergeant (Pearson) in those early days of training as 'a regular soldier and a gentleman' who was 'scrupulously clean' and 'won us all' by addressing his recruits firmly, but just as importantly, by addressing them kindly. Another man, Company Sergeant Major Bill Hodgson, Cook remembers, 'was also a man apart'. At drill, Hodgson shouted at them, his size eleven boots 'punctuated the thunder of his voice', he was as a good CSM should be, but Cook recalls his humanity: 'I know you think I shout a lot at you but its all for your own good. You cannot work on poor words of command. Don't take it to heart, I mean no harm'. The best, most potent Army discipline was of this kind, not a savage kind.[27]

There were other men whom Cook remembered from his early days – a 'Geordie' who had the foresight to bring his concertina to the barracks: 'he was an expert... it was a pity I lost track of that little fellow, he would find his niche and be welcomed'. Then there was a tall Irishman O'Hara, the song leader of Cook's Company, who had 'just the voice and spirit for the job' and was posted in the front rank on the march where he sang his heart out. Remarkably, perhaps, the officers 'had the good sense to see the value in this' and it was unanimously agreed that O'Hara's Lance Corporal's stripe was well earned. For his singing as much as anything else, was O'Hara identified as a leader, a man whom others would follow, for whatever reason.

## UNIT CULTURE

Luckily, perhaps, Wilfred Cook had found himself in a unit with enlightened leadership; the 1st Battalion had by far the most successful military career of all the battalions of the regiment. Cook describes one incident near Zillebeke in the Salient which suggested to him that the 1st Battalion was composed of men apart. When most were sleeping, the 'Stand to!' was shouted as guns opened up nearby and reports came back that the enemy had broken through Sanctuary Wood. 'All sprung to it with bayonets fixed as we rallied round our Sergeant then off we went in the direction of the woods', headed by Sgt Mjr Drayson. The party came across frightened men of another battalion moving rearward who implored the Northumberlands to turn back as German attackers were hard on their heels, but, 'we carried on following Captain Prideaux and ignored their fears'. After the event, Cook's friend Syd admitted that he had, 'no desire to serve with any men but these. Could any other regiment find men who would turn out like that without a moment's hesitation when it looked like all Hell had been let loose?'.[28] Such was the strength of good leadership and the backbone provided by the NCOs and old campaigners.

The 1st Battalion of the Northumberland Fusiliers was a unit with self-confidence and they made for themselves a reputation for being unstoppable in attack and immoveable in defence. The battalion war record supports this. It was achieved, even late in the war, with raw conscript material, good leadership and a keen interest in learning, developing and teaching the best infantry tactics. Similarly, highly successful regiments like the Guards were, at the outset at least, made solely from regular, professional soldiers and retained their undiluted 'elite' status in the British Army as a result. Some other, non-regular, battalions of the Northumberland Fusiliers struggled with tactics, leadership and did not have the same reserves of experienced men that the 1st Battalion had, difficulties that led directly to a greater number of defeats and failed attacks, retirements and disasters over the course of their war. The origin of these differences was rooted in the psychology of leadership, the degree of professional culture within individual battalions and the effect that had on unit cohesion and confidence. In the professionalism and determination of the junior leadership, then, we find one of the most important underlying controls on the length of a battalion's honours list.

## JUNIOR LEADERSHIP: THE BACKBONE OF THE ARMY

Junior leadership was critical to the success of all operations whether attack, defence, supply or organisation. The prime position the junior leadership occupied in the Army and in its honours lists has been amply shown in previous chapters. In this chapter, the importance of the NCOs in setting an example, providing paternalistic support, leading their men and in giving them courage, is emphasised.

As we have seen, a large proportion of medals were presented for distinguished services rather than spectacular acts of bravery. Most of these were won by NCOs and Warrant Officers. The nature of senior NCO's and Warrant Officer's awards is of great interest, as many award citations appear to indicate that the award was made for a series of unspecified acts over a long period of time. Their citations, are, it is argued, a tribute to their consistent good work, great daring and leadership, no matter what the situation. A survey of the 1st Battalion Northumberland's awards made to senior NCOs supports this: Company Quartermaster Sergeant Crouch's DCM was announced in April 1915, 'For conspicuous gallantry on 7 November 1914, near Hooge, in handling his machine guns with great ability until they were buried by shell fire. He has rendered valuable service throughout the whole period of the campaign'. Company Sergeant Major Cooper was awarded the DCM, 'For conspicuous gallantry in leading forward men who had been checked by the enemy's wire. He showed fine judgment and coolness under fire'. This senior NCO contributed very materially to the success of the celebrated fight at St Eloi on 27 March 1916, by getting the men moving again when pinned down on the wire. Had it not been for his action and good judgement, casualties would have risen as the enemy reorganised and fought back; indeed, his actions contributed to the overall military success of this action. Squadron Sergeant Major Peacock of the Northumberland Hussars came to notice for having to be continually on the move between parties of his men under heavy fire of all descriptions. By doing so he was encouraging his men to be optimistic about the level of danger they faced and by visiting each isolated party, he gave them confidence that they were not in fact isolated, that friends were close by. Setting such a paternalistic example could tip the balance of a battle and acts such as these certainly attracted gallantry awards. These are easily understood acts of gallantry for which they deservedly received the medal for distinguished conduct, yet other awards are less easily understood.

Sergeant Major Myers for example, received his DCM in the King's Birthday Honours list of June 1916, 'For consistent good work and devotion to duty since the commencement of the campaign'. Company Sergeant Major Richardson received his medal in the New Year Honours List of 1 January 1918, 'For conspicuous gallantry and devotion to duty. During the past year he has displayed the greatest energy and coolness, rendering the most valuable assistance to his company commander on several occasions. His gallantry and cheerfulness have always set a most inspiring example to the men of the company under the most adverse circumstances'. Regimental Sergeant Major Pullen received his award of the DCM in the same Honours gazette, 'For conspicuous gallantry and devotion to duty. During the past year this warrant officer has performed continuous good service in the field, and his keen devotion to duty at all times and under all conditions, and his ability and initiative have been of invaluable assistance'.

These senior NCOs, alongside CSM Drayson (MC), received decorations for excellent service over a period of time. These were some of the men who made the 1st Battalion what it was, and whilst they were not singled out to receive an award for a magnificent display of gallantry, they had given something far greater than that to the battalion and to their men – unit cohesion and the confidence and determination to win. Their awards were no less deserved than the man who charged a machine gun. It may be argued that the contribution of those who maintained their fine bearing so consistently, set a marvellous example over a long period, kept smiling in spite of everything and imparted their experience of old-time campaigning was of greater importance than a single act of gallantry. A great many Sergeant Majors were legendary figures and the example they set made those around them capable of anything; they made the British Army a match for the mighty German Army.

Unfortunately, the indiscriminate killings and woundings of that war, meant that the old hands were picked off and replaced by wartime volunteers and conscripts. Lord Moran, in his book *The Anatomy of Courage* (published 1945)[29], noted that by 1917 'the best of that generation had gone'. But even so, the successes of the Army post-1917 suggest that good leaders and willing private soldiers were still found among conscripts. Losses sustained among the junior leadership presented a serious challenge to all units as well as to individuals. Soldier's memoirs dwell extensively on the friends they lost, both at burial services in the field: 'our innermost hearts are furrowed by grief for mates gone west'[30] and over five decades later in the dedication to Norman Gladden's book, *Ypres 1917*, 'Dedicated, to the memory of Personal Friends killed in action'.[31] Remembrance was born on the field of battle. Friends left behind were ever-present in memory, very often alongside a powerful measure of guilt that was centred around the idea that better men than they had died.

The vital importance of the junior leadership may be summarised as follows, much of which will be recognised from points raised in earlier chapters:

1. NCOs and officers in the British Army were instructed to organise and lead; privates were instructed to wait for orders then follow their leaders. Within a command structure, there was no expectation that privates should initiate actions or organise men. The responsibility of the junior leadership for victory or defeat was set.

2. Unit cohesion and fighting effectiveness was best enabled by means of a paternalistic approach and leadership by example. If the leadership looked after their men's supply needs, their physical and emotional needs, the men would look after their leader. They would fight and win for him. They could endure anything with him around; on occasion his smile alone was sufficient to fortify.

3. Victory, capitulation or defeat depended almost completely on the will of the group leader. This was discovered and reported by both German and British Armies during the course of the war. Men without leadership quickly turned into a disorganised rabble of little military value.

4. Leaders were more heroic than those who followed because the leadership had to plan and initiate events that would lead to their own deaths. Enemy riflemen sought out the leadership

when faced with an attacking force. In order to set an example of courage and thereby give their men strength, leaders had to expose themselves to the heaviest fire in order that their men could succeed even if they were gunned down. This behaviour also demonstrated that 'if he can stand out there and live then so can we'.

5. Clarity of orders given and the ability to make the correct decision in a rapidly evolving and threatening situation was the responsibility of junior leaders. This was an aspect that led directly to military success. Those who could function professionally in such conditions were deserving of reward.

These are the reasons why the junior leadership won most of the medals.

# The Sources of Bravery

⤚⤳

Having endured the painful and shocking First of July 1916, 20/190 Private John Johnson would go on to be decorated with both the Military Medal in heavy fighting at Greenland Hill in June 1917 and later a bar to his MM during the desperate rearguard actions of the German Spring Offensive of March 1918. He was very lucky to survive this far, as in March 1918 his battalion was once again nearly wiped out. On transfer to the Italian Front in mid-1918, he was with the 11th Battalion when they were caught by shell and machine-gun fire on the shingle banks of the River Piave, 27 October 1918, and killed. One inevitably speculates that with such fighting experiences behind him, he may have died whilst trying to turn the battle in his favour. Was he doing something that might have attracted a third gallantry decoration, had he survived?

Winning a medal during an attack was not the simplest thing to achieve. Norman Gladden indicated that his experience in no-man's-land had been one of trying to get somewhere forward, by stumbling and running and falling about amongst shell bursts, fountains of earth and falling debris. There was a curtain of explosions, the enemy barrage, which was put down to try to break up an attack as soon as the enemy saw it developing. Through this maelstrom of blasts, concussions, flying earth, muck and dust, the attackers had to move. An orderly advance led by officers and sergeants, under shell and small arms fire, rapidly broke down into a form of individual scramble. A great many men did not see living and fighting Germans, but instead arrived somewhat dazed at the objective, where an aftermath of devastated land and damaged bodies flung about in wild attitudes (and hopefully some Tommies) would be there to meet them. Gladden described the 'charnel house' that was a German trench full of red spattered earth and lumps of body. Soldiers' eyes met the spine-chilling, vacant stares of mortally wounded German soldiers whose mouths were dribbling blood. Men had felt the impacts of lumps of metal thumping into the ground and whizzing past their heads around about. But a good many soldiers never had the opportunity to win a medal and never had to deal with shooting Germans.[32]

In Norman Gladden's case, someone other than him had done that job for him, and had gone on ahead, to be himself killed, or to do more slaughtering of Germans. These were the men to be found surging forwards, willing to shoulder the burden of the fight, to seek out, engage and eject the enemy from his positions. Advance parties would get up to the enemy wire with cutters, or make their way through a gap in the wire, enter the enemy trench, proficiently bomb, shoot and bayonet the occupants, surge forward whilst keeping an eye on the sky above for black shapes of grenades flying about. Bombing fights commonly developed as a preferred means to clear trenches. Working their way along a trench it was a game of chance, the attackers and defenders thinned progressively by injury and death. Some, no doubt, occasionally enjoyed the high stakes of the deadly game and learned that, with luck, they could get away with it. The German infantry officer, Ernst Junger, is widely viewed as a member of that warrior class.

One of many examples of aggressive trench fighting recorded by award citations is this one relating to Corporal William Fraser of the 2nd Infantry Battalion Australian Imperial Forces. His MM recommendation, dated 29 June 1918, relates to how he successfully cleared enemy trenches: 'In an operation against the enemy position South West of Meteren on the night 24/25 June 1918, L/Cpl Fraser had charge of a party to mop up the first objective of the right attacking company. On arriving at objective he led his party down the narrow enemy trench and, though wounded before arriving, he still kept going, killed seven of the enemy and cleared the trench for 200 yards. He set a splendid example of bravery and devotion to duty'.

It is difficult to understand what made some men keen to get to grips with the enemy; certainly some of them appear to have been, some of the time. However, some of those labelled as 'thrusters', who formed part of the forward group, may have found themselves in that circumstance by chance rather than preference. Once confronted with enemy, either their training in bayonet, bomb and rifle fighting came to the fore, or if it didn't they were killed, wounded, froze or fled. It was the former behaviour that tended to attract medals. Considering some of the many published eyewitness accounts, there appear to have been many reasons why men were able to perform great feats of gallantry on the battlefield.

Over time, soldiers gradually gained experience that changed their understanding of the battlefield and its dangers. Under battle stress, men began to get more careless and felt themselves, as a result of continuously strained nerves in a violent environment, to be ready for any suicidal stunt.[33] Death became meaningless and of no great concern to many. Their bravery had not increased; their instincts for self-preservation had been eroded or removed – as they adapted to their environment they became careless with their lives, inured to danger, 'battle-hardened'. Many veteran's accounts contain stories of men who took care of themselves and were killed while others walked about carelessly in heavy shell and machine-gun fire and lived. Their careless behaviour was partly learned from events on the battlefield, as they saw men taken from life at random rather than as a result of their actions; it was one way in which apparently brave actions were facilitated by the intensity and duration of the First World War. But there were many other factors which allowed or caused men to do something exceptional.

## VENGEANCE

Powerful blood-lust motives of revenge and hate could be created by heavy shelling. Being shelled is a peculiar experience of warfare for it is all one-sided. Soldiers cannot fight back whilst being shelled, they have to sit and endure; it breeds a strong desire for vengeance. German soldiers who had endured three weeks of the heaviest and most persistent shelling in history, during the run up to the Battle of the Somme in late June 1916, felt that: 'All longed for an end to it one way or another'. Unteroffizier Friedrich Hinkel of Infantry Regiment 99 recorded his Company's reaction to this stupendous bombardment: 'You made a good job of it, you British! Seven days and nights you hammered on our door! Now your reception was going to match your turbulent longing to enter!'. What the British bombardment bred was 'a searing rage'[34] which found full expression on the 1 July 1916 as a wild vengeful firing which 'slammed into the British masses'.[35]

Aside from the obvious torment, being shelled led to a series of other experiences. The bombardment of late June continued during the month of July as British attacks were launched. 'It was simply terrible' remembered Reserve Leutnant Gruber, a machine gun officer with a Bavarian Regiment, 'We were deafened by fire, terribly tired and indifferent to our fate... Wedged in tight, with our knees drawn up, we entertained ourselves – by discussing dying'.[36] Gruber is not the only one to have bothered to mention adopting this position; Reservist Rabe of the German Reserve Infantry Regiment 15 was one of several men trying to shelter in a shell hole 'with our legs drawn up'.[37] Leutnant Zinnemann, an infantry officer, crawled into his tiny foxhole, 'my knees pulled up tightly and my arms folded in close'.[38] This somewhat 'foetal' position was of practical value because it minimised size, both allowing a man to occupy a small space (a cramped dugout, a shell- or fox-hole) and also helping to contain the body's warmth. Men must have spent a great many hours folded up like this in difficult situations, so that it became a remembered motif for life under shellfire, a thinly disguised search for physical and emotional comfort when there was no comfort to be had. However, J. Gadsby, a machine gunner who got stranded with others in a shell hole on the Somme in late 1916, noted that the cold and wet, combined with long periods in confined conditions brought on 'severe attacks of cramp... the pain was excruciating' as to stand up and try to stretch would be fatal, but 'the rum bottle saved us all'.[39] A man who stood up, was immediately shot through the head, leaving a man in the same shell hole with 'only a dead pal for company'.

The same was true of British soldiers under shellfire. The heaviest German barrage of the war was unleashed on British soldiers early in the morning of 21 March 1918, the first day of the Spring Offensives. There were many untested young soldiers in the line at that time. Lance Corporal William Sharpe of the Lancashire Fusiliers remembered four 18-year-old lads who were new to his Company who all cried, but 'one kept calling 'mother' and who could blame him'.[40] Sharpe seems to suggest that they were all killed when the trench was blown in; such was their brief encounter with war.

The explosion of giant 38cm diameter shells every four to six minutes, night and day by a 'British Big Bertha', recorded the German Artillery Liaison Officer Richard Sapper, caused 'caps, coats and weapons' to be 'flung in all directions' in the dugout. During this time he felt his life was separated from death by never more than four to six minutes. 'The temptation to concentrate on this thought to the exclusion of all else was so great that it took every ounce of willpower to keep working and to stay calm'.[41] His use of the word 'calm' in this situation, appears to be an aspiration, something wished for with the whole of his being, rather than something he truly achieved.

Heavy shelling, unexpected enemy trench raids, trench mortar attacks and sniping activity all resulted in the loss of mates without always being able to fight back. They were not a fair stand-up fight, sometimes stiffened the resolve of defenders to fight, and fuelled the desire to exact vengeance when the opportunity arose.

A great many personal accounts dwell on the tense torture of impotently enduring shelling, yet by way of contrast, some veterans have mentioned how calm they felt when actually in action out in the open, exposed but busying themselves with a task on the battlefield. Passive endurance of shelling or rifle fire, and active participation – even the rushing of a machine gun position – produced very different emotional reactions. The greatest fear might be found in passive endurance; the greatest release from fear might then be found in action, because action allows the individual to make his own decisions and puts him back in control of his own destiny. Action was empowering; it allowed the opportunity for revenge, for getting back at the enemy. It could even be pleasurable. That most symbolic of acts, storming the machine gun, could have been a great thrill after taking a pounding from 15cm shells, air-burst shrapnel and gas. That emotions formed whilst being shelled and gassed for hours or days, could be an important factor in the subsequent behaviour and the winning of medals for bravery. Shelling took men face-to-face with death, so that when that threat was lifted, men experienced the urge for vengeance, they discovered that small arms and machine-gun fire was as nothing to the infantryman. Battlefield conditions change men's minds, allowing them to perform any mad stunt. When asked why he ran at a machine gun post, he may not give the answer we anticipate.

## RAGE

The rage often associated with close quarters fighting was described by Edward Lynch: '...our men charge them... we see one of our fellows savagely bayonet the Fritz who has just shot one of our men. The bayonet flashes. Thrust, thrust, thrust! Three times driven through the poor, screaming wretch before his body hits the ground... Our men, mad with blood lust, are yelling and looking for more to bayonet... "They're killing men!" a new reinforcement man moans in horror... "Of course they're killing 'em. Same as the flamin' Huns did to our coves over there. Expect 'em to be cuddlin' and kissin' 'em?"'.[42] The immediate cause of such aggression was frequently the deaths of friends.

During intense fighting, men could be gripped by 'trench frenzy' which made them capable of remarkable things. When a German Headquarters building that was holding up an attack near Vaux on 1 July 1918 had to be taken, it only fell when 'an irate Irishman who had lost his best buddy started lobbing grenades through the windows'.[43] In his book *Tommy*, Richard Holmes mentions a British soldier who, during the Somme battle of 1916, 'was so enraged that his best friend had been buried alive by a shell burst that he bayoneted three Germans in a matter of minutes'.[44] Holmes thinks that the intensity of the bayonet training itself, meant that soldiers used it when they felt most aggressive, to the point that they were reluctant to show mercy.[45] A German NCO, Unteroffizier Wabnik, involved in a counter-attack on Australian troops at Pozieres on 23 July 1916 described the motivating effect of close quarters trench fighting: 'one comrade after another fell to the floor of the trench, shot through the head'. As a result of seeing these deaths and woundings at close quarters, 'some of the men were gripped by trench frenzy and launched themselves at the enemy with spades, only to be beaten to death with rifle butts'.[46] Such commitment to hopeless actions when the outcome was foreseeable, indicates that men often lost control of their senses, lost their instinct for self-preservation, in the heat of a death struggle. Rage and adrenalin were often lethally combined, perhaps. Such deaths were re-cast as the death of a hero for public consumption, but they were far from that; they could be viewed as the deaths of furious wild creatures.

On 14 September 1914, Sergeant Bradlaugh Sanderson of the 2nd King's Royal Rifle Corps, saw his officer killed next to him by a German Maxim machine gun positioned in a haystack just ten yards in front. The situation was nothing other than deadly, for: 'Bullets were clipping the leaves off the mangolds in front of us. One went through my cap, another hit the safety catch of my rifle, which made me mad'. Sanderson stalked the machine gunner, avenged his officer's death, 'and felt pleased'.[47] This man might not have comprehended being referred to as 'a brave hero'.

As a result of emotion, battle situations could flip extraordinarily quickly. When British soldiers were pressing heavily upon their position, Ernst Junger described how a counter-attack suddenly developed from nothing: 'A subaltern, inflamed with rage shouted: "C'mon boys, who's coming with me?" Bravery, fearlessly risking one's own life, is always inspiring. We too found ourselves picked up by this wild fury'.[48] A bombing fight ensued in which the British were evicted but at high cost to Junger's party. One wonders how running into the face of death can ever be 'inspiring', but in war, soldiers obviously experienced a range of emotional sensations far outside peacetime civilian comprehension.

With the above examples to hand, we see that anger may transform fearful, generally cautious soldiers still conscious of self-preservation, into potent and fearless 'berserk' warriors in a moment. No doubt, some of their berserk sprees gained them bravery medals. But the extent to which these men were in control of their minds and subsequent actions is, very much, debatable. It is quite clear that men's emotions did not remain stable; they experienced rapid swings over short timescales, suggesting that control of their mental state became challenging or impossible. The man, suicidally careless in one circumstance, might take care of himself very keenly when the circumstances were changed. Norman Gladden of the Northumberlands described how, stumbling about in no-man's-land, at times he experienced a disabling panic, yet at others was able to see with striking clarity all around him, to think clearly and logically. He switched between blinded states of dreamlike illusion and acute awareness according to *perceived* level of risk rather than any correct assessment of danger: 'For mortal danger was everywhere, death swept across the field of battle'.

## FEAR

In Joseph Murray's book, *A Call To Arms*, published in 1980, the Durham miner found himself serving in the trenches of France and Flanders with the Royal Naval Division. His diary note for Sunday, 27 August 1916, provides an excellent summary of bravery and fear on the battlefield:

'There are times, yes many times, when each and every one of us would welcome the relief from this torment. It is not cowardice – far from it. It could be bravery. After all is said and done, bravery and cowardice are blood relations; there is a touch of insanity in both. Its only a question of degree and who is competent to judge? Show me the man who has never felt the pangs of fear. I have seen the bravest of men cowering and I have seen cowering men rise and go forward, even give encouragement to others. Fear will make you bury your head in the mud or shelter behind a blade of grass; it will make you run forward without rhyme nor reason or it may completely immobilise you; it is unpredictable'.[49]

Joseph Murray recognised that one of the important underlying causes of battlefield bravery was fear itself; that powerful urge to fight or run.

Gladden wrote that, waiting to participate in the attack on

Messines Ridge during the night of 6–7 June 1917: 'I tried to doze, but could not. We were all subdued, concerned with our most intimate thoughts. I had but one dream, the hopeless dream that I might awake to find it all a dream'.[50] The psychologist Michael Roper has identified a phenomenon of dream and reality becoming blurred, the sounds of battle merging with sleep, and a sleep-like stupor merging with wakefulness.[51] Men ceased to be capable of recognising where they were, what the real situation was, and as Joseph Murray himself experienced, 'In war we repeatedly commit acts that in peace time would be rewarded with the hangman's rope, but such acts in time of war are considered heroic. My brain has become so contorted that, try as I may, there are times that I cannot differentiate between what is right and what is wrong. One moment I am filled with blood-thirsty anger and the next I'm filled with remorse playing havoc with my soul'.[52]

Joseph Murray, without any training in psychology, understood very well the difficulties of defining bravery on the battlefield. A good many infantry soldiers who took the fight to the enemy and received medals for bravery were already changed by battle and by the things they had witnessed. Men who won medals did not necessarily plan what they did, they did not necessarily think in advance. Their minds may have been beaten into a dullness which left them acting without thought, fear, past or future. So how do we now interpret bravery medals and how do we hope to understand the actions of those who won them?

## OBLIGATION (THE SUBJECT MATTER EXPERT)

Many times on the battlefield men found themselves the only person with the requisite responsibility, experience or training. In battlefield situations, this creates an obligation to act because nobody else can. For example, when among 20 men there is only one bomb disposal expert, one doctor or one NCO, the pressure to perform a dangerous task regardless of the danger becomes extremely difficult to resist. When those around are unable to help themselves and one man has training or responsibility, the trained man tends to act and he becomes the leader, irrespective of rank.

Similar pressure comes to bear on men when they know that they have the most experience in a group or they have been in a similar situation before. The greater the experience a man has, the greater the urge to act on behalf of others can become. Further, in the presence of a qualified, more senior or experienced man, the juniors tend to devolve their responsibilities upon him. Quickly, a group divides into those who relinquish any responsibility and the few who take it on. When a dangerous task is involved, it can be very reassuring to have someone more experienced who takes the brunt of it, and it can be very convenient not to have to face the task oneself. A majority may feel they want to shelter, hide or otherwise get away. The result of this is that a hero may very rapidly be 'selected' by his comrades (or self-selected) on the battlefield on the basis of his experience and qualification for the job. The hero is left alone and with the pressure to act or face dereliction of duty; trained men don't like giving up or failing. A fear of failure or of the risks associated with failure (to self, to the group, or to the greater cause) further motivates the hero to act. A threat of court-martial, of letting the side down or of being viewed as a weak link in the group may act as the final push. Inexorably, the hero is part selected, part drawn to the task he is trained to do and part pushed by the Army and his mates to act.

Ultimately, when faced with an unexploded bomb, the ordnance disposal engineer has no choice but to deal with it as best he can. He may do so in order to show his professionalism but he also does it because he knows he is the subject matter expert. When a person is tasked with the job of helping others, most humans will put themselves in great danger to do so. Many so-called brave deeds were performed with the safety and well-being of mates in mind. The officer and the NCO, trained in leadership and usually with plenty of experience under their belts, felt the expectation of the Army, their friends, colleagues and schools, to perform under fire; not to let the side down. Given the specialist expertise, leadership training, rank or experience, men feel increasingly obliged not to follow but to act.

## COOL CALCULATION

There are some award citations which record a pre-meditated form of daring, but they are unusual. In the trenches of the Western Front, men were annoyed by snipers and active enemy machine guns, often during quiet periods in the line. When the front was quiet, trench life was immensely boring, and there was great temptation to relieve that boredom by doing something, by doing anything. In late March 1916, Pte. Trobe of the 1st Battalion Northumberland Fusiliers got his DCM after he left his trench and, 'stalked and shot two enemy snipers who were inflicting casualties on his company'. Similarly, in 1918, Lance Corporal Hogg, from Blyth, was awarded the DCM with the 19th Battalion of the Northumberland Fusiliers when, 'by two daring personal efforts he saved many lives. When his platoon was much harassed by snipers and machine-gun fire he went out, covered by fire from the platoon, and killed a deadly sniper, and again to put a machine gun out of action, which was eventually taken from the enemy'. These actions may have been fuelled by a combination of anger and revenge after comrades were shot dead. It is also possible that their motivation was part rooted in sport (hunting) and even boredom (something to do). Alleviating boredom in the trenches was a concern, leading to some foolish and fatal activities such as dismantling unexploded ordnance purely out of interest, with only a bayonet as a tool.

One remarkable example of dealing with a nuisance sniper was brought to light by author GS, when speaking to Trooper Down, formerly Northumberland Hussars Yeomanry, who was decorated with the DCM for his actions on D-Day the 6 June 1944. He had landed with his anti-tank battery and found himself hungry, perhaps he hadn't been able to eat much on the run-in, through rough seas. Sitting having his dinner, a sniper started taking pot-shots at him. With all the pragmatism of a Northumberland miner annoyed by a wasp, Down carefully put his dinner to one side and said to himself: 'Right, you're for it now, I'm going to get you, you sod'. He went off and shot the sniper, and also destroyed a German armoured vehicle for good measure. He related how he then returned and finished his dinner in peace, but was keen to impress on the listener that:

'the most nerve wracking thing I ever did was meet the King at Buckingham Palace'. Down was not a battle-hardened man, his senses were not dimmed by heavy and violent fighting; he won a DCM, one step removed from a Victoria Cross, because someone disturbed his dinner. With such examples to hand, one must wonder whether a definition of bravery is ever possible.

## HELPING FRIENDS

It is a peculiar characteristic of heroism that it is the observer who sees the hero, yet the observed man feels he is only doing his duty. Participants and onlookers who witness an act of heroism are directly involved in that act and very often perceive that the hero has assisted them in some fundamental way, be it withstanding the strain or the gift of life after resignation to imminent death. And so, a very powerful battlefield motive is that of helping friends, whether they be the men in the immediate vicinity or a larger body of men in their battalion, brigade or division. We have seen how men were motivated to go to war in the first instance largely in support of their mates who enlisted at the same time. The theme is continued in the strength they gained from their 'friends and family' in the trenches, and the immeasurable support that the leadership offered them (from Lance Corporals to Lieutenant Colonels). It may be argued that most heroic acts originate ultimately in helping friends in some way, but at the point of action this underlying motive is sometimes coupled with very strong emotions such as anger or vengeance. There is a large component of 'sticking together' about battlefield heroism and it is this source of heroism that leads directly to the indebtedness of those who benefit from the act.

Stretcher bearers and medics have always been mindful of an overriding duty to rescue the wounded, sometimes their own comrades. These men went into the open with a clear aim, for they knew that another's life hung upon their action or lack of action (a motive that may not have been quite so strong for an infantryman on the Western Front charged solely with killing Germans). To an infantryman, the achievements of the bearers could seem superhuman. Edward Lynch of the 45th Battalion,

First Australian Imperial Force, recalls how, in an attack on the 18 September 1918, two stretcher bearers were seen disappearing into a shell-swept wood to rescue some of his own comrades, their daring feats attracted great interest and admiration from his battalion: They 'charge straight into the jumping, flaring hell... through smoke, flying earth and screeching shell fragments. We watch two brave men going to their doom in an endeavour to rescue a couple of wounded men who are by now probably dead... The bearers disappear deep into the shell-tossed wood and we give them up for dead'. Yet soon they were spotted, 'Here they come! Like two drunken men they stagger out of the smoke, reeling from side to side, but between them on their stretcher, a wounded man on it!'. The two stretcher bearers went back in and extracted the second of two casualties, earning Edward Lynch's full praise; 'Bearers as gentle as they are brave. We've seen something to think about in the past few minutes'.[53] Normal Gladden also held some of his battalion stretcher bearers in high regard, stating: 'The company's stretcher bearer, Private Bell – known lovingly as Kidder Delicate – was a fat, lazy and easy-going person in normal times, who became a fearless, self-sacrificing hero when there was any succouring to be done... He richly deserved his subsequent decoration with the Military Medal'.[54] Contrast these views with that of Wilfred Cook, the battalion stretcher bearer who felt he and the team was simply 'going about our duties'.

Cook recorded the composition and duties of the stretcher bearer parties of the 1st Battalion, Northumberland Fusiliers: 'we had four teams of four men when at full strength. At the call of a runner or signal from HQ we turned out immediately no matter what we were doing. To be told that we were wanted in 'B' trench or elsewhere and approaching to see it under heavy shell fire was no joke but we went in, picked the man up and manhandled him back to safety as quickly as possible. I had very little medical training and the others not much more but the Medical Officer told us to forget the iodine etc., and get the casualty out just as he was'.[55]

Undoubtedly dangerous work, Cook describes how he had to ignore what was going on around him and just get on with doing what was necessary – his job: 'Going about our duties, we were but midgets in the chaos as we made our way to and fro from the front line disdaining the only cover we had on the way, a sunken road. Over the open took less time and time meant lives. Can men become immune to shell fire? There is no alternative here. One just kept on; there was no time for panic. Carrying one case down, we had him shoulder high and were making good progress towards the end of our journey when we heard a large shell coming very close indeed. I actually saw it plunge into the ground almost at my feet and then it burst. Four men with a stretcher shoulder high walked out of the black cloud of smoke and hurling metal, unscathed. Not one of us even ducked'. The Reverend Captain Mellish, VC, saw it all. He had earned his Victoria Cross for rescuing wounded from the battlefield at St. Eloi, 27 March 1916, where Cook's battalion had done so well. He thought it a miracle that the bearer party and patient had not been blasted to pieces. Cook and party simply went on with their work, refreshed after a cup of tea and a snack. Cook would never have accepted that he was brave or did anything other than his duty.[56]

In Afghanistan, 2009, Able Seaman Kate Nesbitt (a Naval Medic attached to the Royal Marines) won the Military Cross. She has joined many others decorated for gallantry in the past, by stating: 'I was just doing my job and the best for my colleagues. I think someone else would have done the same thing'. Later, she reiterated that: 'I was just doing my job'. However, from other statements it is clear that it was the circumstances and her sense of duty that compelled her to act. She knew she was needed, doing nothing would be a dereliction of her duty, so she sprinted the 60 to 70 metres to the casualty while under fire: 'It was adrenalin' she stated, 'being described as a hero is just too much'.[57] This recent example may be described as a lifesaving award, which we may particularly associate with the Army Medical Corps and battalion stretcher bearers in World War One.

Whilst medics and stretcher bearers were strongly motivated by their duty to look out for the wounded as they might their own brothers or sons, soldiers relied on the bearers to get them out if need be and venerated them as angels of the battlefield.

Ration and water carrying parties also knew that their comrades in the front line depended on them for survival. Sidney Rogerson of 2nd Battalion West Yorkshire Regiment thought that ration carrying parties had a particularly dangerous job, 'rarely... did they complete their double journey without casualties'.[58] During the battles around Arras in Spring 1917, 2nd Lieutenant Alexander McKeand of the 20th (Tyneside Scottish) Battalion Northumberland Fusiliers, 'frequently took long journeys in his effort to secure water for the troops', thus he won his MC for materially assisting with the consolidation of captured positions. Company Quartermaster Sergeant Senior was honoured by the award of the DCM when 'he led his party right through the barrage and after five hours' toiling through mud and water located his battalion and issued the ration to his company in a line of shell holes under heavy fire, many of his party becoming casualties. He was the only CQMS whose party reached the front line'. Quartermaster Sergeant Parker was responsible for stores and supplies for the 11th Battalion Northumberland Fusiliers at the Battle of the Menin Road in late September 1917. His efforts, 'largely contributed to the success of the operations' and resulted in the award of his DCM for keeping the men up front supplied (rather than for fighting a battle). To say that QM Sgt Parker largely contributed to the success of the operations is frankly a stupendous accolade as the battle of the Menin Road was, and still is, widely viewed as a great military success. After the war ended in 1919, Sergeant Laing of South Shields, 19th Battalion Northumberland Fusiliers, was awarded his DCM for the 'prompt delivery of stores in most difficult circumstances' since January 1916. His citation further mentioned that 'he never lost an animal killed by enemy shellfire', a remarkable tribute to his ongoing judgement and skill over nearly three years at war. These awards and others demonstrate how important supply was to military success and that such individual contributions, particularly those over long periods of time, should not be underestimated.

Similarly, getting ammunition and replacement weapons up to the front line was done with the lives of comrades in mind. During the Battle of St. Julien, 24–25 April 1915 near Ypres, Ptes Martin and Burrell of the 7th Battalion Northumberland Fusiliers each received the DCM for 'carrying up a box of ammunition to the firing line... across open ground and under a heavy fire from the enemy. These men advanced entirely unsupported and were cheered by their comrades for their bravery'. Regimental Sergeant Major Finch, of Gateshead, 6th Battalion Northumberland Fusiliers, was awarded his DCM during the German Spring offensives 1918 when he 'displayed great coolness and determination in collecting and distributing ammunition under heavy machine-gun and rifle fire after the objectives had been captured'.

Services of this nature are underpinned by the determination to assist comrades whose survival depends upon them. Those who received official recognition in the form of a bravery medal knew that they had done their duty well, but they would not recognise themselves as heroes.

## CIRCUMSTANCES

Identification of a job that needed doing and then acting upon it is another common characteristic of medal winning actions. Lance Corporal Thomas Bryan of the 25th (Tyneside Irish) Battalion of the Northumberland Fusiliers saw his fellow men cut down by a German machine gun during the assault of Vimy Ridge on 9 April 1917. He spotted a communication trench which might allow him to get around the machine gun. He alone got up and worked his way skilfully behind the gun and disabled it, killing its crew. The removal of this obstacle had far-reaching implications, enabling the advance to continue and that part of the ridge to be taken. Thomas Bryan had the Victoria Cross pinned to his chest by the King in front of a huge audience. In many cases, these types of action arise from the particular situations men find themselves in, whereby they become aware of an opportunity to alter a difficult situation and, with their colleagues in mind, take a coolly considered risk. For this reason, the term 'brave hero' seems inappropriate to them, because what they did was motivated by ordinary concerns, the appearance of a clear opportunity, by duty and by training. In this sense, such actions are not at all special and are the natural outcome of battles and military training.

Some of the things men did on the battlefield are more difficult to understand as the objective was not as clear as the elimination of an enemy party, a strongpoint or a machine gun. Pinned down by heavy fire and suffering severe casualties in no-man's-land, men of the 13th Battalion Northumberland Fusiliers went forward with wire cutters and worked at cutting the enemy wire lying on their backs until, very predictably, they were shot through and killed at close range. Lieutenant George Woodbridge and Pte. E. Mawson managed to clear a path through the wire allowing just one man to get through and into the enemy's trench. The rest of the battalion was unable to move. Their MC and MM were the only decorations earned in a failed attack during which many men had performed desperate, hopeless feats and 10 per cent of the battalion had been killed. Lieutenant Woodbridge's MC citation reads: 'For conspicuous gallantry and devotion to duty. At a moment when his company was held up by enemy wire close to their objective, he displayed the greatest gallantry in attacking the wire under very heavy fire, and cutting a way through it for his men. At the moment of completing his task he was shot through the chest.' As was often the case, after months of training, the battalion had marched into the line, gone over the top, been shot to ribbons on the enemy wire and the same evening buses were on hand to take the battered survivors out of the line. No, success meant little in the way of thanks, just one MC and one MM, at the price of hundreds of killed, wounded and missing. The level of reward was not linked to the level of danger, so we may ask, 'where is bravery displayed, if not in the most frightening and dangerous of situations; a failed attack, pinned down in no-man's-land, waiting to be shot?'.

## OTHER ASPECTS OF COURAGE

Bravery, of course, was not only applicable to those who won medals. Only a very few men received official recognition for distinguished services of one kind or another. Not all men felt that their duty was something worth dying for but their experiences required courage, perhaps even bravery.

The following few examples are suggestive that endurance,

courage and stress were abundantly distributed among the soldiers at and near the front.

Noted on my Great Uncle Frank's service record from his time in France and Flanders with the Royal Naval Division (thrown into some of the most testing and bloody battles of the war) there are several notes stating: 'A.W.O.L.' followed by his sentence, Field Punishment number 1. Frank had been wounded in the neck, the finger and the arm; one wound in each of three consecutive battles. His narrow escapes probably suggested to him that he was done for in the next one and perhaps he owed nobody anything, for a day or two, anyhow.

The bald statements on the service record of another Royal Naval Division rating, George Simpson, tend to indicate a more serious negative reaction to being thrown into a war that was not his own. In 1914, George, a 15-year-old miner from County Durham, pretended he was 18 and enlisted in the Hood Battalion of the Royal Naval Division. On the Gallipoli Peninsula he was bowled over by a Turkish sniper and then endured weeks of dysentery at the hospital on Malta before transfer to the Western Front. On his 18th birthday, 13 November 1916, he went over the top in the battle of the Ancre, was shot through both knees and his battalion was utterly decimated. The Hoods did best of all that day, taking every objective, but it was a disaster, for the battle claimed the flower of the Royal Naval Division.[59] For George to have this catastrophe occur on his birthday must have fractured any belief in a mythic guardian he may have had. He may well have had cause to ask himself how his birthday, his own special day so closely associated with his childhood and the safety of his mother, could now be the cause of such a monumental horror. There can be little doubt that this experience and its emotional after-effects were the cause of his future behaviour.

Shipped back to Blighty, apathy and anger seem to have taken ahold of him. In January 1917 he stayed overdue from leave, then forced his way out of the detention room. Again in April he took as much time as he wanted on leave and suffered the consequences. When due to sail for France to rejoin his unit, he revealed that in fact he had enlisted under age, a convenient revelation that meant, as he surely knew it would, that he would remain behind in the UK. At Blandford Camp during July 1917 he was convicted of 'conduct to the prejudice of good order and military discipline' (28 days imprisonment at Parkhurst Prison, pay stoppage). In October he was convicted of the same offence (168 hours detention), and in early November decided to break out of camp and roam around with another soldier's rifle. George no longer feared or cared for what military authority could do to him, he became undisciplined and uncontrollable. And yet, was he not courageous to stand up, in his own way, to the authoritarian might of the British Army?

Other men suffered similar, and worse, emotional trauma but responded quite differently. The service of 20-year-old John Deane, who joined the 1/5th Battalion of the King's Liverpool Regiment, appears to illustrate a transition from shocked young man to brave veteran. His battalion's first attack was at Guillemont during the Battle of the Somme on 8 August 1916 where they suffered heavy casualties of 70 killed, 177 wounded and 64 missing. John was lucky, but the experience must have been terrifying for the 20-year-old. The battalion was sent back to the front, near Delville Wood just four weeks later. On 10 September the *Battalion War Diary* states: 'At 7a.m. the enemy commenced shelling our front and support lines... with 5.9 shells and a few 8' shells. This continued intermittently until 4.15p.m. when it grew into an intense bombardment lasting until 4.45p.m. Casualties: wounded 42, killed 8.'

This proved too much for John and he was evacuated with shell shock that day to a Casualty Clearing Station and on to England. In other words, within four weeks of arriving he had become incapable of performing his duties as a soldier as a result of the concussion of shell explosions. Shell shock victims often exhibited signs of nervous disorder or breakdown such as childlike regression, loss of speech, vision, hearing or all of those senses. In the worst cases they were shadows of men, their bodies and nervous systems rent and contorted so furiously that they had literally lost their minds.

Recovering from this, John Deane went over the top twice in the 3rd Battle of Ypres (on 31 July and 20 September 1917), his

Battalion again suffering heavy casualties. How well he did during these attacks and during a major German counter-attack at Cambrai in late November 1917 is suggested by his citation for the Military Medal, signed by his CO two days after the rearguard Cambrai battle: 'At Grafton Post on the 30 November, 1917, this man employed as a stretcher bearer made several journeys between the front line and the aid post passing through heavy barrages of 5.9 shells. He was compelled to go over the top on two occasions carrying wounded as the trench had been completely blown in. His cheery bearing and devotion to his work were of great value'.

John Deane went through a transition from a defeated young infantryman who did not cope at all with the war, to a brave hero who put his own life before those of his wounded comrades. The battle situation and shelling that had so rapidly and comprehensively broken him previously, produced a 'cheery bearing' as he brought in the wounded not 12 months later. It seems a remarkable turnaround but we should assume that this was neither an exceptional nor a permanent change in his physical and mental state.

We have seen how medals were won in greater abundance in successful military operations. Success often meant lower casualties, and in the case of trench raids success could mean zero casualties. On the other hand, we are mindful of the defeats of the First of July 1916, or recall those Northumberland Fusiliers who were shot through the spine by machine-gun fire at point-blank range whilst cutting wire. High casualties were associated with failure, leading us to the inevitable conclusion that the numbers of medals awarded was lowest when the danger (risk of injury or violent death) was highest. It is obvious that when risk is highest, fear mixed with courage must be present in the highest degree. The courage required to endure shelling has been covered at length. Whilst there are many examples of gallantry awards made for remarkable actions under shell fire, not one has been found for what a great many have admitted required the greatest of courage. Enduring shell fire, we may infer, was recognised simply as part of a man's duty as a soldier. Going over the top was viewed similarly.

We have not encountered a single bravery award made for enduring the storm of steel or for being shot at, wounded or killed. It is clear that a great deal of courage and bravery was expended simply in enduring. That no medals were handed out for enduring those most trying of tests, tells us just how disconnected courage and medals are on the battlefield. If that point may be broadly accepted, at least in generalised terms, then to a degree, so must courage and heroism be disconnected. The heroes of the Great War were carefully selected by the State, and we may recall that most of them did not consider themselves heroes. These war heroes have a point; they were stating plain fact.

In support of the idea that heroism was not at all special and far more widespread than the State officially acknowledged, we may consider those who avoided going to war at all costs; the conscientious objectors, who defied their own State, the mass of their own peers and vehement public opinion. They stood up for what they believed in, against all pressures and suffered jail sentences and deplorable treatment. There is a large measure of Christian self-sacrifice and heroism in their determined stand. They acted, it might very well be said, in the image of Christ himself, who stood up to the Roman authorities at the expense of his own freedom and eventually at the expense of his own life. If Britain's conscientious objectors were not literally crucified, they metaphorically were (and their courage concealed).

Now consider the fathers and mothers whose lives were cast into deep shadow for up to four long years, bearing the load of daily stress. What courage did they need to simply exist from day to day as the casualty rolls lengthened; the war evidently stagnated into an eternity of mutual destruction and War Office letters announcing the deaths of sons and fathers to the community? Waiting under a heavy shell fire of telegrams and the continuous loud reports of newspapers, is what families did. Theirs was as heroic an endurance as that of any soldier, who was at least able to make a contribution to Victory, whilst parents and sisters had to huddle together and bear up (or collapse under the strain).

There were plenty of battlefield activities which required

immense courage but did not win medals. Of the many tasks of the battlefield, one was particularly horrific; that of the burial parties who had to clear up the mess afterwards. Captain Gerald Burgoyne described burying a man as a 'horrid job, lifting his head to get his identity disc' and later had to bury the body parts of British, French and German soldiers, some of whom had been lying there for weeks.[60] Men had to deal with the mutilated bodies of their comrades, a job for at least two men who picked the corpses up by the arms and ankles, placing them often in improvised shallow graves close to the front line. It was always a source of sadness that the buried man would probably be exhumed and flung about once again by shell fire, but it was the best they could do. To know that one might be killed and share the fate of the corpse, in no peaceful grave, was a disturbing thought. Burial parties could not avoid the dead, they had to handle them, look at them, shove their hands into them searching for dog-tags or shovel up the splashed and dismembered remains.[61] Men vomited when faced with these forms of horror, but there was no official recognition of their courage. Only very rarely were men recommended for awards for burying dead, usually under shell fire, but we have no record of any such awards actually being made. For example, preserved in the 8th Battalion Northumberland Fusiliers war diary, an MC recommendation for Temporary Captain William Ash survives: 'On 26 September 1916 at Zollern Redoubt he rendered valuable service after the assault in collecting stragglers and assisting wounded under heavy fire. Later he was in charge of a party detailed to bring in wounded, who were lying about, and to bury the dead, which he carried out under heavy shell fire. As Lewis Gun officer during the tour of the Battalion in the trenches at Beaucourt from 1 December 1916 to 10 January 1917, he displayed marked ability and disregard for danger in personally supervising his gun positions in isolated posts in front of Bois d'Hollande, which were constantly subjected to heavy shell fire'.

Ash was not rewarded with the DSO or MC, almost certainly because the recommendation listed too many separate acts of gallantry over too long a period of time and some of them (burial of dead) weakened, rather than strengthened, the recommendation. And so it was the rainbow colours of the silk ribbon of the gilded Victory medal that became these men's reward; the State recognised no special courage here.

Then there were those who used up their entire reserves of courage dealing with death on an hourly basis – the Padres, doctors and nurses. Padres had to draw heavily on their faith and personal courage in the course of duty as they tried to offer comfort to men passing over the threshold into death. The moments leading to death could be intensely personal and also distressing to witness. Padres had to see hundreds of dead buried every week, stretching their endurance to the limit. This too was part of the Padre's duty which went almost wholly unrewarded.

Nurses saw things that no woman should have to see. They were asked to deal with terribly wounded, dying men and boys over long periods of time in tented or general hospitals, among blood-soaked bandages, infested wounds, hopeless cases, pleading cases, mad men, and it was this daily mental attrition that was particularly challenging. And yet, nurses won most of their medals for bravery when their hospitals were subjected to air raids rather than for the daily courage they mustered simply to do their jobs. One wonders how many nurses had to be sent home with nervous disorders such as neurasthenia or were simply no longer capable of doing their duty, after their courage to go on had collapsed.

The State chose not to make heroes of these people, instead it chose to make heroes of those who did what the State wanted, it persisted with a military expression of heroism to the exclusion of other forms of heroism and courage. This was the model of heroism that was encouraged, nourished and nurtured.

T. R. Fowler has suggested that one of the character traits of the recipients of bravery awards is 'a refusal to be beaten or pushed around'.[62] The description could apply in very equal measure to the conscientious objector, or for that matter, to the deserter who was shot by firing squad, grimly determined that he was right and his country was at that moment outrageously wrong.

## SUDDEN BURIAL

Men faced burial alive when under heavy artillery bombardment, whether in the ready-made tombs of dugouts or out in the open, as heavy shells threw up large fountains of earth from the shell-ploughed land. Burial appears to have been a particularly stressful experience which pushed victims to the brink of death both physically and mentally. Men never received bravery medals for being buried alive, yet it was one of the most stressful events. Soldiers did, however, receive medals for digging buried men out from under earth and debris after shell explosions. They did this frequently under heavy fire themselves, at great personal risk but careless of that risk. After being partially buried himself, Private McIntosh of the 12th Battalion Northumberland Fusiliers won the DCM 'for conspicuous gallantry and devotion to duty... he organised and directed a party in digging out several buried men. He set a splendid example of courage and determination'. This bland citation masks the horror of being buried and of excavating buried comrades.

Leutnant Zinnemann of the German Infantry Regiment 63 had just been blown up by a shell and settled into a small foxhole for some rest when he was blown up a second time, a very near miss. He described the experience as if 'falling down a great hole' with senses reeling and seeing stars. He was buried and successively felt a roaring sound, silent tears, 'terrible cold ice' and a 'great weight crushing me. I feel light headed'. He considered himself receding into a peaceful death but then, hearing someone call his name, he was soon dug out by a rescuer who, 'seized by the Furies... tears at the earth with his bare hands'. Stretched out on the bottom of the damaged shallow trench, Zinnemann gasped for air feeling freezing cold and 'weeping uncontrollably'. When able, he crawled slowly 'on trembling hands and knees' to the doctor where he was sedated.[63] In the front line, still the fountains of clay leapt upwards, claiming victims, tearing men to pieces and burying them alive.

Approximately one per cent of all gallantry awards made to the Northumberland Fusiliers was for digging out buried comrades under heavy shellfire. But it is a German officer, Walter Schulze, who has left a moving account of that furious race to save comrades buried by the blasts of heavy 280mm shells. Walter wrote that: 'There was an appalling crash. From the smoke came a piercing, whimpering scream. I quickly got up and looked for my comrades... all I could see was a mound of earth, out of which came desperate cries for help. At first I could only see Knoblauch.... his eyes stared in terror from his distorted white face... he was only buried up to his waist... Terrified shouts were still coming from the heap of earth. My blood ran cold at the shouts of fear. It was simply dreadful... I worked fast with a spade... Yes! There is a helmet, a head'. Digging frantically, Walter freed this man whose face was as white as a sheet 'from the terrible shock and fear of the incident'. Hearing the receding, suffocating voice of the last man, Walter was then 'gripped by fear' and felt that he would be digging a corpse out of its grave. He was consumed by the 'unspeakable concern that I have not been able to save the poor chap' and this was what motivated him to throw all caution to the wind, expose himself on top of the heap as shrapnel bullets whistled all around, having 'lost all feeling for the danger... I just want to help the unfortunate man down there'. After digging the body out with their hands, Walter noted its blue lips, wild staring eyes, 'a fearful sight!' and then describes in detail his efforts to resuscitate and nurse his friend. He does so to the complete exclusion of any events external to this intense personal experience with the rescued man. Walter records, 'I stay with him constantly, feeling suddenly a warm sacrificial love for this unhappy man... I soothe him and say, "Take it easy, Otto, try to sleep... we'll get you out of here then things will be better". The very helplessness of the man is deeply moving'. Walter felt helpless himself, in fact, whilst trying to perform the function of the man's mother, when Walter needed his own mother to comfort him almost as much: 'all the misery before me will have me crying like a child'. The ending to this does not close the story: 'Finally, as night falls, the ration party arrives and places him in a groundsheet to carry him back. "Get well soon! Keep your chin up!" "You too, Walter." Thank heavens he is away from this hell. Hopefully the poor chap is not beyond help'.[64] It is as much of an ending as was possible to give; men were carried away followed by the hopes of those remaining. But no-one could be sure that the wounded even made it out of the firing line alive, let alone that their graves would remain undisturbed by the ghastly shelling.

## SUDDEN INJURIES, EMPATHY AND MEMORY

It was common for ordinary men, even those in support units behind the lines, to suddenly have to deal with badly wounded comrades. Sapper Frank Jeffrey was serving with the 263rd Railway Construction Company of the Royal Engineers east of Ypres, within half a mile of the front line trenches on 7 December 1917. They were building rail spurs for artillery positions to get ammunition up to the guns, but the German artillery had a good view of their workings and so it got dangerously hot when a barrage of high explosives was put down on them. Shells crashed around, wounding several. While the majority ran for cover, Frank Jeffrey didn't, he rescued his comrades who lay wounded in the open under continued shelling. He was rewarded with the MM for his gallantry under shellfire. This is a common story of self-sacrifice to save mates, a daily occurrence behind the lines on the Western Front.

The aftermath of a shell explosion could be a perturbing and moving experience for everyone in the vicinity. When it happened, some found themselves giving when they needed, acting as mother when they needed caring for. An unknown eye-witness at the 9th Battalion Northumberland Fusiliers Dressing Station, during a battle on 24 October 1918, recorded the streams of wounded coming back from the front line: 'The sight of the stretcher cases on the road affected me very much'. He described 'wrecked and bleeding men, some with huge pieces of their bodies torn off, bones laid bare, men vomiting from internal wounds, others sobbing out their last breaths'. With these scenes around him he saw a battalion runner lean over a particularly bad case and, 'very gently say, "Jack, don't you know me?" and touch his face as lovingly as a mother would her child. How the men feel for each other and how they realise what each other has gone through'.[65] Such care for an unfortunate victim is an outward expression of the carer's own stress.

Soldiers who cared, or grieved, as fathers would their own sons, is a recurrent theme in war memoirs. Some lengthy passages are given to describing the feelings men experienced when confronted with the deaths of young boys on the battlefield. Wilfred Cook became good friends with an experienced and much-respected old soldier known as 'Smiler' McQuade – a man who had been rewarded with an MM for his lifesaving work under heavy shell fire earlier in the war – but who later broke down and had to abandon his duties as stretcher bearer during the Somme battle of summer 1916. 'What is the matter, Smiler?' said Cook upon entering the dugout where the tearful McQuade was sheltering. 'I have been out here from the beginning. Nothing has been too much for me. I don't mind whether a man is still alive or dead I'll bring him out but I don't want another case like the last one'. Smiler, a mature man, a tough miner, was unable to control his emotions. Cook relates that Smiler had picked up a very badly wounded young man with little chance of survival, who, Smiler struggled to relate, 'began to cry for his mother... that broke me. I could not see that and be unaffected. He was only 16 and should never have been here at all, poor kid'.[66] In 1918, a British soldier, himself wounded, saw a 'Saxon boy' who had been crushed by a tank, itself now smashed by shell fire. The boy was moaning: 'Mutter, Mutter, Mutter' (mother, mother, mother). The wounded Englishman dragged himself over to the dying boy and 'takes his cold hand and says, "All right, son, its all right, Mother's here with you"'.[67]

In Michelle Barrett's study of five men's wartime experiences, she claims that the most significant experience in Bombardier Ronald Skirth's breakdown and eventual rebirth as a pacifist, was his encounter with a recently killed German boy. He was sitting just as if he had fallen asleep on the edge of a shell hole, a lock of blond hair from under his helmet resting on his forehead. He died whilst looking at pictures of his parents and a young girl. Rather than repulsion, Skirth was drawn towards this corpse (a lad called Hans, in fact). Skirth identified with the dead German boy, and never forgot him.[68]

As was the case for the dying boy Hans, photographs from home had magical power during the most brutal times. Ernst Junger, the German warrior, remembered an encounter with a British officer in the heat of battle, 'A bloody scene with no witnesses was about to happen', but the British officer pulled a photograph of himself with his family out of his pocket, 'a plea from another world' that saved him. Junger admitted 'that one man of all often appeared in my dreams. I hope that meant he got to see his homeland again'.[69]

In Captain C. J. C. Street's *With The Guns* published in 1916, a fellow officer is recorded as having received 'what he describes as "the shock of his life"' whilst searching for a suitable artillery observation post in a wrecked house near Loos in September 1915. This horror, too, was generated by the discovery of a dead German in startling life position: 'sprawling over a table as though just fallen asleep'. Drawn closer, he ascertained that the German had been writing a postcard 'to a girl in Magdeburg' at the moment when a shell fragment made 'the jagged hole above the temple... and the blood that stained his right side'. Not the shock of the war itself, but the tragedy of love slaughtered by violent death, gave this officer the shock of his life.[70]

After sparing the life of the British officer with the family photograph, Junger let us see his reaction to killing the young. Junger's troops were clearing dugouts and taking British prisoners. Here he did something that affected him for the rest of his life: 'The occupants of a row of dugouts along the side of the path also ran away. I encountered one such as he was just about to leave'. We assume that Junger shot the man through the head at point-blank range, leaving 'my British soldier, little more than a boy' lying there 'looking quite relaxed'. As with Ronald Skirth, Junger found himself drawn to the body, 'it wasn't a case of "you or me" any more. I often thought back on him; and more with the passing of years... sorrow, regret, pursued me deep into my dreams'.[71] We suspect that Junger felt that he could have let the boy go, to run away with the others who had escaped, rather than shoot a lad young enough to be his own son. This was a lad who had, more so than an older man, come direct from his mother's embrace to fight a war. Lingering very close to these young ones there was a mother's presence. The slaying of youth, the slaughter of these innocents, was an aspect that caused soldiers to feel intense guilt, heavy sorrow and deep remorse both during and after battle. Blurring the boundaries of civilisation and brutality, the fog of war extended into the minds of its participants, who had perpetrated deeds that would haunt them.

## THE RUNNER

Experiences of battalion or company runners form part of the story of battlefield bravery. Running messages on the battlefield was a vital military task when other lines of communication had been cut by artillery fire, as frequently happened. Runners were sent to ask for more ammunition or for rations or to report on the situation to Headquarters staff. Front line officers knew all too painfully that at times they were sending young lads to their deaths, but the message had to get through however many times it had to be sent. When telephone cables were destroyed by shellfire it fell typically to the younger members of battalions to 'run' from place to place carrying messages. The particular nature of their courage lies in the absence of comradely support; loneliness made the job a very tough one.

Whereas runners were assigned that duty, in their absence volunteers were called for. Norman Gladden, whilst serving with the 7th Battalion Northumberland Fusiliers on the Somme, relates how, 'I remember the Captain asking for a volunteer to carry a message across the open to another section... a successful journey, he suggested, might well bring a recommendation' (for an MM). Norman, 'paralysed with fear' and 'quite incapable' remembered that one of the old hands in the battalion volunteered.[72] Nevertheless, the runner was engaged in a task to occupy him rather than waiting impotently, and on his travels sometimes came across discarded bounties such as bags of special rations (tea, sugar, tobacco) deposited in a heap by some unfortunate soul. Such prizes were always very welcome in the trenches and made some runners very popular.

Communication between the front line soldiers and the artillery sometimes required the efforts of runners, too, although communication was normally effected by means of firing coloured flares. One of the best descriptions of a runner getting across a battlefield is provided by the German Georg Queri, of Infantry Regiment 163:

*'The telephone is down – all the lines are cut. We'll have to make ourselves understood by means of flares... but the cartridges are buried. Two heavy shells, landing simultaneously, have thrown huge masses of earth on top of the dugout which leads to the flare store. Gefreiter Schoenau heads off to fetch some of the signal cartridges. The first part of his task is to wait and study the impact patterns of the falling shells for five minutes, in order to see if there is a regular gap in the curtains of death through which he could slip. Ah, it appears that initially it will be possible to follow a diagonal course for the first hundred paces. All goes well, very well in fact. Now its a matter of sheltering in a shell hole to work out the next moves – head not too high! Splinters are flying in all directions. Then its off once more, rolling like a barrel from one shell hole to the next, with the splinters whizzing by only a hand's width above. Dive into another shell hole, then one more. Things nearly went wrong there. That thing crashed damned close. Now its possible to move in a number of proper bounds.*

*'Time for a quick breather, further observation, then the move is sideways to the fourth crater on the right. Over there at about two hundred paces distance is Sailly, or rather a number of piles of rubble which offer plenty of cover. That will certainly be needed, because everywhere is being swept by machine gun and rifle fire. So its on with the dance, as the bullets crack by a couple of feet higher. Now its possible to crawl – quick! quick! quick! – CRUMP! That bloody thing was close! Better wait and see if there are more to come! No? OK then, off to the village, which is burning, smouldering, stinking and collapsing with loud crashes and splintering sounds. But here, at least, it is possible to hide away from the small arms fire and make some progress. Now the area is open once more – start running! The shells are not landing so quickly here. Now sniff out the Headquarters of the 2nd Battalion. The first part of the mission is complete and its time to take a proper break, because the return journey with a sack of cartridges will be harder. But there is*

*a pleasant surprise for them up front. The Company is to prepare to be relieved! What a lucky day. Everything the Devil can throw has been negotiated successfully... Fortunately the Regiment had many such men – men who were ready to lay their lives on the line without hesitation if the good of all demanded it. All commanders know how much the troops owed to the work of the runners. For many, life as a runner was life on Death Row, but even when the seemingly impossible was asked of them, they had only one response: 'Yes, Sir!'.[73]*

The job of the runner was an extremely taxing one, as a German Artillery Liaison Officer, Lieutenant Richard Sapper, noted during a violent Somme battle of 1916: 'Now and again the runners appeared; their faces drawn and unrecognisable with the shock and strain. They handed over the reports from the front line wordlessly and were sent out again with orders'.[74] In the context of major actions, a runner's task was not only a case of his luck holding out until he was killed or severely injured; it could be such a violent experience that his power of speech, or the necessity of speech, was removed. On such days as he was needed, he ran alone among monstrous detonations and a falling hail of airborne earth, bullets, shell splinters and shrapnel. Brief moments of contact with humans could be an inconsequential interlude in the physical struggle outside – a struggle that was so intensely physical that his mind was knocked about and snuffed out.

## CHARGING THE MACHINE GUN
The other frightful weapon alongside the shell was of course the machine gun, which was vital in the front line and was also abundantly utilised to provide machine gun barrages. It was most successful in the defence as a means of suppressing enemy movement over the battlefield. It was feared by attacking troops in the open, but was the prime target for enemy artillery and small arms fire. Being attacked when behind a machine gun was described by Leutnant Freiherr von Salmuth who was a machine gunner with a German Guards Regiment: 'It looked bad for us. Naturally the

machine gun was the main target. The gunner was badly wounded. His number two leapt into position and had his shoulder torn off. Leutnant Ziesing fell, shot through the jaw. I was hit on the helmet by a spent round, the NCO next to me was shot through the chest! As I rushed to take over the machine gun, a round came through its cooling jacket and boiling water squirted everywhere'.[75] In major battles, sometimes front line machine gunner's thumbs melted as the gun became red hot and threw out tell-tale clouds of steam after hours of firing, the dead lying in heaps to the front. One gunner described having to be lifted away from his death-dealing weapon as his body had frozen in the firing position after intense hours of murderous shooting, as if the gunner's nervous system itself had been overcome by the rigor mortis of the young men he had taken. Such was the intensity of battle.

The machine gun rapidly gained such notoriety for mass murder that its elimination also rose to become the ultimate act of battlefield heroism. As a symbol of heroism, storming the machine gun remains perhaps the most impressive and easily appreciated act of bravery in popular perception. Given the perceived risk of being killed in the attempt, the futility of attacking a machine gun is evident. This suggests what Dyer described as 'the Glory of self-sacrifice, the blessing of failure'.[76]

Yet, the reality was that the machine gun was not the most dangerous weapon of war between 1914 and 1918; that position was reserved for the artillery. In use, and in shooting an arc of raking fire, the machine gun actually wasted a great deal of ammunition in a poorly aimed spray of bullets which achieved very few hits. A higher hit rate was achieved by aimed rifle fire from a steady body of infantry. With regard to attacking the heavy machine gun, the canny soldier soon learned that the heavy German weapon had a restricted arc of fire, and that by careful observation and a bit of luck, one could work one's way into the blind zone and get around the back of it. Sergeant Edward Cooper gives us a clue about what many knew or at least believed: '...if I got into a certain position, the German's arc of fire couldn't reach me, and I set off diagonally to get into this position'.[77] Thus began his advance to the single-handed capture of an enemy concrete fortification containing several machine guns, for which he won the Victoria Cross. Similarly, Captain A. O. Pollard, VC, MC, DCM confirms that this was not an isolated observation: 'German machine guns were only able to traverse through thirty degrees without moving the carriage on which they were mounted. In normal practice they were arranged in pairs', so he states. However, if one of the pair was destroyed, 'the arrangement broke down, as a gap appeared in what was otherwise an impenetrable barrier. This apparent weakness in disposition was responsible for more than one Victoria Cross earned during the war'. He went on to state, perhaps with exaggeration, that a man, 'could move about in perfect safety outside of its zone of fire'.[78] Lance Corporal Thomas Bryan of the Northumberland Fusiliers, in all probability, took advantage of an opportunity that he saw, be it the arc of fire or of some particular advantage of cover, to get around and behind a machine gun that was holding up his battalion during the attack on Vimy Ridge, 9 April, 1917. He was another who won the VC for knocking out a machine gun, and at the same time having the luck to knock out the key machine gun which was holding up the attack. Probably, Bryan did not have the wider view to realise that his machine gun was so significant to the capture of that infamous ridge. To his local action was attributed major consequences, and so his recommendation passed rapidly along the chain to the King, who concurred. It is quite possible that Thomas Bryan didn't concur.

Machine guns were thus eliminated, in some cases, by clever, cunning men who took their chance. The clever soldier did not approach from the front; he carefully observed and plotted his safest course of attack. But this was not always the case. As a situation deteriorated and a group of attackers was forced to ground, occasionally one or two men took it upon themselves to charge a gun, perhaps because they were angry, or felt that everyone with them would die in vain if nobody acted. Perhaps they felt they were in a no-choice situation. Once pinned down in no-man's-land, they would likely be destroyed by artillery fire. They couldn't stay there, someone had to move, to help their mates get out of danger and into safety.

The Table below shows how the act of storming the machine gun grew in stature between 1914 and 1918; this occurred partly because the types of acts for which the VC was being awarded changed progressively as the war went on and also because of the proliferation of medium and light machine guns later in the war.

| The Victoria Cross for Attacking Machine Guns | | | | |
|---|---|---|---|---|
| 1914 | 1915 | 1916 | 1917 | 1918 |
| 2% | 1% | 13% | 43% | 44% |

**Table 13: The Rapid Increase in Victoria Cross Awards for Capturing Machine Guns, 1914–1918**

By 1917 nearly half of all VCs were given to men who charged and eliminated machine guns; it was the number one VC act of the second half of the First World War. The jump between 1915, 1916 and 1917 is absolutely remarkable, and is as clear an indication as any of what the Generals and the War Office had come to view as the most deserving act of courage on the battlefield. But why? There is a lot of symbolism in the act, and where there is a symbolic act, there is political gain in the creation of indisputable war heroes whose acts are presented as triumphant and glorious and which appear to be designed to mask the horrible reality of war. But the case is not so simple; there is much to consider carefully about this. There is the hero himself, who denies he did anything special. That many men may have charged the spitting weapons from a point of relative safety or from behind, that some men experienced a peak of rage which drove them to careless self-destruction, or that some were in the grip of apathy making it easier to step out, seems likely. That the artillery barrage was a potent and imminent threat that drove men to move rather than wait cowering in fear, is also likely. The men who stormed machine gun positions may have experienced many different emotions in the din of battle and among the heavy concussions of detonating shells and falling earth that knocked their senses about. The motivating factors behind these acts are not always evident when viewed at a distance from battle and may seem quite separate from the promotion of the soldier as hero and the act as heroic.

Nevertheless, the machine gun was certainly feared, it drove men to ground and broke up attacks. In military terms, it was powerful and had a dominating effect on many battles of the First World War. But to understand the act, there is something else to consider, something vital; the audience. It seems probable that the man who got up, while his comrades sheltered, risked his own life in the face of a torrent of bullets primarily to help his mates get off the open battlefield and into the safety of a captured trench. He may be understood, in that limited sense, as a hero already. But for the actor, there was a lot of luck involved and all the emotions of the moment came into play. In tackling the most obvious problem, he felt he was only doing what was required of him in desperate circumstances, and that was his duty to his friends and his job as a soldier. Yet the onlookers, his audience, viewed things quite differently; stuck in a desperate position, with hope waning and waiting to be killed perhaps, they saw a mate get up and do something both unexpected and spectacular; something apparently beyond the call of normal duty. The moment he moved, he became distinct from those who sheltered. The audience watched their friend deliver to them, amidst a hail of bullets, at first the hope of release from certain death and finally the certainty of it. If successful, the onlookers also received the joy of victory over a murderous oppressor. It is David and Goliath of classical mythology. A good story. Among the audience, then, there was a strong sense of relief in getting up and moving into relative safety, then in actively working towards ones' own survival, getting to work consolidating a captured position. All these were a release from danger and from impotently waiting in a hole with one's face pressed into the earth. These were very real gifts, gifts that highlighted the value of the service to those who had recently felt the imminence of death. The one who got them out of such a fix became their rescuer, a lifesaver and a hero who placed himself in the gravest of danger to save his mates. This sensation was driven to the extreme if, in the moment of achieving victory over the enemy, the hero was killed in delivering their safety. The most precious of gifts, in this case, came at the highest cost and in the form of a debt which could never be repaid. Debts that cannot be repaid linger very strongly. In these circumstances, to lay down one's life for one's comrades can be clearly understood as something beautiful, heavy with emotion, most particularly as such a result contrasts so strongly with the terror and danger of the events just experienced by the onlookers.

In arriving at an understanding of the most evocative act of war, the relationship between the act, the rescue of helpless onlookers from death, and the symbolic bronze cross becomes clear; the hero emerges from a dramatic act of theatre involving an audience who witness an actor carrying out an act of extreme and stimulatingly real drama. The hero is created by the power of the circumstances and by his audience whom he rescues. Critically, any one of the audience could have attempted the same feat, but did not. It may not be possible to understand why they did not, but the fact that one man acted, sets him apart immediately from those who did not. By contrast, the hero who is typically motivated by ordinary, if intensified, human emotions, may view the praise and honours heaped upon him as inexplicable. It is not straightforward, in the aftermath, for the hero to comprehend the symbolic and emotional significance of his act from the standpoint of others. But both views are entirely consistent with reactions to life-threatening situations, and they contrast so strongly due to the markedly differing perceptions generated by the different roles of actor and onlooker. As the hero stands up to do what he perceives is a pure necessity, the onlookers' perception changes from negative expectation to one of awe and hope. The gifts received by onlookers are substantial and highly emotive. Self-sacrifice at the moment of victory can very rightly be viewed as supremely glorious to the extent that there is nothing greater than laying down one's life so that others might live. The causes of individual battlefield bravery are mundane; the results are profoundly, yet unfashionably, special.

By such means, the legend of the single-handed destruction

of the machine gun nest took over the military and the public imagination to the extent that it still ranks as the highest symbol of battlefield bravery today. The reason for this is partly the fearsome nature of the weapon but also that such a high proportion of VCs was won for this act. It is significant that the most fearsome symbol of horror in that war, the machine gun, produced the new symbolic hero (whereas artillery was the more dangerous, gun batteries were set back from the infantry battlefield and soldiers did not often come into direct contact with them). Curiously, the new hero emerged at the same time as Sir Douglas Haig was reinforcing his views concerning what acts should dominate the annals of the VC in a large-scale mechanised war.[79] The demise of the lifesaving VC, as well as other symbolic acts, has been charted by M.C. Smith over this period, but the rise of the machine gun destroying hero was insufficiently emphasised. Not surprisingly, perhaps, mention of the use of the bayonet in the execution of enemy machine gunners is present in a significant proportion of these VC citations. The bayonet is mentioned very rarely in citations for MMs and DCMs, perhaps never in relation to MCs and DSOs. The bayonet itself was a largely symbolic weapon which provoked high levels of fear, because of its openly aggressive, murderous and highly personal nature; but it was rarely actually used. The aggressive use of the bayonet was high in the priorities of infantry training depots for the same reasons as the cavalry charge was emphasised by that arm; it was a form of behavioural training more than anything else. Firm intent to use the bayonet was a good way of putting an enemy to flight. When it was actually used as a weapon, in the elimination of the fearful machine gun post, the honours and awards committee recognised that in such actions the man bearing only cold steel had closed with the death dealing machine and had triumphed over it (in the manner that Bellerophon defeated the fearsome and inconquerable Chimaera). When it is borne in mind that the motivation for attacking the position was often to enable comrades to get into cover before they were wiped out by artillery fire, it is plain that self-sacrifice may be added to the triumphal symbolism of the bayonet defeating the machine gun. With such strongly symbolic attributes, the storming of the machine gun post may be viewed as an act consciously and carefully selected by the military organisation as worthy of the highest traditions of classical heroism.

## APATHY

One of the most disturbing aspects of life in the line was living with corpses.[80] Lieutenant Sapper, in the aftermath of a heavy artillery bombardment and British infantry attack, noted a trench that had been turned into 'an area of ploughed up ground', where, in small holes crouched clay-covered, grey bundles – living men. They were sheltering behind the unburied dead, into which: 'Enemy small arms fire thudded repeatedly'.[81] Living among the dead and dismembered, witnessing the progressive dismemberment of the recently alive and the decomposed, was not an uncommon experience and was one that men were least able to deal with. They could try to obliterate these experiences from memory but scenes, smells and noises lived on indelibly in their unconscious, invading their dreams and even their wakefulness for the rest of their lives. Lieutenant Sapper was only able to note the immediate effects of terror: 'One man, screaming terribly, was pulled out from the rubble of a buried dugout; another sat in a puddle of filth singing. His matted hair was plastered to his forehead; madness stared from his bulging eyes. As we passed, he gabbled that he had seen the Devil, yesterday, every day. It had been really comical... and he cackled and clicked his tongue'. Sapper spoke with a young man next, whose 'whole body trembled and he stammered repeatedly... "When are we going to be relieved?"'. These soldiers, recorded Sapper, 'had held out for 14 days without relief, without sufficient food and had beaten off daily the most violent attempts at breakthrough by the British'.[82] They had endured unspeakable torment, they had been mentally broken, but as long as they had physical strength remaining, they would remain in that place and die in that place.

Such men may be characterised as heroes, but were they brave or courageous? By chance they continued to exist amid the unendurable, they survived only in the sense that they were not killed. In those particular circumstances they did not have any option but to remain there and, having experienced battle at that intensity, they no longer had fixed reference points like right and wrong, possible and impossible; they often saw the hitherto unimaginable occur before their eyes. They had been stripped of their ability to understand and react normally to events as a result of the primal force of those events; they had had their senses knocked out of them. This was not an uncommon experience for the men who had won and who went on to win bravery awards in the great battles of the First World War. They had gone through moments, days or even weeks of this. If they survived, we cannot assume that they were possessed of a normal approach to death or a logical reaction to life-threatening situations. How they then performed under heavy shell and machine-gun fire was conditioned by their previous battle experiences. As we saw with regard to John Deane, he was apparently transformed from the cowering and shell shocked to a man exhibiting a 'cheery bearing' under shell fire, but how can we interpret this apparent fearlessness? Is it as simple as it superficially appears; that he rose to the challenge of battle or might something more fundamental have occurred to his state of perception, to his self-preservation instinct and to his ability to deal rationally with violent situations? Deane might be described as a 'battle-hardened veteran', perhaps a hero, but those words don't help us to understand what it was that changed inside his head and what allowed his subsequent behaviour under shell fire to change.

## SETTING AN EXAMPLE

We have seen that setting an example, whatever kind of example, is contagious. It is one of the core ingredients of battlefield bravery and distinguished service in wartime. Whether leading a charge at the enemy, maintaining a cheery bearing in extreme adversity, walking upright to give others courage ('if he can stand up there and live, then so can I'), showing up with hot soup or shouldering the more dangerous tasks voluntarily (so that others need not); in such cases those around about were encouraged rather than discouraged. The effect of a cheerful leader who is ready to provide emotional support to his men in adversity, we have seen, was immense. The effect of a determined leader, with the courage to take control and issue the word of command in adversity, was the difference between winning and losing. Determination and cheery optimism went hand-in-hand. When men have the backing of committed, determined and daring medical services, an Army which also has good leaders becomes fortified to carry out its tasks with a maximum of determination. From somewhere within themselves, the leaders had to find the courage to initiate actions that were all too likely to end in their own deaths. In finding that courage at the moment of extreme difficulty, and in doing it, they were accepting that fate and shouldering its weight. They were putting their lives on the line, having made a conscious choice to do so. Their men followed, and so took much less of the credit.

Setting a good example, maintaining a fine, cheery bearing in battle, paternalism, displays of incredible 'bravery' are all, in fact, related by the effect they have on others; they spread courage, they fortify the group. This is something that goes beyond the act itself, which often had minor or only local tactical importance in its own right, but those who witnessed the act were encouraged to do more, be it attack or defend harder, take more risks to rescue the wounded, or follow the leader and participate. Such is the true function of heroism in wartime and its official reward recognises this importance. This is why heroism is often described as 'inspiring' and it is also, ultimately, why the battlefield leadership was given the lion's share of rewards; because setting the example and initiating their own death was their responsibility.

In order to set such an example and to make that conscious decision to put their lives on the line, the junior leaders of the Great War had fundamentally to believe in the rightness of the cause they were fighting for. Perhaps Britain's soldiers have won the major wars for this reason, rather than being oddly better at fighting than other nations. It seems rather likely that the leadership knew that what they were fighting for was right, enabling them to justify laying down their lives for it. It is unthinkable that without a strong underlying belief in the British State and British values, that soldier's morale and the quality of leadership could have stood so firm in the 20th Century. It is also interesting that ordinary British soldiers, when set an example of this sort, almost invariably 'stuck it out' or followed to the bitter end if need be. Given the choice and shown the leadership, the average Tommy and conscript of 1918, wanted to get the job done, wanted to give of their best in battle; *they wanted to fight.*

# After the Act

The Armistice of 11 November 1918 did not warrant much comment in most unit War Diaries. Participants in this war had survived with their lives; they could look forward with some relief and expectation to going home. Getting home of course took many months of waiting in France for discharge papers. Perhaps those who experienced the greatest relief were those families at home, who had waited through dread, who had dared not hope, for long months and years. But there was a general feeling of loss of purpose within the troops on the various fronts. More seriously, many men were suffering from an underlying trauma, both physical (such as deafness, painful joints and intestinal complaints) and mental. Many were wounded or gassed, leaving eye, lung and other physical damage for the rest of their lives. Most men had by this time, as the Allied Armies with support Corps and light rail construction units rolled forward over the recent battlegrounds, 'seen things that no man should have to see' and others had done things that no man should have to do. An indeterminate number already knew that: 'only the dead have seen an end to war'[83] As if their ordeal had not been enough, Spanish flu swept through military and civilian populations, killing more people than all the battles of the war.

Even more seriously, as Eric Leed has described in his 1979 book subtitled *Combat and Identity in World War I,* a lot of soldiers felt marginalised by the war and utterly disillusioned with 'home' and what that now stood for[84]. Home, although only 30–100 miles away, was what had sent these men to the front to be smashed to pieces by a ghastly industrial machine. The reality of experience at the front included a catastrophic loss of dignity, of self worth and of identity as a human being. Words like glory, self-sacrifice and all that imperial phraseology came to be understood by veterans as a disgusting lie after their experiences. It was the people at home who had allowed this to happen to them, and the industrialists who had profited from their denigrating experiences. This is why some veterans chose to stay out in France helping to exhume the dead and re-bury them in war cemeteries. It is also why some men chose to remain in the Army and volunteered for service in Russia in 1919. If they had had enough of fighting, they had had more than enough of 'home'. There was no 'home' to go back to any more, such was the extent of disillusionment, so argues Eric Leed.

At the same time, many were swept up in the celebrations of the Armistice, yet carrying in their minds the sorrow of comrades gone west. The human damage arising from the war could not be erased. In her book, *Casualty Figures*, Michele Barrett presents the stories of just five different men who reacted to the fighting differently, but who all struggled with their nerves. They experienced not so much fear in battle but horror in its aftermath; living among corpses troubled several of these men. When one of these five got home, Lieutenant John Willis Brown, his mother observed sadly that; 'He hadn't the energy left to be taking anything seriously and he could only cope with the years he had never expected to see, by making a gentle mockery of everything, which anyway only had a slight and relative seriousness after everything he had been through'.[85] At the end of the war many men were at the point of total exhaustion, they struggled to rebuild normal lives and suffered a succession of illnesses in the following years and decades. As a result, in the post-war years, veterans commonly struggled to rebuild themselves and their lives and to keep them from falling to pieces.

Bereaved mothers had a fight on their hands to be allowed to wear their son's medals at remembrance occasions. One mother, at the 1926 parade before the Cenotaph explained that she would wear the DCM and MC won by her two dead sons 'whether the Home Office forbids me or permits me'.[86] For the relatives of those soldiers whose bodies were missing, and who had no known grave, the symbolic focus of grief sometimes became the soldier's medals and bronze memorial plaque. There are many medals and plaques still in 1920s frames, mounted by the family and these became a small memorial that elevated the lost family member to that of soldier hero whose life was given in the service of his country and comrades. Roper has provided an example of a woman whose son Alf was one of the missing; unable to focus grief on a grave site, she 'constructed a memorial in her front room, putting a photograph of Alf in uniform, his two war medals, bronze medallion and pressed poppies into a frame and mounting it on the mantle wall, where it remained until she died in 1929'.[87]

The sight of blind or limbless ex-soldiers had a profound effect on the mood of the nation: In his book *Voices from the Great War*, Peter Vansittart wrote: 'As a small boy in Southsea, I saw streets disfigured by ragged, unwanted ex-soldiers, medalled, but ill, blind, maimed, selling matches, bootlaces, notepaper, trundling barrel-organs or standing with a melancholy dog or monkey beside a decrepit hurdy-gurdy. Whether they were pleading or abusive, resigned or menacing, they appalled me. Their wretchedness suggested that, in overthrowing Germany, they had earned some monstrous penalty now being... enacted'.[88]

Throughout the war, men awarded gallantry medals were hailed in the local and national press as heroes. Having experienced trench warfare and mechanised destruction on a grand scale, we can see how some of these returning men felt when greeted by crowds eager to offer approval and witness the presentation of silverware, watches and other tokens of honour. We can glimpse the complete estrangement from 'home' that Eric Leed has written about.

That medals were usually sent not to the soldier at the Front, but home to next-of-kin, created the opportunity for an unofficial presentation ceremony for men on leave or returning from the war. Such ceremonies were common during and immediately after the war, and a survey of these presentations and what was said at them allows us to explore the early stages of the creation of heroes from ordinary men.

The first case we shall consider is that of Hugh Liddell, a miner of 72 Elm Street, Benwell, Newcastle-upon-Tyne. Hugh had been awarded the DCM and was further honoured upon his return home in September 1916 by the presentation of a gold watch contained in a wooden box. The circumstances and organisation of the presentation are at once remarkable and typical of a great many carried out around the country. The newspaper report ran as follows:

## Benwell D.C.M. – Decoration and Presentation to Corporal Hugh Liddell

*There was a crowded audience at Benwell Cinema, Condercum Road, last night, on the occasion of the presentation of a Distinguished Conduct Medal to Corporal Hugh Liddell of Benwell, for gallant services in France in June last year. After a fine display of war films had been shown, the curtain rose on a large company of ladies and gentlemen on the stage. Councillor John Chapman presided and was supported by the Lord Mayor of Newcastle (Councillor George Lunn), the sheriff (Councillor Wm Bramble), Mrs Wm. Cochran Carr, with Corporal Liddell and Mrs Liddell .*

*After pinning the decoration on Corporal Liddell's breast, the Lord Mayor remarked: 'Your King and country are proud of you; Newcastle is proud of you; Benwell is proud of you; and last and best your wife is proud of you.' (Loud applause). May God bless you and give you many years of life to wear that medal'.*

*Next, with a few remarks, the Sheriff handed over to Corporal Liddell a gold watch, the gift of the owners and Liddell's fellow-workmen at Benwell Colliery.*

*After the recipient had replied, the Chairman said that one-half of the household had received gifts, and he would ask Mrs Cochran Carr to equalise matters by a gift to Mrs Liddell, the gallant Corporal's wife. Mrs Cochran Carr, in a neat little speech, then presented Mrs Liddell with a gold bracelet and wished her every happiness'.*

Hugh Liddell had earned his award working underground in a chamber filled with explosives known as a *camouflet*, the citation being: 'For consistent gallantry and good work, notably on one occasion when after the enemy had exploded a *camouflet*, he rescued a man from the foul gas with no rescue apparatus. Later attempting further rescues, he nearly lost his own life'. In the pursuance of duty and in desperate circumstances, he had toiled for his fellow comrades, and would have willingly done so without much thought until his own life expired. We sense that Liddle's sense of self-worth may have been eroded almost completely by the war, such that it no longer mattered if he died. Of that there can be little doubt. What could he have felt, then, during a lengthy, ritualised proceeding in the presence of old friends and important people, most of whom had nothing to do with the world of war? The ceremony took place in an environment completely separate from the underground workings of the Western Front. A chasm separated these worlds. War films shown would have presented a very unfamiliar version of war (not least because the showing of dead had already been banned as bad for public morale). Hugh Liddell was being honoured, but was also being paraded as an exhibit out of context. Not only was his act of gallantry being placed out of context, but he was out of context, he was an alien.

**Figure 46: Gold Watch Presented to Corporal H. Liddle, Royal Engineers, by Benwell Colliery, Newcastle-upon-Tyne**

Northumbrian newspapers reported the presentations of medals to local men throughout the war. There was great determination that all men who received decorations for bravery would also receive the public thanks and a token of appreciation, typically a silver cigarette case or gold watch and chain, but others received wrist watches, marble clocks, silver tea services and ornamental silverware. Newspaper reports sometimes record what the recipient of the medal said in response to the presentation ceremony. In early February 1916, the first man of Ashington to bring a medal home was honoured by the gift of an inscribed gold watch and chain at the Town's Council Chambers. Private Thomas Page, Royal Army Medical Corps, responded to his gift 'very briefly and modestly, thanking the district for their recognition of his act of duty'. He continued by admitting; 'there were many men… who had done much more than he had, but he had been fortunate in that he had been seen'. The act for which he was awarded his DCM was for rescuing, with another member of the RAMC, a sergeant-major on the 157th Division RFA, who was lying wounded and exposed to the fire of the enemy between two woods at Pilkem, near Loos, on 21 October 1915; the two men carried in the wounded man to safety under fire. Page is telling us that his award was not exceptional; that he was lucky because he was seen doing exactly the same as others who had not been seen. From the pages of an old newspaper, Thomas Page is telling us that his award was, in effect, both unfair and unrepresentative.

At that time, presentations became increasingly formalised under the auspices of various local organisations which raised funds and organised events. A large number of societies had been established for the purposes of raising funds to be spent on honouring recipients of gallantry medals on their return, or the fathers of those recipients who had not returned from the front. Bebside and Cowpen established a 'Military Merit Fund', Ashington had its 'Distinguished Service Recognition Society' and in the port of Blyth, a 'Military Merit and Home Coming Committee' was formed. There were many others, set up by those who felt it imperative that brave local soldiers should come home to a rousing reception and gifts of value. Employees of the Ashington Coal Company could further reckon on receiving an engraved silver rose bowl 18 ounces in weight, in addition to any other gifts they might receive. Returning with bravery medals gained the honour of the pit and of the town. It is important to remember that all of this activity reflects the understanding of those at home to war and heroism, and that the soldier returning from the front may have found it all extremely bizarre. These presentations represent a perpetuation of the pre-war myths of what war meant, and this contrasted violently with the reality of soldier's experiences when placed in the jaws of the war machine 'to have things done to them'.

In the town of Blyth the 'Military Merit and Home Coming Committee' was very active in honouring its local heroes by means of ceremony. This abridged newspaper extract from the *Blyth News* and *Wansbeck Telegraph* of Monday, 30 July 1917, describes one such ceremony in which the crowd revealed the level of their patriotic enthusiasm for their heroes' actions on the battlefield:

*BLYTH HEROES – PRESENTATIONS FOR BRAVERY AT THE FRONT*
*There was a crowded and enthusiastic audience at the Empire Theatre, Blyth, last evening when three presentations to local heroes took place under the auspices of the Blyth Military Merit and Home Coming Committee, the three men being: Corporal Thomas Easton, DCM, Northumberland Fusiliers; Corporal L. A. Atkinson, MM, Northumberland Fusiliers, and Sapper George Longstaff, MM, Royal Engineers. The soldiers who had obtained distinctions were given a hearty reception by their townspeople.*

*When the three heroes made their appearance on the stage they were greeted with deafening applause, which continued for some time. The chair was occupied by Mr George Dunn, JP, chairman of the Blyth Urban Council, and he was supported by Brigadier-General A. Blair, DSO, and Messrs T. C. Heatley, W. Clark, T. C. Blackburn, Charles Nuttall, and C. W. Grainge (secretary).*

*...the Brigadier-General simply pinned the medals to the breasts of Corporal Thomas Easton, Corporal L. A. Atkinson, and Sapper George Longstaff. As each medal was pinned on, the enthusiasm of the audience became unbounded.*

*On behalf of the Merit Committee, Mr Charles Nuttall, BA, made the presentations of a local character. To Corporal Easton he presented a gold watch, to Corporal Atkinson a silver cigarette case, and to Sapper Longstaff a silver wristlet watch.*

Public enthusiasm occasionally reached fever pitch, as revealed by the following examples:

*(BN & WT. Monday 16 September 1918) – LENGTHENING LIST OF BLYTH HEROES. – Three More Presentations – Three more gallant miners, Bombardier James Hunter Eastwood Boynes, Lance-Corporal George Cantley and Private Albert Cannon, from the Cowpen Collieries, have been added to the lengthening roll of honour for gallantry on the battlefield. Councillor W. Clark presided at the ceremony, which took place at the Theatre Royal. The Chairman remarked... so long as Britain had such soldiers she would take no harm. He had pleasure in calling upon Mr J. L. Gibbons to make the presentations. Mr Gibbons said... it afforded him great pleasure indeed to present those little gifts demonstrating their appreciation of those gallant men who had gone from their midst to take part in the great fight. He believed, in regard to the war, they were at the beginning of the end, and that it would not be long before the end was reached, when the blonde beast that assailed civilisation would be strangled and dead at the feet of the Allies. Each of the recipients, on coming forward to receive their gifts, were cheered enthusiastically'.*

Reactions of the popular 'heroes' to some of these ceremonies must occasionally have appeared as a rebuke to the audience for their collective lack of understanding and for their unbounded patriotic fervour, as in this remarkable case which took place during the interval in a Theatre performance:

*(BN & WT. Monday 12 February 1917) A BLYTH HERO. Yet another Blyth hero has arrived home from the front to receive recognition for gallant and courageous conduct.*
*The recipient was Gunner William Brown, of Blyth, a son of the*

*assistant harbourmaster, Mr James Brown, and the nature of the presentation took the form of a beautiful gold watch. The chair was occupied by Mr Chris Hunter, Chairman of the Urban Council, and this gentleman also made the presentation.*

*In handing over the watch, Mr Hunter said it was their pleasing duty to again do honour to another one of the brave Blyth lads who had nobly and gallantly distinguished himself on the field of battle during the present war. (Applause). The recipient, said the Chairman, was one of those heroes who made history at the Battle of Mons a little while after reaching France. (Loud applause). He also took part in the big battles of the Aisne, Ypres, and other conflicts, out of all, they were pleased to see, he had come out unscathed. During the fights their guest had been awarded the Military Medal for bravery (Applause). The circumstances were that on one occasion an 18-pounder gun was in charge of four men who were all wounded by flying shells. Gunner Brown was standing by and at once jumped into the pit and served the gun single-handed until the Germans were repulsed and until the order to cease fire was sounded. (Applause.) That was indeed a brave action, and fully merited the distinction which he had been awarded. (Loud applause.)*

*Proceeding, Mr Hunter said that... Gunner Brown had proved himself worthy of the highest traditions of the British race.... that the father had every reason to be proud of the sons who were fighting for King and country. (Loud applause.) In conclusion the speaker expressed the hope that Gunner Brown would be spared to see through the great conflict, and that the present he was receiving that evening would give him renewed courage when he returned to his strenuous duties at the front. (Cheers.) Mr Hunter then handed the watch over to Gunner Brown, amidst tremendous cheering. Gunner Brown received an enthusiastic reception when he rose to modestly reply: 'It was only a matter of doing my duty, nothing more nor less,' he said, and sat down. This terminated the presentation proceedings'.*

Such a response provides staunch opposition to a view of these men as heroes. Speakers at presentation ceremonies very often took the opportunity to talk in extremely patriotic terms prior to the medal recipient receiving the award and gifts. A man's single act of gallantry on the battlefield, which he may have considered was simply part of his daily duties as a soldier, was elevated by reference to its Regal sanction and then heavily decorated with the floral language of Imperial patriotism:

*(BN & WT. Monday 7 February 1916) – BLYTH D.C.M. – Interesting Presentation to Pte. Clark. – A large and enthusiastic gathering assembled in the Empire Theatre, Blyth, last evening, to do honour to Pte. Wm. Clark, a local soldier, of the 10th Yorks, who has been recognised for the DCM for bravery on the field of battle, and who is at home just now on a few days leave.*

*The country, through the King, was acknowledging that brave deed by investing Private Clark with the DCM. The speaker went on to say that this country had never been slow in acknowledging bravery and heroism. No country on the face of the earth valued more highly bravery and a brave act more than the nation of which all present were proud citizens. Whether on land or sea, the British people were always willing to acknowledge valour and pay homage to brave men. (Applause). It was well that it was so. They must always remember that we were the trustees of a glorious past, of great and noble deeds, and it was their duty to preserve that heritage so that it may be handed down to those who followed them untainted and unsullied. (Applause). The greatness of a nation was not to be judged merely by its material or industrial success, went on Mr Heatley. It was by the devotion of the individual citizen to the country, to duty and to sacrifice. Those principles had animated the heroes of the past, and it was that which inspired the battle cry of Nelson when he exclaimed 'England expects every man to do his duty.' And what was it that was inspiring the men at the front today, but the same grand and noble principles? What was it that inspired them with the confidence that, whatever the day be near or far, we were going to beat the Germans? (Loud applause). Their army and their navy was so inspired, and they could therefore look with every confidence to the future.*

Just three days later, Clark was in attendance at another such ceremony at which he was presented with 'a massive silver tea service and tray' engraved with the following dedication: 'To Pte. W. Clark, from the Committee and Members of the Duke of Wellington Social Club Ltd., Burt Street, Blyth, for winning the DCM'. He was interviewed for the newspaper later in the same week: 'our representative found him in his home in West Row, Cowpen Colliery, having a real homely North-country meal of eggs and bacon'. Having dug out three lads buried by the explosion of a shell, in the open under an extraordinarily heavy shell fire, William Clark admitted that he: 'just walked away as though there had been nothing unusual done… I was only too pleased to get the poor fellows out, and I am sure that any of them would do the same thing for me if they had the chance, and whenever any of the lads see me they come and shake me by the hand, which is sufficient reward in itself.'

Comrades thought nothing of digging out buried friends; it was so obvious a necessity as to go without saying and a task that would be carried out without question under any circumstances by any man in the line. Yet taken out of context back at home the simple act would be elevated to heroism in the defence of the Nation and Empire in the name of God and the King. Men's reactions to such high words were very often disarmingly honest and down-to-earth, in fact almost all recorded responses of these men amount to the same thing: Lance-Corporal Robert Mason, of the Northumberland Fusiliers, on the receipt of his gold watch, stated 'that he only did what others would have done – his duty'. What, then, do we understand of bravery? Those who were there simply and defiantly contradict all the talk of heroes and honour, glory and self-sacrifice.

BN & WT Thursday 24 October 1918, reported that Sergeant Robert Scott of Cambois, Northumberland, had received a wrist watch from the Colliery in a ceremony at Cambois. A Tank Corps man, he had done good work with a Lewis gun whilst dismounted from his vehicle, in order to cover the movement of other men and then extricated himself with the gun safely. Sergeant Scott is reported to have said that: 'I had only done my duty as any other British soldier would do', and he thanked them most sincerely for their kind present. In common with many, he attended another ceremony a few days later, receiving a silver cigarette case from the Secretary of the Social Club, who stated that he 'hoped that Sergt. Scott would be spared to come through the war, and that when in the eventide of his life he was enjoying his *tab* the small gift would recall pleasant memories of the high appreciation and respect in which he was held by the members of the club'. A *tab* is a cigarette in the language of the North-East of England. Sergeant Scott was then given a grand reception, the audience standing up and singing 'He is a jolly good fellow.'

A Sergeant William Scott was similarly honoured in Blyth with a silver cigarette case by the Duke of Wellington Social Club, the presentation being recorded in the *Blyth News* and *Wansbeck Telegraph* of Thursday 15 February 1917. The President of the Club, Mr J. G. Parker, said of Scott that 'they were glad to honour one who at the call of duty, like so many other brave lads, had gone forth to face danger and death for the honour of the Empire and the security of their homeland, and the rights of humanity against inhumanity, aggression and tyranny. After receiving his award of the Military Medal for gallantry under heavy shell fire at the infamous High Wood on the Somme in 1916, Scott said: 'In regard to what I have done, I can truly say that every soldier in my section was entitled to whatever merit I have secured'. This statement was met with applause.

The *Blyth News* and *Wansbeck Telegraph* reported for Thursday 26 September 1918:

*PRESENTATION TO BLYTH HERO – There was a good attendance at the Catholic Schools, Cowpen Village, last night, when the Rev. Father O. Kershaw presented Corpl. J. Stevens, Cowpen Village, winner of the Military Medal, with a beautiful gold watch on behalf of the Bebside and Cowpen Military Merit Fund. Mr M. Gleghorn presided and referred in high terms to the support given the local fund by Father Kershaw. In handing over the watch the rev. gentleman said the attitude of Corpl. Stevens was similar to that of a Blyth hero, who declared that all the men at the front deserved medals as big as saucepans. Corpl. Stevens suitably replied, stating that he had only done his duty, which they all did out there'.*

This extract implies that whatever was being presented to men was small compensation for what the men were actually enduring and experiencing at the front. Make no mistake, the pointed remark that all soldiers at the front deserved medals 'as big as saucepans' was meant as criticism of those at home; the men in the line deserved something far greater than they were getting from those at home. It suggests the gap that that was growing, and implies the threat that all would not be the same when the men returned home.

The *Blyth News* and *Wansbeck Telegraph* reported on Thursday 21 March 1918 that Private J. Wilson, Northumberland Fusiliers, of Ashington, 'who has lost his legs in action, is to be presented with an invalid chair. The presentation was to have been made last night at the Miners Theatre, but the chair had not arrived'. Great Britain sent Private Wilson to France to have his legs removed and Great Britain was good enough to provide him a wheelchair free of charge when he got home. The dark ironies of surgical procedure may not have been viewed by Private Wilson as intended.

Presentation ceremonies did not always take place in the recipient's home town. Nowhere would the gap between an ordinary man's reality and his surroundings have been greater than in the presence of Royalty at the Palace. A miner, separated from his mates, with spades for hands and a common way of speaking, would, understandably, have felt both out of place and out of his depth in a palatial setting. There is in this situation a measure of 'waiting to go over the top'. Trooper Down, DCM, remembered that when he couldn't hold out any longer and had to get to a Royal water closet, he 'had the shock of his life' when he finished off and turned around to find that two richly dressed gentlemen had silently followed him in, bearing clean hand towels. His description is exactly the same as that of Edward Lynch, when he, blundering about in no-man's-land in the dark, came face to face with two dead Germans. They gave him 'the shock of my life'. We have seen how Trooper Down (Northumberland Hussars) had taken on both German snipers and armoured vehicles single-handed in the Normandy beachhead on 6 June 1944. After the water closet incident, he found the award ceremony at Buckingham Palace 'the most nerve wracking thing I ever did'. So too Private William McGee of Coventry, who wrote to his mother on the 23 May 1917 proclaiming: 'I have just had a terrible ordeal to go through… had to step out in front of 5,000 chaps' (to receive his MM). Four weeks earlier he had told his mother of his very near brush with death, in the form of an explosive bullet, on the way over no-man's-land in the attack: '…it glanced off my equipment and I saw no more of it'. Thus, he admitted to his mother without fluster a fearful event that could have seen him laid out flat, yet it seems he found the parade at which he received the medal the more extraordinary and concerning. (Both of these letters remain with his medals in a private collection). Almost certainly he felt that many others deserved the medal more than he did and so his award was a lie.

Silver bowls and gold watches were pretty, and valuable certainly, but couldn't themselves feed a miner's family in time of need. Neither could a medal clothe, nor the honour these gifts brought, heal damaged bodies or souls. Just as in battle, men were preoccupied by ordinary, very human, concerns such as lifesaving, protecting comrades (from enemy fire) and the sadness they saw about them. For these moments, some received official recognition in the field and at home, but as Corporal Wilf Cook put it in his narrative *Men, Horses, Mud and Stew*, what was undoubtedly the most important to him was this: 'it was sufficient that I earned the respect of Smiler and others which was worth much more than any medal'.

What the public award ceremonies tell us about is the vast gulf in understanding between those who had experienced the realities of war and those who had stayed at home and who had been sustained by a diet of lies and patriotic rubbish. The responses of the soldiers at these ceremonies barely disguise their disgust with the home country. It may also be said that the average British soldier of 1914–1918 had at times a greater compassion for the enemy than with the country he was supposedly fighting for. The evidence from presentation ceremonies is saddening.

# SECTION IV:
# A SUMMING UP

## BRAVERY, LEADERSHIP AND DISTINGUISHED SERVICE

Bravery is least likely to be displayed by disheartened or lonely men. Courage can be mustered when leaders are optimistic about getting through and can demonstrate what can be achieved. A smile may be sufficient to encourage. Bravery is very dependent upon the presence of and behaviour of mates. A man does not go into battle with the sole intention of killing his fellow men but put a weapon in his hand and he will do as his mates do. For that to occur, men need to be led. Successful leaders must command the respect and trust of those they lead, so men will follow them anywhere and will do their utmost to assist and protect their leader (we have seen how some men did protect their wounded leaders with their own bodies). Loyalty to group leaders is essential, and that loyalty is typically established by means of the leader's personality, by his care for the men (paternalism) and by his track record of behaviour in previous encounters with the enemy. Among very courageous leaders we find the so-called alpha males, stubborn men who would not be pushed about in battle, who would stand and fight and whose determination provided others with an example they could emulate, but could not draw from themselves alone. Charismatic, yet determined and stubborn, individuals who also cared deeply for the wellbeing of those around them, stood a very good chance of winning medals. These character traits made them more likely to do things that are considered brave.

The presence of such leaders in a group maintains the command structure and changes the behaviour of team members. The maintenance of a command structure in a moment of crisis allows the group to remain functional in the form of leader and led. Command structure implies the maintenance of order within chaos as the leader provides specific logical tasks to group members – keeping them busy with meaningful tasks which benefit the group as a whole. The issue of clear and simple orders in moments of crisis is particularly important for the effective function of the group and to its ability to win the fight. Winning or losing frequently meant the difference between life and death in the face of a determined enemy attack, and so we may view the tough leader as the saviour of his men.

At the point of action, we have seen how simple emotions such as anger, vengeance or even fear can propel individuals forward into mortal danger. Underlying the ability to throw oneself at the enemy, or into bullet or shell fire, is very often the strong urge to assist comrades, either by offering direct assistance (the stretcher bearer) or by consciously trying to set men an inspiring example (for example, officers who needed their men to follow them). A combination of war-related phenomena makes it easier for men to do that; a man's war history up until that point, a degree of apathy, of resignation to fate, can erode a man's survival instincts to the point he is ready for any suicidal stunt. Battle-hardened troops include many who are resigned to fate's course, to whom death is of little consequence because on the battlefield future ceases to exist. The violence of shelling, gunfire, the noise, smoke and chaos of raining debris knocks the ordinary senses from men. The phenomenon of self-sacrifice is enabled by these emotions, experiences and conditions. Battle changes men, in a way that civilians without the experience find difficult to comprehend.

That 'bravery and cowardice are blood brothers' is very relevant; in fleeting battlefield moments, men can exhibit both behaviours, especially in the considerable chaos and uncertainty of battle. There is indeed 'a touch of madness in both'; we may consider the psychologically frail men who exhibit extreme bravery, the shell shocked and the neurasthenic who might act spectacularly, yet unpredictably and without warning. Mental instability was created by the long experience of violent battle and it should be no surprise that those recognised as brave heroes should come from all types of men; the strong alpha male who found himself successful in war stands alongside the mentally shaky who were cowards at times and capable of immense displays of aggression and daring at others. As Ernst Junger put it: 'Brave puny men are always to be preferred to strong cowards'.[89] These men were blood brothers, they were comrades in war.

At a larger scale, the reputation of a military unit is also relevant. Whether by tradition in the case of the Guards and Scots regiments, or by means of recently demonstrated prowess, units developed their own prestige and expected levels of performance. The Scottish reputation for victory stemmed from national pride; men rose to the challenge of upholding national standards, of not letting the side down. This is underpinned by good training and military leadership, but the military aggression generated by such expectations was very effective in cracking the enemy's resolve to stand and fight. It was as much the purpose of infantry bayonet training as it was for cavalry training, to instil in men the instinct that to close with the point of steel 'at any cost' was a secret of success in battle. Even in ordinary infantry battalions we have seen how some fared much better than others due to differing unit culture, expectations and morale. A battalion's self perception was important in providing the background for ready capitulation or for bravery to emerge from its ranks and for military successes to be achieved.

A good many decorated war heroes, most particularly those returning with VCs, were not left in a media darkness. They found themselves, and the acts for which they had earned their dubious fame, elevated to the heroic by a thankful nation (who had not seen them throw a phosphorous bomb into a dugout full of young men). There is a lot about battlefield bravery and the glory that subsequently shines upon men that cannot be squared up against war itself, least of all in the mind of the ordinary soldier. Whereas he may well have experienced pride in his decoration, being the sole proof to others of a job done well among mates, he would undoubtedly recall the faces and voices of the many who were obliterated by that war. He would recall the many acts of heroism that went unrewarded; men being rescued, men without fear, getting on with the job for the ultimate wellbeing of their mates; teamwork, peril and pride. Heroes see their part in these great events for what they were, of no greater significance than a great many of their mates' unrewarded escapades and achievements. Some felt forced into action by circumstances, in which the required task seemed so very obvious. Others were certainly just doing the job assigned to them, that of runner or ammunition limber driver, rather than being brave. After the act, those selected to become heroes found themselves paraded as an example in front of colleagues. Many felt that colleagues had done more than they to deserve the reward which they now received. It could be a worrying process, being held up as a hero in front of comrades, being exposed as something they felt they were not. This explains why some men found the presentation ceremonies more disturbing than being shot. The latter was real and painful but the former was, they ultimately felt, some form of a lie.

Yet, the service that these men gave to their comrades must not be under-estimated. Giving a nation victory, getting a group of men out of a dire situation, rescuing a wounded man ready to meet his end in filth, all amount to something significant. Bravery and leadership on the battlefield meant a lot to men at many levels. In order to emphasise in this summary the importance of leadership and distinguished service, present in so many citations for the DCM, MC and DSO, we may return to the citation for the Distinguished Service Order awarded to Temporary Lieutenant Gwynfryn Jenkins, Machine Gun Corps. It reads as follows:

'For conspicuous gallantry and devotion to duty. He led his four guns to their objective with the infantry assault, and in spite of heavy casualties, placed them in good defensive positions and made complete arrangements for the supply of ammunition, which had run short. He afterwards took charge of two more machine guns when their officer had been killed, and kept all six guns in action for three days in spite of continuous and severe shell fire, which reduced the teams to a minimum. But for his cheerfulness, gallantry and untiring efforts in going from gun to gun and encouraging the men, <u>they could never have stood the strain</u>'.

In this citation we see stated one of the most important aspects of battlefield leadership that underpins the strength of individuals and Armies. It was well known to the men on the ground, it was well known to senior officers behind the lines, and was well known to the Honours and Awards committees back in Blighty. Yet, it seems that since that war ended, civilian historians with no direct experience of the positive effects of good leadership, of cheeriness in adverse conditions, have mostly neglected to focus on these most simple and basic of human needs – emotional support – when describing the ordinary man's experiences and the performance of Armies of the First World War. Many reward citations include elements of paternalistic behaviour cryptically embedded in their wording. In the case of Jenkins, he personally provided ammunition, regular morale-boosting visits and good cheer. It was this kind of activity and behaviour that a great many DCMs and MCs as well as DSOs was made for; not solely for bravery. Individual bravery, on its own, could only provide a part of the resolve of an Army to win through, inspiring as it might be to witness. The Victoria Cross is dominated by readily understood acts of spectacular bravery, suitable for public consumption. Leadership by example, the winning of absolute loyalty of private soldiers by caring for them when in action, by working to maintain their self-confidence; these were major ingredients of large numbers of the other awards. Whilst the elimination of a machine gun by knocking it out or by charging it single-handed unquestionably carries the mark of heroic self-sacrifice, these sorts of acts do not make up the bulk of rewards. Single-handed elimination of the machine gun post was selected as one of the new symbolic acts of heroism and is present in dominating abundance in the annals of the Victoria Cross from 1917 to 1918.

What we see in leadership awards is something a little different from the stunning acts of gallantry preserved and publicised by the VC. The battlefield leadership made victory possible by encouraging men to form a solid defence, to follow a respected, even loved, officer or NCO into danger, and to win. Their leader's smile, his cheeriness in the toughest of moments, was a decisive factor in 'withstanding the strain' and winning the victory. This explains why the more prestigious of bravery medals – particularly the DCM, MC and DSO – were not only awarded for bravery, but also for leadership and distinguished service; it explains why the numerically inferior NCOs and junior field officers walked off with a substantial majority of decorations, and also how the majority of private soldiers found ways to cope with that war; they had good leaders to follow who made sure they had what they needed to get through it. These leaders were not always more brave than the private soldier, but they created or broke group spirit by their personalities and example, defied the enemy or gave way to the enemy when placed under pressure. It was the leader's choice, he who maintained the fighting spirit and self-confidence of the British Army longer than that of his opponents.

Bravery need not be confined to one man; its display affects those who stand in witness, it inspires men to join in and participate. This is why setting an example to others is so important in the control of battlefield behaviour. We will recall how an NCO or officer might stand up and walk about when the bullets were flying, showing 'a total disregard for his own safety'. This behaviour demonstrates to men that 'if he can stand up there and live then so can we'. When reality is at its most dangerous, humans crave to be reassured that it is safe. If that can be demonstrated, then fear can be more easily controlled. Men become encouraged, try to emulate their leader's example, and their will to resist or to win is reinforced. Courage is contagious when such example is set. Aggression can also be contagious, as Ernst Junger reminds us; 'A subaltern, inflamed with rage shouted: 'C'mon boys, who's coming with me?' Bravery, fearlessly risking one's own life, is always inspiring. We too found ourselves picked up by this wild fury'.[90] The effect on a body of men can be transformational, it can turn defeat into victory. The force and suddenness of an attack is critical in giving the enemy no chance to gather himself and prepare to resist. On the back foot, complete capitulation, or a bloodless rout, is much more likely to result. Cautious probing of enemy positions allows resistance to stiffen, battles to stagnate and the casualty roll to climb. Setting the example of decisive action tends not to leave one man out in front, but tends to pull the remainder along and lift their performance too. A magnificent display of bravery inspires others to follow and the enemy to flee. This explains how individual bravery is so important for the wider military action and it explains why military heroes are honoured not only by the handshakes of comrades but also by armies and nations.

From an examination of the underlying reasons for the award of the majority of decorations, it is evident that reward of bravery, on its own, was not the only purpose of these medals. Instead the awards system was used by the King, by the Government, by the War Office, by Field Marshalls and by unit commanders to encourage those who could lead, inspire and imbue men with a strong fighting spirit. This is evident in the hierarchy of awards: the MM and MC were mainly awarded for determined actions during fighting whereas large numbers of the more prestigious DCM and DSO contained elements of inspirational training, leadership and paternalistic emotional support. Tommy needed these from his leaders in order to survive; such support gave him something positive to look up to and emulate as well as giving him the gifts of confidence, strength and hope. All Tommies endured shelling, bombing by aircraft, and many went over the top in attack. Immense courage was required of all, great bravery perhaps. But it was not the isolated act of bravery that the Empire particularly needed; it was leadership, for leadership can turn broken, running men into a solid defence; it can turn a stalled attack, bogged down in no-man's-land, into a successful enterprise and it can triumph over the sternest of human tests. The leadership, in setting an example, gave courage, resolve and determination to others.

If there is anything we ought to carry into our own civilian lives, it is surely the example of paternalistic, caring leadership that has been extensively described in these pages. It is not so much the demonstration of self-sacrifice provided by storming machine guns, although even that holds the message that service to others is a greater thing than service to self. Success in almost any aspect of life depends on developing our own leadership skills, and our own courage in daily life and work.

## CREATION OF THE HERO AND REMEMBRANCE

The hero has been a part of human culture since well before Roman times, but it was the Romans and the Greeks who created the heroic characters that live on in the modern world. Viking literature offers another, dramatic and powerful image of the distilled ancient warrior hero. More recent paintings and the literature of heroes contain the rich symbolism of bravery and heroism as well as religious ideals. Close relationships between the hero, self-sacrifice, glorious death and transition to eternal life are depicted in many of these artistic and literary works. An archaic language of heroism persists in writing and in paintings of war and heroes. These old stories, and more recent ones built from them, condition public understanding of what constitutes bravery and heroism. The hero is part real and part constructed by the society and media we live with. Military heroism remains highly distinct from courage exhibited in civilian life, but it conditions public expectations of non-military heroism. The ultimate purpose of heroism is to create an artificial mythology which allows young men to idealise about the realities of war, which becomes a young male adventure with the possibility of returning a hero. As we have seen, the reality of modern mechanised war can shatter such illusions profoundly. The hero is a product of a mythologising civilian society.

The transition of the ordinary man to hero occurs after the act. It begins informally with handshakes and the recognition of colleagues. It moves to the formal when a man's actions are brought to the attention of officers and a recommendation for reward results; as we have seen the recommendations were ranked in order of merit, a procedure that immediately emphasises the perception of the onlooker rather than that of the actor. At this point the gap between the perception of the actor (the hero) and the onlooker (or co-involved) starts to widen. A rather mundane and widespread battlefield phenomenon is turned into something else as it passes into the first stages of the publicity chain. Heroes do emerge from battle without the help of this process but heroes are selected, produced and promoted by the honours system and by civil structures. The media plays a vital role in the public understanding of heroism and of the promotion of heroes. Without the publicity (the medals, the column inches, interviews, photographs and history books), heroes do not grow substantially in stature and fame (compare Admirals Nelson and Collingwood, for example; men who performed the same services and who died in service but courted the publicity machine very differently). Heroes grow from ordinary men with ordinary motives, through the awards system, through the media, and are illuminated at public ceremonies, interviews and receptions. Honour is imparted by a thankful public who understand heroism largely from the media. In some cases, men become celebrities who play up to the role; Johnson Beharry, VC, has been the subject of portrait artist Emma Wesley (who compared Beharry to Christ[91]). He has become a minor work of art in his own right after having a large VC tattooed on his back. The comparison of Beharry with Christ emphasises the ongoing relationship between heroism and Christian self-sacrifice, between Monarchy, Military and Church – the old state structure. Providing the vehicle for the hero to emerge from this old state structure are, ironically, the artists and the literary media (rather than the scientists), which group also acts as war's most potent critics by means of their own mythologising.

Heroism is found in the eyes of the beholder not in the mind of the hero. Only acts that are viewed as heroic by the outsider are heroic. The outsider includes the Honours committee who decide, under Government and media influence, what is and what is not politically correct to honour in war. The populace is educated; heroes lay down their lives for others or win through against superior, preferably evil, odds. Certain wartime acts fit the bill. Bomb disposal in enemy territory is indisputably in the heroic vein and in addition is not controversial. Destroying enemy souls en masse is heroic (Sampson), but is controversial and definitely unfashionable. Those who throw themselves upon unexploded ordnance to shield their colleagues from the blast are classically heroic. Lifesavers are uncontroversially heroic. It is no coincidence whatsoever that these types of act dominate the honours lists today in spite of the fact that close-quarters fighting still occurs in war.

The State chooses its heroes carefully. Only very particular acts which are perceived as honourable and fit the established storyline, are isolated as heroic. That the most highly decorated men to emerge from the Great War were lifesavers is an indication of the underlying state function in generating a marketable hero. Many other awards contain a component of getting mates out of a nasty situation. In the more violent award citations, the phrase: 'he undoubtedly saved many lives', places the violence into that acceptable, self-sacrificial, heroic mould. Violent acts, which in peacetime would result in the hangman's noose, in war can be suggested to have saved lives and so the act may be transformed by means of a pre-existing heroic ideal into noble acts that set an example for others to follow. The invitation to focus on the lives saved, distracts from the act of killing mothers' sons. In choosing its heroes carefully like this, the state exercises some influence over public perception of war, the killings, the woundings, and of the mechanised violence which the state brings to bear upon soft human souls. That said, there can be no doubt that heroism is real enough in the minds of those who have benefitted from it on the battlefield, where it is unquestionably a case of 'me or him'. That is a reality which is impossible to deny; even if the state is in part culpable, this much stands out. The identification of heroes should not be understood in a wholly cynical fashion, for it truly does bring out from war a series of acts which certainly have remarkable merit. If a country chooses to have an Army for the purpose of backing up international policies with the threat of lethal force, then it must also be prepared to recognise martial excellence, and particularly the distinguished services rendered by ordinary men.

Medals and decorations from the First World War represent state recognition of the country's indebtedness to its soldiers and sailors who rendered distinguished and courageous services in the defence of the nation. They record permanently the deeds of the country's heroes so that they will not be lost. The aim of the Victoria Cross is to honour only those very few whose deeds are selected to stand as an example to soldiers for all time. The scarcity of Victoria Cross awards points to the requirement that, in order to stand for all time, military heroes should be few in number rather than abundant. Whereas just 627 men won VCs, close to 200,000 men received other decorations for bravery in the First World War. Many of these, VCs and others, have stated in speeches, memoirs and in letters, that they were only doing their job, that they had done nothing special or that they had only done what any other man would have done in the same situation. This view is expressed because the soldiers were largely performing acts of duty which came within each man's overall job description, or because what they did was viewed as a necessity under the circumstances. We have seen that this is the case in our examination of each Army Corps and infantry unit in the preceding chapters.

This is probably a fair representation of how military heroes see themselves, but it is not how the military and civilian societies in which they exist view these men. In many cases of bravery and distinguished service, a service provided to others, a form of gift, can be recognised. In the case of the medical man, the service he gave to his patients was rescue from the arms of death on the battlefield, hospital care and a future life. Medics were the 'angels of the battlefield' who provided hope, strength and resolve to the soldiers who faced wounding and a helpless lonely death. In the case of the man who stormed a machine gun post, the gift handed to comrades was release from a terrible fate; waiting to be ripped apart in a shell hole. In the case of a Lieutenant Colonel in command of an infantry battalion, his gift to his men was good cheer, courage, hope and faith in ultimate success by means of his management skill, paternalistic care, charismatic confidence and expert military judgement in battle. Without him, men 'could never have stood the strain', and with him they did. In the case of a Sergeant in the Army Service Corps, his gift was to the Army in supplying the needs of thousands of men for months on end, frequently under heavy shell fire. Without his efforts, many might have died as the front line collapsed for want of materials and sustenance. In the performance of their duties, these heroes of the First World War went the extra mile, and in so doing gave those around them a gift that was very substantial and yet difficult to repay. The debt was amplified many times over in the mind of the onlooker when the hero sacrificed his own life on their behalf at the moment of victory or salvation.

The symbolic recognition that a medal for bravery gives is part of the repayment of these debts. That only about 3 per cent of men received any form of decoration for bravery or distinguished service, indicates the high regard in which their services are held by their comrades and by the State. That only 0.2 per cent of this already small group received the Victoria Cross is a measure of how great a distinction the bronze cross is. And yet, we have seen how all participants in the Great War (including conscientious objectors, deserters and waiting families) made some form of sacrifice and needed to find some level of courage. Participants witnessed acts of bravery and of self-sacrifice, they also knew the great pain that the loss of dear comrades imparted, and they were left with the veteran's guilt. That members of their strongly-knit family and friends locked together by adversity, assisted them and died in doing so, is a very powerful source of guilt. Why did the virtuous heroes die, and yet I, a mere participant who did nothing of merit, who took the lives of others, survive? Some veterans felt guilt for their part in the war, their pillaging of corpses or their 'disposal' of prisoners.

Guilt does not stop at the individual veteran; in the aftermath of war it pervades military and civil authorities. Those who declared war, who ordered men into battle feel guilt. The reigning monarch, to whom soldiers swore allegiance and in small part fought on behalf of, felt guilt too. The nation felt strongly the debt of a great many sacrifices and families felt the guilt that other mothers' sons had died whilst their own came home; they felt joy and relief in the midst of a national tragedy. In some way, and at all levels, these debts must be repaid, and the sorrow of what was done had to be dealt with. In the immediate post-war era, the construction of war memorials and highly structured cemeteries allowed the nation and individuals to collectively settle the debts. Remembrance rapidly became deeply entrenched in British society as a symbolic means of mass grieving for a collective mistake and collective loss. Taken together, these are the reasons why war medals, those giant monuments to the missing, and the myriad of small community memorials, fountains and church plaques, memorial gates, windows and scrolls retain a sacred character to this day. Those who commissioned and paid for the memorials understood the service that had been rendered to the survivors and the debt that was owed; those who wore the medals understood the debts that could not be repaid. War veterans, civil and military societies and the Royal Family itself, grieved the loss, expressed the loss, and dealt with it in these ways. State, Monarchy and populace, including masses of the working class, were brought close together in shared melancholy ritual. Sorrow is a great leveller. Remembrance is part of the repayment of debts as well as the absolution of personal and national guilt, but it too is a creation of society and the State. The nature of annual remembrance in this country projects a single aspect of winning that war – the nation's sorrow -– from 100 years ago, down through the generations. The scale of loss between 1914 and 1918 is reflected in the scale of its remembrance and continued heavy poignancy; why on the 11th do I weep somebody else's tears? As a glorious counterpoint to war, heroes were created and are celebrated. Yet, both these ways of remembering the Great War are heavy with myth; they serve to obliterate the ordinary, happy-go-lucky Tommy who dealt with the war on his own terms and did his job remarkably well. The horror of World War One was nowhere near so great as to entirely break the resolve of ordinary men; the horror itself is but a small part of the total story, large parts were cut out and buried by writers such as the war poets who found fruitful ground in the horror motif. But employing his own brand of battlefield psychology, having within his unit a father officer and soldier brothers, Tommy's smiling robustness shines out from behind the veil of sorrow which was drawn down over the war and from behind the mask of heroism that was placed over his face.

What should never be forgotten is the ordinary Tommy, smiling from a box-brownie photograph, alive with his mates, doing the job. His deeds, motives and legacy prove something a little surprising to we who live 100 years after; that the ability to perform such feats in battle is present somewhere within all of us, only the circumstances are missing to bring it out. Courage and bravery are an abundant human trait, rather than being present in a select and special few. In this sense, bravery is not at all special. Yet within those who benefit from heroism, those lifted up off the field of battle and carried away to safety, it provokes enduring admiration, a profound indebtedness and a desire to recognise and remember. That urge is taken up by the state and the heavily managed phenomenon of heroism is laid before us. As many winners of bravery medals state, they were just doing their jobs, that anyone in their position would have done the same and they do not feel that the words brave hero apply to them.

This is not modesty, it is the truth, for courage, bravery, heroism even, were traits displayed by a very wide range of individuals between 1914–1918, from mothers to conscientious objectors, to shell-shaken artillery observation officers.

In this sense, it is paradoxical that on becoming a hero, the myths of heroism are dissolved. What's left isn't what we thought it was.

# Bibliography

Abbot, P. E. & Tamplin, J. M. A. *British Gallantry Awards.* Nimrod Dix & Co, London, 1981. ISBN: 9780902633742

Arthur, Max. *Symbol of Courage. A History of the Victoria Cross.* Sidgwick & Jackson, 2004. ISBN: 0283073519

Ashcroft, Michael. *Victoria Cross Heroes.* Headline Publishing, 2007. ISBN: 9780755316335

Ball, Tony. *The Northumberland Fusiliers and the Somme, 1916: A Case Study in Unit Deployment, Tactical Order and Casualties.* Journal of the Society for Army Historical Research, 2007, vol.85, pp.310–345

Barrett, Michele. *Casualty Figures. How Five Men Survived the First World War.* Verso Books, 2007. ISBN: 9781844672301

Buckley, Captain F. *War History of the Seventh Northumberland Fusiliers.* T. M. Grierson, Printers, Newcastle-upon-Tyne. (No publication date, but c.1920s).

Callin, Reverend R. W. *When the Lantern of Hope Burned Low.* The Story of the 1/4th Northumberland Fusiliers (T.F.) during the German Offensives of March, April, May, 1918. J. Catherall & Co., Hexham. (No publication date, but c.1920s).

Cook, Wilfred. *Men, Horses, Mud and Stew. The Little Fusilier's Great War.* Tommies Guides, 2009. ISBN: 9780955569845

Cooke, Captain C. H. *Historical Records of the 19th Service Battalion Northumberland Fusiliers (Pioneers).* Published for private distribution by the Council of the Newcastle and Gateshead Incorporated Chamber of Commerce, 1920.

Cooke, Captain C. H. *Historical Records of the 9th Battalion Northumberland Fusiliers.* Published by the Council of the Newcastle and Gateshead Incorporated Chamber of Commerce, 1928.

Crook, M. J. *The Evolution of the Victoria Cross: a study in administrative history.* Midas Books, 1975. ISBN: 0859360415

Crutchley, C. E. Machine Gunner 1914-1918. *Personal Experiences of The Machine Gun Corps.* Pen & Sword Military Classics, 2005. Reprint of 1973 Edition. ISBN: 1844153592

Donovan, Tom. *Hell At The Front.* Tempus Publishing, 2006. ISBN: 0752439405

Dorrington, N. *'Live and Let Die' – The British Army's Experience of Trench Raiding 1915-1918.* Journal of the Centre for First World War Studies, vol.3, 2007

Dyer, G. *The Missing of the Somme.* Phoenix Press, London, 1994. ISBN: 1842124501

Fowler, R. T. *Courage Rewarded: The Valour of Canadians Under Fire 1900–2007* Trafford Publishing, 2008. ISBN: 9781425170240

Fussell, Paul. *The Great War and Modern Memory.* Oxford University Press, 2000. Reprint of 1975 Edition. ISBN: 9780195133325

Gladden, N. *Ypres 1917.* William Kimber, London, 1967. ISBN: 0718302354

Gladden, N. *Across the Piave: A personal account of the British Forces in Italy, 1917–19* H.M. Stationery Office Books, 1971. ISBN: 0112900704

Gladden, N. *The Somme 1916.* William Kimber, London, 1974. ISBN: 71830313X

Griffith, P. *Battle Tactics of the Western Front. The British Army's Art of Attack, 1916–1918.* Yale University Press, London, 1996. ISBN 9780300066635

Holmes, Richard. *Tommy: The British Soldier on the Western Front 1914–1918*. Harper Perennial, 2005. ISBN: 0007137524

Holmes, Richard. *Shots From the Front. The British Soldier 1914–1918*. Harper Press, 2008. ISBN: 9780007275489

Jerrold, D. *The Royal Naval Division*. Naval & Military Press reprint, 1995. ISBN: 9781843422617

Junger, Ernst. *Storm of Steel*. Allen Lane, 2003. ISBN: 0713995947

Kenyon, David. *Horsemen in No Man's Land. British Cavalry and Trench Warfare, 1914–1918*. Pen & Sword Books, 2011. ISBN: 9781848843646

Leed, Eric. *No Man's Land. Combat and Identity in World War I.* Cambridge University Press, 1979. ISBN: 9780521285735

Lewis-Stempel, John. *Six Weeks. The Short and Gallant Life of the British Officer in the First World War*. Orion Books, London, 2011. ISBN: 9781409102144

Lynch, E. P. F. *Somme Mud. The Experiences of an Infantryman in France, 1916–1919*. Bantam Books, 2006. ISBN: 9780553819137

Marix Evans, Martin. *1918: The Year of Victories*. Chartwell Books, 2003. ISBN: 9780785816355

Military Secretary's Branch, General HQ. *Instructions Regarding Recommendations for Honours and Awards (1918)*. Naval and Military Press, 2000. ISBN: 9781897632574

O'Moore Creagh, Sir, and Humphris, E. M. *The Distinguished Service Order 1886–1923*. J. B. Hayward & Son, London, 1978. ISBN: 0903754126

Percival, John. *For Valour. The Victoria Cross*. The Leisure Circle, 1985. ISBN: 0423017004

Pollard, A. O. *Fire Eater: The Memoirs of a V.C.* Naval and Military Press, 2005 Reprint. ISBN: 9781845742553

Rimington, Major-General M. F. *Our Cavalry.* MacMillan & Co., London, 1912.

Roskill, Captain S. W. *The Art of Leadership.* Collins, London, 1964.

Sandilands, Brigadier H. R. *The Fifth in the Great War. A History of the 1st and 2nd Northumberland Fusiliers 1914–1918.* G. W. Grigg & Son, Dover, 1938.

Shakespear, Lt. Col. J. *A Record of the 17th and 32nd Service Battalions Northumberland Fusiliers (N.E.R.) Pioneers: 1914–1919.* Northumberland Press Limited, 1926.

Shakespear, Lt. Col. J. *Historical Record of the 18th Battalion Northumberland Fusiliers.* Published by the Council of the Newcastle and Gateshead Incorporated Chamber of Commerce, 1920.

Shakespear, Lt. Col. J. *Thirty-Fourth Division, 1915–1919: The Story of Its Career from Ripon to the Rhine.* Naval and Maritime Press, 2001. ISBN: 1843420503

Sheen, John. *Tyneside Irish: A History of the Tyneside Irish Brigade.* Pen & Sword, 1998. ISBN: 085052587X

Sheldon, Jack. *The German Army on the Somme, 1914–1916.* Pen & Sword Books, 2005. ISBN: 9781844152698

Sheppard, Ruth. *Extraordinary Heroes.* Osprey Publishing, Oxford, 2011. In conjunction with the Imperial War Museum. ISBN: 9781849083898

Smith, Melvin Charles. *Awarded for Valour. A History of the Victoria Cross and the Evolution of British Heroism.* Palgrave MacMillan 2008. ISBN: 9780230547056

St. Clair, William. *The Road to St. Julien. The letters of a stretcher bearer from the Great War.* Pen & Sword, 2004. ISBN: 1844150178

St George, Andrew. *Royal Navy Way of Leadership.* Preface Publishing, London 2012. ISBN: 9781848093454

Stewart, G. And Sheen, J. T*yneside Scottish: 20th, 21st, 22nd & 23rd (Service) Battalions of the Northumberland Fusiliers.* Pen & Sword, 1999. ISBN: 0850526310

Street, C. J. C. With The Guns. Naval and Military Press, 2004 Reprint. ISBN: 9781843427001

Vansittart, P. *Voices From The Great War.* Jonathan Cape Ltd., 1981. ISBN: 0224019155

Watson, A. *Enduring the Great War. Combat, Morale and Collapse in the German and British Armies, 1914–1918.* Cambridge University Press, 2008. ISBN: 9780521123082

Williamson, H. *Wet Flanders Plain.* Gliddon, Norwich, 1989.

# References

**INTRODUCTION**

1. Ball, 2005
2. Roper, p.16
3. Soldiers Died in the Great War, CD-Rom, Naval and Military Press, 2004

**SECTION I**

1. Instructions Regarding Recommendations for Honours and Awards (1918)
2. Fowler, p.96
3. Crutchley, p.83
4. Williamson, 2011
5. Crook, 1975 (and specifically p.68)
6. Instructions, paragraph 46
7. Instructions, paragraph 30
8. Instructions, paragraph 35
9. Griffith, 1996
10. Chris Baker, http://www.1914-1918.net/crime.htm, accessed 6.3.10
11. Barrett, p.133
12. Crutchley, p.81-82
13. Griffith, p.11
14. Holmes p.365
15. Griffith, 1996
16. Griffith, Chapter 11, pp.192-200
17. Crutchley, p.159
18. Crook, p.104
19. Crook, p.107
20. Watson, 2008
21. Watson, p.179-182
22. Smith, 2008
23. Abbot and Tamplin, 1981
24. Holmes p.79

25. Williamson, 2011, p.381 and p.405
26. Fowler, p.59 Wintringham T. And Blashford Snell, J.N. Weapons and Tactics. Hammondsworth, 1973 p.157
27. Dorrington, 2007
28. Sheldon, p.106

## SECTION II

1. Abbot & Tamplin, p.285
2. Crook, p.24, and Chapter 10, pp.100-116
3. Sheldon, p.185
4. Junger, p.195
5. Crutchley, p.42
6. Crutchley, p.77
7. Crutchley, p.51
8. Crutchley, p.52
9. Crutchley, p.49
10. Crutchley, p.114-115
11. Crutchley, p.158
12. Griffith, p.166
13. Smith, p.157
14. Smith, p.158
15. Kenyon, 2011
16. Kenyon, p.192-193
17. Rimington, p.2
18. Rimington, p.5
19. Rimington, p.32
20. Pease, p.177
21. Pease, p.191-192
22. Pease, p.204
23. Pease, p.199
24. Watson, chapter 5; pp.140-183
25. Watson, chapter 6; p.185-231
26. http://www.susandoreydesigns.com/genealogy/clirehugh/Winterbottom.pdf (consulted 29th June 2011)
27. Holmes, p.273
28. Smith, p.157-158
29. Watson, p.141-144

30. 2$^{nd}$ Bn NF History, p.274-276
31. Instructions, paragraph 45
32. Watson, p.143-144
33. Shakespear, (18th Bn.), p.185
34. Sheen, p.93.
35. Stewart and Sheen, p.104.
36. Stewart and Sheen, p.99
37. Sheen, p.94
38. Sheldon, p.158-159
39. Sheen, p.104
40. Sheen, p.105
41. Sheen, p.105
42. Stewart and Sheen, p.157
43. Shakespear (34$^{th}$ Division) p.101

## SECTION III

1. Roper, p. 254-257
2. Barrett, p.22-23
3. Stewart & Sheen, p.78
4. Barrett, 2007
5. Holmes, p.151
6. Holmes, p.63-64
7. Crutchley, p.59-60
8. Fussell, p.72
9. Holmes, p.528-534
10. Holmes, p.173
11. Holmes, p.197
12. Cook, p.146
13. Gladden, The Somme, p.75
14. Holmes, p.62-63
15. Barrett, p.74 and p.78
16. Crutchley, p.66
17. Lynch, p.58
18. Junger, p.196
19. Lynch, p.418
20. Lynch, p.58
21. Cook, p.122

22. Moran, p.109
23. Cook, p.171
24. Holmes, p.348-349
25. Cook.
26. Cook, p.17
27. Cook, p.23
28. Cook, p.64
29. Moran
30. Lynch, p.101
31. Gladden, Ypres 1917.
32. Gladden, Ypres 1917, p.130-132
33. Roper, p.179
34. Sheldon, p.134-135
35. Sheldon, p.142
36. Sheldon, p.184
37. Sheldon, p.201
38. Sheldon, p.233
39. Crutchley, p.68-69
40. Holmes, p.66
41. Sheldon, p.204-205
42. Lynch, p.374
43. Marix Evans, p.113
44. Holmes, p.384
45. Holmes, p.384
46. Sheldon, p.215
47. Van Emden, Soldier's War, p.53-54
48. Junger, p.213
49. Murray, p.75
50. Gladden, Ypres 1917, p.59
51. Roper, p.262
52. Murray, p.187
53. Lynch, p.376-377
54. Gladden, Ypres 1917, p.71-72
55. Cook, p.109
56. Cook, p.129
57. *Western Morning News*, Friday September 11th, 2009. Plymouth newspaper.

58. Holmes, p.288
59. Jerrold, p.183-207 (specifically pages 205-207)
60. Holmes, p.297
61. Roper, p.208-209
62. Fowler, p.15
63. Sheldon, p.233-234
64. Sheldon, p.219-222
65. 9NF History, p.116
66. Cook, p.129-130
67. Williamson, Henry, 1989. (quoted by Dyer, p.49)
68. Barrett, p.70-72
69. Junger, p.233-234
70. Street, p.128
71. Junger, p.241
72. Gladden, Somme 1916, p.112
73. Sheldon, p.335-336
74. Sheldon, p.205
75. Sheldon, p.257
76. Dyer, pp.9-10
77. Percival, p.63
78. Pollard, p.59
79. Smith, Chapter 8; p.152 - 164
80. Barrett, p.69-70
81. Sheldon, p.206
82. Sheldon, p.206-207
83. George Santayana's *Soliloquies in England* (Scribners, 1924, p. 102), Soliloquy #25, 'Tipperary').
84. Leed, 1979
85. Barrett, p.47
86. Roper, p.222
87. Roper, p.219
88. Vansittart, introduction, p.ix.
89. Junger, p.124
90. Junger, p.213
91. National Portrait Gallery, painting reference NPG6803, web link consulted 11th November 2011: http://www.npg.org.uk/whatson/display/2008/recent-commision-johnson-beharry.php

# Index